rainb

DIRECTC

GW00363812

The indispensable
Internet Directory
to
World Wide Travel

You can use this directory to:

travel the world from your computer

plan every aspect of your business and holiday travel

buy your tickets and insurance

arrange your travel finances

book accommodation, tours, and car hire

take advantage of attractive special offers,

and save money.

Happy Travelling!

rainbowdirectories

WORLD WIDE TRAVEL

First published in the United Kingdom in 2000
by

Dragon Publications Limited
PO Box 24076
LONDON
NW4 3ZR

Other titles in this series are in preparation.

Printed and bound in Finland by
WS Bookwell Oy

All manufacturing processes conform to the environmental regulations of the country of origin. Nordic Environmental Label, Licence no. 444-004.

This book has been printed with the pages laid cross-weave, which means that it stays open when laid down. We think that this is a useful feature in a directory.

The publishers and researchers have done their utmost to ensure the accuracy and currency of all the information contained in this publication. However, they cannot accept responsibility for any loss or inconvenience sustained by any person as a result of information and advice contained, nor as a result of any transactions carried out with third parties. It is the purchaser's responsibility to determine the suitability of the publication, for whatever purpose.

© **Dragon Publications Ltd. 2000**
dragonpublications.com

ISBN 1-903524-00-8

Contents

Staff and Contributors

Editor	Moshé Elias
Researchers	Ivana Baierova
	Petra Hausknecht
	Fei Kwok
	Konstantin Leidman
	Maciek Lozinski
	Susan Pentreath
	Mauro Poletto
	Daniel Weinberg
Cover & Internal Layout	Gee-Design

Introduction

Travelling has never been easier. Modern transportation makes the whole world accessible and millions of people now travel every year. The choices seem endless, with new destinations being explored all the time.

This has coincided with the phenomenal development of the Internet, which allows an enormous potential for choice for those with access to it. There is of course, the flip side. There is now so much to choose from that it can quickly become very confusing.

Because of the vast number of sites, the enormous quantity of information available and the overlapping of subject material, you can spend a good deal of time and money searching the Internet before finding the exact nugget of information you want. Search engines can give you so many references to your enquiry that you can end up in a labyrinth from which the only way out is to switch off.

rainbowdirectories are designed as friendly guides to take you directly to the web site you want to access for information, to conduct transactions, or simply to entertain yourself.

What we have done in this guide is to provide a directory of the best Internet travel sites that we have found on the World Wide Web. The list is by no means of every site, that would be impossible. We have included only those we believe are the best of what is currently available. We hope that our choices will help you plan your travel quickly and conveniently.

Some of the sites listed in this directory provide information only, while others will allow you to make bookings and purchase goods and services online. Please heed all warnings before making purchases and communicating your personal or financial details over the Internet. Most sites allow you to make payment in a variety of ways. If you are in any doubt about the organisation represented in the web site, then take whatever steps are necessary to clarify.

Although the information contained in the Health web sites may prove useful, you should always seek qualified medical assistance for your specific condition.

What is the Internet?
The Internet is a giant network of computers spanning the globe.
It connects anyone with a computer and a modem to anyone else with
a computer and a modem.

What started in the 1980's as a project to collect and securely save and
disseminate information within the US Defence organisation, came into
the public domain with the ending of the Cold War. The network received
a boost after 1990, when private organisations offered services to process
information for general use.

The commercial potential of the Internet was recognised once
telecommunications technology had improved sufficiently to allow fast
data transmission at a reasonable cost. The first commercial web site
joined the Internet in 1991. The phenomenal expansion of the network,
coupled with competition between service providers has driven down
prices, making the Internet accessible to home users. There are now
more than 2,000,000 web sites, and the number is growing daily.

How do I access the Internet?
To access the Internet, you need a computer with a modem attached to it
and connected to a telephone line. You also need to subscribe to any of the
Internet Service Providers and have a copy of one of the Internet browser
programs installed on the hard drive of your computer. You connect to the
Internet via your Service Provider, and then use the browser software to find
and view the particular web site you want.

What will I find at a Web Site?
A World Wide Web document, or web site, is like a file in a filing cabinet,
except that it stores its information in a variety of visual and sometimes
aural forms. You may read text, see images, as well as hear sound.

The best web sites are crammed with useful information on every
conceivable topic, much of which you can act upon. Many sites are interactive
and may even allow you to play games on them, joining other players from
anywhere in the world. The data on most sites can be downloaded to your
computer so that you can make a hard copy of the information.

How to use your rainbowdirectories WORLD WIDE TRAVEL book.
Every journey requires many different services and when all these are put
together, a traveller, whether for business or pleasure, has a lot to attend to
when planning each trip. This book has been designed so that you can

research and make all of your travel arrangements conveniently with your computer and the World Wide Web.

The Contents page lists the categories. The web sites are arranged regionally and then alphabetically within each category. The Index will help you to locate a particular web site if you cannot find what you are looking for in the Contents.

Each web site entry is set out so that it contains:
its name
its Internet address (URL)
a review of the web site
an e-mail address (if available)

Many commercial web sites allow you to make reservations and pay for products and services via the Internet. These facilities are noted in the reviews where appropriate.

If you like this book and find it useful, look out for our other Internet directories on World Wide Shopping and World Wide Sport which will be available in your bookshop soon.

Online Shopping Tips
Many of the sites we have listed allow you to make bookings or buy goods online. Here are some points you should bear in mind:

■ Check if the site has secure online payment or reservation facilities. We have focused on those that do, however make sure you are happy to pay by another method if there are no secure facilities. Most ordering screens on secure servers are prefixed https:// and often display a closed padlock symbol on your web browser.

■ Never give your personal or credit card details to an insecure site. Never fax your complete personal or credit card details to any company. Always black out part of the information to prevent it being intercepted and misused. Never send these details by e-mail, as this is very insecure.

■ Check for delivery options, costs and minimum order values. Delivery costs may vary enormously depending from where the goods are being shipped. Courier services are usually more expensive than regular post, but they are faster and the items are usually insured in transit. Minimum order values may make ordering from a site uneconomic, unless you are spending a lot.

■ Check the retailer's returns policy before you buy in case of any problems with the goods.

■ Take account of local tax and any duties payable in your calculations if you are booking from an overseas site.

■ Check the local compatibility of any electrical purchases.

■ If the goods are priced in a foreign currency, make sure you are getting a fair exchange rate. Some sites have currency converters so ensure that what you are being charged converts correctly into your own currency.

■ Print or take a screenshot of the order confirmation screen after paying with your credit card as your proof of reservation.

■ Ask for an e-mail confirming your order or reservation. You can also print this and keep it as your record.

■ Note the company's contact details where possible, in case of any problems. We have listed e-mail addresses where available, but you may also want to note their telephone and fax numbers.

■ If you are having your purchase delivered by courier, get a tracking number when you complete your order. You can then use this to check the progress of your delivery later, on the courier's own web site.

■ Check if your orders are insured in transit – some credit card companies insure all purchases made with their card, but it is always worth checking.

■ When an item is delivered, check the packaging carefully before signing for it. If it has been damaged in any way, do not accept delivery and have it returned.

With a little help from our friends ...
The Internet is changing at a considerable rate, and trying to keep up with those changes is a never-ending exercise. Although all the Internet addresses contained in this directory were correct at the time of printing, don't be alarmed if you find that a few do not work or have changed when you try to access them. The problem may only be temporary, so it might be worth trying again later. If you find that an address has changed, or if you know of other useful travel sites, please let us know via e-mail at: email@dragonpublications.com. We'll try to include them in our next edition.

Accommodation

Africa

Bed and Breakfast in South Africa

www.bedandbreakfast.co.za
Bed and Breakfast throughout South Africa. Choose the State on the map, then the region. The rest follows.
e-mail: Info@bedweb.co.za

City Lodges Hotel Group

www.citylodge.co.za
A small hotel chain operating in South Africa, with online credit card booking service.
e-mail: not available

Fortes King

www.fortesking-hotels.co.za
A South African hotel chain that works in with vacation ideas. You can book online with a credit card.
e-mail: via online form

Golden 5 City

www.golden5.com
Golden City is a large resort in the Egyptian province of Hurghada on the Red Sea Coast. Accommodation is available in the Beach Village, villas, palaces and hotels. All the information you need is there: pictures, facilities, services, dining out, shopping and sports.
e-mail: not available

Hotel Sea Cliff Dar Es Salaam

www.hotelseacliff.com
A single hotel in Tanzania making its contribution to local tourism. It has a good range of facilities and you book by e-mail.
e-mail: Information@hotelseacliff.com

Kapani Safari Lodge

www.kapani.com
In Zimbabwe you have a choice of the safari lodge itself or two bush camps. Contact is by post, phone, fax or e-mail.
e-mail: Kapani@super-hub.com

South Africa Accommodation Guide

www.doorway.co.za
This is the biggest accommodation database in South Africa. There is no booking service but a good place to start searching for deluxe hotels down to campsites.
e-mail: via online form

Victoria Falls Safari Lodge

www.vfsl.com
Accommodation within a few miles of the Victoria Falls, either in the hotel or one of the Lokothula self-catering lodges, or in a 700 year old village with the local people. You can book online.
e-mail: Res@saflodge.com

Asia

Aitken Spence Hotels

www.aitkenspence.com
This is a resort and hotel chain in Sri Lanka and the Maldives. In addition to hotel information you will find facts for tourists.
e-mail: Hotel@aitkenspence.com

Amari Hotels and Resorts

www.amari.com
Ten luxurious hotels in Bangkok and Thai resorts with a short guide to Thailand. There are pictures, a room catalogue with prices and details of

public facilities. You can book online.
e-mail: Email@amari.com

Asia Hotel Group

www.asiahotel.co.th
Asia Hotel Group has three hotels;
the Asia Bangkok, the Asia Airport and
the Asia Pattaya Beach. Each hotel has
basic information with photographs
about its location, room plans, prices,
restaurants, amenities and conference
facilities. There is a booking form,
which can be printed and faxed.
e-mail: sale@asiahotel.co.th

Asia-Hotels.com

www.asia-hotels.com
The best hotels in most Asian countries.
Clicking on the country gets you a list
with the price range and a short
description of the hotel. Click on the
hotel name and all the facts are laid out.
e-mail: Asiahot@asia-hotels.com

Bali Hotels & Accommodation Co.

www.travelideas.net
This site covers hotels and holiday
resorts in parts of Bali and Thailand.
Each region has a list with brief details
and prices. Follow the links for more
information or booking online using
the secure credit card service.
e-mail: Bali.Direct@virgin.net

Bangkok Budget Hotels

www.thaihotel.com
A Bangkok hotel directory for budget
travellers with prices guaranteed
between US$10 and $35. Hotels are
listed by city district, each with a sample
price. If you like the price, follow the link
to a large-scale map for location, rates
and nearby attractions. You can book
online.
e-mail: Enquiry@thaihotel.com

Bangkok Hotels Guide

www.bangkokhotelguide.com
The site alphabetically lists more than

170 hotels in Bangkok, with links to
travel information, flights, car hire and
a restaurant guide. The more luxurious
hotels have internal links to pages
with brief details, maps, prices and
a reservation form.
e-mail: Info@bangkokhotelguide.com

Banyan Tree Hotels & Resorts

www.banyantree.com
Banyan Tree owns luxury hotels in
Thailand, Indonesia and the Maldives.
The home page features press releases,
an online brochure, request form and
special offers. Clicking on a hotel brings
up a good deal of information about
rates and reservations, location, villas,
dining and corporate facilities. Each
page has a photograph and useful links
to maps and other information. Booking
is possible online using a credit card,
and you can put yourself on a mailing
list for special offers.
e-mail: reservations@banyantree.com

D'MA Pavilion Hotel

www.sino.net/amtel/
The official site of the D'MA Pavilion
Hotel in Bangkok, Thailand.
The homepage contains a brief
description of the hotel and links to
room rates, a reservation form and
further information. Linked pages
contain a brief description and
photographs of each facility offered
at the hotel, including suite layouts,
menus, bars, as well as entertainment,
banquet, business and recreational
facilities. A location map is also
available
e-mail: toll@samart.co.th

Dusit Group

www.dusitgroup.com
Thirty hotels mainly in Thailand,
with a few elsewhere in Southeast Asia.
Each hotel is separately detailed.
You can book online.
e-mail: Rachel@dusit.com

Heritage Hotels of India

www.heritagehotels.com
This web site provides little more than links to 14 hotels owned by Heritage, many of which were stately homes. The hotels are described with photographs, lists of amenities and local attractions. Reservations cannot be made online; complete a form and the hotel will contact you. The site is poorly designed but if you want a taste of Indian history and enjoy traditional Indian art in character settings, this is where you should go.
e-mail: heritagehotels@planetindia.net

Hotel Equatorial

www.equatorial.com
This chain owns hotels in Burma, China, Malaysia, Singapore and Vietnam. Each hotel has a good picture gallery, e-mail addresses, location map, prices and details of facilities.
e-mail: Dgibbens@equatorial.com

Hotels and Lodging in Turkey

www.lodgingturkey.com
The most popular hotels in the regions around Istanbul, Cappadocia, Ephesus, Pammukale and Mediterranean Coast. Each region is briefly described with a list of accommodation. Click on your choice and you get details, pictures, rates, services and a link to a reservation form. There are links to tour operators and yacht charters.
e-mail: Lodgingturkey@superonline.com

Hotels in China

www.cbw.com/hotel/
Part of the Chinese Business web site contains a list of selected hotels from all provinces in mainland China, Hong Kong and Taiwan. Some hotels in each province are highlighted; follow these links for pictures, location, facilities, services, activities and discount offers.
e-mail: Editor@cbw.net

Hotels in India

www.hotels-india.com
Hotels are listed for most cities in India, including heritage hotels in palaces and castles. Each city has a well-presented catalogue of hotels with pictures, details of location and facilities and a link for online reservation.
e-mail: Info@hotels-india.com

Japan Hotel Association

www.j-hotel.or.jp/english/
The site has information on most Japanese hotels, listed by Prefecture. Links take you to pages with details and a booking form.
e-mail: not available

Keells Hotels

www.keells.com/jkhome/hotels/index.htm
Ten hotels offering a thousand rooms in Sri Lanka account for more than ten percent of all hotel accommodation in the country. You can book online.
e-mail: htlres@keells.com

Nepal.com: Hotels

www.travel-nepal.com
This site lists all Nepalese hotels by category and name. A few are described in detail with prices, local activities and pictures.
e-mail: Feedback@travel-nepal.com

Oberoi Hotels & Resorts

www.oberoihotels.com
Thirty hotels in six Asian countries and you choose them off a map. There is a link to a world wide hotel reservation system where there are no Oberois.
e-mail: via online form

Phuket Hotel Guide

www.phuket.com/hotels/
Hotels and resorts in Phuket, the popular Thai holiday centre. There are listings and a search engine giving location, seasonal prices, discounts and special offers and

photographs to help you decide.
e-mail: not available

Shangri-La Hotels

www.shangri-la.com
Luxury hotels in South-east Asia and the Pacific Islands. There is a lot for you to look at and enjoy on this site of good quality hotels.
e-mail: via online form

Staying in Pakistan

www.rpi.edu/dept/union/paksa/
The site has links to the home pages of Pakistan's best hotels listed by city. Clicking on the hotel name connects you to its web site.
e-mail: Malika@rpi.edu

Taj Hotels, Resorts and Palaces

www.tajhotels.com
This is India's largest chain with 49 hotels in 34 locations across South Asia, graded as luxury, business and leisure. Each hotel has online e-mail for reservation, details of facilities and services in guestrooms, public areas and restaurants, local attractions and a calendar of events.
e-mail: Trn@tajhotels.com

Australasia and Oceania

Accommodation Line

www.accomline.com.au
This is an accommodation finder and reservation service for hotels in Australia, New Zealand, Singapore and Bali grouped by city, each of which has a list of highlighted names. Clicking on one takes you to an information page. You can book online by using the secure payment form.
e-mail: Hotel@cia.com.au

BABS - Bed and Breakfast Site

www.babs.com.au
Bed and Breakfast accommodation in Australia. Information is listed with

enough choice to suit everyone. Rates, facilities, photos, a booking form and how to get there are all nicely laid out.
e-mail: not available

Duxton Hotels

www.duxtonhotels.com.sg
The Company owns five hotels, three in Australia, one each in Singapore and Thailand. The home page has links to each hotel and enquiry e-mail. The hotels are fully described with a visual tour, map, facilities and sample menus. You can reserve your room online over a secure server and take advantage of special deals.
e-mail: duxton@singnet.com.sg

Fiji for Less

www.fiji4less.com.fj
Budget accommodation in Fiji with a list of hotels and hostels with prices, discounts and special offers. You will also find details of the country's main attractions.
e-mail: not available

Flag Choice Hotels

www.flag.com.au
Flag Choice Hotels manages approximately 500 hotels across Australia, Papua New Guinea and New Zealand. The home page has links to the following pages: business traveller, leisure traveller, reservations, hotel pass, external links, and a search engine. Information on individual hotels can be obtained by completing an online enquiry and reservation form. Online reservations are possible, and full contact details are given for each hotel. There are external links to travel agents and a hotel directory. The search facility consists of a drop-down menu for each hotel or location.
e-mail: reservations@flagchoice.com.au

Hotels New Zealand

www.hotel.q.co.nz
This site is a network of independent hotels all over New Zealand. They are

all described separately and must be contacted individually.
e-mail: not available

Kingdom of Tonga: Hotels
www.vacations.tvb.gov.to/hotnuk.htm
This is part of the Tonga information centre. Hotels are listed by island with contact details for each.
e-mail: Tonga@value.net

Kiwi Camps
webnz.com/kiwi-camps/
The web site lists campsites in both islands of New Zealand. Use the map to pinpoint your location and you are linked to an internal page with everything you may want to know and a booking form.
e-mail: David@kiwi-camps.co.nz

Metro Inns
www.metroinns.com.au
Large resorts to intimate inns in Australia and Oceania. Pick the category and region and your accommodation comes forth in full detail. You can book by freephone, e-mail or the online form.
e-mail: Metrores@ozonline.com.au

Outrigger Hotels and Resorts
www.outrigger.com
You can start by downloading the brochure in PDF format. Then check out this chain of hotels and resorts in Australia and the Pacific Basin.
e-mail: via online form

Rydges Hotels & Resorts
www.rydges.com.au
Luxury hotels in Australia, New Zealand and Dubai. Choose your hotel from the pull down menu, and full details are shown, or alternatively use the map.
e-mail: via online form

Caribbean

Carib Villas
www.caribvillas.ch/indexe.htm
This Swiss company offers villas for rent or sale in the Caribbean, mainly in the Dominican Republic. The home page describes the company and staff, and has links to their two main complexes. Each villa has a page containing photographs and information about the resort and its surroundings, local activities and amenities. A German language version of the site is also available.
e-mail: caribvillas@datacomm.ch

Caribbean Destinations
www.caribbeandest.com
A villa rental company giving personalised service for short term rental of private vacation homes on many of the Caribbean islands. The home page has a map of the area, with buttons to access each island, giving a list of available villas. Information includes prices and amenities and some photos of the villas and their environs. You can request further information about specific villas using the form provided.
e-mail: island@caribbeandest.com

Heart of Caribbean
www.hotcarib.com
Villas on the Caribbean islands of Bonaire, St. Martin, Barbados and St. Lucia. The villas are listed by island and size, each with a photo gallery and details of facilities. Booking is by telephone.
e-mail: Villas@hotcarib.com

Where to Stay in the Caribbean
www.wheretostay.com
This is a huge database of all types of accommodation in the Caribbean. You can browse alphabetically or view lodges by island. Each feature has links to internal pages with information about the islands, some with web sites and

e-mail addresses, prices, credit card acceptability, activities and photos.
e-mail: via online form

Europe

48 Castles in Germany

www.germancastles.com
Accommodation in forty-eight castles and mansions in Germany is available on this site. Each comes with a picture, short description, location and a link to either an external web site with more detailed information or a request form if there is no dedicated page. There are links to other web sites with general information on castle accommodation.
e-mail: via online form

A Bed and Breakfast agency for Madrid

www.madridbandb.com
You will find more than twenty B & B hotels in Madrid on this site with all the information you require. A map tells you how to get there.
e-mail: not available

A Bed and Breakfast agency for Paris

www.parisbandb.com
Use the map to help you choose from more than twenty B & B hotels in Paris. All the information you require including how to get there is on site.
e-mail: not available

A Bed and Breakfast agency for Rome

www.romebandb.com
A map will direct you to over twenty B & B hotels in Rome. There are pictures, accommodation details and how to get there.
e-mail: not available

Accommodation Online UK

www.accom.co.uk
If you are looking for Bed and Breakfast accommodation in the UK start here.

Search by location from regions to counties and towns. Each B & B is described with facilities, rates, e-mail address, photos and a booking form. If you cannot find accommodation in a particular town, e-mail them for help.
e-mail: Johnlyon@fasttrack.co.uk

All Hotels in Russia

all-hotels.ru
This database and reservation system will find you a hotel in Russia and the European part of the former Soviet Union. Log in the city or pick from the list and a selection of hotels appears. Choose one by name and you get all the information you need to book online.
e-mail: www@cnetworks.net

Alp'Azur Hotels

www.nova.fr/alpazur/
This company runs hotels in St. Tropez and along the nearby peninsula. The hotels are listed by location and star rating and each is shown with photographs and price list. You can book online but the server is not secure. Other pages have information about local attractions and societies, restaurants and business. The text is mainly French with a few pages in English.
e-mail: alpazur@aol.com

Alpine Classics Hotels of Switzerland

www.alpineclassics.ch
The map divides the Swiss Alps into regions with a list of selected lodgings in each. They are simply described with photos, facilities and an e-mail link for contact.
e-mail: Alpineclassics@centralnet.ch

Astron Hotels

www.astron-hotels.de
4 and 5-star hotels in Germany and Austria. Choose your hotel from the map or by clicking on its name on the

list. Details are ample and you can book online.
e-mail: Info@astron-hotels.de

Atlas Hotels

www.atlas-hotels.com
Atlas owns three hotels in Holland. You can view a hotel by clicking on its name or by clicking on the map. For each hotel there are several pages covering rooms, staff and restaurant, each containing photographs and a short description. Prices are listed on a separate page, and rooms at all hotels can be reserved online. There is even a page containing sample recipes, you can send recipes or e-mail the chef. The 'interesting links' page contains external links to the Dutch national railway, Schipol Airport and the Dutch tourist board, amongst others.
e-mail: info@atlas-hotels.com

Auberges de Jeunesse

www.fuaj.org/eng/
This is the French branch of the Youth Hostel Association and the web site tells you how to join. You will find a list of cities hosting their hostels and each hostel has its address, tariff, dining facilities and opening times.
e-mail: via online form

Austria Hotel Guide

www.abserv.co.at/abserv/hotel/
The site contains an accommodation and rent-a-car guide for Austria. Select your hotel by location or by activity, for example skiing or golfing, and details will appear including prices, a map, pictures and a reservation form for both hotel and car.
e-mail: Koberger@abserv.co.at

Automobile Association

www.theaa.co.uk/hotels/index.asp
This site is part of the Motoring & Travel section of the AA web site and is a searchable database of 4,000 hotels in

Great Britain and Ireland. You can search by choosing a region, then narrow the criteria according to your main priority, either price, hotel quality, accommodation type, or food quality. For each hotel there is a photograph, an AA rating, a description of the venue, facilities, location and a price guide. There is also a link to a detailed map of the area showing nearby AA-listed hotels. Online credit card reservation and booking are possible.
e-mail: theaa@hotelres.co.uk

Bettoja Hotels

www.bettojahotels.it/pmlserv2.htm
Bettoja Hotels operates in Italy. Their site is available in English, Italian, French, German, Spanish and Japanese. The homepage describes the group and links to pages about Rome and Florence, a daily newsletter, price lists, business facilities and an enquiry and reservation form. The Rome and Florence pages contain basic tourist information and maps, and link to a list of local Bettoja Hotels. Hotel pages are well laid out with photographs and description of the amenities, local attractions, a local map and a direct e-mail link.
e-mail: via online form

Bilderberg Hotels & Restaurants

www.bilderberg.nl
Their 24 hotels are located around Holland. Apart from well-displayed hotel rooms and conference facilities, you will find chain-wide offers and details of local beauty spots. You can book online and text is in English, Dutch and German.
e-mail: Info@bilderberg.nl

Camping en España

www.vayacamping.net/en/
There are more than 1,200 regionally catalogued campsites fully detailed with facilities, prices and photos on this web

site. The search engine does not seek out campsites with particular facilities but there are enough in each location that something is bound to suit.
e-mail: Info@vacayacamping.net

Camping in Sweden

www.camping.se/index_en.html
This database has all the campsites in Sweden with current camping packages and discount card offers. You choose your location from the map and a list of campsites appears; click on one and you get details, prices, web site and e-mail addresses.
e-mail: Adm@scr.se

Camping NET

www.camping.ch
The search engine will find you a campsite in Switzerland. Choose the region, type and facilities you want and up comes a campsite to match your specification with addresses, telephones, facilities, services, equipment suppliers and prices. Text is in English and German.
e-mail: Info@camping.ch

Campingguide

www.camping.no/index_eng.html
This Norwegian campsite database has links to camping organisations in other countries. Choose your region on the map and a large-scale map appears. Most campsites are fully detailed with facilities, photos, web site and e-mail addresses.
e-mail: Larsen@rbl.no

Caravan & Camping Ireland

www.camping-ireland.ie
Choose a County in Ireland for your camping holiday then click on the campsite name and you get all the information you need, including how to get there by car. You can book online.
e-mail: via online form

Chateaux & Country

www.chateauxandcountry.com
Over 130 French castles turned hotel are described on this web site. You can find accommodation by name, location or by filling a multi-criteria search form to get you what you want. Every castle is listed with facilities, activities, prices, a photo gallery and other castles nearby.
e-mail: via online form

CountryCottages

europvacationvillas.com
Europe-wide vacation rental company with a portfolio of cottages, villas, apartments and mansions. Choose a country, an area of interest and a date, then select from 13,500 properties. Make your selection and you will receive details, a price list, maps and suggestions on how to enjoy the surroundings.
e-mail: not available

Countryside Hotels

www.countrysidehotels.se
This operator owns 29 picturesque hotels in beautiful surroundings in Sweden. Each hotel is fully described and you can book online.
e-mail: Info@countrysidehotels.se

Croatian Tourist Index

business.hr/tourism/
Lists of local hotels, motels and camping sites throughout Croatia. You can search accommodation by location or from an alphabetical index. Some lodges allow booking online.
e-mail: via online form

Cyprushotels.com

www.cyprushotels.com/Entrance.asp
The search engine helps you choose accommodation by location or rating. Each category has links to pages with information and room facilities, entertainment, conference arrangements and a reservation form. Most hotels indicate their rates.
e-mail: x-rm@x-rm.com

Dansk Kroferie

www.dansk-kroferie.dk/
Eighty of Denmark's best reputed
inns and hotels with more than 3,000
rooms can be accessed on this web site.
Use the map to pick your region, then
the lodging and you will find all the
information you need to book.
e-mail: Kroferie@dansk-kroferie.dk

Denmark Hotel List

www.dkhotellist.dk
Danish hotel chains, private hotels,
conference centres and restaurants
are listed on this site. You can search
accommodation by standard, location
or name. Each comes up with pictures,
facilities, room details and an e-mail
address for reservation.
e-mail: Info@dkhotellist.dk

Der IHA Hotelführer

www.iha-hotelfuehrer.de
This database of German hotels has a
search engine to help you find accommodation. First choose the region on
the map, then a smaller region within.
Next choose the city, room type, what
you expect in the way of facilities, or a
hotel chain if you prefer and full details
appear. You can order a brochure and
make your reservation online.
e-mail: not available

DirectHotel

**www.directhotel.com/EN/home/home.
html**
To find a hotel in France, first choose
the region on the map, then the city.
Each hotel appears with price information,
facilities and a link to a registration form.
Additional links take you to the French
Railways, flight and car reservation centres.
e-mail: not available

DK Camp

www.dk-camp.dk
Denmark's campsites are listed with
details of discounts available. You can

find a campsite in an area of your choice
and order a brochure in PDF format.
Some of the campsites have their own
web sites.
e-mail: Info@dk-camp.dk

Dorint Hotels & Resorts

www.dorint.de
Operating in Germany, Switzerland
and the Czech Republic, they list their
hotels separately. You can book online
and order a free brochure.
e-mail: Info@dorint.de

Esperia Hotel Group

www.esperia-hotels.gr
Esperia own a small chain of hotels
on Rhodes. Each hotel has a photo
gallery, list of general and room
facilities, tour operators, nearby
attractions and prices.
e-mail: Esperia@esperia-hotels.gr

France Hotel Reservation

www.francehotelreservation.com
This well designed site in English
and French contains hundreds of
hotels in France. The online booking
system lets you choose your hotel to
suit your own criteria. All this can be
done on the homepage by regional
location or within Paris on the street
plan. Each hotel is rated and briefly
described - facilities, local attractions,
prices and numerous photographs
allowing a virtual tour. Hotels can
be booked online via a secure form.
Special features include Hotels of
the Month and personalised booking
services for travel agents and business
travellers.
e-mail: info@francehotelreservation.com

France Villas

www.francevillas.com
This site provides information and
online booking of more than 500
villas in France. You can browse by
Department or complete a request

form, choosing location, all other
requirements and specifying your
budget.
e-mail: Loc@francevillas.com

Great Southern Hotels

www.gsh.ie
This Irish chain owns hotels all over the
country. Choose your hotel off the map
or by clicking on its name. Each hotel is
detailed on separate pages showing all
its features, e-mail address and booking
form.
e-mail: Res@sales.gsh.ie

Hotel Continental Skopje

www.contimak.com
A hotel in Skopje, the capital of the
former Yugoslav Republic of Macedonia.
You will find a good catalogue of rooms
with photos and prices and an online
reservation form.
e-mail: Contimak@contimak.com

Hotel Edda

www.edda.is
Sixteen hotels in Iceland's most
picturesque locations. Check the details
and book by e-mail. Text is in English,
Icelandic and German.
e-mail: Icehotel@edda.is

Hotel-Net.cz

www.hotel-net.cz
A database of hotels in the Czech
Republic. Fill in the request form,
choosing the city, distance from centre,
hotel category, room type and period
of stay and up comes a list of suitable
hotels. Then follow the hotel link for
more specific details.
e-mail: not available

HotelNet Nederland

www.hotelnet.nl
The home page has logos of major
Dutch hotel chains; follow the link to
each chain. Additionally a search engine
will help you find a hotel anywhere in

the Netherlands, matching your
requirements with what is available.
e-mail: Info@hotelnet.nl

Hotels in Bulgaria

www.internet-bg.bg/hotel.htm
The site has links to eleven of the
most representative hotels in Bulgaria.
Each hotel comes with information
about prices, location, facilities and
local attractions.
e-mail: Lnd@lnd.internet-bg.bg

Hotels in Greece

www.filoxenia.com
The search engine helps you find any
type of accommodation, any time,
anywhere in Greece. Take your pick, as
many have internal links with pictures
and online booking.
e-mail: via online form

Hotels Virtuales

www.hvsl.es
The company owns hotels and
apartments in Spain. This site is slow
because of the large number of images
but otherwise it has all the information
you need about their operations on
the Spanish mainland and islands. You
access the hotels by clicking on a location.
Reservations can be made online and
there are links to airline web sites.
e-mail: hvpost@hvsl.es

Hotels-in-Ireland.com

www.hotels-in-ireland.com
This database lists hotels in Ireland
by region and category. You can find
out more by following internal links
to hotels. There is a currency converter
and you can book online.
e-mail: not available

HotelsPoland

www.hotelspoland.com
On this site you will find current special
offers for each city and information
about accommodation with prices in

US$, as well as local attractions. If you prefer, you can stay at a castle where all facilities, prices and links to car rentals are provided.
e-mail: Poland@hotelspoland.com

Hungarian Tourism Site

www.miwo.hu/index.en.phtml
This is a Hungarian Travel Site but is mainly concerned with accommodation. You can search by region, city, name, category and services or make a combined search involving all these. The database contains more than 2,600 hotels with over 6,500 photos.
e-mail: not available

Husa Hotels

www.husa.es
Although this site is not very clear, it covers 180 hotels in Spain with text in English,Spanish and French. Most hotels have their own pages with enough information to help you make your choice. Their online booking service is run by Hotel World, which is linked into the system.
e-mail: not available

Inter Hotel

www.inter-hotel.com
The company owns and manages 200 hotels throughout France. The site offers special packages to leisure and business travellers in both English and French. You can find your hotel by clicking its location on the map, on a city list or by keyword search. Each hotel is adequately detailed and links to local information and online booking are provided. A useful icon system describes facilities available at each hotel.
e-mail: information@inter-hotel.com

Italian Camping Guide

www.camping.it
Campsites in Italy are listed regionally, so pick out the one most suitable. Some campsites are named only with

an address and telephone number, but most are fully detailed with sports grounds, services and operating season.
e-mail: Genial@camping.it

Italian Itineraries

www.italian-itineraries.com
Here you have villas, country houses and city apartments for rent in Italy, with links to property sales and car rental. Each region has highlighted lists of accommodation. Clicking on a villa name links you to a page with lots of information about it.
e-mail: Info@italian-itineraries.com

Italy Hotel Reservation

www.venere.it
The search engine will connect you with most hotels in Italy. Choose the region on the map or from the text, then the city. Each hotel is listed with address, telephone, rates and facilities. You can check room availability online.
e-mail: not available

Jurys Hotel Group

www.jurys.com
Budget accommodation in Ireland and the UK.
e-mail: Info@jurys.com

Kanika Group

www.kanika-group.com
Click the pictures on the map of Cyprus and you get a datasheet about the hotel and local attractions. Book with the online form.
e-mail: Info@kanika-group.com

Les Castels

www.les-castels.com
Les Castels own campsites throughout France. Click the map on your chosen location and you get a list of campsites, each of which has a separate page with pictures, a local map, a guide on how to get there, tariffs and list of facilities.
e-mail: Mail@les-castels.com

Libertel Hotels

www.libertel-hotels.com
A good list of budget accommodation in 50 two and three star hotels across France and Belgium, in both English and French. Each hotel page will give you more detail about prices, room style and local attractions. There is an online reservation form, but online payments are not possible. There are inks to Westin Demeure Hotels and the Pavillon Ledoyen restaurant.
e-mail: info@libertel-hotels.com

Logis Of Ireland

www.logis-ireland.ie
Logis manages a group of hotels and guesthouses in Ireland. From the home page you can search by region (click on the map to bring up a list of hotels in that region), or see a list of all hotels, with addresses and rating. Some hotels have hyperlinks to their own pages, which contain photographs, more detailed information about the location, facilities and price lists.
e-mail: via online form

London Bed & Breakfast

www.londonbandb.com
More than twenty B & B hotels in London are listed on this site with all the information you require and a map.
e-mail: not available

MAX

www.camping.hu
You will find 500 Hungarian campsites listed by city, a few of which have e-mail and web site addresses. A new, more up-to-date site is under construction.
e-mail: Camping@mail.matav.hu

Minotel

www.hotelnet.co.uk/minotel/
Minotel operates a chain of hotels throughout Europe. Although their site is sparely illustrated, it is available in nine European languages. The home page has price lists, e-mail links for reservations and comments as well as information about the hotel group. The first link is to a map featuring links to hotels in 31 countries. Click on a country to display a list of Minotels in that country, click on a hotel to see prices, location, amenities, and photographs. There is an external link to Switzerland Tourism, a partner site.
e-mail: europe@minotel.ch

Orbis Hotels

www.orbis.pl/index2.html
The largest chain of domestic hotels in Poland. Clicking on the map takes you to a page with all the information you need and a reservation form.
e-mail: Kontakt@orbis.pl

Orient Express Hotels

www.orient-expresshotels.com
Twenty hotels mainly in Europe along the famous Orient Express train route. Details are nicely laid out and you can book online.
e-mail: not available

Pestana Hotels and Resorts

www.pestana.com
In Portugal and the Azores.
Each hotel in the chain is fully detailed with a catalogue of nearby golf courses. The site has links to local airlines, car rental companies and travel agents in Portugal and Spain.
e-mail: Cph.reservas@pestana.org

Portugal Accommodation

www.portugal-info.net/accommodation.htm
This site has links to holiday apartments, residential rental agents, hotels and inns mainly in Lisbon and the Algarve. You will also find links to flights, property and vehicle rental.
e-mail: not available

RAC Hotel Finder

www.rac.co.uk/services/hotelfinder/
A database of over 3,000 RAC accredited hotels across the UK and Ireland. Two types of search are possible: a quick search, if you know which hotel you're looking for, and a tailored search, where you enter a combination of requirements. The hotel information is very brief, just consisting of an address, contact details, rates, and facilities. Features of the site include a call back system, where you check the boxes next to the hotels you are interested in, then the automated RAC booking service will call back with availability, detailed information and possibility of reservations. There is also a Route Planner, where you enter the departure and arrival addresses, and the service e-mails you with the best route.
e-mail: via online form

Relais & Chateaux

www.relaischateaux.fr
The web site brings together more than 4,000 French castles, country houses and restaurants reputed by quality of service. You will find all their details online and can even order a guide.
e-mail: not available

Ringhotels

www.ringhotels.de
This web site is a co-operative of personally managed, middle-sized hotels in Germany. To find a hotel, choose a Land - German administrative region - then a smaller region within the Land. Each region gives a list of hotels. Click on the hotel name and all is revealed. You can book online.
e-mail: Info@ringhotels.de

Roteiro Campista

www.roteiro-campista.pt
Choose the region in Portugal on the map, then choose the campsite from the region map. Each campsite has a list of facilities, tariff table for various services and seasons, a photo gallery and a detailed map. There are links to camping equipment manufacturers and shops.
e-mail: Info@roteiro-campista.pt

Sercotel Hotels

www.sercotel.es/
The company owns 70 hotels in the main cities of Spain, Andorra and Portugal. and has an attractive web site in English and Spanish. To find a hotel, either use the drop-down menu or click on the map. Lists of hotels in each area link up with individual hotel pages. Each hotel is described concisely with all the information you may need.
e-mail: reservas@sercotel.es

Silence Hotels Austria

www.silence-hotels.co.at/silence-hotels/engl/index.html
There are eighteen family-run hotels in quiet and remote regions of Austria, mainly in the mountains. The web site tells you something about the host family; if you want to book, complete the enquiry form.
e-mail: via online form

Sokos Hotels

www.sokoshotels.fi
Thirty-seven hotels in twenty-five Finnish cities. Choose the destination on the map then the hotel from the list. Prices are tabulated separately and you can book by phone or fax.
e-mail: via online form

Sorat Hotels

www.sorat-hotels.com/index.htm
Sorat controls a group of about 20 hotels, many of which are unusual or avant-garde, in major German cities. The simply laid out site, in English and German, features online booking, an event planner and a brochure request form. There is no search engine but

hotels can be viewed by clicking on a list or a map. Each hotel is fully described and there are external links to national railway and local tourist information web sites.

e-mail: headoffice@sorat-hotels.com

SunScale

spain.sunscale.com
This is a database of 300 hotels in more than forty Spanish cities. All the information is clearly set out with a currency converter. You can check room availability and book online.
e-mail: via online form

Swedish Hotel Guide

www.hotellguiden.se
A simple search engine gives you a list of hotels in Sweden with addresses, telephone and fax numbers. There are also web site and e-mail addresses to other hotels.
e-mail: via online form

The Parker Company

www.theparkercompany.com
The Parker Company rents villas all over Italy, from cottages to castles. The home page contains links to the villas, travel tips, a discussion forum, an events calendar, car rental, phone rental, vineyard tours, a cookery school and the Tuscany Institute. You can see lists of villas in each region in table format with price and size details. Clicking on a particular villa brings up several photographs and much more detailed information about it, as well as activities in the surrounding area.
e-mail: italy@theparkercompany.com

The Tartan Collection

www.regionlink.com/grampian/tartan/tartan.html
Covers 24 Scottish hotels owned by this group. The home page has links to each hotel, providing pictures, descriptions of facilities and location, proprietor,

contact details and prices. Although booking information (including terms and conditions) is given, online booking is not possible.
e-mail: not available

TOP International Hotels Europe

www.top-hotels.de/indexe.htm
The web site combines 230 selected 3 and 4 star hotels in Europe. Use the map to choose your hotel then follow the link to its home page. A booking form is available.
e-mail: via online form

Travel UK

www.travel-uk.com/tuk/travel-uk-data.htm
A directory of accommodation for the whole of the UK, with a comprehensive guide to restaurants. On the home page you can search under town listing, restaurant name or establishment type.
e-mail: via online form

Travillas

www.travillas.com
Villas for rent in Portugal are listed regionally and by resort. Each villa can be viewed, read about and booked online. There are details of facilities, services and staff, local activities and prices in Euros, US$ and Sterling.
e-mail: Villas@travillas.com

UK Parks

www.ukparks.com
This is a directory for campsites, chalets, caravans and equipment hire in the UK. Choose what best suits you and the search engine does the rest, giving you full details and a price list.
e-mail: not available

Latin America

Camino Real Hotels & Resorts

www.caminoreal.com
This Mexican hotel chain operates in twenty resorts around the country. Loads

of information, a currency converter and online booking make it easy to transact.
e-mail: Feedback@caminoreal.com

Cascada de las Animas

www.cascadadelasanimas.cl
This private ranch, 60 km from the Chilean capital Santiago, offers accommodation in cabins or at a campsite. There is a range of leisure activities and eco-tours, a healing centre with a range of healing programs and a meeting hall.
e-mail: cascadaa@ctcinternet.cl

Chile Hotels Reservations

www.chile-hotels.com
Chilean hotel listings, reservations and links to flights, transport, car hire and tour booking services. Hotels have brief descriptions and links to pages with pictures, services and reservation forms.
e-mail: Chilehotels@gochile.cl

Five Sisters Lodge

www.fivesisterslodge.com
Five Sisters Lodge is a resort in a beautiful part of Belize. It offers suites, rooms and cabanas, local attractions and guided tours with combined prices.
e-mail: Fivesislo@btl.net

Middle East

Bed and Breakfast and Holiday Apartments in Jerusalem

www.bnb.co.il
Rooms in more than fifty private lodgings are available for rent. If you find one on the list supplied with names, addresses and phone numbers, use the e-mail to book. If not, about half of them have individual pages, which you can check out for more details.
e-mail: not available

Dan Hotels

www.danhotels.co.il
Dan operates a chain of ten luxury hotels in Israel. The homepage features

a travel agents link, conference facilities, package deals, and useful tips for visitors about what to wear, climate and geography. For each hotel there are photographs, maps, contact details and a vast amount of other information including banquets, restaurants, suites, hot deals, services, kids activities and local attractions. Online reservations and bookings are possible, using a secure server.
e-mail: via online form

Dedeman Hotels & Resorts

www.traveler.net/htio/custom/dedeman/
There are thirteen resort hotels in Turkey's favourite tourist destinations. Click the image on the map and the hotel is revealed. You can book by credit card online.
e-mail: not available

Israel Kibbutz Hotels

www.kibbutz.co.il
This online catalogue of kibbutz accommodation in Israel has a map. Click on a region and you get a list of accommodation. Other features include tour itineraries from each kibbutz.
e-mail: Yael@kibbutz.co.il

Isrotel

www.isrotel.co.il
A small chain with eight hotels and resorts in Israel with local information and instant booking by e-mail.
e-mail: Cro_asst@isrotel.co.il

North America

1st Travellers Choice

www.virtualcities.com/ons/oonsadex.htm
This is a database of Bed and Breakfast and Country Inns in the USA and Canada. You can search for accommodation either by location or activity, for example, fishing, skiing or even weddings. Each inn has details

of rates, local activities and guidance on how to get there.
e-mail: 1stone@virtualcities.com

AH & MA Online

www.ahma.com
Over a thousand lodgings with 1,400,000 rooms from hotels to campsites across the USA. First pick the State, next the city, then what you prefer, and you will see a list of possible choices.
e-mail: Infoctr@ahma.com

America Inn

www.americinn.com
A database and reservation system for 17 US States must be useful. Match your itinerary with the map and you more or less have it made.
e-mail: Americinn@Americinn.com

Amerihost Inn Hotels

www.amerihostinn.com
Hotels and inns in many US States. Each lodge has its own page with details and a booking link. All information is clearly laid out with local attractions, restaurants and a guide to getting there.
e-mail: Beckys@americahostinn.com

Bed and Breakfast Inns of North America

cimarron.net
Bed and Breakfast in North America with inns listed by State.
e-mail: Daniel@bestinns.net

Campgrounds & Trailer Grounds in Canada

www.myvacationguide.com
Campsites in Canada are listed by Province, tourist region or nearby town. Each campsite has a photo gallery and list of facilities. There are links to private pages containing another catalogue of Canadian campsites and travel resources.
e-mail: not available

Cedar Creek Treehouse

www.cedarcreektreehouse.com
A cabin located 50 feet up a giant cedar in Mt. Rainier National Park in the USA. You can rent it and see for yourself what the web site shows in a picture gallery.
e-mail: not available

Concord's Colonial Inn

www.concordscolonialinn.com
This extraordinary site features an inn said to be haunted by a previous resident. Apart from the usual information about local attractions, room rates, dining and a reservation form, you will find comments made by guests who stayed in the eerie room 24.
e-mail: Info@concordscollonialinn.com

Delta Hotels

www.deltahotels.com
Canadian hotel chain listed by Province and city. Details are sufficient and booking is by e-mail.
e-mail: via online form

Fairmont Hotels and Resorts

www.fairmont.com
North American hotels and resorts for business and leisure. Details are well laid out, including how to get there.
e-mail: not available

Grand Heritage Hotels

www.grandheritage.com
US listed historic houses used as hotels. Their history, environs and well-appointed facilities are set out in enough detail to book online.
e-mail: via online form

Historic Hotels of America

historichotels.nationaltrust.org/
This site has 145 historic US homes converted into hotels. The facilities of the hotels are fully described, many have their own sites where you will find more details and online booking. You can order a brochure.
e-mail: not available

Keddy's Hotels & Inns

www.keddys.ca

This chain operates hotels in three regions of Canada: Nova Scotia, Prince Edward Island, and New Brunswick. The hotels are listed in these regions and can be accessed by clicking on the navigation bar. Each hotel is well described with room rates, dining and other facilities. Good maps show you the locations and local attractions are fully detailed. Credit card reservations can be made via secure server, or by phone.

e-mail: not available

Knights Inn

www.knightsinn.com

US guesthouses listed by State and linked to a reservation service. Get yourself a free catalogue.

e-mail: via online form

La Quinta Inns & Suites

www.travelweb.com/TravelWeb/lq/common/laquinta.html

Budget accommodation in the USA offering more than 33,000 rooms in some 300 cities. Each inn is listed separately and you can book online.

e-mail: via online form

Loews Hotels

www.loewshotels.com

The web site has more than accommodation in North America. At the same time as booking accommodation online, you can arrange car rental and check out a travel guide.

e-mail: via online form

Microtel Inns and Suites

www.microtelinn.com

Budget accommodation in North America. Each state has its highlighted list and clicking on a hotel name takes you to its page. Information is ample and there are several discounts on offer.

e-mail: via online form

Milner Hotels

www.milner-hotels.com

Milner Hotels runs five hotels in North America, which are listed by location. For each hotel there are photographs and a description of the rooms, facilities and services. There are links to a reservation request form (no online booking), maps and room rates. There is also a page of external links for local information about airlines, car rental, weather forecast, tourist bureaux, restaurant guides, and other local city web sites.

e-mail: milnerht@ix.netcom.com

Motel 6

www.motel6.com

A motel chain in central USA. Use the map to access the motel, then make your booking.

e-mail: not available

Omni Hotels

www.omnihotels.com

Omni operate forty-two luxury hotels mainly in the USA. Their impressive web site has a sound file, animations and a tour of the hotels. You can get yourself on their mailing list, register in the travel agents section and book online. To view the hotels you select a state, then choose the hotel from the list that appears. Each hotel is fully described and as an extra you can download location maps, a photo library and get a weather forecast.

e-mail: via online form

Phoenix Inn Hotels

portland.citysearch.com/E/V/PDXOR/0008/32/95/

There are eleven Phoenix Inns located across North America. Each hotel is described separately with room rates, special offers, conference facilities, amenities, maps, local attractions and restaurants. There is an online form to request further information but booking cannot be made online. You can get

local information by using the link to
Portland.Citysearch.com.
e-mail: not available

Ramada

www.ramada.com/ctg/cgi-bin/Ramada
The Ramada chain operates over 1,000
hotels all over the world. From the home
page of their user-friendly web site you
can directly access media information,
special packages, an event and meeting
organiser, franchise information, and a
full description of the three types of
accommodation offered. The customised
search engine allows you to specify any
combination of country, region, price
range, amenities or features. Each hotel
is adequately described and external
links take you to currency converter and
weather forecast sites. Online availability
check and booking are possible.
e-mail: via online form

Red Roof Inns

www.redroof.com
The Red Roof site is disappointing,
but as the company manages more
than 300 moderately priced hotels
across North America it is worth
visiting. By searching with a unique ID
or by city or State you will have enough
information about their hotels, facilities
and nearby restaurants. You can make
your booking online by credit card.
e-mail: gwhitcomb@redroofinns.com

Renaissance Hotels and Resorts

www.renaissancehotels.com
Mainly North American with a few
hotels and resorts scattered elsewhere.
Information is ample and booking is
simple.
e-mail: via online form

Rodd Hotels and Resorts

www.rodd-hotels.ca
A Canadian hotel chain with lots of
facilities and good in-house services.
e-mail: Rodds@rodd-hotels.ca

Shilo Inns

www.shiloinns.com
They have built 45 inns in nine western
States of the USA. Information is fairly
detailed and you can book by freephone
or e-mail. There are links to local guides
and event calendars.
e-mail: Groupsales@shiloinns.com

Shoney's Inn

www.shoneysinn.com
Use the alphabetical list or click on
the map to choose from the seventy
US inns on this web site. You will find
a map, contact details, how to get there
and a booking form.
e-mail: not available

South Seas Resorts

www.ssrc.com
A chain with accommodation in seven
resort areas in Florida. Each page details
special offers, recreation facilities,
restaurants and public rooms, facilities
and services. You can check prices,
availability and booking procedures.
e-mail: not available

StudioPLUS

www.studioplus.com
Comfortable deluxe studios in ninety
locations in North America, intended for
long-term stays by business travellers.
Check out the contact addresses and
book by e-mail.
e-mail: Extstay@extstay.com

Super 8 Motels

www.super8.com
US motel chain. Search on the maps or
fill a request form. As a friendly gesture
you get the local weather forecast.
e-mail: via online form

Taylor Hotel Group

www.taylorhotelgroup.com/index.htm
This hotel chain owns three luxury
hotels in Idaho and Montana, western
USA. The home page contains only a

map and four links: to each hotel and to a Special Offer page. The hotels are adequately set out with a local road map, selected features, daily rates and external links to a local travel guide and event calendar, a fishing report, and FAQ. Reservation can be requested via an online form, but booking is not possible.
e-mail: not available

Terracana Resort & Chalets

www.terracana.com
Log cabins in the Canadian Rockies with online contacts and e-mail booking.
e-mail: Booking@terracana.com

The Vacation Connections

www.lodging1.com
There are hundreds of places to get away to in Wisconsin USA. To view them click on the Search button and enter the name or click on the map for a list of accom- modation, then call the number to book.
e-mail: bill@lodging1.com

Towne Place Suites

www.towneplace.com
This US group is a member of the Marriott chain of hotels. Find your hotel by location, then use the contact information online to book. Local amenities are clearly detailed, including the nearest airport.
e-mail: via online form

Travelodge

www.travelodge.com
They offer almost 600 lodges throughout North America's business, resort and leisure areas, varying in size between 25 and 200 rooms. Each hotel is listed separately and you can book online.
e-mail: via online form

Tree Houses of Hana, Maui

www.maui.net/~hanalani/
The site briefly describes a small tourist village built in the tree-tops. Previous visitors give you their comments.
e-mail: Hanalani@maui.net

USA Campsites

www.usacampsites.com
This vast database of campsites in the USA is listed by State. For each you will find an address and a phone number. A few have their own web sites.
e-mail: Customer-service@ usacampsites.com

USA Groups Inc.

www.usa-groups.com
This is a free hotel reservation service for group travellers wanting quality accommodation in Washington DC for business meetings, conventions, student and senior citizen travel, or family reunions. They promise to provide the most cost-effective accommodation. Complete the form, use the telephone, or e-mail to book.
e-mail: Usagroups@aol.com

Vacation Link

www.vacationlink.com
North American home exchange directory with some world wide offers. If you want to swap your yacht as well you can do so online.
e-mail: via online form

Westin Hotels & Resorts

www.westin.com/cgi/t3.cgi/main.taf
The Westin group includes Starwood, which owns the Sheraton Hotels. They operate 110 hotels world wide. The homepage of this well-designed site will link you to company news, hot deals, meeting facilities and a section for official travel agents. Searching for a hotel can be done either by clicking on the world map or by choosing a combination of city, area and type of facility. Each hotel is amply described and external links forecast the weather and help you with flight and car reservations. A special feature is the

online meeting planner for business customers. Online reservations are possible.
e-mail: via online form

Wingate Inn

www.wingateinns.com
Some 70 inns in western and southern States of the USA. Click on the State, then the inn name and up comes a list of facilities and services, local restaurants, how to make a reservation and how to get there.
e-mail: via online form

World wide

3rd Age Home Exchange

www.3rdage-home-exchange.com
A home exchange service world wide for senior citizens. Over 50's register free. Don't forget to say how far you are from shops and local transport.
e-mail: not available

Barceló Hotels

www.barcelo.com
This Spanish chain has hotels in Spain, Turkey, Czech Republic, North and Central America and the Caribbean. Select the country, then click on the hotel list that comes up and you get lots of information, pictures and an e-mail link for reservation. Text is in English, Spanish and German, however, the site can only be viewed with Navigator 4 or Explorer 4 or later.
e-mail: not available

Bass Hotels and Resorts

www.basshotels.com
Type in your destination city and this world wide hotel chain will come up with suggestions. The map shows you where they are and other information tells you what to do when you get there. You can book by e-mail.
e-mail: HI GuestRelationsEMEA@ basshotels.com

Best Western

www.bestwestern.com
Best Western is a chain of 3,800 hotels world wide. The home page features a Quick Search facility, where hotels can be searched by location or date of travel. Searching brings up a list of hotels that match the criteria, with availability if known. Each hotel listing includes a photograph, information about facilities, rates, location and local attractions and events. Once you have found your hotel, rooms can be booked online. There is information on special deals and a mailing list.
e-mail: via online form

Four Seasons Hotels

www.fourseasons.com/index.html
Four Seasons operate luxury hotels and villas in Asia, the South Pacific, Europe, the Middle East and North America. The home page features new hotels, event planning, city reviews and vacation information. Each hotel is described with all its facilities, photographs, special packages, printable fact sheets, map, airport directions, local attractions and business facilities. You can check rates, availability and book online.
e-mail: via online form

Helnan International Hotels

www.helnan.com
Hotels in Egypt, Saudi Arabia and Denmark with a database and reservation form. There is enough information to transact but if you want more use the e-mail form provided.
e-mail: helnan@ritsec2.com.eg

Hilton Hotels

www.hilton.com
Hilton Hotels operate world wide. This is a good, easy to use site, but crowded with banner ads and links. The homepage contains links to Hilton Japan (dual-language site) and a drop-down menu for quick navigation. There is a

keyword search facility, which helps you search the entire site by location or categories such as special offers, casinos, business packages and so on. Each hotel is clearly described: there are photographs and information about amenities, location and airports. Many hotels offer special packages and reservations can be made online by credit card.
e-mail: via online form

Holi-Swaps Vacation Home Exchange
www.holi-swaps.com
At least 5,000 homes to exchange in more than 60 countries with free membership in the first year. That can't be bad.
e-mail: not available

Holiday Inn
www.basshotels.com/holiday-inn
Holiday Inns are part of the Bass Hotels group. Their home page contains links to the other divisions of the group. The site gives a lot of local information through external links to newspapers, maps, weather, airlines and car rental firms. The Bass Priority Club offers a journey planner and customised quotes to frequent travellers. Hotels can be searched only by location with each hotel amply described and with clear driving directions. Online booking is possible.
e-mail: via online form

Home Exchange
www.homeexchange.com
A database of homes to swap for holidays around the world. You can browse as a guest but you must register as a member to use the service.
e-mail: Admin@homeexchange.com

Home Exchange International
www.heig.com
A world wide home exchange database

with a bonus - links to cheap flights and travel tips.
e-mail: not available

Homestay Friends
www.we-friends.com
This database is for housekeepers and home minders seeking employment. To register yourself fill in the form and upload your photo, then search the web site for a suitable post.
e-mail: Festival@we-friends.com

Hostelling International IYHF
www.iyhf.org
The International Youth Hostel Federation has hostels world wide. Their web site tells you how to join the Federation and lists discounts for members. There are links to national YH pages, most of which are available in English.
e-mail: not available

Hostels.com
www.hostels.com
This is the largest grouping of hostels world wide, listed by continent and then by country. You will find the address and telephone number of each hostel. There are useful tips for budget travellers, links to budget transport pages and online travel stores.
e-mail: not available

Hotelguide.com
www.hotelguide.ch
The site claims to be the largest hotel directory on the Internet, with information on over 20,000 hotels world wide. Just type in the city name and you get a list of hotels with internal links to pages containing all the information you need, accepted credit cards, a reservation form and currency converter.
e-mail: Service@Hotelguide.com

Hotels and Travel on the Net
www.hotelstravel.com
This is a truly excellent web site with

links to more than 120,000 hotel web pages in over 120 countries. There are links to local guides, maps, transport and cultural pages. More than 100 hotel chains world wide, including small regional chains, are linked on this site. There are also links to flight and car reservation centres.
e-mail: Comments@hotelstravel.com

Hotels Concorde

www.concorde-hotels.com
Over 70 hotels, mainly in France, with a few others scattered around the world. Use the map, then choose the hotel and all is revealed. You can book online with help from the currency converter.
e-mail: via online form

Hotelweb

www.hotelweb.fr
Several French hotel chains combine on this web site to provide a database of more than 3,000 hotels world wide. Choose the chain, then the city, then the hotel and book online.
e-mail: not available

Howard Johnson Hotels & Inns

www.hojo.com/ctg/cgi-bin/
HowardJohnson
Howard Johnson operates world wide, with over 500 hotels in four categories. The site is lively and the home page contains special offers, packages for corporate travel and franchise information, which can be requested online. You can access your chosen hotel by location using the maps, by categories listed or with the search engine to select a combination of location, price and amenities. Each hotel is clearly described and there are external links to a currency converter and weather forecasts. Reservations can be made online.
e-mail: via online form

Hyatt Hotels & Resorts

www.hyatt.com
Hyatt Hotels, incorporating Park Hyatt, Grand Hyatt, and Hyatt Regency,

operate luxury hotels around the world. The attractive site with links to a vast amount of information is simple to use. Its features include a special offer finder, online meeting planner, mailing list and external links to travel agents. You access the hotels and resorts using a destination keyword or via the world map provided. The hotel information can be downloaded with a fact sheet that contains a lot more useful data about the hotel and surroundings. Online reservations are possible and a currency converter is provided.
e-mail: via online form

Ibis Hotels

www.hotelweb.fr/HOTELWEB/
i_gindex.htm#NIVEAU-0
Ibis operates 450 hotels world wide. This is an attractive site in English and French but navigation can be a little difficult, as there is no fixed menu bar. Reservations can be made through travel agents listed for each country, but the location map does not include hyperlinks. Information about their hotels is not generous and the reservation request form does not permit you to book online.
e-mail: not available

ILA - Chateaux and Hotels de Charme

www.ila-chateau.com
Two hundred independent hotels around the world combine on this web site. Most of them were previously aristocratic homes in charming locations. Each hotel is separately described with pictures and an e-mail address for reservation.
e-mail: Info@ila-chateau.com

InnSite

www.innsite.com/index.html
This site is a huge directory of inns and bed and breakfast accommodation world wide. The home page is crowded with banner ads but once into the site it

is well designed and simple to navigate. You can browse the site by country, keyword or specific feature.

Extra features include a travel-related bookstore, newsgroups and links to world accommodation and travel associations. Although online booking is not possible, each venue is fully documented and has a contact for reservation. External links bring you maps and local weather forecasts.
e-mail: info@innsite.com

Inter-Continental Hotels and Resorts

www.interconti.com
Inter-Continental own and operate hotels all over the world. Select the continent then the country and you get a list of hotels, each of which has an internal page with details of location, facilities, weather, a currency converter and meeting fact sheet in PDF format. There are special promotions for leisure and business travellers.
e-mail: Inquiry@interconti.com

International Chapters

www.villa-rentals.com
The site is maintained by an agency, which rents villas on behalf of the owners. There are villas in Britain, the Caribbean, France, Greece, Ireland, Italy, Morocco, Spain and its islands. Listings are in country groups, each villa having its own internal page with picture gallery, facilities, services and equipment, distances from local attractions and staff details. You can order a brochure online.
e-mail: Info@villa-rentals.com

Jewish Travel Network

www.jewish-travel-net.com
A database of home exchange, rental, home stays, B & B's and hotels for orthodox Jews. Transactions are open to members only.
e-mail: Jewishtn@best.com

Kempinski Hotels and Resorts

www.kempinski.com
The German level of luxury, which the web site makes plain, spread over Europe and the Middle East. Text is in English and German, you can download a fact sheet and book online.
e-mail: Kempinski@vertikal.de

KOA Kampgrounds

www.koakampgrounds.com
You will find more than 500 campsites in the USA, Canada, Mexico, Spain and Japan. Each country has a map; clicking on a campsite links you to a descriptive page. All prices are in the national currency without a converter. Additional features include discount cards, FAQ, and vacation ideas.
e-mail: via online form

Le Meridien

www.lemeridien-hotels.com
World wide French hotel chain, well catalogued and with easy online booking.
e-mail: not available

Maritim Hotels

www.maritim.de
Hotels in Germany, Tenerife and Mauritius that you click off the map. Road maps tell you how to get there.
e-mail: Info.vklon@maritim.de

Marriott Hotels

www.marriott.com
Marriott International own 1,800 hotels and inns world wide. The home page lists all hotels in the chain and current special offers. A search engine will seek out accommodation including apartments and conference services in a city of your choice. Each hotel has details of services, room facilities, sports and recreation facilities, local attractions and a map of the environs.
e-mail: via online form

Millennium Hotels & Resorts
www.mill-cop.com
There are two hotel chains on this
database spanning the USA, Europe
and Southwest Pacific. Maps for each
will help you choose your hotel.
You can book online.
e-mail: via online form

Mövenpick Hotels & Resorts
www.movenpick-hotels.com
The chain operates in Germany, Holland,
Switzerland and the Middle East.
Everything is neatly set out so you can
book online using the currency converter.
e-mail: via online form

Pan Pacific Hotels
www.panpac.com/index.html
Pan Pacific run sixteen luxury hotels
in the Pacific Rim and four more in North
America. The home page lists all the
hotels by country and has links to special
offers, toll-free reservation numbers, and
company information. The hotels are fully
described with contact details, room rates,
services, restaurants, sample menus,
meeting and banqueting facilities. The
Bangkok hotel in the chain is linked to a
separate site (www.bangkok.panpac.com).
Online booking is possible over a secure
server. Japanese text is available.
e-mail: not available

Park Plaza International Hotels, Inns and Resorts
www.parkhtls.com
This international hotel chain offers
luxurious accommodation world wide.
Choose the continent on the map and a
highlighted list of hotels appears. Click
on the hotel name and it is described in
full detail.
e-mail: Trizzo@parkhtls.com

Peninsula Hotels
www.peninsula.com
The classy web site reflects the style of
this Asian and US hotel chain. Each

hotel has information on local
attractions, maps and a list of special
packages in addition to details of its
services and facilities. You can book
online.
e-mail: Tph@peninsula.com

Places To Stay
www.placestostay.com
This is a world wide Internet
accommodation booking service
catalogued by continent and country.
Each hotel is briefly described with
facilities and local attractions. You can
check room availability and book online
using the secure credit card service.
e-mail: not available

Prince Hotels
www.princehotels.co.jp/english/
Prince Hotels runs sixty-two hotels in
Japan and nine more world wide -
North America, Malaysia, Australia
and Hawaii. This web site covers thirty
Japanese and nine world wide hotels in
four groups which you can access via a
hyper-linked map. Each hotel has pages
with details of room rates, restaurants,
banqueting halls and other facilities,
local maps and information. Online
booking is not possible but you can
request reservations. Text is in English
and Japanese.
e-mail: not available

Radisson Hotels
www.radisson.com
Radisson operates world wide.
There are two versions of the site and
you are better off with the low graphics
option as the other is extremely slow
to load. A special feature is a customer
profile called My E-scapes, which sends
customised e-mail alerts to registered
clients. You search for your choice of
hotel by country, then the hotel page
gives you the details and maps you
require. Reservations can be made
online and there are external links to

companies with reciprocal arrangements - airlines, car rental, financial institutions and telecommunications.
e-mail: via online form

Regal Hotels

www.regal-hotels.com/regalhotel/pages/regal.cfm

Regal owns and operates luxury hotels in North America and Asia. The web site is attractive with some animation and lots of images. It runs a monthly newsletter, a meeting planner, and a guest-book. External links take you to travel agents and to American Express. Hotels can be selected from a list or by clicking on a world map. Each hotel has photographs, street maps, information about amenities, meeting facilities, room rates, special offers and local attractions. You can book online.
e-mail: info@regalhotel.com

Sheraton Hotels & Resorts

www.sheraton.com

The site has a search engine that allows you to select by city, country and hotel requirements. When a match suiting your requirements is found you get a list of hotels with internal links to pages with pictures, prices, facilities, weather information and forms to book your room, car and flights.
e-mail: via online form

Stay 4 Free

www.stay4free.com

Accommodation exchange and home stay for backpackers, businessmen and gays. Register free and the world is at your service.
e-mail: Info@stay4free.com

The Leading Hotels of the World

www.lhw.com

Every hotel in this database is regarded as unique, luxurious and providing guests with an extraordinary level of comfort and service. Only those

countries world wide with hotels satisfying the exacting criteria are included. If this is your scene, enjoy it; if not enjoy the web site.
e-mail: not available

The Surf-X-Change

www.geocities.com/TheTropics/Shores/5177/

A site for surfers living near surfing beaches. New visitors should check the Explanation page for details of how the accommodation scheme works.
You need to register to use the site fully. Otherwise click on the area of the map where you want to go surfing and you are given a list of all surfers living there with details. Links take you to other surfing sites.
e-mail: Surf-x-change@geocities.com

TravelWeb

www.travelweb.com

TravelWeb is a world wide hotel and flight-booking service offering special deals and online shopping facilities. The site is easy to navigate with the database accessed by location, date, price range, hotel chain and amenities. Each of these will produce a description of the hotel including availability, prices, facilities, local attractions, distance from airport, and sometimes a link to the hotel's own web site. There are external links to local maps, weather forecasts and a currency converter. Reservations can be made via secure central online booking system or directly with the hotel.
e-mail: travelweb@travelweb.com

Unusual Villa Rentals

www.unusualvillarentals.com

This is a catalogue of luxury villas and castles in the Caribbean, Mediterranean, Africa and South Pacific. Each region has a list of lodges and internal links to pages providing details and picture galleries. Few villas are priced, so fill

in the online request form if you find something you like.
e-mail: Inquiry@unusualvillarentals.com

Vacation Rentals by Owner

www.vrbo.com/vrbo/
The site offers privately let villas all over the world. Each villa has a picture gallery, location and seasonal rates. Send your enquiry direct to the owner's e-mail address.
e-mail: not available

Villa Rent International

www.villa-rent.com
Villas all over the world. Each continent has a list of villas; clicking on a name gives more details. The villas are briefly described with pictures and prices and an enquiry form can be completed for more information.
e-mail: via online form

Villas of Distinction

www.villasofdistinction.com
The site contains a huge collection of villas situated on all continents. The villas are listed by country with a breakdown to individual units including seasonal rates. To find out more fill a request form specifying your destination, facilities, staff and price range.
e-mail: via online form

Welcome to Ritz-Carlton

www.ritzcarlton.com
The site lists hotels by continent. Click on the town name and you get rates in local currency for rooms of different standards, a reservation form and useful tips for business travellers.
e-mail: via online form

Worldexecutive

www.worldexecutive.com
A search engine helps you find luxury hotels in cities world wide. There are discount offers for business travellers in more than fifty cities, as well as city guides and links to official guides.
e-mail: via online form

Wyndham Hotels & Resorts

www.wyndham.com
The chain has more than 300 hotels with some 70,000 rooms in North America, the Caribbean and Europe. Selecting your destination and then the hotel gives you all the details you need. You can order a brochure.
e-mail: not available

Airports

Africa

Airports Company South Africa

www.airports.co.za/acsa/
This is the official site of the Airports
Company South Africa. It provides
information about the company, as
well as flight schedules, facilities and
weather at nine airports in the country.
e-mail: via online form

Airports of Mauritius

mauritius-airport.intnet.mu/
Although being redeveloped, the
International Airport at Plaine Magnien
in the Republic of Mauritius is in use.
At the moment the site is a single page
in English and French giving local
weather news, flight schedules and little
else. A more comprehensive site is to
be posted on the Internet.
e-mail: airport_info@intnet.mu

Asia

Airports Authority of Thailand

www.airportthai.or.th/html/bkk.html
Five of the most popular tourist airports
in Thailand are represented on this site;
Bangkok, Chiang Mai, Hat Yai, Phuket
and Chiang Rai. There is General
Information, Terminals, Complete

Services, Airline Information, Contact
Information and facts about each city.
Tourist attractions, site maps and guest
books are listed on the home page.
All information is available in English
and Thai.
e-mail: aatcom27@ksc.th.com

Chiang Kai-Shek International Airport

www.cksairport.gov.tw
Chiang Kai-Shek International Airport
is in Taiwan's official web site. Searches
are possible under five main subjects:
Flights, Transportation Services,
Immigration, Airport Facilities and
Travel Services. Links to postal services,
aviation, museum, food and airport
shops are also available. Information
is in both English and Chinese, however
the Chinese version can only be read
if you have the right software.
e-mail: via online form

Fukushima Airport

**www.kajima.co.jp/site/fukushima/
index.htm**
Fukushima Airport is 20 kilometres
south of Koriyama on the main Japanese
island of Honshu. In addition to details
about the airport, transport and links to
airlines, hotels and travel agents, there
are a few words about the culture and
history of Fukushima.
e-mail: motoo@pub.kajima.co.jp

Hiroshima Airport

**www.pref.hiroshima.jp/kukou/kutai/
airport/index-e.html**
Hiroshima airport serves the southern
part of Japan, and the site is in Japanese
and English. The home page has an
overview of the airport runway.
To the right of the picture, you will
find nine subjects: Domestic Flights,
International Flights, Ground
Transportation, Terminal Map, Phone
Numbers, Air Network, Chuo Shinrin
Park, Airport Village and Hiroshima

Nishi Airport Information. Links to other information and contacts are available under each subject. One point to note is that there are seasonal variations for both domestic and international flights.
e-mail: kutai@pref.hiroshima.jp

HKG - Hong Kong International Airport

www.HkiD.Com/people/hkg/
Hong Kong International Airport at Chek Lap Kok. Click on the "News" navigation bar and you will find information about ground transport, terminal services and tourist attractions, among others. Alternatively, you can go to the HKG Site Index box to search for a specific topic. Links to airlines, hotels and travel agents, as well as a history of Hong Kong's previous airport are also available.
e-mail: hkg@hkid.com

Kaosiung International Airport

www.kia.gov.tw/
Kaosiung is the second city and main port of Taiwan. This well presented site allows you to access information by clicking either the images or subject titles on the home page. The eight topics cover as much information as you will need but further enquiries can be made by e-mail or phone. The text is in English and Chinese.
e-mail: kia@kia.gov.tw

KL International Airport, Malaysia

www.jaring.my/airport/
Everything you could possibly want to know about Kuala Lumpur International Airport, including arrivals, departures, duty free shopping, how to get there, and airport regulations. Pay special attention to this subject!
e-mail: airport@po.jaring.my

Komatsu Airport

www.pref.ishikawa.jp/k_air/
Komatsu Airport lies in the Hokuriku region in the centre of Japan. Flight

schedules, airport facilities, links to tourism and travel agents are well laid out. A good introduction to the history and culture of the region takes up a large part of the web site.
e-mail: e120800@pref.ishikawa.jp

Macau International Airport

www.macau-airport.gov.mo/
Macau is a former Portuguese colony in southern China. The airport web site has comprehensive information including Flight Information, Airport Guide, Facilities, Duty Free, Tourist Information, Transportation, Technical Information and Cargo. Links to travel agents, airlines and local attractions are also available, all in English, Chinese and Portuguese.
e-mail: via online form

Mactan Cebu International Airport

www.bluewateresort.com/air.html
The Mactan Cebu International Airport is the premier airport in the southern Philippines. The Maribago Bluewater Beach Resort is a 15-minute drive away. Drivers from the resort or a taxi from the airport will whiz you over. The web site gives you a list of international and domestic carriers, but for flight details consult the airlines.
e-mail: not available

Nanjing Lukou International Airport

www.lukou-airport.com
Nanjing Lukou International Airport is in Nanjing, China. All information is in English and Mandarin under six subjects on the home page, but because the headings are not particularly clear, you may have to visit them all to find a sub directory. For example, transportation and tourism information is found under Profile and News. Banking, visa and other immigration information is listed under Passenger Services.
e-mail: njlkia@public.ptt.js.cn

Narita Airport

www.narita-airport.or.jp
Narita Airport in Japan is shown in this
simply designed site. Information about
flight schedules, access to the airport,
services, maps and a directory are easy
to locate. Restaurants, Duty Free
shopping and airline counter directories
are neatly listed under separate titles.
Links to Customs, hotels, and tourism
are also available.
e-mail: naal@naa.go.jp

Niigata Airport

www.pref.niigata.jp/sec25/en/index.html
Niigata Airport is approximately 25
minutes from Niigata City in Japan.
It serves as a commercial and military
airport with routes to Russia, North and
South Korea, China, Southeast Asia and
the Pacific Islands. Part of the web site
is still under construction and English is
presently limited to ground transport
and links to two airlines - Aeroflot and
Korean Airlines.
e-mail: not available

Osaka International Airport

www.ocat.co.jp/english/menu-e.html
Information about Osaka International
Airport in Japan, in Japanese and
English. There is detailed information
about International Flight Check-Ins,
World Travel (tourist offices, travel agents
and airline offices), a map and links to
other useful travel related contacts.
e-mail: via online form

Singapore Changi Airport

www.changi.airport.com.sg
You will find information about airport
services, flight schedules, airline contacts,
shopping and dining at the airport,
transit hotel links, flight connection
advice and free tour offers. In addition
to this English version, the information
is also available in Chinese, Japanese
and Malay.
e-mail: caasinet@pacific.net.sg

Subic Bay International Airport

www.subicnet.com/sbma/airport.htm
Subic Bay International Airport is the
gateway to the Subic Bay Zone in the
Philippines. Links on the home page
connect you to flight schedules,
airport layout and transportation,
airlines, a telephone directory, leisure
centres and the seaport with a fine
photo gallery.
e-mail: via online form

Yuzhno-Sakhalinsk Airport

www.airport.sakhalin.ru/english/
The airport of Yuzhno-Sakhalinsk is
the gateway to the Sakhalin region of
the Russian Far East. The web site is
well documented and you will find all
the information you need to use the
airport. There are links to airlines, a
directory of useful telephone numbers
and other information sites.
e-mail: bagrov@airport.sakhalin.ru

Australasia and Oceania

Alice Springs Airport

www.aliceairport.com.au
Alice Springs Airport serves the very
beautiful tourist areas of the Northern
Territories of Australia. The web site
gives you a lot of information about
airport services, flight schedules, car
parking and airline contacts. If you need
more, then phone, fax or e-mail the
airport with your enquiries.
e-mail: via online form

Auckland International Airport

www.auckland-airport.co.nz
Detailed information about New
Zealand's Auckland International
Airport. In addition to basic facts
about airport layout, transportation
and flight schedules, there are links
to consulting services and investor
information. Customs regulations
and procedures can be found under
Passenger Information. Airport

contacts, airlines and financial services are all online.
e-mail: via online form

Brisbane International Airport
www.bne.com.au
Brisbane International Airport serves south-east Queensland, Australia. This user-friendly site sets it out completely with a visitors' guide to Brisbane, Moreton Bay, the Gold Coast and other places in the environs. Online links to general contacts, business and government sites are worth a look. If you have Navigator or Explorer 4.0 or later you can enjoy the Flash movie online.
e-mail: info@bne.com.au

Hawaii Airports
kumu.icsd.hawaii.gov/dot/airhaw.htm
The home page has links to the airports on eight islands. Information covers services, facilities, transportation and flight schedules. Highways and harbours State-wide also get a mention.
e-mail: via online form

Perth International Airport
www.perthairport.net.au
The Perth International Airport web site is imaginatively designed. The home page has titles that take you to Australian and international flights and circled pictures reveal other information about the airport and its services. There are additional links to Government Sites, Australian and other international airports, travel, tourism and airlines.
e-mail: via online form

Sydney Airport
www.acay.com.au/~willt/yssy/
Everything you ever wanted to know about Sydney and its airport, including airport services, food and shopping, transportation and tourist tips. Links to other web sites and associations are available. You can join the web site e-mail list to obtain more information about the airport and city of Sydney.
e-mail: willt@acay.com.au

Caribbean

Airports Authority of Trinidad & Tobago
www.airporttnt.com
Tobago is served by Crown Point International Airport and Trinidad by Piarco International Airport. There is ample information about flights, airport services, transportation, fast facts about the region and a directory of useful telephone numbers.
e-mail: via online form

Caribbean International Airport
www.virtualmauritania.com/airport/
The Caribbean International Airport, General Santiago Marino, leads you to sunny Margarita Island and the marvellous tourist attractions of Venezuela. By clicking either the subject titles or navigation bars on the home page of the web site you will find interesting tourist features in addition to other travel information.
e-mail: via online form

Princess Juliana International Airport
www.webcarib.com/airport/
Princess Juliana International Airport, located on the island of St. Maarten in the Caribbean, is within 8 hours flight of any major city in Europe and 4 hours from South America. More than 20 daily flights connect the island with 40 destinations world wide. The web site has Airport, Visitors' and Business Guides and the home page has links to airlines, accommodation, local transport and other sites.
e-mail: via online form

Europe

Aeroports de Paris

www.adp.fr

Aeroports de Paris includes two airports in Paris, France: Roissy-CDG Airport and Orly Airport. Information is available both in English and French. You will find topics including flight timetables, car hire, shopping, food and accommodation. A practical guide to Customs regulations and other travel related subjects are also available.

e-mail: via online form

Airport Authority - Flughafen Zurich

www.zurich-airport.com

Designed to meet the needs of both leisure and business passengers, the Zurich Airport web site provides information on five main subjects - News, Visitors, Passenger Services, Flight Information, and All about Us, in English and German. Alternatively, you can make a specific enquiry using the search facility.

e-mail: via online form

Amsterdam Airport Schiphol

www.schiphol.nl

The site for Amsterdam Airport in the Netherlands has a very straightforward design, with 26 subjects neatly laid out on the home page. These include Arrivals, Departures, Timetables, Airport Guide, Maps, Traffic Information, Weather, Jobs, Shopping and Facilities. Links to travel agents, regional airports and a miscellaneous directory are provided separately and are worth further exploration. By clicking the "Buy Fly" navigation bar, you will find the best offers available.

e-mail: via online form

Athens International Airport S.A.

www.athensairport-2001.gr

This web site uses of Quick Time 3.0 and Flash Technologies to provide a stunning experience of the new Athens International Airport in Greece, due to be completed in 2001. By choosing the Flash option on the home page, News, Site Map, Contact Points, Career Opportunities, Flights and Airline Information come out one by one like an aircraft landing, with sound effects. The interactive map is innovative and gives a vivid picture of the airport. Languages on the web site include Greek and English.

e-mail: not available

Birmingham International Airport

www.bhx.co.uk

Birmingham is in the heart of the UK. Information on the site is simply organised under three subjects: Passenger Information, Corporation Education and General Information. Passenger Information details holidays, scheduled flights, airlines, hotel accommodation and airport facilities. Telephone contact numbers to reserve hotels and flights are listed.

e-mail: via online form

Bournemouth International Airport

www.bia.co.uk/bournemouth/

Bournemouth International in the UK has a web site full of traveller-friendly information about hotels, car hire, jobs, airport advertising, airlines and tickets. Use the on-site link to latebreaks.com for money saving opportunities.

e-mail: not available

Brussels Airport Official Website

www.brusselsairport.be

Brussels Airport web site greets you in: English, Dutch, German, French and Spanish. To access information, simply click on titles such as Airport News, Arrivals, Timetable, Telephone Directory, Flights, Shopping Services or Airfield. Alternatively, use the Table of Contents box for a quick search. This site contains some advanced functions which older

browsers might not show at their best, so the latest browsers are recommended.
e-mail: info@brusselsairport.be

Brussels Charleroi Airport

www.charleroi-airport.com
Brussels South Charleroi Airport, 55 km from the capital of Belgium, is ideal for those wishing to travel in central Northern Europe. The navigation bars on the home page take you to airport news, flight schedules, ground transportation, airport maps and on-site links to airlines and tourist matters. Text is in English and German.
e-mail: mail@awex.wallonie.be

Copenhagen Airport

www.cph.dk
Copenhagen Airport is the main air terminal in Denmark. Finding your way around the web site is easy. All airport facilities are clearly laid out with lots of information about special offers at the shopping centre, transportation and travel planning guide. Text is in English and German.
e-mail: via online form

Cork International Airport

www.foundmark.com/AerRianta-Cork.html
Cork International Airport is one of the fastest growing airports in Europe and is a gateway to Southern Ireland. The airport web site has information under many separate topics, including airport news, flight schedules, airport services, airlines operating from the airport and transportation. Links to travel agencies and many other local services are also provided in an information box at the bottom of the home page.
e-mail: via online form

Discover Dusseldorf International

www.duesseldorf-international.de/e/plaene/index.html
Dusseldorf International Airport in

Germany. The English home page has flight schedules, airport maps, trains and road transport details. Text is in English and German.
e-mail: via online form

Euro Terminal

www.euroterminal.com
The Euro Terminal web site provides very comprehensive links to the major airports, airlines and to travel information throughout Europe. All of the linked official airport web sites are in their native languages. Links to sites providing information on accommodation, travel agents and tourist offices are based on your choice of destination. There is a travel planner assistant which quickly helps you to plan a trip, including booking flights and accommodation. If no immediate match is found, you can make a reservation request direct to one of the registered agents or airlines listed.
e-mail: visit@euroterminal.com

Frankfurt Airport-Information

www.frankfurt-airport.de
With Flying Franky as your guide, information is available in English and German, with many help tools. You can either use the flying tool to search for your subject or click on the text links. The online travel service and travel planner are helpful.
e-mail: via online form

Geneva International Airport

www.gva.ch/en/default.htm
Geneva is the main city in the French speaking region of Switzerland and this web site is in English and French. Information about arrivals, departures, flight offers, shopping, services and airport access are available from the boxes on the left side of the home page. There are seven other topics which link to news, other web sites or to the airport management.
e-mail: via online form

Istanbul Airport

www.dhmiata.gov.tr

Istanbul Airport has a well designed web site, but with the majority of the information in Turkish. Information in English is limited to flight arrivals and departures. As there are no links to the airlines, you may find it best to use the contact numbers listed or the e-mail address for further information.
e-mail: info@dhmiata.gov.tr

JSC Tolmachevo Airport

www.tolmachevo.ru

Tolmachevo International Airport is in Novosibirsk, a large industrial, scientific and cultural city in central Russia.
The air route via this airport is one of the most convenient and cost-effective ways to get from Europe to Southeast Asia. It has most of the facilities you would expect at an international airport, all explained on the web site.
e-mail: ivc@tolmachevo.ru

Kastrup, Copenhagen International Airport

www.kastrup.dk

Copenhagen, Denmark, has two airports one at Kastrup and the other at Roskilde. Kastrup is the International Airport and gateway to Denmark. Its web site describes airport services, flight schedules, and other subjects of general interest. Text is in English and Danish.
e-mail: via online form

Keflavik International Airport

www.randburg.com/airport/

Keflavik International Airport in Iceland is one of the most sophisticated and secure airports in the world.
You can check out terminal facilities, transport, hotels, restaurants and links to shopping, tourism, and other subjects on Iceland.
e-mail: via online form

Latvia General

www.eunet.lv/VT/general/tavia.html

Riga International Airport in Latvia, located 7 km from the city. There are details of layout, facilities, services and airlines using the airport; rail, ferry and road transport.
e-mail: not available

Liege Airport

www.liegeairport.com

This Belgian airport handles both passenger and cargo transportation. Click the Passenger navigation bar and you will find information about airport facilities, flight schedules and tour operators. Liege Online in the left corner of the home page has links to other useful information.
e-mail: liegeairport@sab.be

London Luton Airport

www.london-luton.co.uk

Luton Airport is to the north of London. This user-friendly site provides information about the airport, as well as thirteen other topics on its home page. These include facts about the airport, destinations, parking, airlines, tour operations, cargo and development. Special offers and an on-site parking booking service with discount rates are two very useful features. Links to airlines, travel agents, travel and educational organisations are also available.
e-mail: via online form

Malta International Airport

www.maltairport.com

Malta International Airport. Click on the home page navigation bars and you get flight schedules, airport services and facilities and a directory of tax-free shopping. There are links to Malta Tourism Authority.
e-mail: via online form

Manchester Airport

www.manairport.co.uk
Manchester Airport is a gateway to the UK. Designed for easy and quick search, the web site provides about 12 main subjects accessible by clicking either on icons or navigation bars. Information such as flight schedules, airport services and facilities, shopping, food and the tourist attractions in Manchester are well presented. Links to airlines, travel agents and other transportation companies are provided under a series of sub headings.
e-mail: via online form

Marco Polo - Venice Airport

www.veniceairport.it/vce/ita/home.asp
Venice is a beautiful city in northern Italy, and the web site is in English and Italian. You will find very detailed airport and travel information on nineteen subjects on the home page. Links to the day's flights, airline companies and weather forecasts are clearly listed under headings in the middle of the page. There is a News box on the right side of the home page which gives the latest airport and transport news.
e-mail: via online form

National Express - Airports

www.eastmidsairport.co.uk
National Express run a coach service in the UK. This site offers information about Bournemouth International Airport, East Midlands Airport and Stewart International Airport. By simply selecting your airport on the home page, you will find information about airport facilities, flight schedules and links to many other services.
e-mail: via online form

Oslo Airport

www.osl.no:81/osl_web_norsk.html
Oslo, capital of Norway, has English and Norwegian versions of this site. The Arrivals/Departures section includes flight schedules and a timetable. Ground Transportation advises about road and rail access. Shopping/Dining provides a directory of airport shops and restaurants. Passenger Service introduces the local culture and travelling information about Norway. There are also public inquiry e-mail addresses under each of these subjects.
e-mail: irene.snelling@osl.no

Port Lotniczy Wroclaw SA

www.airport.wroclaw.pl/index2.html
Wroclaw International Airport is in Poland, and the information on the web site is available in both English and Polish. Information about schedules, location, terminal layouts, services and airport news is available on the home page. Links to airlines and their official web sites, customs, travel agents and transportation are available under the Services heading.
e-mail: airport@airport.wroclaw.pl

Sheremetyevo International Airport

www.sheremetyevo-airport.ru
Sheremetyevo International Airport serves Moscow, Russia. Click the "eng" link on the home page for guidance on airport layout, transportation, flight timetables, parking, a telephone directory and airlines operating from the airport. All information is available in English and Russian. Links to tourist information for Moscow are available.
e-mail: not available

Sofia Airport Web Site

www.sofia-airport.bg
Visitors to Bulgaria will find lots of useful information at this site - Airline Offices in Sofia with links to airline pages, Information Phones, a Sofia City map with a street index, Borders and Visas, Weather in Bulgaria and Euro Weather. Text is in English and Bulgarian.
e-mail: welitchkovz@sofia-airport.bg

Spanish Airports

www.aena.es/homepage.htm
A link page to forty airports on the Spanish mainland and islands. Click on Aeropuertos Españoles, then select the city you want to visit and you will find an English version for each airport.
e-mail: via online form

The French Airports

www.aeroport.fr
This web site covers 29 French airports. Click on the specific airport and you enter its home page, which gives you Today's Flights, Schedules, Airport Services and Facilities and useful links to local travel information. Text is in English and French.
e-mail: via online form

UK and Ireland Airport Guide

www.a2bairports.com
This is one of the largest guides to all airports in the United Kingdom and Ireland. Clicking on a particular airport brings a wealth of information about local transportation, accommodation, holiday packages, flight schedules, airport maps and other visitor services. You can submit your comments via a feedback mailbox.
e-mail: not available

Vienna International Airport

www.viennaairport.com/englisch/
Vienna is the historic capital of Austria and has long been a major crossroads of Europe. The site provides information grouped in five topics, Airport Information, Services, Vienna Airport plc, Euro Centre Airport and Airport in the Centre of the Europe. Under these topics, you will find information on hotels, flight tickets, food, transfers via Vienna and links to other travel related contacts. Text is available in English and German.
e-mail: via online form

Latin America

Panama City- Bay County International Airport

www.pcairport.com
This official web site is part of Panama City, Florida. Information is grouped into three main subjects: Airlines, Airport Information and NW Florida Information. Links to different airlines, tourist development councils and travel agents are available by selecting each of the subjects. Links to tourist attractions in Panama City are accessible via Panama City Online, at the bottom of the home page.
e-mail: via online form

Rio De Janeiro International Airport

www.aviationbr.com/gig/
Well designed with enough information to make it worth a visit. The home page has eleven links with topics covering airport services, airlines, flight schedules and whatever else a traveller needs to know. More importantly there are very useful links to official Brazilian web sites and information about other airports in the country.
e-mail: via online form

Middle East

Bahrain International Airport

www.bahrainairport.com
Bahrain International Airport is at the strategic and geographic centre of the Gulf States. In addition to information about the airport authority and local Customs regulations, you will find travel tips and transport information. Useful links to other official Bahrain web sites, travel agents and hotel operators are also available.
e-mail: via online form

Fujairah International Airport

www.fujairah-airport.com
Fujairah International Airport is on the

east coast of the United Arab Emirates and is well located to benefit from commerce between East and West. On the home page you will find details of transportation, services, passenger assistance and tourist tips for Fujairah City.
e-mail: via online form

Israel Airport Authority
www.ben-gurion-airport.com/english/main.htm
This site available in English and Hebrew. Information includes airports and schedules. However, there is a disclaimer from the airport authority for those who rely on the information provided, so you may want to consult other related travel or airline sites or contact the particular airport for confirmation.
e-mail: via online form

Kuwait International Airport
www.kuwait-airport.com.kw
You will find nine separate topics including: DGCA, airport, flight schedules, weather forecasts, airport hotels, duty free and facts about Kuwait on this neat interactive site. Links to information and contacts are available under each subject on this is clear and straightforward site.
e-mail: via online form

Sharjah International Airport
www.shj-airport.gov.ae
Sharjah is in the United Arab Emirates, a short distance from Dubai. This site provides a great deal of information about the city and its culture. You will find airport information including facilities & services, airlines and flight schedules. Additional information about Customs, job opportunities and weather, as well as links to other airports, hotels, banks, hospitals and travel tips to other cities are also provided from search boxes.
e-mail: via online form

North America

Aeroports de Montreal
www.admtl.com
This web site provides information for Dorval and Mirabel airports in Montreal, Canada, in English and French. You can either click on one of the four icons on the top of the home page or on the subject headings at the bottom. There is general information about the airports as well as customer services, environment, airline contacts, flights, weather and local attractions.
e-mail: via online form

Airport Authority of Washoe County
www.renoairport.com
Reno Tahoe International Airport and Reno Stead Airport are included on this site. To access the information just click on the images on the home page of each airport or use the Quick Link boxes. These give you all you need to know, with online booking instructions.
e-mail: kmatthews@renoairport.com

Albany Airport
www.albanyairport.com/index1.html
Albany Airport is a gateway to New York City. All information is easily accessible with links to online parking directions. The New York Airport Management web site has information about other New York Airports.
e-mail: info@albanyairport.com

Alpena County Regional Airport
www.oweb.com/upnorth/transport/
Alpena County Regional Airport is a warm and friendly airport on the sunny side of Michigan's Lower Peninsula in the USA. Northwest Airline operates daily flights to Detroit Metro Airport and Chippewa County International Airport. You will find all airport services adequately set out and links to car rentals, Alpena Travel Service as well as a

calendar of local events and festivals.
e-mail: apn@northland.lib.mi.us

Austin-Bergstrom International Airport

www.ci.austin.tx.us/newairport/
Austin-Bergstrom International Airport opened in May 1999 to replace Robert Mueller Municipal in Austin, Texas. This friendly web site gives you lots of information and a virtual tour of airport facilities.
e-mail: via online form

Bermuda International Airport

www.bermuda.bm/airportops/
Bermuda is a popular tourist destination. Information on the airport web site is neatly organised under five subjects: Passenger Information, Scheduled Flight Arrivals & Departures, Shopping, Food & Beverages, Aircraft Handling and The Year 2000 Problem.
e-mail: via online form

Boca Raton Airport

www.bocaratonairport.com
Boca Raton Airport is in Southern Palm Beach County, Florida, USA. Information is neatly presented and the airport seeks to reflect the beautiful and popular city of Boca Raton. You will find airport services, transportation, food and lodging in easy reach on the web site, which is designed for business travellers and tourists alike.
e-mail: via online form

Burbank/Glendale/Pesadena Airport

www.bur.com
Burbank/Glendale/Pesadena Airport is the closest airport to Hollywood, the Valley and downtown L.A. in California, the USA. In less than 10 minutes from the airport you can be in Disney Land, NBC, Warner Brothers and Universal Studios. The web site gives all relevant information about airlines and a good on-site directory about flying from Burbank Airport to other American cities.
e-mail: via online form

Cherry Capital Airport

www.tvcairport.com
Cherry Capital Airport offers services to over 300 domestic and international destinations from Traverse City, Michigan, USA. The web site gives you all the usual airport services, Toll Free phone numbers to all airlines and links to US Maps and traveller information.
e-mail: tvair@tvcairport.com

Chicago Midway Airport

www.ci.chi.il.us/Aviation/Midway/
Chicago Midway Airport covers one square mile in the south of the city, just ten miles from the downtown area. Before O'Hare International Airport came into operation, it was the busiest airport in the world for three decades. Clicking on 6 boxes or 6 images on the home page gives you information about the airport, a map, useful phone numbers, parking facilities, travel and flight schedules.
e-mail: via online form

Chicago O'Hare International Airport

www.ci.chi.il.us/Aviation/Ohare/
In an Internet survey conducted by CIC Research Inc, passengers rated Chicago O'Hare International Airport the world's favourite airport. On this web site you will find information about the terminals, services, parking, airport concessions, transportation, airlines and links to a multitude of companies operating through the airport. You will also discover a lot about Chicago city, where to go and what to do there.
e-mail: via online form

City of Klamath Falls International Airport

www.mhmdesign.com/kfairport/
The official web site of Klemath Airport in Oregon, USA, provides straightforward

and simple information. There is a map of the airport and four boxes on its home page. Horizon Air gives flight schedules, Business tells you about airlines, restaurants and other local information, car rental and travel agents provide contacts to local companies.
e-mail: imt@cdsnet.net

Decatur Airport

www.decatur-airport.org
Decatur Airport is one of five Park District airports in Illinois, USA. In addition to tourist traffic it operates a feeder service to St. Louis's Lambert International Airport and Chicago's O'Hare International Airport. Online links to TWA, United Airlines and National Car Rental are especially useful.
e-mail: via online form

DeKalb Peachtree Airport

www.pdkairport.org
DeKalb Peachtree Airport is regarded as one of best airports in Atlanta, USA. Visitors' Information on the homepage takes you to all you need and a photo gallery.
e-mail: via online form

Denver International Airport

www.flydenver.com
The web site of Denver International Airport in Colorado, USA, has a Quick Navigation Box or buttons to access information. There are links to airport services, flights, airlines, accommodation, car rentals and travel tips.
e-mail: via online form

Houston Airport System

www.ci.houston.tx.us/has/
The Houston Airport System is the 4th largest in the USA and the international gateway to South Central United States. The web site covers George Bush Intercontinental Airport in Houston, William P. Hobby Airport, Ellington Field and CBD Heliport. There is a lot of

information about flights, accommodation, car rental, local travel tips and airlines via their links.
e-mail: not available

Lambert St. Louis International Airport

www.lambert-stlouis.com
There is a good deal of information in this well-designed web site for travellers using this airport in Montana, USA. All you need to know about airport services, transportation, airlines, weather, St. Louis, and so on are easily accessible from links on the home page. There are good maps and anything not listed is obtainable from the Airport Authority through on-site contact numbers.
e-mail: via online form

Lehigh Valley International Airport

www.lvia.org/
Lehigh Valley International Airport is a hassle-free alternative to big-city airports and the gateway to Eastern Pennsylvania and Northern New Jersey, USA. This site is packed with information about flight schedules and destinations, subjects of interest to visitors, airport maps, free online services, local, regional and tourist attractions.
e-mail: via online form

Lester B. Pearson International Airport

www.lbpia.toronto.on.ca
The Greater Toronto Airports Authority operates Lester B. Pearson International Airport in Canada. This official site has information about the airport and Greater Toronto Airports Authority, detailed traveller and airport visitor information and tourist tips. These topics cover local attractions, car rental, hotel accommodation, airline services and flight details. There is also a telephone directory which you can use for further exploration.
e-mail: via online form

Los Angeles World Airports

www.lawa.org

Four airports located in the Los Angeles area; LAX, Ontario, Van Nuys and Palmdale are linked to this site. Separate sections are available on flight schedules, airport layouts and services, ground transport, local maps, tourist attractions and hotels. There is also information about local business opportunities and employment.
e-mail: infoline@airports.ci.la.ca.us

Louisville International Airport

www.louintlairport.com

Louisville International Airport serves Kentucky, USA. The home page links you to all the information you need about airline services, flight schedules, local transport and travel news.
e-mail: admin@louintlairport.com

McCarran International Airport

www.mccarran.com

McCarran International Airport is part of the Clark County Airport System in Nevada, USA, and serves Las Vegas. Airport, airline and flight information is clearly stated. There is an on-site search engine and links to Las Vegas tourism and business web sites.
e-mail: via online form

Melbourne International Airport

www.mlbair.com

Melbourne International Airport is on the beautiful coast of Florida, USA. The holiday spirit of the place is reflected in this enjoyable web site. There are six terminal-like links on its home page and by clicking on the symbols you get the information you are looking for, ranging from air and passenger services to children's entertainment.
e-mail: via online form

Memphis International Airport

www.mscaa.com

Memphis International is the main airport in Tennessee. Apart from subjects important to travellers, this user-friendly site has links to business and employment opportunities and a local weather report.
e-mail: via online form

Metropolitan Washington Airports Authority

www.metwashairports.com

The Metropolitan Washington Airports Authority operates two airports: Washington Dulles International Airport (IAD) and Ronald Reagan Washington National Airport (DCA). This site provides information about ground transportation, airline listings, flight schedules and status, airport facilities, air cargo and general aviation activities for both airports. Links to the home pages of airlines and their ticket booking services are provided. Under Links of Interest you will find airport information directories and airlines from around the world.
e-mail: not available

Miami International Airport On-Line

www.miami-airport.com

Miami is the main airport of Florida, USA. This site has a wealth of information with links to flight schedules, CNN, European Airports International, American Association of Airport Executives, Commercial Aviation Resource Centre, Greater Miami Visitor's Bureau, the Beaches Hotel Association and a host of other official sites.
e-mail: emurray@miami-airport.com

Monroe County - Airport

www.co.monroe.ny.us/airport/

This official site of Monroe County provides a complete overview of Rochester International Airport in the United States. You can either search for topics with the navigation box or click directly on the headings set out on the home page. Detailed transportation maps and helpful telephone numbers

are provided for easy reference. Although the overall design is somewhat plain, the site provides a list of well-selected links to many useful web sites. A visit to these links is recommended.
e-mail: via online form

Nashville International Airport

www.nashintl.com
Nashville is a major airport in Tennessee, USA. You will have no difficulty getting all the information you require from this well-designed web site. When you click on the Check Your Flight icon you will find flight schedules. There are links to government sites, airlines and local travel agents.
e-mail: via online form

Norfolk International Airport

www.norfolkairport.com
This site is designed for a quick search from eight main subjects. By selecting the navigation bars located at either the top or bottom of the homepage, you will find information on flight schedules, airport information, online flight guide, weather and site maps. Links to local attractions and transportation are also provided.
e-mail: via online form

Oakland International Airport

www.flyoakland.com
Oakland International Airport is the gateway to the Oakland Greater Bay Area in California. You will find your way around their web site with ease. The A-Z index is very helpful and should answer most of your questions. There is a network to assist international travellers and lots of useful information about local events, activities and tours. Several services can be booked online.
e-mail: via online form

Official John F. Kennedy International Airport

www.panynj.gov/aviation/ jfkhomemain.html
An attractive site with a lot of information, including transportation to and from JFK, La Guardia and Newark airports, getting around JFK, airport terminal services, tourist information, facilities for the disabled, as well as links to other US and international airports. There is information about local sight seeing, museums and events.
e-mail: not available

Orlando International Airport

www.fcn.state.fl.us/goaa/
Orlando International Airport is conveniently located in the heart of central Florida, USA, between downtown Orlando and the many attractions the State has to offer, including Disneyland. You can navigate the site by clicking on either the images or the subject titles listed on the home page. All information is clearly set out, but if you have further enquiries, you can make them online.
e-mail: via online form

Pilot Age - Airports of Southern California

airports.pilotage.com
This site provides a list of Southern California's airports. From here you can visit thirty-eight separate airport web pages, each containing information about the airport, aviation services, food and accommodation, transportation, local attractions and businesses. Instructions are provided on take off and landing for those arriving in their own aircraft. There are also links to other web sites of local interest.
e-mail: Airport@ci.santa-monica.ca.us

Port of Portland - Aviation System

www.portofportland.com/Aviation.htm
This is part of the web site of the Port of Portland, Oregon, which operates Hillsboro, Troutdale, Mulino and Portland International airports. Between them they handle both commercial and smaller personal and business aircraft. In addition to details about airport

services, there are links to Portland area weather reports, airlines and a travel guide.
e-mail: not available

Raleigh-Durham International Airport

www.rdu.com

Raleigh-Durham International Airport sits in the heart of the Research Triangle of North Carolina, USA and handles more than 7 million passengers each year. Nine subject headings give you information about the terminal, transportation, airlines, travel tips, maps and other news, or you can search the index.
e-mail: info@rdu.com

Salt Lake City Airport

www.ci.slc.ut.us/services/airport/

Salt Lake City International Airport is the gateway to the attractions of Utah, the Mormon State of the USA. This is the web site of Salt Lake City and information about the airport is listed under seven titles specific to airports. There is also a Fast Facts navigation bar to help you find information more rapidly. This web page is in Adobe Acrobat format so if you do not have an appropriate viewer, download it from Adobe's web site.
e-mail: via online form

San Francisco International Airport

www.sfoairport.com

A well designed site offering a series of clear airport terminal maps and detailed descriptions of ground transportation, with costs of travelling between the airport and local hotels by bus, taxi or railway. Flight schedules and airline information is also well presented. Clicking on an airline's name takes you to its web site. An Airport Yellow Pages section allows you to access the web sites of other airports and major airlines world wide. City and airport job opportunities are listed separately.
e-mail: comments@sfoArts.org/

San Jose International Airport

www.sjc.org/

San Jose International Airport is the gateway to Silicon Valley in California, and the web site provides information quickly and easily. On the home page there are friendly instructions on how to use the navigation bars to search from its eight major sections such as flight schedules, airport maps and services. Once in a section, a directory is displayed in the black horizontal bar above each page. Links and contacts are available for further exploration.
e-mail: not available

Santa Monica Municipal Airport

pen.ci.santa-monica.ca.us/ resource_mgmt/airport/

Information about airport office hours and general services. There is a section dealing with specific information on flight schools, pilot supplies, aircraft maintenance and aircraft charter companies based at the airport, with contact telephone numbers. Other useful features include information on local tourist attractions and restaurants, links to the City of Santa Monica web site, aviation related events, emergency aid, local flying clubs, hotels and updated traffic reports.
e-mail: Airport@ci.santa-monica.ca

Seattle-Tacoma International Airport, Port of Seattle

www.portseattle.org./seatac/

This web site has general information about Seattle-Tacoma International Airport, and the Port of Seattle. There are links from the airport home page to individual airlines and their web sites as well as business links, local attractions and employment information. There are domestic and international city guide links and a useful collection of airport terminal maps and local street maps. You can contact the airport management by completing an online public opinion survey.
e-mail: not available

State of Alaska

www.dot.state.ak.us/external/
This is the web site of the State of Alaska. On the home page of the Department of Transportation and Public Facilities you will find the Alaska Airport System. This covers all the airports in Alaska. While Fairbanks is the pivotal transportation and distribution link to interior Alaska, Anchorage gets the bulk of the international traffic. Information about the airports, flight schedules and other matters of interest will appear by clicking appropriately on site links for each airport.
e-mail: marllyn-burdick@dot.state.ak.us

Tampa International Airport

www.tampaairport.com
The airport serves the West Coast of Florida, USA. This is an amusing site with information accessed by clicking titles or cartoon images. Subjects cover news, travel tips, airport services, parking and transportation, flight schedules and transit, a telephone directory, local places of interest, air cargo, weather and business matters.
e-mail: via online form

Tucson International Airport

www.tucsonairport.org/
Tucson International Airport is in Texas, USA. This is a good web site with lots of information set out under ten headings on the home page. You will find all you want to know about the airport, airline services, flight schedules, business matters, local transportation and travel agents. There are flashing navigation bars that provide news and a program of events.
e-mail: via online form

Vancouver International Airport

www.yvr.ca
Vancouver is on Canada's Pacific coast, and the airport web site has information

on airport guides, flight information, transportation & parking, services & facilities, shopping & food, economy & commerce and links to other travel related subjects. The site is well organised and links to travel news web sites are very helpful.
e-mail: via online form

Williamsburg International Airport

www.phf-airport.org/business.html
Williamsburg International Airport is the main airport in Virginia, USA. The web site is designed for quick and easy search. The home page, apart from information about business development possibilities, has links to maps, passenger services, emergency information and others, each of which is elaborated in its own page.
e-mail: via online form

Yeager Airport

www.yeagerairport.com
Yeager Airport is in Charleston, West Virginia, USA. The home page has 15 links which give you lots of information about airline services, flight schedules, business matters, transportation, car rentals, travel agents and more. Daily domestic flights out of Yaeger take you to many of the larger American cities, all of which are listed.
e-mail: fly@yeagerairport.com

World wide

Airwise: The Airport and Air Travel Guide

www.airwise.com/navigate/ hub-frame.html
From this excellent site you can access all major US and fifty international airports. You can book your flight, reserve accommodation and rent a car through the links provided. The Airwise Discussion Forum seeks your opinions on travel matters.
e-mail: feedback@airwise.co

Boats

Africa

Travco

www.travco-eg.com
Cruise the Nile with scuba diving and travel packages as extra attractions. The Nile map shows all the destinations. Contact is by e-mail.
e-mail: main@travco-eg.com

Asia

Andaman Princess

www.siamcruise.co.th/home.htm
Cruising the Andaman Sea and Gulf of Thailand. Links connect you to company information, destinations, schedules and fares. For more information fill the request form or contact them by e-mail.
e-mail: contactus@siamcruise.co.th

Irrawaddy Flotilla Company

www.wild-dog.com/irrawaddy/home.html
Based in the UK, they cruise the Irrawaddy River in Burma. Ships, cruises, services and a good map of the Irrawaddy are all detailed but other information must be obtained from the UK sales agent. You can contact them by e-mail.
e-mail: zaber@wild-dog.com

Songline Cruises of Indonesia

www.songlinecruises.com
Songline Cruises operates in Indonesia, offering a variety of cruises including diving and wildlife adventures, sailing on traditional Bugis Pinisi schooners. The map shows all the ports of call. Click on any ship and you will see her itinerary. For contact use the online addresses.
e-mail: info@songlinecruises.com

Star Cruise

www.starcruises.com
Star Cruise, based in Singapore, is the leading Cruise Line in the Asia-Pacific Basin. Clicking Enter on the home page takes you to another page with Fleet, Cruise Itineraries, Destinations and Enquiries. This excellent site allows you to install Flash 4.0 for better viewing. You can also visit Genting, the Leisure & Entertainment Centre. Text is in English and Japanese.
e-mail: via online form

Turkey Baranta Yachting

www.baranta-yachting.com
Cruising the Turkish coast on a 25-meter yacht takes you into bays and ancient places inaccessible by road. They recommend two weeks on board but this is optional. Equipment to windsurf, fish and kayak is carried on board.
e-mail: Ulysse22@wanadoo.fr

Victoria Cruises

www.victoriacruises.com
Victoria Cruises sail China's Yangtze river, Asia's longest. Home page links take you to sailing dates, schedules, fares, facilities and what you need do to get on their fascinating cruises. There are pictures of destinations and external links to a China travel guide. Contact is by e-mail.
e-mail: info@victoriacruises.com

Australasia and Oceania

American Hawaii Cruises

www.cruisehawaii.com

Cruise your way around the Hawaiian islands of Oahu, Kauai, Maui and Hawaii. The home page has links to Islands, Experience, Vessel and Special Offers. If you like, order a brochure and contact them by e-mail.
e-mail: via online form

Aranui.com

www.aranui.com

Cruising the Marquesas in the South Pacific. In the Destinations link you have a map of the Islands; clicking on one gets a photograph and description of that island. Contact them by e-mail or through their agents.
e-mail: aranui@mail.pf

Coral Princess Cruises

www.coralprincess.com.au

Coral Princess Cruises operates in Australia. The home page gives you access to all their itineraries and destinations - Great Barrier Reef, Kimberly Coast, Across the Top and so on. A map of Australia has much the same information. Contact is by e-mail. Text is in English and German.
e-mail: cruisecp@coralprincess.com.au

MTS Papua New Guinea

www.meltours.com/index.html

Cruising around Papua and New Guinea with diving services and tours as an extra. The map is of Sepik river where most of the action is. External links lead to Air Niagini and more. You can book online.
e-mail: melanesian@meltours.com

Norwegian Capricorn Line

www.ncl.com.au

Wonderful cruises in Australasia and the South Pacific. Internal links take you to loads of information about destinations, ships, maps and more. You can book by online e-mail form.
e-mail: via online form

Paradise Cruises

www.paradisecruises.com

Sunset dinner cruises in Hawaii. Ships and schedules are well presented. External links take you to the Polynesian Cultural Centre, Hawaii Homepage, news and more. Contact is by e-mail.
e-mail: info@paradisecruises.com

Caribbean

American Canadian Caribbean Line

www.accl-smallships.com

On offer are 25 cruises in the Caribbean and Central America in winter, the USA and Canada in summer. The home page has links to Cruises, Ships, Contacts and more. A map helps you choose where to visit and then reveals a load of information.
e-mail: info@accl.mallships.com

Blackbeard's Cruises

www.blackbeard-cruises.com

Live aboard a sail ship and scuba dive in the Bahamas. The home page links you to lots of information about rates and schedules, weather, dive sites, FAQ and video clips of their cruises. You can book online.
e-mail: sales@blackbeard-cruises.com

Cape Canaveral Cruise Line

www.capecanaveralcruise.com

To take the virtual tour cruising the Bahamas and Key West you must have Quick Time 4.0 installed. All the other information is viewed normally with accompanying music. Contact is by e-mail.
e-mail: via online form

Royal Caribbean International

www.rccl.com/1.0.html

If you want to cruise around Europe, the Caribbean, Central and North America take a look at this excellent web site.

Choose your cruise on the map and you get all the information you need. There are several useful external links and you can ask questions by e-mail.
e-mail: via online form

Windjammer Barefoot Cruises

www.windjammer.com
Based in the USA, Windjammer Barefoot Cruises voyage extensively in the Caribbean. The home page has links to the Fleet, Cruise Director and travel agents. You can order a brochure and book online and use the Coconut Telegraph to share information and gossip with Windjammer Shipmates.
e-mail: windbc@windjammer.com

Windward Lines

www.infinetworx.com/windward/contact.html
The Windward Islands in the Caribbean have their own inter-island passenger and cargo ocean services. You will find details about the company and how to contact their agents, as well as external links to Island tourist boards.
e-mail: not available

Europe

A2Beurope

www.a2beurope.com
Claims to be the UK's most comprehensive online ferry guide and has details about holiday deals as well as ferry information. Select your preferred route, departure date and time from the drop down menus and you are given full details of sailings. Click the Enquire Now button, and you have an online enquiry form to complete. Once submitted, you will be contacted by phone or e-mail. There are also links to other A2B information and booking sites.
e-mail: via online form

Adriatica

www.adriatica.it
Adriatica operate between Italy, Croatia and Greece. The home page welcomes you with music and links take you to everything you want to know, with a good look inside their ships. There are booking centres all over Europe. Text is in English and Italian.
e-mail: iadrnav@port.venice.it

Afloat in France

www.bargeaif.com
Cruise the waterways of Europe. Take a look at all there is on offer then contact them by e-mail.
e-mail: aifbarging@compuserve

Blakes Boating Holidays

www.blakes.co.uk/frame.htm
Blakes offer inland cruises from Scotland to Florida, Holland to the Norfolk Broads. The home page of this very good site has links to lots of information and Waterways of the World. You can order a brochure online.
e-mail: Boats@Blakes.co.uk

Brittany Ferries

www.brittany-ferries.com
Routes between the UK, France and Spain. Select the route and month and the search engine gives you the sailings. Check out fares, order a brochure and book online if you wish. Text is in English and French.
e-mail: not available

Caledonian MacBrayne

www.calmac.co.uk/index.html
On this wonderful web site you can explore the Western Isles of Scotland while following the links on the home page. This is a very beautiful part of the UK and well worth a visit. You can book online, write comments in the guest book or enter the discussion forum.
e-mail: reservations@calmac.co.uk

Captain Morgan Cruises

www.captainmorgan.com.mt
Captain Morgan Cruises offer cruises off
Malta you can book online. Prices, terms
and sailing dates are listed. They also
offer safaris and helicopter tours.
e-mail: info@captainmorgan.com.mt

Color Line

www.colorline.com/Default.htm
Cruises in Norway, Denmark and
Germany. All the information is on the
site and there is an external link to the
Norwegian Tourist Guide, with text in
English and Norwegian.
e-mail: colorline@colorline.no

Condor Ferries

www.condorferries.co.uk/index.html
They serve the Channel Islands, St. Malo
and the UK. The home page has links to
routes with schedules, fares and the
fleet, with a virtual look around the
vessels, hotlines, a map and special
offers. There are external links to tourist
boards, Channel Island and Brittany tour
operators and accommodation guides.
You can conveniently book online.
e-mail: condor@weyquay.demon.co.uk

Continental Waterways

www.continentalwaterways.com
Barge holidays in France, Holland and
Belgium. The site has a lot of information
and if you want to be kept up-to-date give
them your e-mail address. You can book
online, order brochures and books. There
are links to several interesting sites.
e-mail: sales@continentalwaterways.com

DFDS Seaways

www.seaeurope.com/default.htm
Sea services between Britain, Denmark,
Sweden, Norway, Germany and Holland.
All the information you need is neatly
presented and the map has destinations
and schedules. You can book online and
order a brochure by e-mail.
e-mail: admininfo@dfdsusa.com

Estonian Shipping Company

www.eml.ee
They have a variety of passenger and
shipping services in Western Europe
and the Baltic. The home page has
internal links to their operations and
external links to World Ports and other
subjects of interest.
e-mail: online@eml.ee

Euro Cruises

www.eurocruises.com
Sea and river cruises in and around
Europe. Take your pick on the home
page, follow the links and take a look at
the special offers. Contact is by e-mail.
e-mail: eurocruise@compuserve.com

First European Cruises

www.first-european.com
US based and operating in Europe, the
Caribbean, South America and Africa,
their home page connects you to all you
need to know about their cruises.
e-mail: not available

Golden Sun Cruises

www.goldensuncruises.com
The Greek Islands in the Aegean Sea
must be one of the world's favourite
cruise areas. Follow the links on the
home page or use the search engine
to get your information. You can order
a brochure if you wish.
e-mail: gscruz@goldensuncruises.com

Hoverspeed

www.hoverspeed.co.uk/eng/index.asp
Hoverspeed is a fast car and passenger
ferry service operating between Britain,
France and Holland. The home page of
this lively site has internal links to a car
buying scheme, fares and schedules, a free
prize draw and external links to SeaCat,
Orient Express Trains and more. Use the
quick menu for travel, shopping and
exclusive offers. You can book online. Text
is in English, French, German and Dutch.
e-mail: not available

Irish Ferries

www.irishferries.ie/index.html
Ireland's largest ferry services operate
Ireland-Britain and Ireland-France
routes. Links on the home page connect
you to well presented information. You
can book online and request a brochure
by e-mail.
e-mail: info@irishferries.ie

Jadrolinija

www.jadrolinija.tel.hr/jadrolinija
Jadrolinija operates ferries between the
Croatian Adriatic ports and routes to
Italy and Greece. The site has timetables,
fares and facilities on each route. A list
tells you where you can book in Europe.
e-mail: jadrolinija@jadrolinija.tel.hr

KD River Cruises of Europe

www.rivercruises.com/index.htm
Cruising the Rhine and Moselle rivers,
the waterways of Holland, the Main,
Elbe, Saar, Neckar, Danube and French
rivers. The map shows you the routes
and the text tells you everything you
need to know about the ships and
cruises. You can also order a brochure
and video.
e-mail: not available

Ma-re-si Shipping

www.sms.com.mt/maresi.htm
Based in Malta, they provide scheduled
services between Malta, Sicily and Italy.
The home page has schedules, fares and
useful information regarding taxes, tickets
and so on. Contact is by e-mail.
e-mail: mail@sms.com.mt

Minoan Lines

www.minoan.gr
A coastal passenger shipping company
operating in Greece and Europe.
The home page links with Italy-Greece,
Greek Islands, cruises and more, routes
of which are shown on maps. Contact is
by e-mail and text is in English and Greek.
e-mail: info@minoan.gr

Norwegian Coastal Voyage

www.hurtigruten.com
You get a very large choice of Norwegian
coastal voyages. Browse the menus and
check out the ports, ships and routes
before choosing. Timetables and cabin
availability are shown online, and you
can send an electronic postcard to a
friend. Text is in English and Norwegian.
e-mail: booking@ovds.no

P & O Stena Line

www.posl.com
Regular sailings between Dover and
Calais. The home page has links to a
timetable, fleet details, what you can
do aboard ship, or when in France,
and how to book your crossing.
You can order a brochure for free.
e-mail: not available

Paleologos Shipping & Travel Agency

www.greekislands.gr
Ferry services in the eastern
Mediterranean to the sound of music.
The home page links up with several
other ferry lines. You can book online.
Text is in English and Greek.
e-mail: info@greekislands.qr

Poseidon Lines

www.ferries.gr/poseidon/
Named after the Greek god of the sea,
the lines operate year round services
between Greece, Cyprus and Israel.
Links take you to enough information
to book online or by e-mail.
e-mail: paleologos@her.forthnet.gr

SeaFrance

www.seafrance.com
Ferry services between Dover and
Calais. Fares, sailings and onboard
services are well presented and the
instant fare calculator is a great help.
You can book online. Text is in English
and French.
e-mail: not available

Silja Line

www.silja.com

Operating between Sweden, Finland and Denmark, they set out routes and schedules in good detail with a map. External links take you to Finnair, Welcome to Stockholm, Scandinavian Seaways and the Finnish Tourist Board. Text is in English, Swedish and Finnish.

e-mail: not available

Smyril Line

www.smyril-line.fo

Services between Denmark, the Faroes, Iceland and the Shetlands. Aside from schedules and fares you get a bit about the region and accommodation availability. Text is in English, German and Danish and contact is by e-mail.

e-mail: office@smyril-line.fo

Stena Line

www.stenaline.co.uk/traveluk/ Stena_Line_UK/

Their ferry services connect Britain, Northern Ireland, Republic of Ireland and Holland. Fares and schedules, vessels and ports are all linked to the home page with maps and photographs. You can book online and order a brochure by e-mail. Text is English and several other languages.

e-mail: info@stenaline.com

White Horse Fast Ferries

www.birnbeck.co.uk/home.mhtml

A Thames ferry service offering travel between London's famous landmarks. The home page connects you to ferry service details, timetables and fares.

e-mail: fastferries@whitehorse.co.uk

Latin America

Canodros S.A.

www.canodros.com/index.html

Based in Ecuador, they offer cruises in the Galapagos and the Amazon Rain Forest. There is information about natural history, excursions, vessels, itineraries and special cruises. For additional information use the e-mail form.

e-mail: eco-tourism1@canodros.com.ec

Cruceros Australis

www.australis.com/index.html

Cruises between Chile, Patagonia and Tierra del Fuego. The home page gives you lots of choice and access to view ship plans, cabins and safety. You can book online. Text is in English and Spanish.

e-mail: fguillem@nisa.cl, vluco@ altavoz.cl

North America

Alaska Cruises

www.glacierbaytours.com

Cruises in Glacier Bay and Alaska's Inside Passage. There is a wonderful photo gallery to tempt you to their scenic and adventure cruises. You are informed about weather, what to wear and a lot more. Order a brochure, video and request information inline.

e-mail: not available

Baylink Ferries of Vallejo California

www.baylinkferry.com/index.shtml

These ferries operate between Vallejo and San Francisco. Links take you to schedules, fares, terminals, routes and tours. The map highlights the crossings with sound and text. There are links to several sites about Vallejo.

e-mail: via online form

BC Ferries

www.bcferries.bc.ca

These ferries operate between west mainland Canada and the islands, with routes clearly shown on the maps. Travel information is well set out with site search and links to other useful pages. Text is in English, French and German.

e-mail: not available

Catalina Cruises
www.catalina.com/cruises2/
Based in the USA, they travel to the Catalina Islands. The home page has links to schedules and fares, whale watching, private charters and more. Contact is by e-mail.
e-mail: info@catalinos.net

Dandy Restaurant Cruise Ship
www.dandydinnerboat.com/thedandy.htm
The Dandy is a restaurant-riverboat based in Old Town Alexandria, near Washington D.C. The home page tells you about cruises, tours, menus, dinner-dances and lots more fun on the Potomac River. You can book by e-mail.
e-mail: dandy1@erols.com

Delta Queen Steamboat
www.deltaqueen.com
You can cruise along the Mississippi and nine other US rivers by steamboat. The home page has links to all the vessels, rivers, a Steamboatin' History, special offers and lots more. Click on a river name on the map and up comes regional information. There are links to other river-related web sites.
e-mail: via online form

Disney Cruise Line
disney.go.com/disneycruise/
The itinerary includes stops in Nassau, the Bahamas and Castaway Cay. The home page links you, among other subjects, to the Disney World Experience. To plan your vacation use the helpful links, then have some fun with this entertaining web site or shop online. You can also register at Disney.com.
e-mail: not available

Lake Champlain Ferries
www.ferries.com/index.html
The map shows the routes served by these North American ferries and the home page links up with cruises,

charters and other information including employment opportunities. Contact is by e-mail.
e-mail: lct@ferries.com

River Barge Excursion Lines
www.riverbarge.com
Click on any region of the US map and you find information about it, with river barge excursions in the area. There are links to Schedules & Fares, River Rendezvous, and other exciting river sights. You can order a brochure and check employment opportunities online. External links take you to several local and national web sites.
e-mail: not available

SeaEscape Cruises
www.seaescape.com
Cruises in South Florida with music accompanying a 3-D ship tour sounds like lots of fun. The home page has links to all cruise information and onboard entertainment. You can book online or by e-mail.
e-mail: sales@seaescape.com

Steamship Authority
www.islandferry.com
Ferry services from mainland USA to Martha's Vineyard and Nantucket. Schedules, fares and reservations are linked to the home page as is information about the islands and how to get to their terminals. There are commercial external links.
e-mail: not available

Washington State Ferries
www.wsdot.wa.gov/ferries/default.cfm
This is the largest ferry system in the USA. Follow the home page links to fares, schedules, route map, tourist information and more. You can book online or contact them by e-mail.
e-mail: wsf@wsdot.wa.gov

World Explorer Cruises

www.wecruise.com
World Explorer Cruises offers voyages of Discovery, Learning and Adventure to Alaska. The home page takes you to a lot of useful information and a map of Alaska. By clicking appropriately you will find cruise schedules and itineraries. External links connect you to the Alaska Travel Industry Association, State of Alaska, AAA Club and more.
e-mail: info@WECruise.com

Worldwide

Aquanaut Cruise Lines

www.aquanautcruise.com
There are two cruise areas - the Galapagos Islands and European Rivers. Follow the links on the home page to loads of information and a good look at the ships. Ask for a free brochure by e-mail.
e-mail: Divercruise@aol.com

Carnival Cruise

www.carnival.com
The home page of this charming web site has links to everything you need for a wonderful cruise on their Fun Ships around the Caribbean or Central and North America. You can book online and external links connect you to news, jobs, FAQ, contacts and downloads.
e-mail: not available

Celebrity Cruises

www.celebrity-cruises.com
Based in Miami, they operate in Alaska, the Caribbean, Trans-Canal and Europe. Celebrity Experience on the home page takes you to information about the ships, activities and entertainment; Destinations tells you where you can cruise. Fares and agents are listed.
e-mail: via online form

Clipper Cruise Line

www.clippercruise.com
From the US they sail to the Caribbean,

Western Europe, Greenland and the High Canadian Arctic, Central and South America, Antarctica and the Pacific. All itineraries are online with fares and departure dates. Availability will be confirmed by e-mail.
e-mail: SmallShip@aol.com

CruiseWest

www.cruisewest.com
Cruises in Alaska, Mexico, California, Columbia & Snake Rivers and British Columbia & Islands. The home page has several internal links, most interesting of which is Destinations. External links take you to travel sites on their routes. You can order brochures and videos; contact is by e-mail.
e-mail: Info@cruisewest.com

Cunard Line

www.cunardline.com
All the glory of this distinguished luxury cruise line, in operation since 1840. There is information about the fleet both past and present, cruises around Europe, Africa and the Americas, voyage specials and agents world wide. You can order a brochure by e-mail.
e-mail: via online form

Expedition Cruises

www.societyexpeditions.com/index.html
Cruises to Antarctica, Alaska and the South Pacific. The home page has links to all the usual information, onboard lectures and the zodiac. Use the online form for more information.
e-mail: not available

Freighter Travel

www.freighterworld.com/index.html
Travel by freighter world wide. To find out why, follow the link on the home page. The world map gives you itineraries when you click on each area. Contact is by e-mail.
e-mail: freighters@freighterworld.com

Global Quest

www.odessamerica.com

Cruises throughout the world from the Russian Waterways to the Galapagos. Information is well set out and there are Hot Deals to tempt you. Contact is by e-mail.

e-mail: global@globalquesttravel.com

Holland America line

www.hollandamerica.com

Based in Seattle, they operate world wide. Click on "When was the last time you acted on a dream" and you see the itineraries on offer. Or use the Cruise search. You can book online. Additional features include a Career Centre, Video order, Literature Request and more.

e-mail: not available

Lindblad Special Expeditions

www.expeditions.com

Cruises all over the world with a list of expeditions you can access by region, departure date, time and cost. Order a brochure or download their newsletter; book by e-mail.

e-mail: explore@specialexpeditions.com

Norwegian Cruise Line

www.ncl.com

They offer a flotilla of cruises to forty countries on four continents. Links from the home page lead you to all you need to plan and book a vacation. For the best view of the site, you will need Internet Explorer 4.0 or Netscape Navigator 4.0 or higher. Text is in English and German.

e-mail: not available

Orient Lines

www.orientlines.com

Cruise your way to the most exciting and exotic parts of the globe. The home page has a map with links to all the cruises on offer. These are divided into six regions, all accompanied by beautiful photos. Other features include ship details, news & events, special offers, travel agents and more. A free brochure is available on request.

e-mail: info@orientlines.com

P & O Cruises

www.p-and-o.com

Peninsular and Orient, with a long heritage of sailing the world, is UK based. The diversified fleet includes several modern cruise ships that ply the seas world wide. Choose the Links option at the top of the home page to find all P & O companies including P & O European ferries, P & O North Sea ferries and P & O Australian. These contain routes, vessel details, sailing times and the latest special offers.

e-mail: not available

Premier Cruise Lines

www.premiercruises.com/main.htm

The US-based Premier Cruise Lines operate in Europe, North and Central America. Home page links lead you to everything you need to know about the ships, where and when they go. External links take you to group cruising, news and beyond cruising. You can book online.

e-mail: info@premiercruises.com

Princess Cruise Line

www.travelandcruises.com

Princess Cruise Line operate in Europe, the Caribbean, Central and North America, and if you are so inclined, a special 65-day World Cruise aboard the Island Princess. The home page has links to a variety of cruises and details about each can be accessed through the Specials link.

e-mail: not available

Radisson Seven Seas Cruise

www.rssc.com

Radisson is based in the US and operates world wide. The home page of this excellent site illustrates all the ships;

by clicking on one you get detailed information about its operations. Other topics covered are About RSSC, Port profiles, cruise calendars and a virtual tour for which you will need an IPIX plug-in - just follow the instructions to download it.
e-mail: not available

Renaissance Cruises

www.renaissancecruises.com
Based in the USA, Renaissance sails the Mediterranean, South Pacific and to destinations in Asia and Africa. Clicking on Destination gives you information on prices, ports and excursions, national holidays and weather. There is a chat line and you can book your trip online.
e-mail: not available

Royal Olympic Cruises

www.royalolympiccruises.com
Royal Olympic Cruises are based in Greece and travel world wide. The home page has offers and information about Destinations, Cruise Calendar and Enrichment Programs. Welcome Aboard gives you company news and fleet details. There are contact addresses and you can order a brochure online.
e-mail: not available

Sail with the Stars

www.sailwiththestars.com/homepage.shtml
They cruise around Mexico, the Caribbean and Alaska. The home page has lots on upcoming cruises, holidays, photo memories and a video library. There are external links to a host of local sites. Contact is by e-mail.
e-mail: crusstars@sailwiththestars.com

Seabourn Cruise Line

www.seabourn.com
The home page of this US based company shows the ships. Clicking on one gives you information about the vessel and itineraries, while other links

take you to Intimate Cruising Styles, Destinations, Value Programs and so on. You can make contact by e-mail.
e-mail: seabourn@aol.com

Ship Pax Information

www.shippax.se/index.html
This is a database of ferry and cruise companies world wide, providing an excellent source of passenger shipping details. Home page links take you to lots of information and photographs. The web site of each operator can be accessed separately and you can order a CD-ROM or floppy disk with all the vessels depicted.
e-mail: info@shippax.se

Star Clippers

www.star-clippers.com
Based in the USA, they cruise the Caribbean, Mediterranean and to the Far East. The home page has links to Cruises, News, Specials and a photo library. Use the search engine to select a Travel Agent or Tour Operator and shop online if you wish. Text is in English, French, German, Spanish and Dutch.
e-mail: not available

Swan Hellenic Cruises

www.swan-hellenic.co.uk
Ocean cruises in the Mediterranean and Adriatic, expedition cruises in unseen Caribbean, the Arctic Circle and river cruises on the Rhone and Danube. The home page sets out the cruises by region with more about touring and lectures. Contact and ordering a brochure are by e-mail.
e-mail: swan_hellenic@easynet.co.uk

The Cruise Ship Center

www.cruise2.com
They claim to be the largest Cruise Source on the Internet, designed to help you find the best cruise at the best price from 194 cruise lines world wide. The Visitor Site Guide on the home page has

an alphabetical Menu that explains everything you need to know to book your cruise or just have fun searching the web site.
e-mail: not available

The World of ResidenSea
www.residensea.com
Travel the world without leaving home, with a floating community aboard a luxury vessel, constantly in motion around the globe. The site tells you about the ship, route and what the press says. Contact is by e-mail.
e-mail: bryn.freberg@rsea.no

TravelPage.com
www.travelpage.com
A database of cruise operators and cruise ships world wide, with links to the appropriate web sites. There are extensive descriptions of all the major cruise ships, with photographs. There are also lots of other features to enjoy including links to destinations, hotels and resorts and air travel.
e-mail: info@travelpage.com

Union - Castle Line
www.union-castle-line.com
The Union-Castle Line is UK based. Click on the flag on the home page and another page opens; choose Sector Cruises and you get a map of the area. Now click on the Voyage link and you'll find the information you need. There are several other useful links and you can order a brochure online.
e-mail: mailbox@union-castle-line.com

Windstar Cruises
www.windstarcruises.com
The home page of US based Windstar Cruises has links to Experience, Voyages, Foremast Club, Internet Offers and a Virtual Cruise where you will see a video clip of ships and destinations. Internet Offers gives you savings on your bookings. You can order a video or CD-ROM and book online. The offices are listed with contact details.
e-mail: windstar@windstarcruises.com

Buses & Coaches

to travel as much as you wish anywhere along the route. You can book online.
e-mail: Bazbus@icon.co.za

Translux

www.translux.co.za
Translux operate long distance routes in South Africa, Zimbabwe and Zambia. Travel Options tell you what services are offered. The Information section covers the routes taken and gives details of the coaches. No online reservations, however there are telephone numbers for the various offices.
e-mail: translux@mweb.co.za

Africa

African Elephant Tours

www.african-elephant-tours.co.za
Based in Durban, South Africa, they operate throughout southern Africa from Cape Town to Malawi, Namibia to Mozambique. All tours are detailed and have pictures. For prices, availability and to book, complete the enquiry form.
e-mail: Info@african-elephant-tours.co.za

Greyhound Coach Lines

www.greyhound.co.za
A nation-wide coach company operating throughout South Africa. Timetables, fares, discount passes, coach charter, facilities and services are clearly set out.
e-mail: via online form

Springbok Atlas

www.springbokatlas.co.za
These South African tours vary with the season, so be sure to check the schedules. All tours show period, rates, itinerary, services included and a picture gallery.
e-mail: not available

The Baz Bus

www.icon.co.za/~bazbus/
A hop-on hop-off bus service for backpackers between Cape Town and Victoria Falls. A valid pass allows you

Asia

Bali: The Online Travel Guide - Transport

home.mira.net/~wreid/bali_p2t.html
The bus connections between major cities on the island are part of an unofficial web site on tourism in Bali. You will find prices, journey distances and times for each route.
e-mail: not available

Fez Travel

www.feztravel.com
Fez Travel provides a hop-on hop-off bus service in Turkey. The well illustrated site has route maps, details of tours and things to do and see in Turkey. The FAQ section deals with most of the queries you might have, and it is possible to book tickets and arrange airport pickups online.
e-mail: feztravel@feztravel.com

Hong Kong Travel Tour & Sightseeing

hongkong-tour.com
Touring Hong Kong, Kowloon and Macao by coach with a few short trips in mainland China. Timetables, itineraries, prices and photos accompany each tour. You can book online.
e-mail: Sam@asiatravel.com

Kramat Djati

www.nusaweb.com/krmdjati/index.html
A transportation and travel company
operating in the Indonesian islands of
Sumatra, Java and Bali. The route tables
give distances, journey times and fares.
Information regarding local transport
and taxi services can be very useful.
e-mail: Krmdjati@idola.net.id

Lucknow Online

www.lucknowonline.com/
businessdirectory/bd_stransportbus.htm
Bus services between Lucknow
and Delhi and other destinations in
Uttar Pradesh in India. The page has
timetables and contact numbers of bus
stations within the State.
e-mail: not available

Metrobus Group of Malaysia

www.transweb.com.my/metrobus/
default.htm
This page of the Malaysian transport
web provides a table with destinations,
departure times and ticket prices for
Metrobus, an inter-city bus and courier
company.
e-mail: Metrobus@tm.net.my

Nankai Highway Bus

www.nankai.co.jp/bus/
A bus network with inter-city and
long-distance connections on Honshu
island in Japan. All routes are detailed
with timetables, fares and maps clearly
showing the terminals in departure
cities. Services, coaches, discount
passes and offers are detailed.
e-mail: not available

Singapore Coach Tours

www.travelasia.com.sg/rental2.htm
Coach tours around Singapore and trips
to Malaysia and Indonesia. Each tour is
briefly detailed with photos and prices.
e-mail: not available

Thailand Online - Chiang Mai: Bus Schedules and Fares

thailine.com/thailand/english/
north-e/chmai-e/transp-e/bus-e.htm
This page is part of the Thailand
information site and has details of
bus services in Chiang Mai State only.
Timetables cover routes within the
state and to Bangkok. Fares and
journey times are listed.
e-mail: not available

Varan

www.varan.com.tr/english/index.htm
From Istanbul to many Turkish and
international destinations by coach.
The site has the routes and details of
the booking centre. Pick a route, check
price and availability, then book your
seat online.
e-mail: not available

Australasia and Oceania

Australian Tours

www.world.net/Travel/Australia/aatkings
Described as Australia's premier tour
operators, the ATT Kings web site is concise
and contains a range of information about
its services. There are pictures of destinations
and route maps as well as a small
number of links to other Australian travel
and tourism sites. There is no online booking
facility but you can order a brochure.
e-mail: not available

Bronzewing Tours

www.ideal.net.au/~proex/
Short coach tours, usually three days,
anywhere in Australia with a choice of
safari, educational and bush walking
tours. All tours are priced with an
itinerary, pictures and brief description.
e-mail: not available

Buslines Australia

www.buslines.com.au
This is a database and directory of links
to all Australian local and inter-city bus

services. Links take you to inter-city home pages where you will also find municipal bus routes in the larger cities.
e-mail: not available

Ekahi Tours
www.ekahi.com
Guided coach tours to the most exciting parts of Maui in the Hawaiis to see different aspects of the island. Tours have picture galleries, fares, services and other travellers' opinions.
e-mail: Tour@ekahi.com

Firefly Express Coaches Australia
www.fireflyexpress.com.au
Daily coach services between Melbourne, Sydney and Adelaide in Australia. Each route has timetables, itineraries and fares.
e-mail: Enquiries@fireflyexpress.com.au

Hawaii Tours
www.fly-hawaii.com/above/
They take you on air-conditioned sightseeing coach tours on all the main islands of Hawaii. Each island is individually listed with tour prices, itineraries and the attractions you visit en route.
e-mail: Sales@polyad.com

Intercity Coachlines
www.intercitycoach.co.nz
This hop-on hop-off bus service operates on the two main New Zealand islands. A system of passes allows unlimited regional travel. Pass holders are also eligible for accommodation discounts.
e-mail: Info@intercity.co.nz

Magic Travellers Network
www.magicbus.co.nz
This New Zealand-wide bus company has a nation-wide timetable with discount passes and online booking.
e-mail: Info@magictn.co.nz

Moruya's Historic bus tour
www.morning.com.au/go/historybus/welcome.html
A bus tour around the historic landmarks of Sydney, Australia. Prices and timetables are available, and group bookings possible for a minimum of 6 people. To book you can phone, fax or e-mail.
e-mail: mtronson@sci.net.au

Overland Australia
www.overlandaustralia.com.au
Safari Australia by coach to the wildest parts of the continent. There are four distinct tours, fully detailed with itineraries, pictures, accommodation, buses, meals, maps and costs. Other tours are briefly described and priced.
email: Overland@overlandaustralia.com.au

Oz Experience
www.ozexperience.com
Australian adventure transport network of coaches. Routes and prices are listed in the Trip and Price guide link. In order to book a seat online you must already have bought a ticket from one of their Australian ticket offices. There is an enormous list of budget accommodation throughout Australia via the Accommodation link.
e-mail: enquiries@ozexperience.com

Sheppard Touring
sheppard.touring.co.nz
7-day and 14-day tours throughout New Zealand. The site has all the details of itineraries, prices, facilities and services. There is a currency converter and distance calculator.
e-mail: Sheppard@xtra.co.nz

Waipawa Buses
www.wbuses.hb.co.nz
Coach charter for group tours throughout New Zealand. Choose a tour category, then your destination and you get the details you need.
e-mail: Info@wbuses.hb.co.nz

Welcome to the World of Transit

www.transitregency.com.au

Transit provide a range of coach services in south Australia from day trips to airport transfers. Their well presented and easy to use site has details of the destinations they travel to, with clear route maps. You can book tickets online with a well-designed form.

e-mail: info@transitregency.com.au

Westbus Australia

www.westbus.com.au

Bus services in Western Australia. Clicking on your route gives you the timetable. The company also offers bus and courier services.

e-mail: Buses@westbus.com.au

Caribbean

Jamaican Tours

www.nwanet.com/carlton/carlton.htm

A private owner offers coach tours to the most interesting parts of Jamaica. He describes his buses and displays pictures of the tours. To book, complete the enquiry form and you will be picked up at the airport and assisted with accommodation.

e-mail: Jumo@n5.com.jm

Metro Servicios Turisticos

www.metrost.com

The bus company of the Dominican Republic has a good web site with clear timetables, fares and tariffs for courier services. The coaches are displayed and you can book online.

e-mail: Mexpresso@metrost.com

Europe

ABUS

timetable.svt.cz/cgi-bin/start.pl?uk

The Czech national coach network. The route planner gives all daily connections between cities. Though you can view itineraries they are described only in Czech.

e-mail: not available

âebus

www.cebus.cz

Regular coach services between Prague and Brno in the Czech Republic. Timetables, fares, discounts for regular travellers and details of where to find their buses.

e-mail: Doprava@cebus.cz

Auto Cars

www.binet.lv/clients/auto-stars/latvian/plus/index.htm

Latvian coaches running regular services to Minster and London and tours to different locations in Europe from Scandinavia to Italy, St. Petersburg to Spain. Tours have detailed itineraries, costs and numbers to call for reservations.

e-mail: Autostars@apollo.lv

Autobusni Kolodvor Zagreb

www.akz.hr/Eng/Time-table/time-table.html

The main bus station in Zagreb has its own site with timetables of all bus companies serving the Croatian capital. Choose your destination and you get timetables for all services, fares and seat availability.

e-mail: Vladislav.Valicek@zg.akz.hr

Autotrans

www.autotrans.hr/eng/index.html

The Croatian branch of the Eurolines group provides domestic and European connections. Each route is shown with timetables and fares with discounts for frequent travellers.

e-mail: not available

BSI - Bus Terminal in Iceland

www.bsi.is

A bus network operating throughout Iceland. Click on a route and you get a timetable for the whole itinerary at different times of the year. There are contact numbers for bus stations and organised tours with a timetable to download in PDF format.

e-mail: not available

Bus Eireann

www.buseireann.ie
Buses throughout the Republic of Ireland.
All information is clearly set out with
maps, FAQ, special services for schools
and an enquiry form for more information.
e-mail: via online form

Cambridge Coach Services

www.cambridgecoaches.co.uk
Details of connections between
Cambridge, Oxford, Norwich and the
London airports, with timetables for
each route and ticket passes for
frequent users.
e-mail: not available

Caravella Italia

www.seeitaly.com
Two-week tours to the most interesting
regions of Italy. Scheduled tours cover
the most popular destinations, but if
you prefer to travel as a group, plan your
own tour or choose one of the themed
tours and visit the places of particular
interest.
e-mail: Info@caravella.com

Cars de Brie

www.les-cars-de-brie.com/index.gb.html
Chartered tours anywhere in western
Europe. A catalogue of the fleet and
onboard services are shown online.
e-mail: Les-cars-de-brie@wanadoo.fr

Contus

www.contus.hr
Inter-city coaches in Croatia with
frequent connections between Zagreb,
Split and Zadar. Timetables, fares,
special offers, facilities and services are
all clearly set out. Click the British flag
on the home page for English text.
e-mail: Contus@contus.hr

Dubrovnik Bus Services

**dubrovnik.laus.hr/dubrovnik2/html/
bus_services.html**
Domestic and international timetables
for coaches departing from Dubrovnik,
Croatia.
e-mail: not available

Eurolines France

www.eurolines.fr
This is a branch of the Eurolines
consortium connecting domestic bus
services throughout Europe. Since each
branch maintains its own timetable you
have to visit the national web sites for
information. Details of French bus
connections with other countries in the
network include timetables and fares by
age group. You can book online.
e-mail: not available

EuroLines Spain

www.eurolines.es/eurolini/ruta_reg.htm
This is the Spanish branch of Eurolines.
To plan your journey, choose your
destination outside Spain and the route
you wish to travel. The timetable and
fare will appear. You can book online.
e-mail: not available

Eurolines UK

www.eurolines.co.uk
Eurolines UK is the British part of
this pan-European bus service. This well
presented site gives you details of their
routes, updated prices and special
deals, with links to European tourist
boards and details of travel insurance.
Tickets and a variety of brochures can
be ordered online; a feedback page
allows you to comment or make
suggestions about Eurolines or their
web site.
e-mail: welcome@eurolines.co.uk

Eva Transportes

www.eva-transportes.pt
Regular inter-city connections between
towns in southern Portugal with an
additional route to Seville in Spain.
Each service has timetables and special
offers.
e-mail: Info@eva-transportes.pt

Express Bus

www.expressbus.com

A consortium of 30 companies covering most of Finland, with services to other Scandinavian countries and Russia. Although the English part of this site is tangled with Finnish, a little patience will unravel everything. Timetables are quite clear.

e-mail: not available

Halkidiki Bus Service

halkidiki.com/ktel/

This page provides information on bus services in the Greek peninsula of Halkidiki. Text is in English, Greek and German.

e-mail: Ktel@halkidiki.com

Intertours Romania

www.intertours.ro/en.html

See Romania's best attractions by coach or ride one of their regular services to Budapest. All tours are fully described.

e-mail: Office@intertours.ro

KTEL.org

www.ktel.org

This organisation brings together several privately owned Greek bus companies into a large network. There are detailed maps of their services and contact numbers to all main bus stations.

e-mail: Praxis2@ibm.net

Kyiv's Central Bus Station

koiwww.relc.com/kiev/transpor/buses/buse.htm

This site has details of Kiev's Central Bus Station activity, services, timetables, platform and bus numbers.

e-mail: not available

Lasta

www.lasta.co.yu/english/first.htm

Inter-city connections between Serbia, Montenegro and Bosnia with connections across Europe, through membership of Eurolines group. Timetables and fares with online booking.

e-mail: Splasta@eunet.yu

Lomond Tours

www.lomond-tours.co.uk

Mini-bus tours to the historical and natural attractions of Scotland. Itineraries, prices and special offers are set out, but for more information use the enquiry form. You can book online.

e-mail: not available

National Express

www.nationalexpress.co.uk

National Express operates a bus service throughout the United Kingdom. Their comprehensive web site contains up to date information about services and schedules. Tickets can be booked via an online form. There are useful suggestions for days out, weekend breaks and links to other public transport and tourism sites.

e-mail: info@nationalexpress.co.uk

Nord Tour

www.archangelsk.ru/nordtour/english/

Nord Tour offer sightseeing trips in Northern Russia. There is a wealth of information about the areas they visit. The links section is comprehensive and there is also a list of useful contacts in the region.

e-mail: not available

Norway Busekspress

www.nbe.no

Norway Busekspress offer luxury coach travel throughout Norway. Their web site contains timetables and local travel information linked to relevant sites. Whilst it is not possible to book over the Internet, enough contact information is provided to help you plan your journey.

e-mail: administrasjon@nbe.no

Panturist Osijek
www.iridis.com/panturist/
Domestic coach services within Croatia
and international routes to Austria,
Bosnia, Germany, Switzerland and
Yugoslavia. Itineraries, timetables,
contact numbers and fares are clearly
set out.
e-mail: not available

Prestov Bus Transport
**www.presov.sk/PRESOV/DOPRAVA/
dopravuk.htm**
Part of the site of Presov in Slovakia has
bus information listed alphabetically by
destination. Click on the initial of your
destination and you get the timetable of
all services.
e-mail: not available

PTA Bus Routes
**engine2.maltanet.net/pta/routes/sites/
pta/frames.htm**
This is the bus network page of the
Maltese information site. There is a
network map, an interactive list of
routes with schedules and detailed
information about each specific route.
e-mail: not available

Rede National Express
www.rede-expressos.pt/index_uk.htm
The Portuguese national coach
network serves most destinations in the
country. Online you will find timetables,
discount offers and contact details for
booking offices in major Portuguese
cities.
e-mail: Rede.expressos@mail.telepac.pt

Scottish City Link
www.citylink.co.uk
Buses between main Scottish cities.
A network map, journey planner,
discount cards and timetables are
available, but little fares information.
Use the e-mail link for enquiries.
e-mail: Info@citylink.demon.co.uk

South Iceland Bus Service
www.selfoss.is/sbs/
SBS specialise in travel around the south
of Iceland. This simple site has pages
relating to services, destinations and
schedules, with some pictures and
information about the places they visit.
There is no online booking nor feedback
section. Text is in English, Icelandic and
German.
e-mail: sbs@selfoss.is

SP UAB Toks
www.autobusai.lt/indexE.htm
Coaches within Lithuania and to many
international destinations. Choose your
departure and arrival cities and the route
planner gives timetables, itinerary and
seat availability at Vilnius coach terminal.
e-mail: Toks@post.5ci.lt

SPA Coaches
**www.highlanderweb.co.uk/highland/
tourist/spacoach.htm**
Excursions in the Scottish Highlands in
season. Itineraries, departure points and
prices are listed. Book by phone.
e-mail: not available

Take-A-Guide
www.take-a-guide.com
British company offering coach tours in
Britain, some countries in Europe and in
New York. Their tours are briefly described.
e-mail: Tag@take-a-guide.com

Touraine Evasion
tourevasion.com/anglais/anglais.htm
Mini-bus tours throughout the Loire
Valley visiting the most interesting
castles in the region. Maps, itineraries
and prices come online with a booking
system.
e-mail: Toureva@tourevasion.com

Welcome to Petrabax
www.petrabax.com/index.htm
You start the journey with a flight from
the USA, then go on to a range of tours

covering different aspects of Spain, Portugal and Morocco. Each tour is described either online or in PDF format with pictures, maps, itinerary and all services. You can book online.
e-mail: not available

Latin America

ADO's Linea Uno Transportation

www.uno.com.mx/luno-engl.html
Inter-city bus services in southern Mexico. Choose your destination on the map and check timetables. You will find travel times, fares in Mexican Pesos and pictures of the coaches.
e-mail: Info@uno.com.mx

Belize Bus Schedules

www.belizecentral.net/bus_schedule/schedule.html
Buses in Belize. The network covers four areas of the country. Identify your departure and destination and you get daily schedules, name of operator and fares.
e-mail: not available

Eternautas Viajes Historicos

www.eternautas.com
There are several enjoyable coach tours available in and around Greater Buenos Aires in Argentina. All the information is online and text is in English and Spanish.
e-mail: Informes@eternautas.com

Flecha Amarilla Web Site

www.flecha-amarilla.com/eindex.htm
Local and inter-city Mexican bus services. The site has a ticket booth to check fares and seat availability. Frequent travellers are entitled to discount passes.
e-mail: Comentarios@flecha-amarilla.com

Groupo Pullman de Morelos

www.inetcorp.net.mx/pullman/eng.html
This Mexican bus network runs services between Mexico City and destinations within a three-hour journey radius. Check out the map, timetables and the link to a Mexican Travel Guide.
e-mail: Gpopullm@inetcorp.net.mx

Hop on the Bus

www.yellowweb.co.cr/crbuses.html
Part of the Costa Rican Yellow Pages web site has information on bus services within the country. Clicking on a destination gives the timetable and fares in local currency.
e-mail: Hitcom@yellowweb.co.cr

Tica Bus

www.ticabus.com/Eindex.html
This is an international bus company with daily services connecting all Central American countries. Itineraries and timetables for all major routes.
e-mail: Ticabus@ticabus.com

North America

Agape Tours

www.agapetoursinc.com
Texas based with coach tours within the State and throughout the USA. The event calendar lists trips by departure date. Destinations are briefly described and prices include all services listed.
e-mail: Agape@wf.quik.com

Alaska Skagway Gold Rush Tours

www.ptialaska.net/~grt/index.htm
Tours to see the remains of the Alaskan gold rush in Skagway and its scenic surroundings. The site takes you on a virtual tour of the excursion route and you can download a free brochure in English and Spanish.
e-mail: Grt@ptialaska.net

Alaskabus Company

www.alaskabus.com
Anywhere in Alaska and the Canadian Yukon territory. They provide the coach, driver and guide. You organise the group, choose the route and pay the

charges. Sample tours give you an idea of what you can do and an enquiry form helps you book the tour.
e-mail: Tours@alaskabus.com

Bermuda Public Transportation

www.bermudabuses.com
Bus services on Bermuda Island. The island map shows the routes; click on one and you get the details. There is a fares page with local zone and travel pass tariffs.
e-mail: Info@ptb.bm

Bus On Us Motor Coach Tours

www.busonus.com
Tour the US Midwest by coach. Schedules, itineraries, maps, prices and what you get for your money are given online with fleet details and a booking facility.
e-mail: Fun@busonus.com

California Parlor Car Motorcoach Tours

www.calpartours.com
Coach tours all over California. The table has all tour details, accommodation, meals, costs and internal links to itineraries and pictures. Text is in English and Japanese and you can download free brochures.
e-mail: Reservation@calpartours.com

Crossroads Adventures

www.xroadsusa.com
Crossroads offer adventure holidays in the USA, Alaska and Canada, coach tours with budget camping or hotel accommodation and special tours for youngsters. Take a look at the catalogue online; clicking on highlighted names gives you itineraries, services, costs, optional activities and a map.
e-mail: not available

Croswell Bus Lines

www.croswell-bus.com
You can choose your own route with this coach company that specialises in

extended tours to and from all points in the USA. They also organise group accommodation.
e-mail: Tracy@croswell-bus.com

Dillon's Bus Service

www.dillonbus.com
Scheduled services and budget coach tours in and around Maryland and Washington DC. Their budget tours are briefly described and priced.
e-mail: not available

DRL Coachlines

www.drl.bigkahoona.com/coach.html
Bus services right across the Island of Newfoundland. Timetables, fares and bus charter arrangements are listed.
e-mail: not available

Eastern Bus

www.easternbus.com
Daily connections between New York and Miami; timetables, fares and discount offers. Chartered tours can be arranged to many destinations in the US and Canada.
e-mail: Easternbus@worldnet.att.net

Fehr-Way Tours

www.fehrwaytours.com
These are scheduled coach tours to various destinations throughout the Canadian provinces of Winnipeg, Manitoba and Saskatchewan and chartered tours to many more destinations throughout North America. Click on a tour for details, pictures and a map and get more information by filling the enquiry form.
e-mail: via online form

Go West Adventures

www.gowestadventures.com/english.html
Scheduled coach tours to Los Angeles, Beverly Hills, Hollywood, Santa Monica, Disneyland and the Grand Canyon. There are details of the tours with prices and travellers' opinions.
e-mail: Reservations@gowestadventures. com

Greyhound Canada
www.greyhound.ca
This is the Canadian arm of the famous US giant. There is a route planner to help you get from A to Z and a fares reckoner. They also operate courier and charter services.
e-mail: not available

Greyhound Coaches
www.greyhound.com
Greyhound operate coaches throughout North America. There is a page for every possible aspect of coach travel from scheduling to lost baggage claims on this detailed site. There is also a useful fare finder which helps you work out prices quickly and efficiently. The site map allows easy navigation and there is an online customer satisfaction survey to complete if you wish.
e-mail: via online form

Lakefront Lines
lakefrontlines.com
Regular scheduled services between Cleveland, Ohio and Michigan, Indiana and Kentucky with casino and theatre tours as an extra. There are details of both services with timetables, prices, pictures and tours.
e-mail: Lakefrnt@lakefrontlines.com

Nagel Tours
www.nageltours.com
Based in western Canada, they run tours to some of the most interesting regions in the country. Their tours are fully described but if you want to find out more, order a free catalogue.
e-mail: Nagtours@telusplanet.net

Nava-Hopi Tours
www.navahopitours.com
The Grand Canyon would be enough, but when the other natural attractions of north Arizona are part of the package, you get a tour that cannot be missed. Their tours are described online with

operating season, cost, route maps and a reservation form.
e-mail: Navahopi@aol.com

Old West Tours
www.oldwestours.com
Coach tours to California's most famous historic places. Tours go to old whisky factories, inns, gold mines and other relics of the Wild West. Every tour is fully detailed.
e-mail: Info@oldwestours.com

Rocky Express Backpacker Bus Tours
www.backpackertours.com/TrueNorth/
Coaching around the Canadian Rockies. Tours are designed mainly for backpackers seeking adventure on small budgets. Prices, itineraries and pictures are all available.
e-mail: not available

SMT Group
www.smtbus.com
Coaches running regular services throughout eastern Canada and chartered tours to various destinations in North America. Check out the route planner, type in the names of departure and destination cities and you get a timetable and prices for the regular services. You can book by credit card.
e-mail: SMT@smtbus.com

Sojourners Ministries
www.busesnbeds.org/index.html
If you are a foreigner residing in the USA and want to see the country by coach check out this site. You get to see the most visited attractions and stay in budget accommodation. The itinerary of each tour is set out and priced. You can book online.
e-mail: Office@busesnbeds.org

West Coast City and Nature Sightseeing
www.vancouversightseeing.com
Customised group tours in western Canada. Charter the coach, choose from

their suggested tours, or design your own. Text is in English, German and Mandarin.
e-mail: Westcoast@ vancouversightseeing.com

World Wide

Adventurebus

www.adventureplanet.com
International bus tours for backpackers with the emphasis more on adventure than comfort. The Himalayas, South America, Alaska, Africa and the USA are some of the areas visited. Prices, itineraries, pictures, and online booking forms are all available.
e-mail: Info@adventureplanet.com

Gray Line Worldwide Sightseeing Tours

www.grayline.com
Gray Line offers holidays with a difference. Their world wide tours include sightseeing trips by motor-coach, double-decker bus or van, in addition to overnight packages, airport transfers, charters, multi-lingual tours, convention services and customised tours. You can request brochures and book online.
e-mail: info@grayline.com

Trafalgar Tours

www.trafalgartours.com
British company that tours the world by coach. Choose the region and you are offered a list of tours from the country's best to themed excursions. The itineraries tell you what you see, where you stay and what you eat. You can book online.
e-mail: Anlinho@wellwin.com

Car Hire

Africa

Cabs Car Hire

www.southafricarent.co.za/index.html
Cabs offer car rental in South Africa, with several useful links, including a rates calculator, currency converter, booking form, accommodation and weather information. The site is easy to use, and has a map of South Africa with a distance calculator (your browser must be Java enabled for this facility). The company also offer airport transfers, with all rates clearly explained.
e-mail: cabs@southafricarent.co.za

Comet Car Rental

www.cometcar.co.za
If you need a car in South Africa, you can choose from a large range of economy and executive models on this site. Vehicles and rates are displayed with a few bonuses added. An online reservation from is provided and contact can be made by fax or phone.
e-mail: comet@iafrica.com

Econo Car Hire

www.natron.net/tour/econo/carhiree.html
Namibian car rental site with some details and an online enquiry form. There is a link for camping equipment hire. Text is in English and German.
e-mail: econo@natron.net

Egypt Tourism Net - Car Hire

www.tourism.egnet.net
This is the car hire link of Egypt Tourism Net. Several companies advertise their vehicles with rates and discounts and not much more information.
e-mail: not available

Kenya Web - Car hire

www.kenyaweb.com/business/carhire.html
Car hire directory for Kenya, mainly for well known international companies. Information is restricted to contact details.
e-mail: not available

Odyssey Car Hire

www.iwwn.com.na/odyssey/odyssey.html
Odyssey is based in Namibia, offering sedans, minibuses and two 6-seater aircraft, with vehicles and rates shown. Camping equipment can also be hired. They offer direct transfers from the airport for rentals of longer than 10 days, as well as free emergency air transport to a hospital. Rentals are paid in advance and credit cards are accepted. No online form is available but you can contact them by e-mail, fax or phone. The site is clear and easy to use, with a link to travelling in Namibia.
e-mail: odyssey@iwwn.com.na

RMS Car Hire

home.global.co.za/~rmscar/
Established car hire company in Johannesburg offers four groups of well equipped vehicles. Rates are displayed but more information is available on online enquiry and reservation form. Alternatively contact them by e-mail.
e-mail: rmscar@global.co.za

Sun-Trek

www.suntreksafaris.com/car.html
This is a Kenyan travel company which also offers car hire and a chauffeur service. It has affiliations in the UK,

Zimbabwe, India and Tanzania.
There is an online enquiry form for the latest rates; vehicles are not displayed.
e-mail: info@suntreksafaris.com

Sunnyland Travel Car Hire

www.sunnylandtravel.com
A company in Tenerife, offering car hire, flights and excursions on the island. The cars are displayed with prices in pesetas. There is an online reservation form and a list of contacts is displayed on the main page.
e-mail: advertising@mail.canary-isles.com

Super-Rent AVIS

www.explore-africa.de/car-rental/index-g.htm
South African company offering pickup and drop off in major locations in the country. Vehicles types are displayed without pictures but rates come with a currency converter. There is an easy to use booking form and credit cards are accepted. You can order a free mobile phone if you wish and good road maps. This site also has German text.
e-mail: schlorf@kapstadt.de

Tenerife Car Hire

www.trc-cars.com
This is a Spanish company based in South Tenerife. On offer are small 3-door cars, convertibles and 9-seater minibuses. These are all displayed with a price list. You can make your enquiries online, and use a convenient currency converter. An airport shuttle service is available at additional cost.
e-mail: info@trc-cars.com

Tonys Car Hire

www.sacarhire.co.za
Although they operate in South Africa, you can rent their cars over the border in Zimbabwe, Botswana and Namibia with free delivery and pickup service. Rates and conditions are shown and an online booking

form provided. Major credit cards are accepted.
e-mail: tony@SaCarHire.co.za

Western Cape Car Rental

www.kapstadt.de/denny/index-g.htm
If you want to hire a car in South Africa with free delivery and collection, you will get all the information you need from this web site. Their vehicles come in four price groups and a map shows you where to find them. There is an online booking form and major credit cards are accepted. There are links to safari tours and a currency converter. Text is in English and German.
e-mail: schlorf@kapstadt.de

Asia

Car Hirers

www.carhirers.com
Car Hirers is recognised by the Indian Department of Tourism. Their well presented site displays cars and rates clearly. They accept credit cards with discounts for bulk bookings and long-term contracts. Online reservation is available.
e-mail: info@carhirers.com

Enesty Hire And Drive

www.biznet.com.my/enesty
Malaysian company, based in Kuala Lumpur and Sepang airport, offers cars, jeeps and 6-seater vans. Vehicles and rates are displayed and booking can be made online with the facility to pay by credit card via secure server.
e-mail: enesty@pd.jaring.my

Istanbul - Transportation

www.istanbulcityguide.com/trans/html/whitin_city.html
This is a link on Istanbulcityguide.com with several car hire companies advertised, including local and international organisations. Information is restricted to contact details.
e-mail: not available

Pattaya Rent-A-Car

www.pattayacar-rent.com
A car and truck rental company from
Thailand, based in Pattaya City.
Information is sparse but an online
form is available. Hire rates are given
with a currency conversion link. Credit
cards are acceptable.
e-mail: hcrental@cscoms.com

Sampo Car Rental

travel.cybertaiwan.com/transpor/car/
sampo.htm
They operate six offices serving the
whole of Taiwan. Rental procedures
are simple, all you need are a national
ID card and driving licence. Although
there is no online booking form, phone
numbers are provided for all locations.
They offer a complete range of vehicles,
though they are not displayed.
e-mail: not available

Australasia and Oceania

Abell Hire

www.abellhire.co.nz
New Zealand company with a large
selection of vehicles and depots around
the country. Their site is easy to navigate
and contains information about the
types of vehicles and rates, as well as
a booking form. A local map is also
included to help you find them.
e-mail: abell@lynx.co.nz

Ace Tourist Rentals

www.acerentals.com.au
Based in Brisbane, Australia, they offer
budget, tourist and executive car hire
in Australia and New Zealand. The
information contained in the site is
comprehensive and includes rates and
conditions of hire. One service offered
is collection from the local airport.
You can make bookings, including
specifying the type of car and period
of hire and pay via a secure encrypted
server. There are also links to motels
and other budget accommodation
in Brisbane.
e-mail: info@acerentals.com.au

All Seasons Campervans

www.allseasonscampervans.com.au
Based in Sydney, Australia, this
company has camper vans for hire.
Their site is easy to navigate and very
clear, though a little slow to download
because of the number of images.
The company offers free delivery and
collection anywhere in Sydney, and can
even meet you at the airport on arrival.
All the types of vehicles offered are
shown, but there is no booking form.
The site also contains useful links to
Australian tourist offices.
e-mail: camper@bigpond.com

Australian Motor Vehicle Rentals

www.atn.com.au/carhire/carhire.html
An omnibus site with links to car
rentals throughout Australia. Choose
the State and vehicle type and all
available locations appear.
e-mail: not available

Cars In Hawaii

www.carsinhawaii.com/index.htm
This well-presented site has all the
information you need to make a
reservation online and pay by credit
card. The vehicles are divided into six
groups from economy to luxury. Map
locations, rates, vehicles, and contact
details are all shown.
e-mail: sales@carsinhawaii.com

Casuarina Camper Trailer Hire

www.comcen.com.au/~casuarina/
index.html
Australian company offering jumbucks
and golf tourer campers for short or
long term hire. Their site is easy to
navigate, with good contact information
and a map of their location. There is no
booking form available.
e-mail: casuarina@comcen.com.au

Central Rent-A-Car

www.central-rent-car.com.fj
Fijian car rental company located in Suva, Nadi Airport and Lautoka offering six vehicle types. Rates and terms are displayed with discounts for weekly and monthly rentals. Credit cards are accepted.
e-mail: centralrentals@suva.is.com.fj

Fiji, Transportation, Rental Cars

www.fijifvb.gov.fj/transpt/rntl_car/rntl_car.shtml
This page is part of the Fiji Tourist Board web site. It offers links to a range of companies from international to local car hire. To make contact select the specific company link, as there are no other details available.
e-mail: not available

Mini-Cost Auto Rentals

www.auto-rent.com.au/main.html
Australian company offers a wide range of vehicles including campervans, motor homes, 4WDS, minibuses, cars, trailers, luxury cars, limousines and vehicles for the disabled, with free pick up and delivery in the Sydney area. There is an online booking form. Terms and conditions are clearly explained but it is not stated if credit cards are accepted.
e-mail: laurie@auto-rent.com.au

No Worries

www.atn.com.au/no_worries/welcome.html
Sydney based company offers car rental, car sales, and hotel accommodation in Australia and New Zealand. There is a pick up service at Sydney airport. Rates are mentioned and you can book online, but it is not clear if credit cards are accepted.
e-mail: no.worries@a1.com.au

Travel Mall Car Hire

www.oztravel.com.au/travel_mall/mainpages/TM_cars.html
Lists of car and camper-van hire

companies in Australia and New Zealand. You can book online or by fax and use credit cards via a secure server.
e-mail: not available

Caribbean

Aruba Car Hire

www.arubatourism.com
Part of the Aruba Tourist Board web site, with links to car hire companies, from large international organisations to small local firms. You can also hire a bicycle, moped, scooter or motorcycle. Use the link of the specific company for contact.
e-mail: not available

Auto Rentals Barbados

www.skyviews.com/autorentals
Local authorised agents for Hertz, with a fleet of on and off road vehicles. They provide free pick up and delivery service and free road maps. All vehicles and rates are clearly displayed. Reservations can be made online with payment possible by major credit card.
e-mail: caddy@sunbeach.net

Cayman Auto Rentals

cayman.com.ky/com/cayauto/index.htm
A simple map of Cayman Island, pictures of cars for rent and you can book online with a major credit card.
e-mail: cayauto@candw.ky

Coconut Car Rentals

www.coconutcarrentals.com/index.htm
You can rent a car from four locations in Cayman Island, book online by major credit card and expect a discount.
e-mail: coconut@candw.ky

Courtesy Rent-A-Car

barbados.org/tours/courtesy/index.htm
Long established Barbados company opens seven days a week with several types of vehicles on offer, including

jeeps. An online reservation form is available and a link which provides a virtual tour around Barbados.
e-mail: courtesy@goddent.com

Efay Rent-A-Car

www.efay.com
Jamaican company shows their vehicles with rates in US dollars. Credit cards are accepted but there is no online reservation form. An Airport Shuttle service is available free of charge, and they also offer a chauffeur service. The web site is well presented with an FAQ section and some useful and interesting links about Jamaica.
e-mail: reservations@efay.com

Island Rentals

www.bonairenet.com/island/indexisl.htm
All you need to know to rent a car in Bonaire and you can book online with a credit card.
e-mail: info@islandrentalsbonaire.com

Jones Car Rentals

barbados.org/tours/jones/index.html
The vehicles offered by this Barbados company include small or executive cars, vans and jeeps. They are displayed with rates and credit cards are accepted. You can book with an online reservation form.
e-mail: jonescarrentals@caribsurf.com

Just Jeep Rentals

cayman.com.ky/com/jeep/index.htm
Jeeps on Cayman Island. All the information is clearly set out and you can book online by credit card.
e-mail: justjeep@candw.ky

National Car Rentals

barbados.org/tours/national/national.htm
Barbados company with online booking form. Credit cards are accepted, vehicles and rates are displayed. Free delivery and pick up at your hotel is also available.
e-mail: via online form

Premier Auto Rentals

www.barbados.org/tours/premier/index.htm
This company from Barbados shows their vehicles with hire rates. They have small, medium and large automatic cars as well as mini mokes. Credit card payments are accepted and a 10% discount is available for booking online.
e-mail: autorentals@caribsurf.com

Toyota Rent a Car

www.toyotacarrent-aruba.com
Aruba car hire web site with all cars and rates displayed on the main page. You can book online and credit cards are accepted.
e-mail: toyota.rentacar@setarnet.aw

Wander Services

barbados.org/tours/wander/vehicles.htm
Barbados company offers a full range of cars, including mini-mokes, jeeps and sedans. Rates are clearly displayed, with free delivery, 24-hour emergency service, shuttle to airport from anywhere on the island and 10% discount if booked online.
e-mail: wandering@sunbeach.net

Europe

Agile Rentals

www.agilerental.co.uk
Algile operate in the UK, and their web site displays a good range of vehicles, with free delivery and collection from Heathrow Airport. Online booking is possible but rates are not stated.
e-mail: info@agilerental.co.uk

Alpha Car Hire

www.landweb.co.uk/carrentals/
London based company offers a good selection of cars including top-of-the-range models. Airport collection and delivery come free. Major credit cards are accepted but there is no reservation form. They also have a car sales section

with over 1,500 cars and a link that
explains the British Highway Code.
e-mail: carrentals@landweb.co.uk

Anglo Budget Rental

ourworld.compuserve.com/homepages/
ANGLO_BUDGET_RENTAL/
Based in the UK, offering three
categories of budget car rental on this
simple web site. Reservations can be
made by e-mail or telephone. Credit
cards and cheques are accepted.
e-mail: 106064.224@compuserve.com

Argus Rent A Car

www.argus-rentacar.com
This Irish company's web site is in
English, French and German. There
are thirteen categories of vehicles, in
several locations around the country.
Rates are shown for all groups of cars
for low, middle and high season. You
can view prices online in several
currencies. You can make reservations
and payments by secure server online.
e-mail: info@argusrentacar.com

Asprokavos

www.travel-greece.com/ionian/corfu/
asproka/index.html
This Greek travel agency offers car hire
in Corfu. The only contact information
on this simple web site is a telephone
number.
e-mail: not available

Atlas Car Rentals

www.atlascarhire.com
Irish company with eight groups of
vehicles, shown with rates. Their
courtesy bus runs to and from the main
entrance of Dublin airport. There is an
online quotation and reservation form
and major credit cards are accepted.
A map of their location is included on
the web site.
e-mail: enquiries@atlascarire.com

Belgard Self-Drive

www.itw.ie/belgard/
This Irish company offers both
commercial and tourist car hire on this
simple site. Vehicles are displayed and
an online quotation is available. Credit
cards are accepted.
e-mail: belgard@itw.ie

Blue Chip Cars

www.bluechipcars.co.uk
If you are looking to hire a top of the
range performance or executive car in
the UK, this company may have it.
Vehicles and rates are clearly shown and
an online booking form is provided but
it is not known if they accept credit
cards. The car photo gallery is very
impressive.
e-mail: sales@bluechipcars.co.uk

Business Car Hire

www.businesscarhire.com
London based company with top of the
range vehicles and chauffeur service, but
their cars and rates are not displayed.
You can contact them by e-mail, book
online and pay by credit card.
e-mail: enquiries@businesscarhire.com

Capital Car Hire

www.capital-car-hire.com
This Irish company shows its full range
of vehicles with rates. Quotes and bookings
are available online. Vehicles can only be
booked by group and not by specific
model. There is a theft protection
scheme and credit cards are accepted.
An online form is provided for contact.
e-mail: via online form

Car Hire In Biarritz

www.touradour.com/towns/biarritz/
citer/gb/index.htm
This company operates from Biarritz in
the French region of the Basque Country.
Their cars range from economy to
4WDs; rates are shown and reservations
can be made by e-mail or phone.

The site includes links to holiday accommodation, a towns index, activities in the French Basque Country and access to their parent company, Nationalcar in Europe and the USA.
e-mail: via online form

Carnies Self Drive Hire

www.carnies.co.uk
Scottish company offering 4 types of car with rates shown in French, German and US currency. They accept credit cards. Contact them by e-mail, phone or fax.
e-mail: Trefoilcars@Btinternet.com

Classic Car Hire

www.yorkshirenet.co.uk/visinfo/ccch/
UK company with classic self-drive sports cars and convertibles including Morgan, Caterham, Porsche, Ferrari, E-Type Jags and others to suit your taste. If you are so inclined, look in the wedding hire section. All cars and rates are displayed and there is an online booking form. Please check availability before booking.
e-mail: info@classic-car-hire.co.uk

CorfuXenos

www.corfuxenos.gr/def-e.htm
This Greek travel agency also offers car hire in Corfu. The site is easy to navigate and you can choose from six groups of vehicles. A reservation form is provided and they accept credit card bookings.
e-mail: cfuxenos@corfuxenos.gr

Crete Car Hire

www.kalithea.demon.co.uk
Economy cars to mini buses in Crete. The only contact is an online enquiry form. There are useful links to tourist information.
e-mail: via online form

Cyprus Rent-A-Car

www.cylink.com.cy/leas/
Cars are displayed and rates are quoted in Cypriot currency. Online booking is possible and credit cards are accepted. You can contact them through a 24-hour phone service or by e-mail.
e-mail: dakis@cylink.com.cy

Czechocar Rent a Car

home.earthlink.net/~czechocar/index.html
Czech company offering five types of vehicle from rental locations nation-wide. Fees and vehicles are displayed, they offer a 30% discount with some travel programs. Contact information is provided.
e-mail: czechocar@earthlink.net

Elite Rent-A-Car

www.elite.ch
Based in Geneva, they offer a very large range of vehicles as well as chauffeur service. Vehicles and rates are well displayed in this site, which includes links to a currency converter, weather forecasts, hotels, guides and maps, airlines and a distance chart. Enquiry and reservation can be done online.
e-mail: elitereservation@elite.ch

Eurostyle

www.eurostyle.uk.com/welcome.htm
UK company offers performance and executive cars. All vehicles are displayed with rates but without online booking form. This can be done by fax, e-mail or phone. A map shows their location. This site uses Macromedia Flash, therefore a Shockwave plug-in may be necessary to view it. Graphics are very detailed but information is in short supply.
e-mail: info@eurostyle.uk.com

Expressway Car and Truck Rental

www.venicecar.com
If you need a car in Venice, they offer short, medium and long-term rental. Rates are displayed in Italian lira but not the cars and booking is possible only by phone and e-mail. Vehicles are in the economy car and van range.
e-mail: reservations@venicecar.com

Lanterna Villas

www.lanterna.co.uk/car.htm
They rent cars from Faro Airport in Portugal. The car rental page shows car types and rates for low, mid and high season, conditions of hire and other general information. Bookings are best made by e-mail or telephone.
e-mail: sales@lanterna.co.uk

McCausland Car Hire

www.mccausland.co.uk
Based in Belfast, Northern Ireland, offering car rentals, airport parking and a cab service, as well as ten different tours of up to four people at a time. The site is simple and easy to navigate. Hire rates of cars, buses and minibuses are available with an online booking form, maps and advice about travelling in Northern Ireland.
e-mail: Car.hire@mccausland.co.uk

SOS Driver

www.sosdriver.com
This very simple site offers car hire and chauffeur service in France. Tariffs and vehicles are clearly listed with terms and conditions. Rental can be tailored to your requirements and pick up arranged. Contact is by post and e-mail.
e-mail: info@sosdriver.com

The UK Car Rental and Van Hire Company

www.ukcarandvanrental.co.uk
This company operates from Britain's main airports. You can select a location and make an enquiry via e-mail. There is no online booking form.
e-mail: reservations@ukcarandvan-rental.co.uk

U-Drive

www.u-drive.co.uk
U-Drive operate in the south of England and provide car and commercial vehicle rental. Vehicles and rates are clearly explained, with a booking form and maps of locations. There is contact information on the main page, with a local free phone number.
e-mail: info@u-drive.co.uk

VRS UK

www.heathrow-car-rental.co.uk/
Default.htm
UK company offering car and van rental from London Heathrow and Gatwick airports. The site is clear and easy to follow, with contact information on the main page. The range of vehicles and rates are clearly explained, with enquiry and reservation forms.
e-mail: enquiry@heathrow-car-rental.co.uk

Yellowcar

www.yellowcar.com
A good range of vehicles in Spain. Rates are in Pesetas and Euros and you can book online with your credit card. Airport collection and return are part of the service. Text is in English, German, French and Spanish.
e-mail: yellowcar@ctv.es

Latin America

Al Rent a Car International

rentacarbariloche.com/index_english.htm
Cars in Argentina, Chile and Uruguay. Good range of vehicles, well presented with pictures, rates and information about insurance, tourism, and more. You can book online.
e-mail: not available

Elegante Rent A Car

www.eleganterentacar.com/carsf.htm
Costa Rican company with more than 200 vehicles in six categories. Vehicles, rates and conditions of hire are clearly stated in English and Spanish with online booking and credit card transactions possible via the Internet. A map of the country is also shown.
e-mail: info@eleganterentacar.com

Full Fama's Rent a Car

chile-travel.com/fullfama.htm

Chilean car rental with eight different vehicle types and special discounts for business and institutions. Chauffeur service available. There are contact details online.

e-mail: fullfama@chilesat.net

Imbex Rent a Car

www.imbex.com

Car rental in Bolivia with mainly 4x4 vehicles. Rates are advertised and a booking form provided online.

e-mail: info@imbex.com

Mapache Rent A Car

www.mapache.com

Based in Costa Rica with a simple site showing vehicles, rates and special offers. Online reservation is available and they accept credit card transactions via the Internet. Contact information is on the main page.

e-mail: mapache@sol.racsa.co.cr

Mega Rent

www.megarent.com.br/english

Mega Rent are based in Brazil, and this site is available in Portuguese, Spanish and English. They hire economy, intermediate, executive and off-road vehicles with a 10% discount for online reservations. Telephone contact details are given.

e-mail: via online form

Poas2

www.mercadonet.com/poas.html

Costa Rican car hire with links to insurance facilities and online booking. This well-designed site shows you the cars on offer. Links take you to immigration and other official matters.

e-mail: customer@carentals.com

Trancura

www.trancura.com/car.htm

This travel company offers car hire in Pucon, in Southern Chile; unfortunately the only contact is a phone number and an e-mail address.

e-mail: carhire@trancura.com

Middle East

Capital Rent a Car

www.capital-car.com.lb

You get free delivery and collection anywhere in Lebanon and a weekly car wash when you hire from this company. Tourers, 4x4, luxury cars and convertibles are displayed with online booking; other services include professional bodyguards on request.

e-mail: Capital.Car@inco.com.lb

Fadi Escorted Car Rental

www.fadi.com.jo

Jordanian car rental company with chauffeur-driven, air-conditioned cars with mobile phones for business and pleasure. No pictures or rates are available, but the enquiry form will get you answers. There is a link to local tourism and travel tips.

e-mail: info@fadi.com.jo

Palestine - Car Hire

www.palestine-net.com/tourism/rentals.html

There are two car rental companies advertised on the Palestine-net. The only information available is name, location and phone number. There are recommendations for tourists driving into Israeli controlled areas.

e-mail: not available

Pery

www.yellowpages.co.il/homepages/English/01644087000000000/index.html

Israeli car hire with a modern fleet of private and commercial vehicles with mobile phones, free door to door and airport service and credit card arrangements. Contact is by mail and phone.

e-mail: not available

Sinsal.com

www.sinsal.com

This is a car rental directory for Bahrain, Jordan, Kuwait, Lebanon, Qatar and the UAE. Companies listed are both local and international with contact details provided.

e-mail: not available

North America

Budget Rent A Car

www.budgetrentacar.com/home.html

This site is for the American company, offering seven types of vehicles in the USA and British Columbia. Vehicles are clearly displayed but without rates. A rates and reservation form is available online and payment can be made by credit card via secure server.

e-mail: not available

Europe By Car

www.europebycar.com

This is an American company offering seven categories of vehicles in Europe from economy cars to mini vans. Students and teachers get discounted rates. The well laid out site has an online form for price quotations, an FAQ section and a service for official EAA International Driving Permit Translations. For a small fee you can order the official EAA Translation of your driving license, recognised in many countries.

e-mail: via online form

Only Cars Dot Com

www.onlycars.com

This US web site brings together major American car rental companies. On the online enquiry form you enter the city or airport code, dates of hire, car type and company you prefer. Rental conditions are not shown nor can you pay by credit card.

e-mail: via online form

World wide

Alamo Rent-A-Car

www.freeways.com

American company operating in Europe and the Americas. Lots of information on this well organised web site, with discount schemes for online booking, an extensive FAQ section and various pick up and drop off locations.

e-mail: crelations@goalamo.com

Autoeurope

www.autoeurope.com/cgi-bin/runbin.exe?AE:link::file=carmenu.html

US based and represented in Europe, North America, the Middle East, Australia and South Africa. Select the country on a scroll down menu and you will be offered several vehicle types, illustrated and with rates displayed, chauffeur driven cars and GSM mobile phones. There are links to hotels, flight reservations and an FAQ section.

e-mail: via online form

Avis Galaxy

www.avis.com

This well-known US Company has an international network of more than 4400 locations. Their impressive fleet is attractively displayed online and by selecting your desired country you can see their rates. The FAQ section and a world wide telephone directory will help your enquiries.

e-mail: via online form

Bnm.com

www.bnm.com

This is an online reservation centre operated by about 100 car rental companies in major US and international airports. You can access your chosen airport and make a booking by clicking on a map, with discounts available for online reservations. Cars for the disabled are available.

e-mail: via online form

Discount Car and Truck Rentals

www.discountcar.com/English/default.cfm
Based in Hamilton, Ontario, they have
over 200 outlets in Canada, USA,
Morocco, Jamaica and Australia. Though
their vehicles are displayed, rates,
reservations and pickup locations must
be requested via the online form.
e-mail: via online form

Dollar Rent A Car

www.dollar.com
An American company with an
international network of offices and
impressive fleet of vehicles. A map of
locations leads you to each office and
rates are shown for each type of vehicle.
For Europe use their affiliated company,
Europcar.
e-mail: rhelpdesk@dollar.com

Hertz Rent-A-Car

www.hertz.com
This is probably the world's best known
car hire company. The well-designed
site is worth a visit; it is easy to browse,
has several useful links and allows you
to reserve a vehicle online practically
anywhere in the world. Several major
credit cards are accepted.
e-mail: via online form

Pelican Car Hire

www.itsnet.co.uk/car/pelican/
UK company with agents world wide.
Rates, types of vehicles and conditions
of hire vary from country to country.
Rates are shown for each country with
a phone number and e-mail address.
You can pay by credit card and take
advantage of a 10% discount for
Internet reservations.
e-mail: pelican@travel.itsnet.co.uk

Rent-A-Car

www.reserve-a-car.com
American company offering car rental
world wide. You can reserve your car
online and pay by credit card via a
secure server. Rates are shown only
in US dollars. Little other information
is available.
e-mail: via online form

Rent-A-Wreck

www.rent-a-wreck.com
This is an American car rental company
with locations in Norway, Sweden and
the United Arab Emirates. A US
freephone number will connect you to
their main office.
e-mail: raw@rent-a-wreck.com

Thrifty Car Rental

www.thrifty.com
An American company with offices
world wide. Vehicles include economy
cars and jeeps. Pick your location, time,
date and vehicle, and enquire via online
form. The site has links for franchise
opportunities, travel agents, careers and
airlines. They also offer airport parking
within the USA.
e-mail: via online form

National Car Rental

www.nationalcar.com/servlet/DocHand
ler/index.html
US company offering car rental world
wide. A large variety of well displayed
vehicles is available. Enquiries and
reservations can be made online,
though an FAQ section may already
have all the answers you need. You may
find navigating this site a bit confusing.
e-mail: not available

Worldwide Car Hire with Choice Cars

www.choice-cars.com
This is one of the world's largest leisure
car rental brokerage companies, which
uses the best car hire company in each
territory for most destinations in the world.
Several classes of vehicle are presented
with rates, but only the European section
contains pictures. Enquire using the online
form or telephone.
e-mail: via online form

Cyber Cafés

Africa

CyberGates

www.cybergates.net
This café in Khartoum, Sudan provides Internet access with peripheral services, programming, troubleshooting, maintenance and a range of courses.
e-mail: cybergates@cybergates.net

Gerardo's Internet and Rockmusic Bar

www.arrakis.es/~fordinal/
The first Internet bar on the Canary Island of La Gomera. You can surf and e-mail to the sound of grunge and rock from the 60's to the present. They serve snacks and drinks, will create a home page for you and on Fridays and Saturdays between 1030 and 1330, offer Internet courses. They open 1030 to 1500, 2030 to 0200 daily and charge 1,200 pesetas per hour.
e-mail: fordinal@arrkis.es

The Blue Lizard Internet Café

www.lizard.co.za
Situated at the hub of Zonnebloem, Cape Town, South Africa, the café offers full access to the Internet. You can e-mail, play network games, IRC, hold live video conferences, ftps, print with full DTP

services, research, and take a four hour comprehensive computer course. The café plays acid jazz, drum and bass, world music, current hot singles and 70's and 80's tracks. There is a full bar and you can check their drinks list on the web. They open 1000 to 1800 weekdays, and at the weekends they start at 1000 with no set closing time but generally between 0200 and 0500.
e-mail: info@lizard.co.za

Westdene Internet Café

www.westcafe.co.za
Restaurant, pub and café all in one in Johannesburg, South Africa. You can drink and eat while surfing the net on one of eight Pentiums, connected to a 64K dedicated line. Cuisine is diverse from all over Africa and meals are served in the traditional African style. Rates for 15-minute slots vary with each program so check them out before you start.
e-mail: steve@westcafe.cn.za

Asia

Bali @Cyber Café and Restaurant

www.singnet.com.sg/~hchua/cafe.htm
If you have trouble finding it, ask for directions to the Swiss Restaurant in Pura Bagus Taruna, Legian on Bali Island, the café is nearby; or download the map from the Location link on the home page. When you get there you can send e-mail, surf the web or watch a multi-media VCD programme; chat over the net or have an interactive game on the web. 15 minutes will cost you Rp 5000, about US$2, with discounts for longer periods.
e-mail: Bl-cafe1@idola.net.id

Cybermaster

members.xoom.com/sabahcyberm/
Click the button and the map will show you where they are in Api-Api centre, Kota Kinabalu, Sabah, Malaysia. You can

surf the Internet, play games, scan, print and design web pages; watch TV, listen to music or have a drink, paying 0.10 RM per minute using the 17 inch monitor and 0.20 RM for the 38 inch.
e-mail: cybermasterkk@hotmail.com

Easylink

www.visitnepal.com/easylink
This is the first cyber café for the use of foreigners in Nepal, located in the heart of Thamel, Kathmandu. High-speed Internet connections come in friendly and peaceful surroundings with beverages and snacks. In addition to real time chats, Mirc & ICQ, scanning, colour and laser printing, web design and phone, fax and e-mail communications abroad, they offer car rentals and accommodation. Discounted rates for students and groups are available.
e-mail: easylink@visitnepal.com

Explorer Internet Café

www.explorer.cybersurf.co.th
Cold beer, coffees, juices, burgers and snacks come with the most reliable Internet service in Pattaya, Thailand. You can e-mail with Pop accounts, mail incoming monitor, AOL, Hotmail, Rocketmail and others without waiting. Scanners and colour printers are available.
e-mail: info@cybersurf.co.th

Future.com

www.india-future.com
The most up-to-date cyber café in Calcutta, India is located near Belgachia Metro station. You get all Internet related services in a friendly atmosphere, from e-mail to web page design and hosting. They are equipped with Telnet, FTP, Browsing, e-mail and chat, photo-scan, CD writing and colour printing. They open daily 1000 to 2100.
e-mail: futurecom@vsnl.com

Hyperlink Internet

www.kfnet.com.my/hprlk/
The cyber café in Malaysia gives Internet access, computer and web page design courses, has network games, printing and scanning facilities. You can shop for furniture, computers, a variety of printed products and rent space. E-mail is not available so to contact them, use the online form. Prices are shown on the site.
e-mail: not available

Internet Café Paniqui

www.paniqui.com
Located on Burgos Street, Paniqui, Tarlac in the Philippines, they offer nine terminals, all running Windows 98 with a choice of Internet Explorer 5 or Netscape 4. They have network games, Internet chat, fax, scanning, design and web services, computer sales, repairs, tutorials, membership and unlimited access for 500 pesos per month.
e-mail: not available

NetCafe 2000

www.lipacity.com
Batangas in the Philippines. Apart from snacks, coffee and soft drinks they offer Internet access, printing, computer rentals and peripherals, accessories, licensed software and training. Membership brings many service benefits and a reduced hourly charge of P45; non-members pay P60.
e-mail: netcafe@lipacity.com

The Cyber Beach Café

www.cyberbeachcafe.com
Espresso and Internet services just off the coast road of Patong Beach Phuket, Thailand, a favourite hangout for young people. They sell a range of cafeteria food and drink side by side with second hand books. Check your e-mail and surf the net in good company.
e-mail: info@cyberbeachcafe.com

Tibtronic Cyber House

www.angelfire.com/in/tibtronic
A Tibetan cyber café next to the Post office in McLeod Ganj, Dharamsala, India. Eight of the latest high speed computers are networked together using Windows NT as a router. All can be used simultaneously to access the Internet with a fast 56k modem connection. They have a colour printer, scanner and a computer for hire with free tutoring. Drinks are hot or cold. Monday to Saturday 0830 to 2000, Sunday 0900 to 1930.
e-mail: pnamgyal@hotmail.com

Universe

www2.mozcom.com/~trigem1/index.html
A chain of cyber cafés in Manila, Philippines. You can surf, chat and e-mail with no minimum charge; you pay for what you use at P 1.50 per minute. There are lots of discounts for extended use leading up to the Universe Gold Card, which allows you unlimited access for a month for P5,000.
e-mail: fkl@universecafe.com

W@rung Kopi

www.geocities.com/SouthBeach/2354
This traditional Indonesian café in Jakarta is dedicated to the net traveller. You can visit other cyber cafés around the world or search the net. You can seek help on the Problem@ page, or just talk about any of your problems.
e-mail: warungkopi@geocities.com

Yagmur Café

www.citlembik.com.tr
Click on the map link on the home page to find where they are located in Istanbul, Turkey. They have a fast functional leased line for Internet connections with regular events like Quake II competitions. When e-mailing using, IRC, USENET or other Internet services, please follow the Netiquette guidelines; displaying pornography is strictly forbidden and may lead to prosecution. Hourly rates are shown on the site.
e-mail: not available

Australasia and Oceania

Coffee Cove Online

www.coffeecove.com
Located at the corner of University and South King Streets in Honolulu with six PC workstations and high-speed Internet access, the café serves coffee, soft drinks and snacks. You can surf the net, e-mail or join a chat room. Their mini library has something for everyone, including the daily papers. Students, soldiers and senior citizens get discounts off the standard rate of $6 per hour. They open weekdays 0700 to 0000, weekends 1000 to 0000.
e-mail: not available

Coffee Haven

www.coffee-haven.com
Both Macintosh and Windows NT/98 based systems are used in this Honolulu café with live music every night except Sunday. The site has useful links to Honolulu, maps, search engines, chat links, newspapers and so on. The café charges $4 per hour for Macintoshes and $6 per hour for Windows.
e-mail: not available

Cybernet Café

www.internet-cafe.org/cybernet
Cybernet Café in Melbourne was the first Internet café to open in Australia. Enjoy your coffee and cakes while browsing the web or reading an extensive range of Internet magazines and books. Their Training School runs two classes a week introducing the Internet and web authoring to students. They have a range of charges beginning at $6 per half-hour and stay open Sunday to Thursday 0011

to 2200, Friday and Saturday
1100 to 2300.
e-mail: cybercafe@internet-café.org

Live Wire

www.livewire.co.nz
In Auckland, New Zealand, they provide
connections to the Internet, e-mail,
word processors and network games.
They have ten Pentium 133 Mhz, 8
Pentiums 266 Mhz and four Pentium 300
Mhz. All computers are installed with
Windows 95 and Office programs, like
Word and Excel. Printing and scanning are
included in the normal hourly rate of $10.
e-mail: livewire@livewire.co.nz

Surfnet

www.surf.net.au
Located in the heart of Manly, Australia
they provide Internet access, scanning
and e-mail facilities. You can play the
latest games including GL Quake,
Quake 2, Unreal and Fifa 99 or take a
course at competitive rates in word
processing and printing.
e-mail: info@surfnet.net.au

The Internet Café

www.aloha-cafe.com
This is Honolulu's premiere cyber café
equipped with international keyboards in
more than fifteen Western languages
and Kana for Japanese users. Twelve
Apple Macintosh computers with the
latest software including Java enhanced
Netscape and the Microsoft Office
series run a high-speed network. Colour
and laser printers, fax and copying
facilities are also available.
e-mail: surfbum@aloha-café.com

Caribbean

Cyber Café

www.cybercafe.aw
Royal Plaza Mall 204 in Oranjestad,
Aruba is where you can access the
Internet or play computer games.

Internet services include America
Online, Compuserve, e-mail, ICQ, chat
and videoconferencing. Cyber guides
will assist you to create a web page or
advertise on the web, or any task you
wish to perform on the computer. They
charge $5.75 per 33 minutes and open
Mondays to Saturdays, 1000 to 2130
and Sundays, 1200 to 2000.
e-mail: Bizopp@cybercafe.aw

Europe

2zones

www.2zones.com
Woolstraat 15 in the centre of Antwerp,
Holland is the address. They offer
internet access, computer training,
graphic design, web site development
and a host of other services, including
five servers giving fast access to the
Internet, a fast colour laser printer,
scanner and up to 4 zip drives for
storage. On weekdays they open 1130
to 0000, 1130 to 0130 at the weekends.
e-mail: 2zones@s-dreams.net

Avenue Cyber Theatre

www.cybertheatre.net/en/
The Cyber Theatre is located at the
Avenue de la Toison d'Or 5, Brussels,
Belgium and opens daily except Sunday,
1000 to 2300. As the name implies the
café offers online access with live shows,
seminars and networking activities. They
have more than 100 computers, both PC
and Macintosh with an extensive range
of professional and recreational
applications, fast network connection and
a team of professionals to assist. They
have a range of prices with discounts for
students and holders of EURO<26 cards.
e-mail: nmichils@cybertheatre.net

Babel

www.babel.dk
Fully equipped Internet café in
Copenhagen to surf, scan, print, design
and program web sites. Coffee and

snacks keep you alert. Their rates start at DKK30 per hour or you can buy Surfcards for up to five hours a day for the whole month and save money.
e-mail: chris@babel.dk

C@fe.net
www.cafenet.uk.com
A regular café with relaxed atmosphere, cable TV lounge, daily newspapers, board games, great coffee, interesting lunchtime and evening menus and hi-tech cyber connections. Located in East Sheen, London, their IT services include Internet access, e-mail, newsgroups, chat lines, Telnet, games, several software programs and a CD-ROM library. They charge £5 per hour and open 1100 to 2100 Monday to Thursday, 1100 to 1900 Friday and Saturday and 1230 to 1900 on Sunday.
e-mail: cafemail@cafenet.uk.com

Café On Line
www.corfu-net.gr/online/
The home page has a few travel links about Corfu, a discussion board and a location map showing their café at Kapodistriou Street, Spianada Square. They open daily 1000 to 0100 and offer Internet access, free e-mail, online games, scanning and printing.
e-mail: Café_online1@yahoo.com

CyberCentral
the-bureau.com
Access to the Internet from the Palma cyber café is via high speed ISDN connection to seven workstations. Web design, computer courses and full office services come with food and drink. All computers have the latest Windows software, Internet Explorer and Netscape browsers. You can surf, e-mail, chat and use their computer peripheral services on weekdays 1000 to 2030 and Saturday 1000 to 1800.
e-mail: info@cybercentralpalma.com

Dot Com Internet Café
www.dotcom.uk.com
Internet café, bistro, bar and snooker club rolled into one, above a fitness club, opposite Portobello Green in London. Specialised services include web layout and design and inexpensive Internet and computer training courses at all levels of competence. The bar sells a range of health and energy drinks, freshly-brewed coffee, wines, spirits and beers.
e-mail: dotcom@dotcom.uk.com

Hyperactive the Internet Café
www.hyperactive-cafe.co.uk/index2.htm
At Central Station Crescent in Exeter, Devon, England, Hyperactive give friendly helpful Internet access at affordable prices. Their other services include e-mail, word processing, scanning, faxing, desktop publishing, training and single or multi-player games, Telnet, IRC, ECQ, FTP and more. They open on weekdays 1030 to 1930, Saturday 1000 to 1800 and Sunday 1200 to 1800. Their standard rates are £5 per hour, £4.50 for students and £4 for under 16's.
e-mail: enquiries@hyperactive-café.co.uk

Hypercorner Internet Café
www.hypercorner.gr
102 Agiou Loannou Street, next to Deree, the American College in Athens, Greece. The café offers a full range of Internet services from 16 PC's with more than 200 PC games and a wide range of peripherals like printers and scanners. To keep you nourished they have a range of snacks, sandwiches, beverages, beers and cocktails. They open Monday to Thursday 0900 to 2000, Friday 0900 to 0000 and Saturday 1200 to 0000, charging between $2.50 and $8 per hour.
e-mail: administrator@hypernet.hypercorner.gr

Inetpoint.CZ

www.inetpoint.cz/en/index.htm
Check the home page for their location
in the centre of Prague, close to
Wenceslas Square. They have eleven
PC Pentium II, 333MHz computers with
64 Kbps fixed link connection to the
Internet. You can surf, e-mail, print,
laser scan and do high quality copying.
They charge 25 CZK per 15 minutes.
e-mail: inetpoint@inetpoint.cz

Interlink

www.interlink.it/index_en.htm
A café in Torino, Italy with full
staff-assisted Internet services, e-mail
facilities, PC's with dedicated connection
and interactive courses. The home page
lists international search engines,
archives of e-mail addresses, e-mail
domains, newsgroups, yellow pages,
and other useful references.
e-mail: not available

Internet Café

www.internetcafe.it/frameuk.html
In San Lorenzo, near La Sapienza
University, Rome, where you can access
the web using Netscape, Explorer, AOL,
Telnet, FTP, or take courses at all levels
of competence from helpful cyber
guides or chat, ICQ and e-mail. They
have the latest video games and organise
Quake tournaments. On weekdays they
open 0900 to 1400, weekends and
holidays 1700 to 0200.
e-mail: info@intercafe.it

The Cardiff CyberCafe

www.cardiffcybercafe.co.uk
They offer a high-speed connection to
the Internet; you can play games,
e-mail, or just surf the web. Software
includes web browsers, chat programs,
video conferencing, ICQ, Internet
games, Telnet, AOL, Compuserve and
FTP. They also run courses from word
processing to graphics packages, from
basic surfing to designing your own web

page. They charge £1.75 per 15 minutes,
£4.50 per hour; check the Members link
on the home page for discounts.
Opening times on weekdays 1000 to
1900, Saturday 1000 to 1800, Sunday
1100 to 1700.
e-mail: info@cardiffcybercafe.co.uk

The Internet Café Astoria

www.astoria.com.mk
Part of Café Astoria in Skopje,
Macedonia is linked to the Internet.
They provide full computer, electronic
and Net services, organise web promotions
and train users. Check prices in the
services section against 900 denars for
10 hours use a month as a member.
They open 0900 to 2300 weekdays,
0900 to 0000 on Saturday.
e-mail: Astoria@astoria.com.mk

Vortex Madrid

www.geocities.com/mfbodoque/
vortexmadrid.html
Vortex Madrid offer 15 Pentium II computers with speeds of 400 Mhz, 64
RAM, in an area of 75m2. The closest
cyber café to El Prado and Reina Sofia
museums, they exhibit the work of local
artists and speak Spanish, English and
Italian. They open daily 1000 to 0000
and charge 500 pesetas per hour.
e-mail: vortexmadrid@yahoo.com

Waves

sites.waldonet.net.mt/waves
The café is situated on the beautiful
sea front promenade in Malta.
Comfortable, air-conditioned with a fully
stocked bar makes it just the place to
sip a cocktail while browsing the web or
sending e-mail. The four PC terminals -
Pentiums 200MMX - are high speed
semi-digital with full stereo sound,
chat lines, choice of browsers -
Netscape or Explorer and e-mail -
Eudora Light or Netscape - with printer
and floppy drives.
e-mail: waves@waldonet.net.mt

Web 13

www.web13.co.uk

The café is in the centre of Edinburgh, Scotland with full electronic services including Internet, e-mail, word processing, desktop publishing, graphic design, multimedia, scanning, printing, faxing and photocopying. They offer consultancy services, web design and development, site management, computer training in co-pilots, word processing and other software skills, web page authoring and promotion.

e-mail: info@web13.co.uk

Webshack

www.webshack-cafe.com

Webshack at 15 Dean Street is London's centrally located cyber café. It has an ergonomic design and vibrant atmosphere. The café offers great coffee and the bar is licensed. There are more than 20 Pentium workstations with London's fastest connection to the Web. Multi-level training from friendly staff starts at £20 per hour. They open Monday to Saturday 1030 to 2300, Sundays 1300 to 2000 charging £5 per hour, £3 for half an hour.

e-mail: rupal@webshack-café.com

Latin America

CyberCoffee1 Internet

amberisle.com/Cybercoffee1

They provide Internet and e-mail services in San Pedro Town, la Isla Bonita, Belize. You get instant access to America Online, AOL Instant Messenger 2.0, FTP & Telnet Access, e-trade, Schwab, Wells Fargo, Hotmail Messenger & Chat, Netscape Netcenter, Yahoo Pager & Yahoo, International FAX service, MS Office, Adobe Photoshop, Photo Image Digitising Service and much more. They offer professional tutoring, web authoring and personal page editing. The first 15 minutes cost

B$5.40, thereafter B$1.67 per 5 minutes 0830 to 2100 Monday to Saturday, 1500 to 2100 Sundays and Holidays.

e-mail: Cybercoffee1@aol.com

Eva's Online

www.evasonline.com/home.htm

Free tourist information to travellers coming to Belize with reasonable Internet connections and e-mail services. They are located in the picturesque town of San Ignacio in Western Belize. The site has links to tours, lodges, hotels, and other local information.

e-mail: evas@btl.net

Middle East

Café Ole

www.ole.com.kw

Located in a shopping and entertainment centre in the Salhiya Complex in Salmiya Kuwait, they offer international cuisine in a hospitable environment.

All computers are equipped with the latest software, network games and high speed Internet access, Adobe Photoshop and other desktop publishing software. Ole Smart Cards have plans with graduated discounts. They open daily from 1000 to 0000 and charge KD1 per hour.

e-mail: not available

Carma Cyber Club

www.al-carma.com/index.html

Multi-purpose Internet café in the heart of Ramallah, Palestine. They have 20 multimedia workstations with audio equipment, high quality graphics cards, floppy and CD drives and large capacity HD's. They provide internet access, printing services, scanning, photocopying, digital photography, web page hosting and design and other services. The home page has a review of Internet cafes in Palestine and a Palestine Web Index Directory.

e-mail: cafe@al-carma.com

Inbar

www.isralink.co.il/inbar999/
Eat, drink and relax while you surf the web, chat on IRC or e-mail at the corner of 87 King George in Tel Aviv, Israel. Computers are charged out at NS0.70 per minute with students and soldiers receiving discounts. No foreign floppy disks are allowed in the system. Internet lessons are available with personal tuition at NS140 per hour. They open Monday to Friday 0900 to 0100, Saturday 1600 to 0100.
e-mail: barak@isralink.co.il

Ur Internet Culture Café

www.ur.com.jo/ur/cafe.htm
The café at Jordan University Street, Amman, Jordan is well appointed and air-conditioned with 12 modern systems, scanners, colour printers and all popular Internet programs. They assist customers and offer training. They open around the clock every day of the year and charge 2JD, approximately US$3 per hour.
e-mail: Culture@ur.com.jo

North America

Access Caffe

www.access-caffe.com
This is Philadelphia's premiere Internet café, located at 1207 Race Street. They feature high bandwidth Internet access from DCAnet and offer web site hosting for personal and commercial home pages. You can Web browse with Internet Explorer and Netscape, Telnet, FTP, e-mail, chat, read and post news, and enjoy multi-player games in a quiet, relaxed atmosphere. The restaurant section has a full Americana menu, home made pastries and gourmet coffee.
e-mail: ihung@access-caffe.com

Bistro

www.bistro.net/service.htm
At $5 her hour everyone is welcome to use the Internet services of this cyber café in Edmonton, Canada. Other services include photocopying, scanning, colour and laser printing. The café menu is on the homepage.
e-mail: not available

Bontu Internet Café

www.bontu.com
Fresh coffee, snacks and soft drinks in a relaxed atmosphere a mile away from the heart of San Francisco where you can surf the web at high speed with a fast DSL connection. Their other facilities include laser printers, scanners and digital cameras. Senior citizens and full-time students get a 10% discount on an hourly rate of $8. Open weekdays 0900 to 2000, and 0900 to 1600 at the weekend.
e-mail: bic@bontu.com

Bytes Café

www.bytescafe.com
The first full service Internet Café in Edmonton, Canada with high-speed ISDN access, e-mail, Chat, MIRC, Telnet, games, colour printing and other office services. They have a three level system of charges with good discounts for members; non-members start at $3 for 15 minutes.
e-mail: not available

Café Internet

www.cafeinternet-bend.com
Check out the menu of this café in Century Village, Bend, Oregon, on the home page. The eight Multimedia Pentiums offer Internet access, word-processing, graphics programs, games and full office services. They charge $2 per 15 minutes and open weekdays 1000 to 1900, Saturday 1000 to 1800 and Sunday by appointment.
e-mail: cafeinternet@bendcable.com

Café & Internet of America

www.cafeina.net
They have ten PC's and one Mac in this Miami café. You can surf the web using

AOL, Internet Explorer or Netscape, chat and correspond by e-mail. Their scanners, digital cameras, laser and colour printers are thoroughly modern and they produce business cards, flyers, CV's and will fax anywhere. Weekday opening is 1200 to 2000, Saturday 1200 to 1800 and charges start at $3 per 15 minutes with discounts for longer use.
e-mail: not available

CafeMyth.com

www.cafemyth.com
Food, coffee, a juice bar, live events and computer classes on request in Washinton DC. They have five Intel-based PC's and two iMacs equipped with MS Office97, AOL 4.0, Quake II and other software. There is a minimum $2 charge per use with normal rates of $8 per hour; students get 50% off.
e-mail: info@cafemyth.com

Cyber Java

www.cyberjava.com
Located in the famous Hollywood Boulevard, Los Angeles, USA they provide Internet access and serve coffees, javas, delicious smoothies, sandwiches, salads and pastries and charge $2.50 for 15 minutes or $9 per hour to use the equipment. Opening times on weekdays are 0700 to 0000, 0800 to 0000 at the weekend.
e-mail: mail@cyberjava.com

Matrix Interactive Café

www.matrix-cafe.com
They are the largest, fastest and best connected cyber café in Calgary, Alberta, Canada with 18 high-speed machines with accelerators and sound blasters for the smoothest and most intense audio-visual online game play available. Weekdays 0800 to 2100 and Saturday 1200 to 0200 with a range of rates depending on method of payment.
e-mail: not available

Sub-Link

www.sub-link.net
Internet and computer services in Yakima, Washington. Access the Netcam link and find out what is happening at the café, what members are doing or chat with others. Membership entitles you to 30 days unlimited Internet access, one e-mail account and one alias and 5 megs storage space for a personal home site; free access to printing, scanning, digital cameras, desktop and web publishing, software packages, such as Corel, Microsoft Office Suite and more. They also sell and service computers.
e-mail: not available

Surfnsip Internet Café

www.surfnsip.com
Sip cappuccino while you check your e-mail, chat online or surf the net. Other services include consultancy, training, videoconferencing, FTP, scanning, printing, games, multimedia, use of digital cameras and web design. They use Word, Excel, Office 97, Publisher, Front Page, Visual Basic and Winzip software. The café is located on Indian Shores in Florida.
e-mail: surfnsip@surfnsip.com

The World Café

www.worldcafela.com/homepage.html
This is the ultimate multimedia venue in Santa Monica, California, with six multimedia Internet access computers in a Jungle Patio environment. Every night except Monday, from 1800 to 2300, you can cruise the ultra high-speed fibre optic T-1 connection with a cyber guide preparing you for the ride. The Tiki Kiosk and Jungle Room are available for private events and web site launch parties. Regular www classes and seminars are held at the café.
e-mail: teck@interworld.net

Destinations

Africa

Africa Insites

www.africa-insites.com
The web site covers Zambia, Uganda, Lesotho and Namibia. Links on the home page take you to tour operators, game parks, safaris and package tours, car rentals and shopping guides for each country. You have information on accommodation and how to get there, the country itself, its people and business matters.
e-mail: robyn@africa-insites.com

Africa Online

www.africaonline.com
Guides to the Ivory Coast, Kenya, Ghana, Swaziland, Seychelles, Zambia, Zimbabwe, Tanzania and Uganda. Apart from general articles there is a lot of travel information with emphasis on safaris in the host countries.
e-mail: not available

Canary Isles

www.canary-isles.com
The site describes every aspect of tourism on the Canary Isles. Hotels are listed in 10 languages with photos, prices, e-mail addresses, facilities, near-by beaches and lots more. You have leisure centres, estate agents,

nightlife venues, flights, restaurants, insurance, shopping, touring, adult entertainment and a huge photo gallery.
e-mail: not available

Cape Town City - South Africa

www.capetown.co.za/outcont.html
Information about Cape Town including events, music, clubs, restaurants, on a simple list click the Go There button for details about any item.
e-mail: via online form

City of Cape Town Home Page

www.ctcc.gov.za
Most of this site presents the city's attractions, reserves, national parks and zoos. There are lists of sports operators and restaurants, galleries, theatres, cinemas and a link to an unofficial guide to local clubs and bars. Accommodation ranges from hostels to luxury hotels.
e-mail: not available

Complete Online Guide to Alexandria

www.alex-guide.com
Alexandria is on Egypt's Mediterranean coast. The web site tells you all you need to know to plan your trip there, with a photographic guided tour. There are lists of hotels, estate agents and shops, as well as information about the local beaches.
e-mail: beshay@beshay.com

Congo Pages

www.congo-pages.org/welcome.htm
Lots of pictures of the life and culture of the Congolese people and lots more of the country's extraordinary wildlife. Travel information is a little sparse.
e-mail: D_R_Congo@yahoo.com

Destination Chad

www.lonelyplanet.com.au/dest/afr/cha.htm
Travel information in plenty on this site with advice about getting around, visas, embassies, history, culture and a

calendar of events. There is a map of Chad, but regrettably we get no pictures.
e-mail: not available

Egypt Tourism Net

www.tourism.egnet.net/
An excellent on-the-spot guide to Egypt. All the ancient sites are described on separate pages reached by clicking on a list or a map. You will find practical information about the country, its hotels, car rental companies, restaurants, travel agents, Nile cruises and the best diving spots in the Red Sea.
e-mail: egyptour-subcribe@egroups.com

Eritrean Network Info Center

www.eritrea.org
Apart from a short hotel guide and a description of the country's main attractions, the site concentrates on the people, culture, history, traditions, food, dress and festivities of the country. There are a few interesting maps.
e-mail: not available

GambiaNet

www.gambianet.com
There's something for everyone in Gambia from travel information to daily local and national news. Jokes, shopping and sports are added for good measure. A few pictures would have been nice.
e-mail: info@gambianet.com

Ghana Tourist Board

www.africaonline.com.gh/Tourism/
There is some information about the country and investment opportunities and more about tourism. There are links to hotels, restaurants, shopping and tours and some good pictures.
e-mail: not available

Go2Africa.com

www.go2africa.com
The guide covers several countries in Africa. The main attractions in each country are set out with a lot of other travel information. You can book your whole holiday online.
e-mail: Info@go2africa.com

GORP Zimbabwe Tourist Information

www.gorp.com/gorp/location/africa/zimbabwe/zimbabwe.htm
This site gives essential travel information about health matters, visas, climate and currency. There are good links to Zimbabwe's national parks, which would be that much better with more pictures.
e-mail: not available

Harare, Zimbabwe

www.sunshinecity.net
Using Harare as a base you can enjoy the country's outdoor attractions - safaris, rafting, canoeing, bungee-jumping and parachuting. There are lists of hotels and other accommodation, restaurants and other amenities.
e-mail: not available

Introduction to the Maldives

www.maldive.com
Water sports including scuba diving, windsurfing, water-skiing and fishing are featured with all the other travel information on the site. There are travel tips, dress codes and a list of travel agents.
e-mail: not available

Kingdom of Morocco

www.kingdomofmorocco.com
Royal Air Maroc maintains this site, with its review of Morocco's history, arts and crafts, cuisine and dress. Hotels and tour operators are listed but with few links.
e-mail: not available

Malawi - The Warm Heart of Africa

www.members.tripod.com/~malawi/
Information, though brief, is sufficient to plan your trip to Malawi. There are hotels, some with their own web sites, a phrasebook, maps, currency rates and

a link for online booking of flights, car rentals and hotels.
e-mail: fukula@ntlinc.8m.com

Malawi Tourism web site

www.malawi-tourism.com
Simply presented but with enough links for things to do in Malawi, places to see, where to stay, parks, contact information and a few good pictures.
e-mail: not available

Mauritius Welcomes You

www.mauritius.net/
You will find information about the island's hotels, restaurants, package tours and a few travel tips.
e-mail: Mtpa@btinternet.com

Miftah Shamali - North Africa

www.i-cias.com/m.s/
This omnibus web site covers Algeria, Morocco, Mauretania, Libya, Tunisia, Egypt and the Sudan. Each country has its own internal guide featuring main cities, attractions, hotels, internal transport, safety, health and climate.
e-mail: i-cias@i-cias.com

Motherland Nigeria

www.motherlandnigeria.com
A colourful site packed with travel information. You will find all you need on travel agents, weather, culture, restaurants, transportation, airlines, currency conversion, maps, city tours and more.
e-mail: webdiva@motherlandnigeria.com

Republic of Botswana

www.gov.bw/
Botswana has game reserves and parks with a full complement of hotels, small and large and campsites all over the country. There is information on local transportation and National Park regulations.
e-mail: not available

Republique Togolaise

www.republicoftogo.com
A calendar of events and descriptions of the main cities make up the bulk of the web site. There is a little information for the traveller but a request form will get you more if you need it.
e-mail: not available

Reunion Tourist Board Guide

www.la-reunion-tourisme.com/Adefault.htm
Though some links are broken, the web site of this small island is beautifully illustrated. There is a map with enough general information and links to hotels and restaurants to plan a trip.
e-mail: not available

Senegal Online

www.senegal-online.com
There are five recommended tours through the cities and national parks of Senegal. Every major city has a list of hotels, some with links to their own web pages and you also get a quick look at the country's history, culture, literature, music and arts.
e-mail: delbende@worldnet.fr

Sudan Page @Sudan.Net

www.sudan.net
Everything you need to know about Sudan, from tourist information to national statistics. There are links to maps, languages, culture, accommodation, weather and government.
e-mail: muaz@sudan.net

Tanzania Tourist Board

www.tanzania-web.com/home2.htm
The National Parks, coastal resorts, safaris and Mount Kilimanjaro make Tanzania a very desirable holiday destination. Follow the links and you get to coastal resorts, tour operators, accommodation, safari parks and a map to select what you want to see. You will get all the

guidance you need to plan your trip from this site.
e-mail: 100711.3161@compuserve.com

The Seychelles Super Site

www.sey.net
Full of travel information and pictures of the archipelago. You will find lots on how to get there and away, travelling between the islands and whatever else you need for a very enjoyable stay.
e-mail: Info@sey.net

Tourism and Travel in Uganda

www.visituganda.com
The site deals mainly with 10 organised tours of Uganda. Prices are quoted in major currencies. You can book by e-mail. If you want to go it alone you can plan your trip with other information available on the site.
e-mail: utb@starcom.co.ug

TourWeb Namibia

www.namibiaweb.com
Accommodation goes the full range from hotels to campsites, most of which have independent web sites. Safaris are well described with pictures and you can book online.
e-mail: info@namibiaweb.com

Travel and Tourism Guide to Tunisia

www.tourismtunisia.com
The official web site of the Tunisian Tourism Office, with detailed information about the culture, accommodation, places to visit, things to do, where to eat, shopping and festivals in the country.
e-mail: info@tourismtunisia.com

Uganda Tourist Board

www.visituganda.com
The map of Uganda shows all its nature parks, the focus of tourism in the country. Other links connect you to holidays, accommodation, wildlife,

people and climate. The site is easy to navigate with lots of fine pictures.
e-mail: utb@starcom.co.ug

Visit Kenya

www.visit-kenya.com
Kenya is synonymous with safaris. This is well reflected in this site, which has a good map and a slide show of the country's best attractions, including the capital Nairobi, the coastal regions and game reserves. There is also a currency converter, weather and other general information.
e-mail: help@Visit-Kenya.com

Welcome to the Republic of Angola

www.angola.org
There is a lot of information about Angola to assist travellers but only a few links specifically for tourism. You will have to work your way through the text. Some of the pictures are excellent.
e-mail: angola@angola.org

Welcome to Tunisia

www.tourismtunisia.com
General facts about the Tunisian government, society, culture, crafts and tourism. The Tourism page takes you to the main cities, with descriptions and photos. There are also lists of hotels, travel agencies and car rental companies in each town on the interactive map.
e-mail: info@tourismtunisia.com

Zanzibar Net

www.zanzibar.net
Facts about the island and its history, with tips on how to get there. The major tourist attractions are described, and you will find photos of the local art. The main diving sites are shown on an interactive map. There are links to airlines and shipping companies.
e-mail: feedback@zanzibar.net

Zimbabwe Parks and Scenic Wonders

www.gorp.com/gorp/location/africa/
zimbabwe/zimbabwe.htm

Zimbabwe's most beautiful natural
resources are on show, with eight
locations described and photographed.
e-mail: not available

Asia

A to Z of Azerbaijan

www.azerb.com

True to its name, the site has information
in alphabetical order, with everything
you need to know down to details of
cash machines. There are several
descriptive articles about the country.
e-mail: a-z@azerb.com

A Travel Guide to India

www.osho.com/travel/t-arrive.htm

This is a comprehensive guide for travel
in India, especially to Bombay and Pune.
Advice on tour information, flights,
transportation, hotels in both cities
and travel agents in India are available.
Special directions on hygiene are given
and it says "A traveller is advised to buy
bottled mineral water at airport stalls
before he starts his journey in the country".
You have been warned! Information is
available in English and Hindi.
e-mail: via online form

Adil Najan's Pakistan

www.mit.edu/people/anajam/
pakistan.html

This chatty unofficial site briefly
introduces the country, then takes you
on a guided tour. The largest cities are
featured with a good deal of information
about the people, culture, crafts, music,
cuisine, religion and sports.
e-mail: anajan@mit.edu

Afghanistan Online

www.afghan-web.com

A well presented site with a photo
gallery and a wealth of information from
geography to sport and links to a chat
room, religion, movies, news and the
economy, languages and politics and a
section about Afghan Woman.
e-mail: qazi@afghan-web.com

All India

www.allindia.com

All major Indian tourist centres and
eight main cities form the centrepiece
of this site. There are also descriptions
of the smaller cities, off-the-beaten-track
locations and places of pilgrimage.
e-mail: via online form

Asian Travel Info

www.asiatravel.com

Travel information for popularly
visited countries in Asia. You can
book your hotel, hire a car and enjoy
a picture gallery.
e-mail: not available

Bangkok Thailand Today

www.bangkok.thailandtoday.com

This is a complete guide to the Thai capital.
Choose your accommodation by location
and price and up come a list of hotels and
a booking form. All travel information is
easily accessible and you can shop online.
e-mail: not available

Bengal on the Net

www.bengalonthenet.com

Calcutta and Bengal are nicely illustrated
on this site. A calendar of events and
entertainment guide help you decide
what to do and see.
e-mail: not available

Cambodia - A hidden kingdom

home.hkstar.com/~l281868/cambodia.htm

The ancient temples of Angkor Wat
are a wonder by any standard. The web
site tells you about them and the rest
of the country, with a few helpful tips,
visa requirements and also lists hotels,
restaurants and duty free shops.
e-mail: not available

Ceylon Tourist Board

www.lanka.net/ctb/
It's all here, including the country's finest beaches and a pictorial guide to national parks and museums. Hotels can be booked online, a calendar of events and a list of travel agents help you complete your travel plans.
e-mail: Ctb_dm@sri.lanka.net

China Vista

www.chinavista.com/travel
You can book your hotel and flight online. There are several interesting articles to read, a virtual tour of the main attractions, a regional guide to the best restaurants and loads of recipes.
e-mail: not available

Darjeeling and Tourism

www.visit-darjeeling.com
This guide to the hill station of Darjeeling, famous for its tea plantations, has some details of hotels, entertainment and tours.
e-mail: Dpa@visit-darjeeling.com

Delhigate.com

www.delhigate.com/main.htm
Delhi online with links to transportation, accommodation, maps, weather and restaurants. There is advice for women tourists and warnings about bad businesses. A few more pictures would enliven the site.
e-mail: theteam@delhigate.com

Discover Mongolia

www.discover.mn
This exotic country is described in encyclopaedic detail from history and folk festivals down to travelling off the beaten track. Travel features tell you how to get there and away, profile the capital Ulan Bator and list package tours.
e-mail: not available

Dragon Tour

www.welleslian.com/dragontour/
This is said to be the most complete online travel guide to China. Thirty-one provinces are fully covered with links to transportation, tours, survival advice, weather, customs, hotels, food and a quiz for a bit of fun.
e-mail: not available

East Java

www.eastjava.com
Java Man lived here. Links connect you to the best accommodation in the region, recreation, restaurants, a shopping guide and natural attractions.
e-mail: not available

Goa.com

www.goacom.com
This very colourful web site of Goa is a full travel guide to the city, with links to accommodation, places of interest and everything else you may need for a visit. Organised tours, maps, pictures and a calendar of events come with brief notes on the culture of this former Portuguese colony.
e-mail: via online form

Government of Brunei Darussalam

www.brunet.bn
The country's traditions are explained with accompanying do's and don'ts. There are descriptions of the main attractions, lists of hotels, travel agents, shopping centres and restaurants.
e-mail: not available

Guide to Japan

www.japan-guide.com
Everything you ever wanted to know about Japan is on the site, or comes through external links. Kimonos, music, gardens, tea ceremonies, baths, geishas, swords, calligraphy, bonsai trees, ikebana and origami come with the hotel and tour guides. The Japanese Hotel Reservation System also helps

you find accommodation in temples and palaces. The food guide has traditional recipes, eating etiquette and a list of recommended restaurants.
e-mail: not available

Hong Kong City of Life

www.hkta.org
This is a colourful and fun site with a whole battery of fascinating sights and information about Hong Kong. You can view the site in many languages just by clicking the appropriate flag. The home page has links to best buys, sightseeing, festivals, events and most importantly where to eat, with a list of 8,700 restaurants in Hong Kong.
e-mail: not available

Hong Kong Terminal

www.zero.com.hk/hkta/hkta.html
The accommodation guide to Hong Kong and Kowloon on the site is particularly good, with access to booking centres for most hotels. There is an introduction to Chinese culture, a calendar of events and other travel information.
e-mail: Admin@zero.com.hk

Hotels, Resorts and Tours in Asia

www.travelasia.com.sg
A comprehensive site which includes links to cruises, coach tours, Singapore Airlines, car rentals, hotels and air fares right across south-east Asia, as well as India, China, Japan, Australia and New Zealand. Click on the country in the onscreen map, or select from the list for further information.
e-mail: not available

India City.com

www.indiacity.com
Guides to the major cities of India. Each city listed has separate pages with information on transport, accommodation and restaurants, sightseeing, shopping, local events and festivals. There are even handy maps so you don't get lost.
e-mail: not available

Indian Tour Operators

www.rrindia.com
Information about tours all over India, including to the mountains, beaches and islands, cultural tours, places of interest, wildlife tours, you name it, it's here. Choose from the lists and full details are provided.
e-mail: info@rrindia.com

Indian Travel and Tourism - Delhi

www.delhitourism.com
This is a general guide to the city with advice on what to do and where to stay. You are bound to find something to interest you in the touring guide and recommended day-trips.
e-mail: via online form

Inner Mongolia Home Page

www.bupt.edu.cn/regnet/inmon.html
Several good pictures bring to life the third largest of China's autonomous provinces. You will find plenty on economy, transportation, agriculture, city guides, industry, education, climate and some helpful travel notes.
e-mail: chemin@bupt.edu.cn

Istanbul City Guide

www.istanbulcityguide.com
A comprehensive guide to the capital of Turkey with information about hotels, weather, shopping, food and drink, sightseeing and transportation. Click on any of the text links on the home page for more details.
e-mail: via online form

Jakarta Online

www.jakarta.go.id
You get a quick sketch of Indonesia's history, geography, climate, dress, people, culture, religion and language and then a bit more. Hotels are listed by district. A guide covers both indigenous and western entertainment, while restaurants and food are amply illustrated. A map of the city shows

its museums and galleries.
e-mail: team@jakarta.go.id

Japan Travel Updates

www.jnto.go.jp
Links to hotels, restaurants, domestic
air travel, railways and roads, city
guides, regional tourist information,
contacts, visas and maps fill this well
organised web site.
e-mail: not available

Japanese Castles

**www.digimad.com/obershaw/castle/
index.html**
This site is for castle enthusiasts.
Information covers history, construction
and details of every castle, with
photographs.
e-mail: Obershaw@digimad.com

Kerala Tourism

www.keralatourism.org
The site comes with music and a picture
gallery. Hotels are listed with prices and
phone numbers; festivals, the weather, a
map and other information about this
Indian state are all linked online.
e-mail: Deptour@md2.usnl.net.in

Kyoto City Tourism & Culture Info System

raku.city.kyoto.jp/sight_apr.html
Kyoto is often described as Japan's
most beautiful city. The site features
its temples, castles, historical buildings
and museums. There are links to places
to stay and eat, shopping centres,
a calendar of events and a few
suggested tours.
e-mail: not available

Leg Manila

www.legmanila.com
This comprehensive guide to the capital
of the Philippines has information about
entertainment, nightlife, exhibitions,
events, shopping, restaurants and bars
and much more. Select your topic of

interest and there are two fast search
engines to help you find your way
around. The restaurant guide also
includes major cities in the rest of the
country.
e-mail: via online form

Malaysia Tourism Promotion Board

www.interknowledge.com/malaysia
This well illustrated site contains useful
links to tourist offices, accommodation,
travel tips, business conventions, history
and culture. It also includes a contact
information form.
e-mail: mtpb@aol.com

Nepal

www.catmando.com/tn/
A good tour guide on this site has
every attraction laid out with text and
pictures. Hotels with prices, embassies,
airlines and travel agents are all listed.
External links take you to guides on
hiking in Nepal, weather and an Everest
Live Camera.
e-mail: Shrestha@catmando.com

New Asia - Singapore

www.travel.com.sg
A city of many cultures, Singapore
offers a diversity of experience.
There is a lot to see and a lot to do,
all of which is set out on the web site.
A search engine helps you find
accommodation with online booking.
The entertainment page gives you
the full picture of everything on offer.
e-mail: stb_sog@stb.gov.sg

North Korea

www.dpr-korea.com
This is an official site with some
information about travel and some
about politics in the country. Take
special note about visas and moving
around in North Korea. US and South
Korean citizens are denied entry.
e-mail: sakai@dpr-korea.com

Peter M. Geiser's Internet Travel Guide

www.datacomm.ch/pmgeiser/index.html
This is an unofficial guide to Cambodia, China, Tibet, Myanmar, Laos, Indonesia, Singapore and Vietnam, and has a lot of useful information. Apart from recommendations on accommodation and restaurants it tells you about the people, events, folk festivals, visa requirements, embassies, border-crossing procedures, money matters, safety, health, transport and books about these countries.
e-mail: pmgeiser@datacomm.ch

Philippine Travel Page

www.nl2k.ab.ca/~gabada/index.htm
Hotels are divided regionally and can be booked online. You can choose to visit beach resorts and volcanoes, play golf and dine on wonderful cuisine that blends Spanish and local styles.
e-mail: gabada@nl2k.ab.ca

Philippines

www.filipino.com
Travel information in good measure, covering all aspects of the Philippines from geography to a calendar of events. There are maps, but a few pictures would be welcome.
e-mail: not available

Planet Tokyo

www.pandemic.com/tokyo
A survival guide explains Japanese culture, gives you a few useful phrases and a list of books about Japan. The site has guides to eating, sleeping and sightseeing. The hotel and restaurant guides give addresses, phone numbers and price ranges and the tour guidecovers areas of interest.
e-mail: not available

Rajasthan Guide

www.rajasthanguide.com
A virtual visit to Rajasthan starts with its attractions, culture and climate. The hotel page is still under construction but meantime you may wish to stay at a fort or palace. There is a lot to interest you in the culture, cuisine, music, festivals, arts & crafts, temples and wildlife of this Indian state.
e-mail: Info@rajasthanguide.com

Seoul City

www.metro.seoul.kr/eng/travel/index.html
A complete guide to Seoul, South Korea, with its royal palaces and tombs, fortresses, parks, entertainment centres and museums. Accommodation, restaurants, transport, night life, sports, airlines and car rental are well presented.
e-mail: not available

Sewasdee Thailand

www.tat.or.th
This general guide to Thailand details the country's history, religion and monarchy. The main tourist destinations, shopping centres, excursions and travel tips are clearly laid out but without information on accommodation.
e-mail: Info1@tat.or.th

Shanghai - ABC

www.shanghabc.com
This informative site, with online booking forms, tells you all you need to know about China's second city. There are guides for accommodation, entertainment, sports, art and culture, eating out, a currency converter, health and consular information.
e-mail: not available

Singapore Tourist Promotion Board

www.travel.com.sg/sog
Singapore's excellent web site is well-structured, comprehensive and easy to use. General and local interactive maps are provided (Flash plug-in is required). Links include places of interest, shopping, accommodation and tours. An online interactive tour is available, with sound (requires Real Audio Player).
e-mail: not available

Ski Japan

www.skijapanguide.com
You will find information on 85 Japanese ski resorts divided by region. Links tell you how to get there, where to stay and what you will find at each resort.
e-mail: not available

Taiwan Tourism Bureau R.O.C

www.tbroc.gov.tw
If you have a ShockWave plug-in you will find this site truly wonderful. Tours, business opportunities, attractions, cities, food and hotels. Travel tips for getting around Taiwan are fully detailed.
e-mail: tbroc@tbroc.gov.tw

Templenet

www.templenet.com
The site gives you a virtual guide to over two thousand temples on the Indian subcontinent, divided regionally. You get a glossary of Indian architectural terms, a guide to styles, as well as local information.
e-mail: Kanniks@temple.net

The Kingdom of Bhutan

www.kingdomofbhutan.com
You will find some travel information and a short tour guide. Take note of immigration and customs procedures and currency. There is a little about the history, geography, people, religion and government of the country; a map, pictures of three major attractions and a calendar of festivals.
e-mail: jdkez@hooked.net

Tourism Authority of Thailand

www.tat.or.th/index-shock.htm
This well illustrated site contains a lot of useful information about Thailand, with links to accommodation, tours, transit, shopping, local food and advice for visitors. Some links are available in PDF format.
e-mail: info1@tat.or.th

Vietnam Online

www.vietnamonline.net/
Accommodation is listed by rating and location and you are told which credit cards are accepted. Museums, art galleries and antique shops, bars, pubs and travel agents are listed on the site.
e-mail: via online form

Virtual Bangladesh

www.virtualbangladesh.com
You can do a virtual tour of Bangladesh, chat online and receive up-to-the-minute news on this very lively and colourful web site. Links take you to business and the economy, education, entertainment, travel, sports, recipes and a whole host more.
e-mail: info@virtualbangladesh.com

Virtual Borneo

www.virtual-borneo.com
This web site covers the Malaysian part of Borneo. You will find links to a hotel booking centre, tour companies and other travel information.
e-mail: not available

Visit Malaysia

www.tourism.gov.my
Malaysia is divided into twelve regions, each fully described for the traveller. A search engine helps you choose accommodation by rating, then produces a list of internal links to appropriate hotels.
e-mail: tourism@tourism.gov.my

Australasia and Oceania

About New Zealand

www.purenz.com
This wonderful web site has stacks of information and booking facilities. You can find accommodation, excursions, transport and lots more, all beautifully illustrated.
e-mail: via online form

Australia Tourist Guide

www.hotelcity.com/australia/info.htm
There are links to airports, airlines,
accommodation, weather, car rental
and some basic travel information
about Australia. Pretty basic really.
e-mail: not available

Australian Holidays

www.austtravel.com.au
With the online search engine you can
access accommodation, holidays and
tour operators in Australia. There is a
calendar of events and other useful
information about each State and a
photo album.
e-mail: not available

Complete Guide to Bora Bora Island

www.boraboraisland.com/index.html
This is part of the web site about French
Polynesia. What to do is out of doors in
the main, like scuba diving and sailing
and what to see includes tropical
lagoons, relics of World War II and
village arts and crafts. Accommodation,
tour packages and boat charters can
be booked online.
e-mail: not available

Destination Queensland

www.queensland-holidays.com.au
This packed web site lays it all out for
you. Organised tours put together all
your needs with prices and booking
forms. If you prefer to go it alone, you
can choose accommodation from fifteen
regions. A destination guide helps you
search towns and excursions, shopping,
the arts and entertainment, restaurants
and everything else for a good stay.
e-mail: qttcinfo@qttc.com.au

Discover New Zealand

www.discover.co.nz
A comprehensive guide to a beautiful
country. Links on the home page take
you to information about accommodation,
the sights, the great outdoors,

ski holidays, action holidays, travel
tips and lots more. There is also a
link to Fiji.
e-mail: web@new-zealand.com

Fiji Islands Travel & Accommodation

www.bulafiji.com
The web site helps you plan your
trip, fills you in on geography, history,
etiquette, language, money, health
and reading guides. You can select
accommodation by price, location
or name. All the other information
is well laid out with links to recreation,
transport and shopping. Text is in
English, German, Spanish, Portuguese,
French and Japanese.
e-mail: via online form

Fiji Visitors Bureau

www.fijifvb.gov.fj
Available in seven languages, with links
for transportation, accommodation,
car hire, activities, a currency converter,
visitor information and FAQ. There is
also a visitor information form where
you can request more details about
this island paradise.
e-mail: fiji@primenet.com

Hawaii State Vacation Planner

www.hshawaii.com/vacplanner/
main.html
As the site name implies you can plan
your holiday on any of the six main
islands. Good pictures enhance the
information you get by following the
online links. Navigation is easy, the
maps are clear and you get weather
news.
e-mail: not available

Melbourne Visitors Guide

www.melbourne.8m.com
This is essentially a general information
and tour guide with recommended city
excursions and river cruises. There is no
accommodation or eating-out guide.
e-mail: not available

New Caledonia
www.new-caledonia.com/eng.htm
There is a wealth of information, lots
of maps and good advice for travellers
on this site. Excursions are mainly
outdoors, visited by land, sea and air.
When you're done there are museums,
and good restaurants.
e-mail: not available

Pacific Islands Travel
www.pi-travel.co.nz
This omnibus site covers most of the
main islands of the South Pacific. Each
island or group has a little story, a list
of accommodation where reservation is
possible with members of the Pacific
Travel Organisation, and local travel
information. Beautiful tropical beaches
offer you a view of paradise where you
can swim, dive and fish to your heart's
content. There are external links to
Australia and New Zealand sites.
e-mail: via online form

Palau - The Adventure in Paradise
www.visit-palau.com
Diving in the warm tropical ocean is the
main attraction of these paradise islands.
Accommodation and restaurants are
listed with price ranges; tour operators,
a map and details of the island's capital
make up the rest of the site.
e-mail: pva@palaunet.com

Papua New Guinea
www.papua-new-guinea.com
You can check out visa and customs
regulations, find out about the country
and follow links to other guides and
web pages for hotels and restaurants.
International hotel sites help you book
accommodation.
e-mail: betty@mail.com

Samoanet
www.samoanet.com
There are links or e-mail addresses to
a few hotels, a local transport guide,

airlines serving the region, as well as
other Pacific web sites.
e-mail: not available

Solomon Islands
**public-www.pi.se/~orbit/solomons/
solomon.html**
There is a good picture gallery, links to a
few hotels, guides to local customs and
traditions and diving in the surrounding
seas.
e-mail: mmccoy@ozemail.com.au

Sydney.sidewalk
www.sydney.sidewalk.com.au
Although the site is still under construction,
it shows signs of becoming a good guide
to Sydney. A search engine takes you to
the arts, entertainment, shopping and
sport, a guide to local beaches and golf
courses, local events and restaurants
and a host of articles about the city.
e-mail: feedback@sidewalk.com.au

Tahiti Travel Net
tahiti.net/
The islands of French Polynesia are
described, one per page of the web site.
You will find guides to accommodation,
tour packages and boat charters, all of
which can be booked online. Sea sports
are high on the list of activities. Apart
from the scenic beauty of the islands
you can look over World War II relics
and village arts and crafts.
e-mail: not available

The Federated States of Micronesia
www.visit-fsm.org
This web site has a big picture gallery
with lots of information about the local
environment, geography, history, people
and culture. You will find lists of hotels
and restaurants, a calendar of events
and tourist sites for all four states.
An entry permit application can be
downloaded.
e-mail: not available

The Official Guam U.S.A. Website

ns.gov.gu
Guam is the capital of the Marianas
in the Pacific Ocean. The web site
briefly describes the islands, the capital
and its places of interest, with sound
effects too!
e-mail: not available

The official tourist website of Auckland

www.aucklandnz.com/index.html
Auckland is neatly described and
an activity guide has addresses to
agents who will take you diving,
cruising, fishing, horse riding,
swimming, kayaking, golfing and a
host of other sports. You will find
links to accommodation, enquiries,
transport and cultural recreation.
e-mail: talk-to-us@aucklandnz.com

Tourism Tasmania

www.tourism.tas.gov.au
Everything you need to know before
planning your trip to Tasmania is nicely
set out and easily accessible, with a lot
to see and even more to do.
e-mail: not available

Tourism Victoria

www.tourism.vic.gov.au/indexo.html
This site gives you enough to find your
way around the Australian State with
interesting expeditions in and out of
the cities, arts and theatres, museums,
sports activities, food and wine.
e-mail: not available

Visit Hawaii

www.visit.hawaii.org
Order a free travel planner online and
it will help you shape your trip. Guides
for each island have hotels and resorts,
local clubs, restaurants and a calendar
of events.
e-mail: not available

Visit New South Wales

www.tourism.nsw.gov.au/tnsw/
The State is divided into travel regions,
each with maps and a search engine
to help you find accommodation, hire
services, tours and local transport with
links to a booking centre.
e-mail: visitmail@tourism.nsw.gov.au

Visit the Cook Islands

www.maui.net/~jbonline/
The site has maps of the islands, some
details about accommodation, scuba
diving and other sports activities, a
calendar of events, tour packages and
picture galleries.
e-mail: jbonline@maui.net

Welcome to Australia's National Capital

www.canberratourism.com.au
There is a lot of information for the
traveller on this excellent site, with a
gallery of pictures and internal links.
It's all here, just click on the search
engine and follow the links.
e-mail: not available

Wellington, New Zealand's Capital

www.wellingtonnz.com
You will find lots of excursions and
walks in the national capital. All the
information you need to plan your trip
is readily accessible from maps and
internal links. Most accommodation
can be booked online.
e-mail: Info@WellingtonNZ.com

Caribbean

Accenting St.Kitts and Nevis

www.stkitts-nevis.com
There is a guide to diving, underwater
attractions and a list of diving operators.
Hotels, restaurants, entertainment
venues, airlines and car rental
companies are all listed with
contact details.
e-mail: Info@interknowledge.com/

Antigua & Barbuda
www.antigua-barbuda.com
The islands are briefly described, a
calendar of events and guide to activities,
most of which are al fresco, put you in
the picture. Hotels, restaurants, car
rentals and tour operators are listed
with contact details.
e-mail: Info@interknowledge.com

Aruba Tourism Authority
www.olmco.com/aruba/
This island, part of the Kingdom of the
Netherlands, is well represented on this
site. There are links to accommodation,
business services, events, nightlife,
weather, places to visit, and transportation.
e-mail: atanjix@netcom.com

Bahamas Tourist Guide
www.bahamas.com
You can explore the site, island by
island, taking in what there is to do
and see. Accommodation services,
local transport including airlines, ferry
companies and car rental agents are
all accessed via links. To round off,
there is a picture gallery and useful
tips for first time visitors.
e-mail: not available

Barbados Tourist Authority
www.barbados.org
All the tourist services are listed - car
rentals, yacht charters, tour operators,
real estate agents, nightlife venues,
restaurants and local cuisine, what to
see and do, health and safety advice and
a photo gallery. There is a directory of
offices world wide, which can be
contacted by phone.
e-mail: not available

Bonaire Government Tourist Office
**www.interknowledge.com/bonaire/
index.html**
This Dutch Caribbean island is well
represented in this web site. There is
information about history, culture,

activities, tourist offices and tour
operators, with a newsgroup for online
discussions.
e-mail: tcbinfo@bonairelive.com

Bonaire Official Website
www.infobonaire.com
You can choose your accommodation
by price range and then book by e-mail.
Tour operators, sports activities and
how to get there, car rental agents and
restaurants are all listed. There is a link
to a complete guide for bikers.
e-mail: Feedback@infobonaire.com

British Virgin Islands
www.islandsonline.com
You can book your hotel online then
discover what else these islands offer.
You can island hop by ferry, follow
internal links to tours, see where to go,
check training courses, sports equipment
rentals, yacht charters, car rental
companies and lots more.
e-mail: Islands@surfbvi.com

British Virgin Islands -
Online Travel Guide
www.b-v-i.com
This web site is an excellent guide to
almost every aspect of the British
Virgin Islands, including transport,
accommodation, dining and beaches.
There is ample information about
airlines and flight schedules,
transportation between the islands,
local tourism and current discount
offers. There are also wonderful maps
of the islands.
e-mail: guide@b-v-i.com

Cayman Islands Tourist Office
www.caymans.com
Links for accommodation,
transportation, events, recreation,
weather forecasts and visitor
information. Further details can be
requested with an online form.
e-mail: via online form

cayman.org

www.cayman.org
Travel information is well set out with guides to accommodation, a map, car rental companies, tour agents, a list of scuba diving operators and descriptions of places to go.
e-mail: Don@cayman.org

Cubatravel

www.cubatravel.com.mx
An unofficial guide to Cuba since the official one is in Spanish. You will find useful information on immigration procedures, what to bring and customs regulations concerning the export of cigars. There is a list of hotels graded by price, the country's top attractions, the best places to dive and how to book a diving trip.
e-mail: Info@cubatravel.com.mx

Curaçao Tourist Board

www.interknowledge.com/curacao
This site offers links for travelling, diving and cruising, the local beaches, architecture, music, sports and recreation, with a page of contact information. The Island Guide page leads to lots of local information.
e-mail: curacao@ix.netcom.com

Dominica.dm

www.dominica.dm
The guide describes the country's attractions, natural resources and national parks. The accommodation section lists hotels, facilities, prices and contact details. There are maps, a calendar of events and immigration regulations.
e-mail: Ndc@cwdom.dm

Dominican Republic Tourist Board

www.ios.uk.com/domrep/
A map, and essential information for the traveller - climate, language, currency and exchange, transportation, entry requirements, economy, major cities and an online contact form.
e-mail: not available

Dominican Republic Travel Guide and Info Center

www.dominican-rep.com
Links on this site take you to mountain biking and private travel guides to escort you through the country. The accommodation section lists hotels all over the country, with reservation facilities. The capital, Santo Domingo, has its own pages with dining and entertainment venues, maps, galleries and embassies. Additional features include travel tips and a currency converter.
e-mail: Contacts@caribe.net

French Caribbean

www.frenchcaribbean.com
The French islands of the Caribbean are covered on this site. Each island has a general guide followed by travel essentials, hotels, cuisine and eating habits, car rentals, where to go, what to see and buy, as well as immigration regulations.
e-mail: Fci@frenchcaribbean.com

Grenada

www.travelgrenada.com
A photo tour shows you the island. Accommodation and other tourist services, car rentals and yacht charters, sports and tour operators and a restaurant guide are all accessible from links. There is a currency converter, a calendar of events and an A-Z index of the island.
e-mail: Info@travelgrenada.com

Jamaica Tourist Board

www.jamaicatravel.com
Lots of good colourful pictures light up the Jamaican web site. There are links to sport, accommodation, activities, food, nightlife and culture.
e-mail: not available

Jamaica Travel.com

www.jamaicatravel.com
You will find a travel planner with six top destinations including their hotels, local sports and places of interest. A culture guide explains local cuisine, the roots of reggae music, local dances and crafts. You can order a brochure online.
e-mail: via online form

Official guide to St.Lucia

www.st-lucia.com
You can book your holiday online after checking out all that is on offer. All the traveller's basic requirements are neatly set out with a map, hotels, restaurants, car rental, a calendar of events and more.
e-mail: Info@interknowledge.com

The Cuban Connection

www.cuba.tc
A map of Cuba, travel tips, cities, car rentals, hotels and accommodation are just a few of the links on this enjoyable site with lots of good pictures. Text is in English and Spanish.
e-mail: not available

The Netherlands Antilles and Aruba

www.ten-ham.com
The general guide to Aruba, Bonaire, Curacao, Saba and St. Marteen gives you a short history, hotel list with links, restaurants, bars, diving schools with links and a picture gallery. Complete a request form and you will be sent more information.
e-mail: Martijn@ten-ham.com

The Official Tourist Guide of Anguilla

www.candw.com.ai/~atbtour/
Travel matters, visa requirements, public holidays and transportation, a short guide to what to do, where to stay and where to eat, are all easily accessible on this site.
e-mail: Dbtour@candw.com.ai

TravelFile

www.travelfile.com
On online travel shopping resource with links to all sorts of useful travel sites listed by destination and type of holiday. If these are not enough, you can use the on site search engine for more specific information. There are also featured articles about travel and travel news links.
e-mail: not available

Trinidad & Tobago Tourism Development Authority

www.tidco.co.tt
Well presented with useful links for tourists, such as accommodation and hotels, maps, natural history, weather forecasts and vehicle rentals.
e-mail: not available

U.S. Virgin Islands

www.usvi.net
This is the web site for St. Croix, St. Thomas and St. John US Virgin Islands. Links take you to car hire, weather, accommodation, maps, restaurants, activities, fishing and tourist information pages.
e-mail: not available

Visit Aruba

www.visitaruba.com
There is a lot to read about the local people, their culture, cuisine and religion. The travel guide details accommodation, a calendar of events with forthcoming carnivals, lists restaurants, night-spots, museums and monuments and of course local sports and tour operators.
e-mail: Info@visitaruba.com

Welcome to Trinidad & Tobago

www.visittnt.com
A calendar of events for the next ten years is posted on this site. Timetables of ferries, maps of cities and diving places, immigration regulations and

climate, car rental companies, yacht charters and restaurants are all there.
e-mail: Tourism-info@tidco.co.tt

Europe

1st in Prague

www.praguetourist.com
Picturesque Prague is laid out for you so you almost walk through the most interesting parts. Hotels of all categories, restaurants with sample menus, cafés and fast food outlets are all at your fingertips. The city has theatres, cinemas, concert-halls, museums, night venues, art galleries, clubs, sports centres, all fully described in the web site.
e-mail: not available

Aix en Provence

www.aixenprovencetourism.com
Aix en Provence is Cezanne's city and the heart of the Provence country, with a rich history of arts, crafts and gastronomy. This French city is replete with museums, galleries and monuments. There are wonderful tours, good accommodation, children's activities and a calendar of events, all of which are described.
e-mail: not available

Albania - Land of Eagles

www.albania.co.uk
The general information about the country is enough for the traveller to find his way around the main towns and choose hotels, restaurants, travel agents and airlines. History and geography acquaint you with the country; details of customs procedures and visa requirements should be noted.
e-mail: not available

Andalucia

www.andalucia.org
The web site is partly in English but contains enough to give you good insights into Andalucia's history, art, tradition and the geography of the

region. There is a search facility for each of the accommodation, restaurant, transport and leisure pages and suggested tours covering major cultural or natural resources, all packed with maps and information.
e-mail: info@andalucia.org

Antwerp City Guide

myplace.to.be/antwerp/
The home page is laid out as if you are visiting for the first time. Weather, money, language, safety, holidays, banking, transport within the city and bicycle routes are all detailed. Guided tours, hotels with sample prices and a comprehensive restaurant guide come in the package.
e-mail: ksawada@ms38.hinet.net

APT Trentino

www.provincia.tn.it/apt/UK/
This well-designed site from Trentino in northern Italy has links to winter sports, a calendar of events, accommodation and more, with lots of good pictures. Though most of the text is in Italian, enough is in English to make it useful.
e-mail: apt@provincia.tn.it

APT Verona

www.tourism.verona.it/index_en.shtml
The site has three virtual tours of the city with lots to see in each. A special search engine will tell you about festivals, exhibitions, theatres, sport and music in the region. Hotels and other services are listed.
e-mail: info@tourismverona.it

Apulia in the World

www.puglia.org
Click the British flag on the home page and you'll find that Apulia has two attractive regions, Lecce and Brindisi, with a long gastronomic tradition. You can choose between regular accommodation, or one of the many campsites in very attractive country, then book by e-mail.
e-mail: wte@impnet.com

Artguide

www.artguide.org

Every art event in Britain and Ireland is chronicled by region and category, while museums and their collections are listed alphabetically. There are also profiles of artists and their work and details of current temporary exhibitions.
e-mail: artguide@cogapp.com

Artsite Belgium Homepage

www.artsite.be

Links take you to galleries, museums and auction houses in Belgium. You get a rundown on the latest exhibitions and permanent collections.
e-mail: not available

Assisi Tourist Guide

www.assisionline.net

The medieval Italian city of Assisi was the home of St. Francis. The home page tells you about the town, hotels, camp sites and for those with long-term plans, estate agents. Museums, churches, theatres and exhibitions, restaurants, pubs and local cuisine are all well documented.
e-mail: not available

Athens Survival Guide

www.athensguide.com

Everything you need to know to survive in the capital of Greece, with basic information about the city, walking tours, accommodation and a comprehensive guide to restaurants. There are also links to other Greek travel sites.
e-mail: not available

Athens Today

www.athens-today.gr

A guide to the capital of Greece. You get a brief history, a list of museums and sights to see, a little about Greek cuisine, restaurants and hotels.
e-mail: not available

Austria Tourist Information

www.austria-tourism.at

The country is well provided with monasteries, churches, castles and palaces, many of which you can see in a general tour - The Best of Austria. Vienna of course has lots of music. Most of the information is in English and you will have no problems finding your way around the site for accommodation, tours, festivals, theatres and a calendar of events.
e-mail: info@auto.co.uk

Austrian National Tourist Office

www.austria-tourism.at

A great deal of information is set out for the tourist in eight languages: hotels, culture, events, a currency converter, transport and travel. Maps are provided with lots of pictures.
e-mail: oeinfo@oewwien.via.at

Backpack Europe

www.backpackeurope.com

Designed to help Americans plan budget trips to Europe, but could just as easily benefit any traveller. There are lots of useful links to camping catalogues, hostel associations, travel gear shops, bus and rail passes. You are advised on what to pack, with special advice for female travellers.
e-mail: Kaaryn@hotmail.com

Balaton net

www.balaton.net

Balaton Lake in Hungary offers hotels, family accommodation and camping sites in picturesque surroundings. Text is in English, German and Italian. Make contact by post or e-mail.
e-mail: infoway@email.datanet.hu

Balearic Tourist Guide

www.baleares.com/tourist.guide/

This site covers all four Balearic Islands. There are excursions, links to all types of accommodation and car rental, lists of

restaurants and if you want the salt wind in your face, there are yacht charter companies in Mallorca and Menorca.
e-mail: balearic@baleares.com

Basel Tourism

www.baseltourismus.ch
You get a brief city tour, a calendar of events and transport information. Hotels are listed with e-mail addresses and some with their own web sites. Gastronomic information is in German with an English version still to come.
e-mail: office@baseltourismus.ch

Bavaria Alpine Net Guide

www.bavaria.com
The most interesting cities and sites in Bavaria including Ludwig II's fairy-tale castles are all described with a list of outdoor activities and hotels. The region's culture and history and an entertainment guide come online. Text is in English, German and French.
e-mail: bang@bavaria.com

Berlin-Info

www.berlin-info.de/index_e.html
A tour of Berlin and its suburb Spandau with one illustrated page for every attraction. There is a search engine for accommodation and links to other Berlin pages, some of which are in German only.
e-mail: not available

Best of Sicily Travel Guide

www.bestofsicily.com
The Sicilian cities described on this site have links to lists of hotels. You also get a short description about the country, its people, crafts, traditions, cuisine, language and travellers' FAQ.
e-mail: questions@bestofsicily.com

Bilbao

www.bilbao.net/
Amongst the general information about businesses, facilities and sports, you can find lists of accommodation, services, restaurants, leisure activities and places to visit in this Spanish city. Text is in Spanish, Basque and English.
e-mail: alcalole@ayto.bilbao.net

British Tourist Authority

www.bta.org.uk
This well-designed site is packed with information about the country, language, culture, places to visit, food and drink, shopping and lots more. There are several links to language courses, a map with a search facility by county and region worth checking out, even if you happen to live in Britain.
e-mail: not available

Brussels Tourism and Information Office

www.brusseldiscovery.com
Twenty theme tours around Europe's capital, for each of which there are pictures and text. You can download brochures in PDF format. If you have QuickTime you can take a virtual walk around Brussels; if not, download it with the link provided.
e-mail: not available

Bucharest Online

www.bucharest.com/bol/
Guide to the capital of Romania, with information on everything you may need to know. There is a search facility as well as an index to help you.
e-mail: not available

Bulgaria.com

www.travel-bulgaria.com
This Bulgarian site has internal links to culture, history, visas, hotels, travel agents, car rental, resorts, a site map and external links to other national web sites. It is easy to navigate and has a good selection of pictures.
e-mail: moreinfo@travel-bulgaria.com

CapriWeb
www.capriweb.com
You get a guided tour of the major
tourist attractions on the islands of
Capri and Procida with a search engine
helping you to find accommodation.
There are maps, facilities and prices.
e-mail: info@capriweb.com

Castles of Spain
www.castlequest.net/spain
View the impressive castles of Spain
with explanations of their history and
architecture. Then order the CD-ROM,
or best of all, make the tour in person.
e-mail: smp@castlequest.net

Catalonia Tourist Guide
www.publintur.es
Whether you are interested in the
beaches, countryside, shopping or
touring Catalonia, you will find links
on the web site. A map shows you
where everything is. Accommodation
in hotels, hostels and campsites is
clearly listed. Text is in English, Catalan
and Spanish.
e-mail: publintur@publintur.es

Central Dalmatia Touristic Page
www.dalmatia-mid.com
Dalmatia is the Croatian coast of the
Adriatic, cleaner and more beautiful
than the Italian side. The site is well
illustrated, has a map to help you find
accommodation, cultural events, tours,
sport, food and whatever else you need
to know.
e-mail: visi_media@dalmatia-mid.com

CityGuide Sweden
www.cityguide.se
The web site covers fifty Swedish cities.
Major cities have separate pages with
information on everything; smaller ones
are briefly described. You will find guides
to entertainment, events, culture, sports
and leisure. Most text is in English.
e-mail: not available

Copenhagen Now
copenhagen.now.dk/english.html
Links cover every aspect of tourism in
the city, museums, accommodation,
restaurants and pubs. Just click on the
spot and you will be told how to get
there and back, how to rent a car and
find local transport.
e-mail: info@copenhagen.now.dk

Corsica invitation to travel
www.corsica.net
Corsica offers horse and bike riding,
rafting, fishing and a host of other
outdoor activities in English, French,
German and Italian with details of
where to do it. You discover the island
by region or theme and some links take
you to official web sites and estate
agents. A search engine helps you find
accommodation and links connect you
to transportation companies and travel
agents.
e-mail: corseweb@internetcom.fr

Crete TOURnet
www.crete.tournet.gr
There are about thirty locations on the
web map of Crete. Each tells you about its
attractions. A guide to the island's culture
and history takes you deep into the past,
covering the Minoan, Greek and Venetian
periods. A search engine will guide you to
accommodation and restaurants.
e-mail: not available

Croatian Tourist Information Services
www.htz.hr/home.htm
The extensive site map has links to history,
cuisine, other maps and plans,
accommodation and lots more. The
pictures are good and you can find your
way around easily.
e-mail: info@htz.hr

Cyclades Internet Server
www.cyclades-greekislands.com
The site covers the Greek islands of

Mykonos, Paros, Antiparos, Siphnos, Santorini and Serifos with information about hotels, camping sites and places of interest. The restaurant guide is in preparation.
e-mail: sunbeam@otenet.gr

Cyprus Tourism Organisation

www.cyprustourism.org
To find what you are looking for, go to the map first. Each region tells you about its attractions, accommodation and cuisine and links you to Cyprus Airways, ferry companies, ports, tour operators, car rental companies and a 7-day itinerary that covers all the island's attractions.
e-mail: gocyprus@aol.com

Czech Republic

www.czech.cz
The official web site of the Czech Republic gives you enough links to build a national profile - climate, population, religion, education, employment, climate, history, arts and culture with many good pictures.
e-mail: not available

Czech Tourism Pages

www.czech-tourism.com
A good overview of the Czech Republic and its main cities with links to hotels, hotel booking services and real estate agents. You will find pages providing useful maps and information about transport, food and drink.
e-mail: mendicott@igc.apc.org

Danish Tourist Board

www.dt.dk
Lots of history and culture together with the more mundane matters of booking accommodation, travel, transportation, restaurants and so on in Denmark. The links are in 10 languages and information is concise.
e-mail: dt@dt.dk

Edinburgh and Lothian's Tourist Board

www.edinburgh.org
All you need to know to have a good time in Edinburgh and the east coast of Scotland with maps, a calendar of events and lots to see and do.
e-mail: esic@eltb.org

Elbalink

www.elbalink.it
The island has wonderful water activities including diving, kayaking, boating and sailing. At least half the hotels have their own web sites and there are campsites aplenty. Etruscan cuisine and vineyards are an added attraction.
e-mail: info@elbalink.it

Estonian Tourist Board

www.tourism.ee
The country is presented by region and then by county. Each county tells you how to get there, where to stay with prices and contacts, where to eat and a little about its history, geography, literature and museums. A list of travel agents, a calendar of events and a photo gallery complete the story. Text is in English and Estonian.
e-mail: etb@tourism.ee

Europe Online

www.europeonline.com
General guides for most European countries. Each country has regional and city guides, booking centres, travel agents, culture information and business links. All pages have English text.
e-mail: Info@europeonline.com

Explore Poland

www.explore-poland.pl
Information covering money matters, embassies, daily life, cuisine, language, fuel prices and problems to watch out for come with local guides and business pages. The link to the Hotels Poland site

will help you find any type of accommodation from campsites to castles.
e-mail: not available

Extensive Armenia

www.cicilia.com
Not only does the site tell you about the country's attractions and culture, all well illustrated, it also includes a wonderful cookbook with about forty recipes.
e-mail: comments@cicilia.com

Faeroe Islands Tourist Guide

www.faeroeislands.com
Bird-watching, fishing, sea sports, folk art, culture and festivals are all part of the island heritage on offer to visitors. There is a good accommodation guide and lots of general information about the geography, history and language of the islands. You may find the text a little small.
e-mail: runi@sansir.fo

Faroe Island Tourist Board

www.tourist.fo/start.html
You can use the map to choose the location you want. Whilst you are at it you can take a guided tour of these northern islands, with lots of good pictures.
e-mail: tourist@tourist.fo

Firenze.net

english.firenze.net
The art page describes this beautiful Italian city's monuments and exhibitions. All necessary travel information is available on the site including cinemas, discos, music, pubs, restaurants, tours, theatres and sports.
e-mail: staff@firenze.net

Flanders Coast

www.flanderscoast.be
A tourist view of the Belgian coast, with brief information and video footage of the major towns. A search engine helps

you to find accommodation.
e-mail: info@flanderscoast.be

French Government Official Site

www.francetourism.com
All sorts of stuff about France and how to get there from the French Tourist Office, with numerous links for general information, accommodation, family activities, where to go, what to see, news, a calendar of events and more.
e-mail: not available

French Travel Gallery

www.europe-france.com
France is divided into its Departments, with a brief rundown of hotels and a link to a general hotel booking centre. An external link has a Paris guide, a calendar of events and information about language courses.
e-mail: not available

Geneva, Switzerland

www.geneva-guide.ch
Geneva is a popular tourist city and this site is packed with information. There are lists of restaurants and car rental companies, a calendar of events and package tours with booking forms provided. The hotel finder has a search engine and online booking facility for the whole of Switzerland.
e-mail: not available

Georgia Travel

www.steele.com/georgia
There are links to accommodation, a travel agency, banking information and flight schedules. There is a good link to a site of the parliament of Georgia which has information and pictures of the main Georgian cites.
e-mail: GeorgiaTravel@steele.com

German National Tourist Board

www.deutschland-tourismus.de/e/index.html
Three detailed maps, extensive information

about towns and cities and lots of good pictures make up this excellent web site. Links take you to holidays, accommodation, weather, transport, a calendar of events and a whole lot more.
e-mail: not available

Gibraltar Home Page
www.gibraltar.gi
The island is fully explored in this web site. Links cover history, politics and finance, tourism and leisure, shopping, passports, visas, currency and much more.
e-mail: tourism@gibraltar.gi

Greek National Tourist Office
www.hri.org/infoxenios
A main map of Greece has links to locations, each with a map and information on how to get there, food and drink, useful numbers and addresses, car hire, shopping, recreation and some history. There are lists of hotels and travel agents with contact details.
e-mail: infoxenios@areianet.gr

Greenland Guide
www.greenland-guide.gl
Greenland's adventure attractions include Ice Golf, observing wildlife and dog-sledding. A travel guide shows the easiest way to get there and provides links to local and international ferry services and airlines. Every city has information on hiking, sailing, accommodation and yes, dog-sledding too.
e-mail: editor@greenland-guide.gl

Greetings from Hvar
www.hvar.hr
Hvar Island is on the Adriatic coast of Croatia. There are ferry and bus timetables to take you to and from the island. Hotels are listed, some linked to an official web site. There is also a gastronomic guide, seven separate excursions, an event calendar and maps.
e-mail: not available

Gstaad Online
www.gstaad.ch
Gstaad in the Swiss Alps is known as a ski resort, but it has much more to offer, including walking, swimming, gliding, golf and sightseeing. The hotels are well documented and you can order brochures and book rooms online.
e-mail: gst@gstaad.ch

Guernsey Tourism
www.guernseymap.com
There is a lot to read about on this Guernsey web site. Travel tips on where to stay, links to services, transport, history, cuisine, leisure, attractions, places to visit, and a map in Javascript give all the information you need to plan a visit to the island.
e-mail: enquiries@tourism.guernsey.net

Guide Web Provence
www.provence.guideweb.com
A brief introduction to the history, geography and culture of Provence. The main cities are described, most with English text, and four recommended tours take you through the unique wine, olive and culinary delights of this French region. Hotels, real estate agents, art and crafts, museums, transport and sports are well covered.
e-mail: not available

Hamburg Highlights
www.hamburg-highlights.de
This web site is a traveller's guide from start to finish, with everything you need to know easily accessible. Accommodation is set out so that you can choose district, price range and facilities; hotels appear with local transport information to get you there. Sightseeing, restaurants, shopping and entertainment are all treated in similar detail.
e-mail: info@hamburg-highlights.com

Helsinki - City of Helsinki

www.hel.fi/english/
Information about this city's one hundred attractions could be interesting if easier to find. There is little order in the web site but you will find timetables for local transport and a calendar of events.
e-mail: tourist.info@hel.fi

Holiday in Denmark

www.holiday.dk
Links to the main regions of Denmark with further links to Danish airports, ferry companies and airlines serving Denmark. The guide has lists of restaurants, cafés, libraries, museums, churches and weather information. Most of the site is in English.
e-mail: sim@sima.dk

Hungarian National Tourist Office

www.hungarytourism.hu
A few more pictures would liven this informative site. There are good links to tourism, culture, travel, accommodation, places to visit, a calendar of events, climate and more.
e-mail: web@hungarytourism.hu

Hungary Tourism Pages

www.hungary-tourism.com
This is one of the four sites created by Infotec Travel to provide information about Hungary, Russia, the Czech Republic and Slovenia. It has general information about the main cities of Hungary with links to both local authorities and hotel pages. Other links give information on transport, food and drink, language, money matters, weather, children's activities and the capital, Budapest.
e-mail: mendicott@igc.apc.org

Icelandic Tourist Board

www.icetourist.is
You can view this interesting site in six languages. Links help you with all your travel requirements; a map has further links to each geographical region.
e-mail: not available

In Milano

www.rcs.it/inmilano/english/
This guide to Milan, Italy, covers many subjects including eating out, shopping, hotels, nightlife, art and culture. The list of restaurants includes their rating, price bracket, payment and contact details. Text is in English and Italian.
e-mail: inmilano@rcs.it

In Your Pocket

www.inyourpocket.com
The omnibus web site celebrates the main attractions of Belarus, Estonia, Hungary, Latvia, Lithuania, south Poland, the Russian enclave of Kalliningrad, Slovakia and Romania. A general introduction deals with the history, geography, people and customs of each country, then launches into the details of travelling in the area.
e-mail: mlufkens@serveur.dtr.fr

Interactive Traveller

www.interactivetraveller.com
Travel news and trends for the business traveller. Reviews of travel sites, new technology to make life for the switched on traveller easier, as well as other topics of interest.
e-mail: js@interactivetraveller.com

Irish Tourist Board

www.ireland.travel.ie
The site is easy to navigate with lots of good pictures and several links to maps, route planners, arts and culture, accommodation, transport, tour operators and a pile of useful addresses.
e-mail: not available

Island of Ischia

www.ischia.com
Ferry and hydrofoil timetables are a must to get to the island's baths for

pleasure or treatment and
excursions from the island to Capri,
Pompei, Naples and Herculanum.
On site you will find all you need to
know about accommodation, car and
boat rental, guided tours including the
environs of Naples and sports like
diving, windsurfing, para- and
hang-gliding.
e-mail: info@ischia.com

Istra

www.istra.com
Istra offers some of the cleanest
and most beautiful resorts along the
Adriatic. Choose your location and you
will find all the information you need.
All types of accommodation are
available and you can book online.
There are links to travel agents, a food
guide, real estate agents and weather.
e-mail: not available

It's Malta

www.visitmalta.com
An excellent site with links to sports,
events, places, hotels, geography,
transportation, history and general
information, a video and an e-mail
address to receive updated news.
Text is in English, French and
German.
e-mail: info@tourism.org.mt

Italian Tourist Web Guide

www.itwg.com/home.asp
Links take you to hotels, tour
operators, a cities index, maps and an
instant online booking form for some
transactions.
e-mail: info@itwg.com

Jersey Web

www.jersey.co.uk
Good accommodation and car-rental
guides, most of which can be booked
online. For tour information you are
asked to fill an online request form.
e-mail: jtourism@itl.net

Kiev Traveller's Guide

www.uazone.net/Kiev.htm
This is part of the Ukraine web site.
It describes Kiev's major attractions,
lists hotels and car rental companies.
There are useful addresses, phone
numbers and a shopping guide.
e-mail: info@uazone.net

Kyiv Navigator

www.kiev.ua:8101
Getting around the capital of the
Ukraine, with information about airlines,
hotels and restaurants, medical services,
embassies, nightclubs and transportation.
Details are limited to lists of names,
addresses and contact numbers.
e-mail: not available

Lake Baikal Home Page

www.baikal.ru
A lecturer at Irkutsk University runs
this web site. He has done a good job
marking out the most beautiful places
on a series of maps and added a photo
gallery and FAQ section about the
region.
e-mail: andrei@baikal.ru

Latvia Tourist Board

www.latviatravel.com
There is a twelve-page introduction
to Latvia's history, culture, traditions,
people, crafts, cuisine, language,
entertainment and shopping. General
information covers everything you
want to know. A link to the Latvian
Hotel Association will help you find
accommodation. Outdoor activities
include bird-watching and cycling.
e-mail: itboard@latnet.lv

Leipzig - City Guide

members.aol.com/wksleipzig/index.html
You will have no difficulty finding your
way around the German city of Leipzig
with the many links on this unofficial
city web site. The virtual tour includes
pictures of the city's most interesting

attractions. There is an accommodation guide, a list of hotels with example prices and some online booking, as well as restaurant and shopping guides.
e-mail: Leipzig@wks-consulting.com

Les deux Alpes

www.2alpeservices.com
If you are looking for exciting ski trails in the French Alps take a good look at this web site. All the information you want on slopes, ski lifts, ski schools and prices is easily accessible, with a lot more about accommodation, entertainment, shops, pubs, bars, health clubs, restaurants, dance halls and libraries.
e-mail: not available

Liechtenstein National Tourist Office

www.searchlink.li/tourist/index.asp
The pictures on the web site give you an impression of the charm of this small mountainous country, with its attractions described and illustrated.
e-mail: not available

Lisbon Pages

www.Eunet.pt/Lisboa
You will find a map with links to each part of the city showing what's on offer, including museums, hotels and discos. There is also a good photo gallery.
e-mail: Hugo.Carvalho@individual.Eunet.pt

Lithuania (Ramunas Personal Page)

www.omnitel.net/ramunas/Lietuva/index.html
An unofficial and brief guide to Lithuania. There are guides to 3 main cities, maps and some history.
e-mail: not available

London Town

www.LondonTown.com
London is celebrated as the world's most interesting city and this web site does it justice. Every category has a search engine that takes you

to loads of detailed information and online booking. Check it out, it's worth a visit.
e-mail: via online form

Luxembourg City Tourist Office

www.luxembourg-city.lu/touristinfo/
You can download brochures in PDF format from this site, including general, accommodation and restaurant guides. The map of the city shows its sixty most interesting places. There are six recommended tours and you can choose your accommodation and restaurant by clicking on its name or location to get details. The Duchy of Luxembourg has a calendar of events.
e-mail: touristinfo@luxembourg-city.lu

Luxembourg National Tourist Office

www.ont.lu/default.htm
You will find an extensive range of links to sport and leisure, culture, history, accommodation, special offers, religions, heritage, museums and more on this easy to use and quick site. Text is in English, French and German.
e-mail: tourism@ont.smtp.etat.lu

Magnagrecia

www.magnagrecia.com
This simple site has information about sports activities and links to three hotels and travel agents in the Italian region of Calabria.
e-mail: magnagrecia@uni.net

Mallorca Market

www.mallorca-market.com
The whole island is documented in this web site. Start with the map, then using the links provided, book accommodation and hire a car. You can preview the sights that await you, check out restaurants and sports activities, and pick up tips about the weather and night-life.
e-mail: index-e@mallorca-market.com/

MeetingVenice

www.meetingvenice.it

The third part of the web site is probably the most useful for travellers. It has a complete accommodation guide and links to estate agents. You will find a lot more about tours, restaurants, road and water transport.

e-mail: not available

Milano In

www.milanoin.it

A guided tour of the city takes you to Milan's famous cathedral, museums, monuments and parks. The shopping guide encourages you to shop till you drop. Hotels are listed but not accessible on the site.

e-mail: not available

Modena Turismo

www.comune.modena.it/infoturismo

Thirteen separate itineraries are on offer to see this historic city. A variety of accommodation is available from plush hotels to a room in a farmhouse. There is a great deal of local information, down to hiring a taxi.

e-mail: not available

Monaco Monte Carlo Online

www.monte-carlo.mc

The site has links to some information and e-mail addresses of hotels, restaurants, shops, travel agents, sports centres and places to visit.

e-mail: info@monte-carlo.mc

Netherlands Board of Tourism

www.visitholland.com

Links for travelling and getting around, tour operators, car rentals, weather, language, eating and drinking. There are also links to city pages with good pictures, an FAQ section and the possibility to get more information with an online form.

e-mail: not available

North Wales Tourism

www.nwt.co.uk

Links on the home page lead you to information on local heritage, a calendar of events, accommodation, eating out and touring, all of which you can access by region, price and interest. Lists then appear to suit your requirements, all of which are provided with some form of contact.

e-mail: croeso@nwt.co.uk

Northern Ireland

www.interknowledge.com/
northern-ireland/default.htm

The official site of the Northern Irish Tourist Board, with all sorts of helpful information about the province in links at the bottom of the home page. You will also find useful travel tips on the site.

e-mail: via online form

Norway Experience
Virtual Guide to Oslo

www.hurra.no

A virtual tour through Oslo. The city map is divided into ten sections, each with more than twenty streets for you to visit. When you are done, you can sightsee, view restaurant menus, hotel rooms and explore museum collections. If you decide to change virtual to actual, get the information online.

e-mail: not available

Norwegian Tourist Guide

www.tourist.no/en/

This well presented site is very informative with links to a map, accommodation, where to go, how to get there, towns and cities, tour suggestions, the outdoors and much else.

e-mail: not available

Novi Sad Municipal Web Page

www.novisad-home.com

Novi Sad is Serbia's second largest city. The site gives you a general overview of

the city, the region and a description of tourist attractions. It also includes pictures of damage from recent NATO bombing.
e-mail: mashad@bellatranti.net

Office de Tourisme de Bordeaux

www.bordeaux-tourisme.com
The UNESCO World Heritage sites in this city are among its main attractions. There are links to local airport and railway web sites; the list of local hotels has descriptions only in French. Restaurants, a calendar of events, tour offers and language courses for foreigners come with English text.
e-mail: otb@bordeaux-tourism.com

Office de Tourisme et des Congres de Paris

www.paris-touristoffice.com
This is as good as an online tourist guide gets. There are search engines for accommodation, museums, monuments, restaurants, transport and a calendar of events.
e-mail: edt@club-internet.fr

Official Tourist Information Office Delft Holland

www.vvvdelft.nl/eng/index.html
A description of the historical town, buildings, museums, churches, and of course there is something about the painter Vermeer. There are city walk guides, links to bus and train route planners, a list of hotels, how to book online and guides to restaurants, pubs and coffee shops.
e-mail: escape.pijnacker@kabelfoon.nl

Parma Italy

www.parmaitaly.com
Giuseppe Verdi highlights this site. You will find some details of hotels with prices, a brief review of places of interest not connected with Verdi, restaurants and local travel.
e-mail: info@parmaitaly.com

Peter Crombecq's Benelux Beerguide

www.dma.be/p/bier/beer.htm
Indulge yourself in the beers of the Low Countries. The web site lists them by country, season, type and flavour, with a catalogue of breweries, pubs and clubs in the Benelux countries.
e-mail: Pcrombercq@antwerpen.be

Pisa Online

www.csinfo.it/pisa/online.htm
You will find all you need to know about tours, restaurants, car rental, entertainment and shopping in this Italian city. Most accommodation listed can be booked online.
e-mail: manager@csinfo.it

Plitvice National Park

www.np-plitvice.tel.hr/np-plitvice/
The National Park of Plitvice is on UNESCO's World Heritage List, and is truly beautiful. The photo gallery goes a long way to encouraging visitors to see for themselves. You will find links to hotels and other types of accommodation.
e-mail: np-plitvice@np-plitvice.tel.hr

Poland Home Page

poland.pl
Lots of pictures and information about Poland covering society, government, art, culture, science and education, economy, tourism and recreation, health and a lot else, most of which is available in English.
e-mail: not available

Republic of Macedonia

faq.Rmacedonia.org
Travel information is divided into summer and winter attractions, with an interactive map and photographs. Hotels have links and there is information about visas, embassies and airlines. The religion, language, history and cuisine - 30 most interesting recipes -

tells you something about the people. You can even study the Cyrillic alphabet.
e-mail: macedonia_faq@faq. Rmacedonia.org

Rodos Panorama

www.rodorama.gr
All the major attractions of this Greek island are presented, with ample information about hotels, restaurants and nightlife in the city of Rhodes.
e-mail: info@rodorama.gr

Romanian Travel Guide

www.rotravel.com
A good travel site with a calendar of events, hotel database, travel agents, an index of other Romanian sites, details about the country, places to visit and even a discussion forum.
e-mail: not available

RomeGuide

www.romeguide.it
The Eternal City of Rome is fully explored and the historical parts of the city are well documented and illustrated. Tours are on offer that will take you through Rome, the Vatican City and environs, leaving no stone unturned. All aspects of travel requirements are covered and you will have no difficulty finding your way around the site.
e-mail: ilsogno@romeguide.com

Russia Tourism Pages

www.russia-tourism.com
This is another page of the Infotec Travel web site. The main cities of Russia are listed with links to both local authority pages and hotel pages. You can access hotel booking services, real estate agents, maps and information on transport, food & drink, language, money matters, museums, weather and children's activities.
e-mail: croc@orc.ru

Scottish Tourist Board

www.holiday.scotland.net/
This beautiful web site is worth a visit just for the looking. It has a wealth of information about Scotland with links to numerous subjects including an FAQ section, local transport, accommodation, outdoor activities, shopping and a tour planner.
e-mail: not available

Shetland Islands Tourism

www.shetland-tourism.co.uk
The Shetland Islands have a strong Viking heritage, explained in the archaeology page of this web site. The other outdoor attractions are bird-watching, wildlife, fishing and sailing. Through links you will find accommodation and complete ferry timetables.
e-mail: shetland.torism@zetnet.co.uk

Skopje Online

www.skopjeonline.com.mk
There are several one-day excursions around the city of Skopje, capital of Macedonia and interesting places in the environs. You have lists of hotels, some with online booking, a calendar of events, shopping, restaurants and lots of night-life.
e-mail: contact@skopjeonline.com.mk

Slovak Tourist Board

www.sacr.sk
An official web site with general and tourist information, useful addresses, hotel links and even a snow report. The pictures are good.
e-mail: sacr@sacr.sk

Slovenia Tourism Pages

www.slovenia-tourism.com
A useful site if you are beginning to gather information about Slovenia, as it contains links to most other sites about the country. You will find information about the main cities, as well as links

to hotels and estate agents, transport, maps, dining, language, currency, weather and activities for children.
e-mail: mendicott@igc.apc.org

Slovenia Tourist Board

www.slovenia-tourism.si
All you need to find accommodation, transport, tourist offices and information, embassies and consulates, weather, health resorts and much more, all in five languages.
e-mail: lucka.letic@cpts.tradepoint.si

Softguide Madrid

www.softdoc.es
The home page puts you immediately in touch with Madrid - embassies, currency, banks, weather and events. Hotels are listed by district with contact information. For a taste of local culture you have the museums, galleries, theatres, cinemas, corridas and flamenco performances.
e-mail: feedback@softdoc.es

St Petersburg, Russia

www.cityvision2000.com/dining/
To start exploring St. Petersburg in Russia, search this comprehensive guide. There is information on hotels and restaurants, shopping, sightseeing, cultural events and entertainment in the city.
e-mail: via online form

Stuttgart Marketing

www.stuttgart-tourist.de
There is a lot to see and do in Stuttgart, all of which is well laid out in this official site. There are suggested sightseeing routes, with descriptions and photos of attractions, as well as details of the parks, zoos, theatres and museums. You can also choose and book your accommodation online.
e-mail: info@stuttgart-tourist.de

Sweden

www.gosweden.org/homepage.html
Useful and interesting links to the history, traditions and culture of Sweden, all well illustrated. You will also find activities and tours, restaurants and city life, transportation, events and accommodation. A map is included.
e-mail: not available

Switzerland Tourism

www.switzerlandtourism.ch/na
Available in seven languages, with good links for visitors. Select your language and point of departure on the home page and subjects covered include accommodation, travel tips, transport and car hire, weather reports, business, and local events, all well illustrated.
e-mail: not available

Tallinn

www.tallinn.ee
A complete guide to what you can find in this Estonian city. Parks, galleries, casinos, churches, concert halls, museums, libraries, theatres, hotels, restaurants and night venues are all listed with maps and information. There are recommended tours and city walks with and without a guide.
e-mail: not available

The Bergen Guide

www.bergen-guide.com/eng.htm
In addition to the usual traveller information, the site has articles about Vikings and local folklore, maps and organised tours, some of which cruise in the spectacular fjord region of the coast.
e-mail: feedback@bergen-guide.com

The City of Perugia

www.perugiaonline.com
Very informative, with cultural attractions in pride of place. Hotels, restaurants and local transport are also well covered.
e-mail: not available

The Fresh Guide to St. Petersburg

www.online.ru/sp/fresh
Practical advice about safety and health, travel tips, guides to hotels, restaurants and entertainment with a little about Russian food and drink.
e-mail: fresh@online.ru

The Official Holland Site

www.visitholland.com
There are some good guides that work their way through walking and cycling tours, holiday packages and routes, art and artists, galleries, theatres, castles, with something about history and safety in the cities. There are profiles of Amsterdam, Delft, Haarlem and several other cities with links to hotels and outdoor activities.
e-mail: not available

The Prado Museum

museoprado.mcu.es
As one of the leading galleries with some of the most famous paintings in the world, this site is a must for art lovers. You can view and read discussions about some fifty works of art. If you order a catalogue of the gallery's complete collection, you can follow it with the site search engine that comes up with a host of paintings to match your choice of school, theme, style or painter. You can also view the gallery hall by hall, or better still you can visit in person and be enthralled.
e-mail: museo.prado@prado.mcu.es

The Tourist Office of Spain

www.spaintour.com/indexe.html
Lots of pictures liven up this site, which has good links to transport and communications, national parks, tourist offices world wide, as well as guided tours and news. Text is in English, German, French and Spanish.
e-mail: not available

The Virtual Guide to Belarus

www.belarusguide.com
The cultural guide on this site gives you good insights into the country's history, literature, cuisine, theatre, music, architecture, icons and costumes. The Touring guide has information on 50 major cities, national parks, forests and rivers.
e-mail: sasha@stm.lbl.gov

Tourism in Burgundy

www.burgundy-tourism.com
This is one of the world's paramount wine regions, well reflected by the web site. The home page describes its geography and climate and tells you how to get there. There are three guided tours around the province and a complete restaurant and wine cellar guide with links to retailing cellars. Accommodation is easy to find online.
e-mail: not available

Tourism in France

www.tourisme.fr/us/index.htm
Packed with information on transport, maps, museums, food and drink and everything French. The search engine will get you tour information by Department and region, find accommodation and places to visit. Navigation is fast and the pictures are good.
e-mail: not available

Tourist Guide of Greece

www.vacation.net.gr
This is a good guide to all the major tourist attractions, cities, archaeological sites and islands of Greece. At each site you are given a quick tour, suggested accommodation and other useful information. You will find a list of tourist operators linked to the Greek Tourism Organisation with a lot more to interest you.
e-mail: not available

Travel Bulgaria

www.travel-bulgaria.com
A sketch of Bulgaria's history, traditions and culture. An external link to the Bulgarian Hotel Association lists most hotels, with separate links to the three most luxurious in the country. The five coastal and one ski resort are described and tour agents listed.
e-mail: moreinfo@travel-bulgaria.com

Travel in Greece

www.travel-greece.com
Click on the map and fasten your seat belt for a virtual trip to Greece. The major cities of each region are described, with pictures. There is also information about accommodation, bars, restaurants and medical facilities.
e-mail: not available

Travel Ireland

www.travel-ireland.com
This is a general link page for tourism in Ireland, where you view external pages like internal ones. There is information on every major city, county and region in Eire and Ulster. You can book accommodation online and there are links to car rental, an entertainment guide, music, libraries, cinemas, activities for children, exhibitions, guided tours, museums, theatre and sports.
e-mail: not available

Turismo de Coruña

www.turismocoruna.com
The Spanish town of Coruña is well described, with lists of entertainment venues, accommodation, restaurants, tourist routes, special offers, photos and maps.
e-mail: info@turismocoruna.com

Turkish Tourism & Information Office

www.turkey.org
Choose either the Flash or un-Flashed option on the first page and you will find plenty of links, including media, currency, geography, culture, tourist information, embassies and consulates, as well as business and economy. The site is well designed with some good pictures, but some links were not available.
e-mail: tourney@soho.ios.com

Val d'Isere

www.valdisere.com
The famous French Alpine village is a favourite ski resort. There is a lot of information about slopes, passes, weather and a school for beginners. There are also an accommodation booking page, restaurant and shopping guides and local bus information.
e-mail: info@valdisere.com

Vienna Guide Services

www.vienna-guide-service.com
Intended for those wanting to be guided professionally around Vienna, the site outlines a few tours and a questionnaire helps you book a tour guide.
e-mail: office@vienna-guide-services.com

Vienna Tourist Board

www.magwien.gv.at/english/
You can download an event calendar all the way to 2002 and get a special discount card for participating museums and galleries. A city guide with a 3-day itinerary will take you to all there is to see. Text is in English, German, Italian and Spanish.
e-mail: not available

Ville de Versailles

www.mairie-versailles.fr
Click the tiny British flag on the home page for the English version, then you can download the map of the city of Versailles and view the palace. Accommodation is clearly listed, with all you want to know about getting around.
e-mail: mairie-varsailles@ mairie-versailles.fr

Visit Amsterdam
www.visitamsterdam.nl
This is a travellers' guide to Amsterdam
with links to online hotel reservations,
airlines, trains, local transport and
car rental, boat and bike services.
The city guide describes the museums,
attractions, diamond factories, canal
cruises, shopping, restaurants, night-life,
with an events calendar and also what
to avoid.
e-mail: not available

Visit Europe
www.visit.ie
On the home page of this user-friendly
web site select a destination via the
Visit European Cities Gateway Site;
you arrive at that city's home page
from where you can access information
about the city, its environs and an
accommodation section. When you
have decided, click the Book Now
button and the server connects you.
e-mail: Tourit1@indigo.ie

Wales Tourist Board
www.tourism.wales.gov.uk
An excellent site for travel and holidays
in Wales. Links include accommodation,
castles, tours and more, all put together
with wonderful pictures.
e-mail: not available

Welcome to Andorra
www.turisme.ad
Andorra offers you breath-taking
mountains and almost tax-free shopping.
If you want to do more than shop, there
are art galleries and gastronomic
excursions and of course a ski paradise,
with hot springs thrown in as an extra.
e-mail: turisme@andorra.ad

Welcome to Brussels
www.a-1.be/site/bxlnew/
This site provides information on everything
but sightseeing. Accommodation,
restaurants, Belgian cuisine, cinemas,

theatres, night venues and shopping
centres are given in detail.
e-mail: not available

Welcome to Ibiza
www.bestof.org
The complete guide to the island has
an online secure hotel booking facility,
currency converter and access to the
property market with direct sales. Every
town has maps, pictures and links to
accommodation, car and boat rental,
diving, insurance, eating out and shopping.
e-mail: dg@bestof.org

Welcome to Islandia
www.arctic.is/islandia/
The web site has pictures of tourist
attractions, a link to hotels, health
information, a short entertainment
guide and the history and politics
of Iceland.
e-mail: not available

Welcome to Lvov
www.lviv.org/eng/index.htm
You will find a calendar of events,
contacts to hotels, restaurants, clubs,
medical information, car rental and
entertainment guides, but there is no
description of what to visit in this
Ukrainian city.
e-mail: info@lviv.org

Welcome to Malta
www.malta.co.uk
Every town on the island is briefly
described and illustrated. The astonishing
archaeological sites are listed, with
organised tours. Some hotels have
linked sites, but most must be reached
by e-mail. Water sports feature high on
the activities list.
e-mail: 0800@malta.co.uk

Welcome to Moscow
moscow.lvl.ru/emoscow.html
Select your option from the home page
and you will find information about the

history and culture of Moscow, as well as useful information on entertainment, business opportunities, hotels and restaurants.
e-mail: www@lvl.ru

Welcome to Moscow Guide
www.moscow-guide.ru
There are several virtual tours around Moscow, or you can see the sights by following the links. The site is packed with easily accessible information on everything you need to know about the city. If you can't go there, you should at least visit this site.
e-mail: info@moscow-guide.ru

Welcome to Munich
www.munich-tourist.de
The capital of Bavaria hosts the world's largest beer festival Oktoberfest. You are offered accommodation packages, a Munich Discount Card and links to hotels, tourist and city attractions and excursions outside the city.
e-mail: not available

Welcome to Portugal
www.portugal.org
The site has an Art & Tradition page that makes you want to see more. As you go from region to region, you get a taste of the cuisine, festivals and crafts. There is a link to another page with travel details and tour operators.
e-mail: not available

Welcome to Romanian Travel Monitor
travel.necomm.ro
Two Romanian travel agents run this site and offer tours to the Riviera, Dracula country, the Danube delta, Prahova Valley and Transylvania. Out of doors you can fish, sail and climb mountains. Be sure to pack plenty of garlic if you go!
e-mail: not available

Welcome to the Isle of Man
www.isle-of-man.com
All the information you need to travel to and around the Isle of Man is clearly set out by region and category. The airport and flight schedules are linked to the local airline. Traditions, folklore, geography and history also get a mention.
e-mail: ts@enterprise.net

Welcome to Travel in Finland
www.travel.fi/int/
The site divides Finland into six regions with links in each to accommodation, sightseeing, adventure tours, the arts and an events calendar.
e-mail: not available

Welcome to Ukraine
www.ukraine.org
Basic information about the Ukraine. The site has links to airlines, travel agents, a list of hotels, embassies, translating services and a little about restaurants.
e-mail: vlad@ukraine.org

Zagreb Tourist Board
www.zagreb-convention.hr
You will find links to culture and history, accommodation, tourist information, business and economy. There is also an online form for requesting additional information.
e-mail: zagreb.convention@ccb.hr

Latin America

Acapulco
www.acapulco-cvb.org
All the tourist attractions in Acapulco, including beaches, bars and clubs, restaurants, shopping and sports centres and hotels are presented, with links to more detailed pages (budget hotels in Spanish only). Car rental, travel companies and airlines are all accessible through links.
e-mail: Cvb@acapulco-cvb.org

An Interactive Mexico Information Resource

www.KnowMexico.com

The site covers the major Mexican cities. Hotels, restaurants, sightseeing and other activities are all listed with car rental companies, hospitals and foreign consulates in some cities.

e-mail: Ears@tonyperez2.com

Argentina Tour

www.argentour.com

Travel information, climate, geography, history, economy, people and maps of Argentina. With a Real Player you can view a video presentation of the country. Text is in English, Spanish and German.

e-mail: lizandrol@hotmail.com

Argentine Tourism, Services and Shopping Guide

www.argentina-guia.com.ar/indexi.htm

A search engine helps you find information by topic. There are links to accommodation with online booking, tours with prices and contacts to the operators. You will also find a photo gallery and information on shopping, health precautions and local events.

e-mail: not available

Belize Tourist & Investment Guide

www.belize.com

Where to stay and what to see and do are laid out for the traveller, just follow the links. Because this is also an investment guide, you get to see some of the country's natural assets. Most activities are outdoors and the scuba diving is good. You can book by e-mail.

e-mail: not available

Bolivia Web

www.boliviaweb.com

This is a big site with lots about local history, business, education, government, health matters and of course travel. Links take you to airlines, car rental and travel companies, city information

and other guides. Some hotels can be booked online, restaurants are listed and several maps provided.

e-mail: not available

Brazilinfo

www.brazilinfo.com/index_en.htm

This easy to navigate site has links to hotels, tourist agents and operators, maps and general information for the whole of Brazil, with many good pictures.

e-mail: not available

Chile: A Country of Opportunities

www.chile.cl/chile-in/index.htm

An uncluttered presentation, with lots of features and links online. Tourist information is plentiful about climate, flora and fauna, internal transportation and there are good maps and pictures of Chile.

e-mail: inforyd@fundacionryd.cl

Colombia

www.colostate.edu/orgs/LASO/
Colombia/index_colombia.htm

Students of Colorado University maintain this site, which has lots of links to politics, business, cuisine, embassies and events in Colombia. Some links have English text.

e-mail: not available

Costa Rica Information Website

www.infocostarica.com

There is a lot of information to help you find your way around and plan your trip. A photo gallery and a short Spanish course get you into the swing. Hotels divided by location, travel agents and car rental companies are listed. You can book online.

e-mail: not available

Ecuador Explorer

ecuadorexplorer.com

You are offered a whole range of activities including mountain climbing,

trekking, bird watching, scuba diving, Spanish language courses, shopping and of course touring. There are guides for where to stay, with online booking, what to eat and how to travel, all with prices and other information.
e-mail: Info@ecuadorexplorer.com

El Salvador Tourism

www.virtualnet.com.sv/tourism/
Hotels, tour agents, car rental companies and airlines are all listed. Tourist attractions are described with photos.
e-mail: Ffernand@citt.cdb.edu.sv

Escape to Puerto Rico

escape.topuertorico.com
Once you have picked out all the travel essentials, ferry services, restaurants and menus, attractions and accommodation by type, city, price and facilities, you can explore the site looking for other items of interest.
e-mail: via online form

Falkland Islands Tourist Board

www.tourism.org.fk
Links on this pleasant and clearly laid out web site take you on a tour of the islands, their geography and climate, who will get you there and who will show you around.
e-mail: manager@tourism.org.fk

Go Chile!

www.gochile.cl
Lots of travel information about Chile. Choose your accommodation by price and you get a list of hotels with online booking. Car rental companies, restaurants, tours, local transportation, flight schedules and a lot more are all online.
e-mail: not available

Guatemala

www.guatemala.travel.com.gt
This tourist guide to Guatemala has a photographic tour of the country. Links take you to maps, transportation,

hotels, tour operators, restaurants and lots more. Text is in English and Spanish.
e-mail: inguat@guate.net

Honduras.com

www.honduras.com
You can explore Honduras and chat online. Links take you to travel matters, culture, history, art, music, cities, language, Honduran football if you are inclined and a weekly news page. To cap off, there is an extensive directory of services. It complements the other Honduras web site at **www.in-honduras.com/travel/tegucigalpa.**
e-mail: feedback@honduras.com

Ipanema.com

ipanema.com
Once you have taken in the information about visas, dress, weather, language, people, history and safety precautions, you will find the nightlife guide, including lists of live music bars, dancing clubs and where to eat. The city tour covers all districts together with lists of hotels.
e-mail: not available

Mexico City Virtual Guide

www.mexicocity.com.mx/mexcity.html
This is a very full guide to the city. A map lists the attractions, with links to the most significant. Hotels divided by area, bars, pubs, restaurants and nightlife venues are listed with links to more detailed information.
e-mail: via online form

Mexico Government Tourist Office

mexico-travel.com
Available in English and Spanish, this well designed site contains information about local culture, geography, history, archaeological sites and embassies and consulates. There is an information request form.
e-mail: not available

Nicaragua's TravelNet

www.centralamerica.com/nicaragua/
This is part of an omnibus guide and
the best one available for Nicaragua.
General information is amply covered
including geography, climate, people,
language, religion, banking hours,
immigration, shopping and cuisine.
The main cities and tourist areas are
detailed, with links to hotels and travel
agents.
e-mail: not available

Panama Info

www.panamainfo.com
The site has links to lists of travel services.
External links take you to hotels, holiday
resorts, entertainment, a calendar of
events, sports centres, tour operators,
real estate agents and language centres.
The site is available in English and
Spanish, with plenty of good pictures.
e-mail: via online form

Panama Travel

www.panamatravel.com
Apart from travel information from
car rental to business opportunities, this
easy to navigate site has a virtual museum
of the Panama Canal and a page of poetry.
e-mail: pataconrico@panamatravel.com

Paraguay - South America
for Visitors

gosouthamerica.about.com/travel/
gosouthamerica/msubmenuPar.htm
There are dozens of links to other sites
covering every aspect of Paraguayan life
from tourism to business opportunities
and UFO sightings.
e-mail: not available

Peru Explorer

www.peru-explorer.com
This is a guide mainly about where to go
and what to do, culture, arts and history.
You will find a lot of information about
Lima, Inca archaeological sites, natural
resources, tips for tourists and a picture

gallery. Adventure sports include rafting,
surfing and climbing.
e-mail: info@explorer.com

Puerto Rican Tourism Company

www.gorp.com/gorp/location/pr/
pr.htm#address
Lots of information for tourists with
plenty of links, but navigating around
the site can be a little confusing.
e-mail: not available

South America Ski Guide

www.southamericaskiguide.com
There are more than thirty ski resorts in
Chile, Argentina and Bolivia and you get
ample information, maps and travel tips
to visit them. To help you along there is
a dictionary of Spanish ski terms and
links to weather reports.
e-mail: Sasg@southamericaskiguide.com

SPGuia: Official Tourist Guide
of Sao Paulo City

www.spguia.com.br
The city's hotels, churches and museums
are featured with text and pictures.
You will also find guides to nightlife,
restaurants, carnivals and a calendar
of events.
e-mail: Wotan@spguia.com.br

Tegucigalpa - Visit Honduras

www.in-honduras.com/travel/tegucigalpa
This is part of the larger Honduras web
site. Travel information concentrates
on the capital city. Hotels with contact
details, restaurants, shopping centres
and entertainment venues are all listed,
together with details about obtaining
a visa.
e-mail: not available

The Belize Tourism Board

www.travelbelize.org
You get a rundown of history, culture,
location, geography and government
with advice on what to see, where to
stay and travel tips, all enhanced with

good pictures and an online virtual tour. If you need more, use the e-mail address and online form.
e-mail: info@travelbelize.org

Venezuela Tuya

www.venezuelatuya.com/tour/ toureng.htm
A great collection of pictures from around this beautiful country greet you on the home page. There is also a detailed map and a guide to eight major destinations with more pictures, local information and a few links to other related sites. Text is in English, French and Spanish.
e-mail: Hrosas@venezuelatuya.com

Welcome to Cancun

www.gocancun.com
How to get to and around Cancun and the Yucatan. Local events, cuisine, dance and shopping are all explained with pictures. You can order a free brochure with more information.
e-mail: not available

Middle East

Bahrain Tourism

www.bahraintourism.com
There are links to some of the tourist attractions and services on this site. Hotels, restaurants, car rental companies, travel agents and a calendar of events are all listed, some in detail.
e-mail: Btour@bahraintourism.com

Discover Israel

www.ddtravel-acc.com
This is just about the most complete travel guide you can get. It covers official institutions, city guides and places of interest, maps, museums, holy places, kibbutzim, news, weather, discount accommodation, restaurants, car rental, customised and private car tours, with discount reservations for all travel services.
e-mail: ddtravel@ibm.net

Go Dubai

www.godubai.com
The city, its everyday life, entertainment for the whole family and tourist excursions are described on this site. There are lists of hotels, restaurants and some links to other tourist sites.
e-mail: Sima@simaint2.co.ae

Israel Government Tourist Info Centre

www.infotour.co.il
Links to local religions and culture, accommodation, places to visit, events, articles, tourist information centres, and car rental in the Holy Land. An interactive map is also provided.
e-mail: hgolan@imot.org

Lebanon Online

www.lol.com.lb
You get a brief tour of the country with links to guide you through most cities. There are four links to hotel pages, a restaurant guide and details of transport within and outside the country.
e-mail: info@webserv.com.lb

Palestine-net. Tourism in Palestine

www.palestine-net.com/tourism
This is a part of a general information site about Palestinian Autonomy. The travel section has links to hotels, city and museum directories, restaurants and Internet cafés, car rental companies and maps.
e-mail: not available

SKILEB.com

www.skileb.com
The six ski resorts in Lebanon are featured in this site with trail maps, prices, hotels, dining and après-ski activities. You will find tailor-made ski packages for Lebanon, Switzerland and France as well as general information about Lebanon.
e-mail: not available

The Jerusalem Website

www.jerusalem.muni.il/english
Jerusalem has over one hundred places of historical and religious significance. If you have a Viscape program you can go on a virtual tour of the city; if not, you can download it using the link. There are internal links to accommodation, restaurants and entertainment.
e-mail: not available

The Travel Guide to Istanbul and Turkey

www.turizm.net
City guides point the way and you can map out all you wish to see in the tourist areas and archaeological sites. Istanbul has a separate section with a restaurant guide, with online booking for guided tours.
e-mail: info@turizm.net

Tourism Section-Yemen

www.yemen-online.com/tourism/
Lots of statistical information and some outstanding pictures. Links take you to general information, currency, hotels, visas, shopping, entertainment, religion and more.
e-mail: not available

Welcome to the Hashimite Kingdom of Jordan

www.welcome2jordan.com
The home page tells you about visas, currency, shopping, hotels, restaurants and the weather in Jordan. The rest of the site describes the many tourist attractions you can visit. The ancient city at Petra is unmissable.
e-mail: mwbseiso@hotmail.com

Welcome to the United Arab Emirates

www.uae.org.ae
The site gives you a list of hotels, most with their own web sites, car rental companies and a brief rundown on places to visit, with a calendar of events.
e-mail: not available

Yemen Tour and Travel Guide

homepages.go.com/~yemenguide/ yemen-travel.index.html
You will find useful tips for visitors and a hotel guide listed by city. There are descriptions of the major tourist attractions, some with pictures. Several excursions include diving, trekking and the outdoors.
e-mail: Jalattab@hotmail.com

North America

Absolutely Florida

www.abfla.com
This is a good guide to travel services with links to reservation centres. You can book airline tickets, hotel and vacation packages online. There are web pages for most hotels, hostels, camping grounds and a list of B & Bs. Activities are catered for with beach profiles and local sights, cultural entertainment and clubs.
e-mail: Info@funandsun.com

AlaskaOne.com

www.alaska-online.com
All you could ever need to know about travelling to Alaska, with information on accommodation, activities, transport, attractions and restaurants. Click on the region you want on the home page map for more details.
e-mail: via online form

AreaGuides USA

www.areaguides.net
A comprehensive site with travel information and business listings for over 500 US cities. Click on the State, then the city, and you find information covering travel services, real estate agents, sports, clubs and restaurants.
e-mail: not available

Bermuda Department of Tourism

www.bermudatourism.com

The guide sets out accommodation services, entertainment and dining, popular sport activities and sightseeing in good detail. There is advice on why and how to organise a group trip to the country.

e-mail: via online form

California Ski Guides

www.skicalifornia.com

The State of California is divided into four ski regions and all the resorts are fully detailed on separate web pages. There is an accommodation guide, up-to-date weather and road condition reports, with trail maps you can zoom in for each resort.

e-mail: info@skicalifornia.com

California Travel & Tourism

www.gocalif.ca.gov/

Maps in PDF format divide the State regionally. Accommodation, tours, travel and dining information are detailed for each. You can book your hotel, airline tickets and car online and order a guide to California. There is a separate guide for cinema lovers showing where some Hollywood films were made.

e-mail: Caltour@commerce.ca.gov

Canadian Tourism Commission

www.canadatourism.com/index_ct.html

Well illustrated and with lots of links, this site divides Canada regionally. You get illustrated travel guides, things to do, places to go and an FAQ section.

e-mail: not available

CanadianRockies.net

www.canadianrockies.net

On offer are guided tours of the region with links to the companies organising them. Check them out and book online. There are guides to the best sports in the area - skiing, fishing and golf,

with maps and assistance. You can choose your accommodation by region and category.

e-mail: not available

Choose Chicago

www.chicago.il.org

The visitors' guide includes travel information, local activities, tour services and advice to the independent traveller. You will also find detailed accommodation and restaurant guides.

e-mail: not available

City of Victoria

www.city.victoria.bc.ca

This is a guide to the city of Victoria, Canada. Travel information includes museums, galleries, gardens, family activities and suggestions for daylong excursions, a calendar of events and local lodging facilities.

e-mail: Publicsrv@city.victoria.bc.ca

DC Online

www.washdc.org

Click on the map and follow the links to the arts and entertainment. Museums, galleries, dance, restaurants, ticket booking offices, sports clubs and outdoor activity operators are all listed, many with their own pages.

e-mail: Info@washdc.org

Discover Alberta

www.discoveralberta.com

The Canadian State of Alberta has travel companies offering tours and adventure holidays to sports resorts and centres. You can visit monuments and museums or take themed driving tours using the maps. Each city has its hotels listed, with an online booking facility.

e-mail: not available

Explore Nova Scotia

explore.gov.ns.ca

The home page gives a general survey of this Canadian State. An accommodation

database has rates and e-mail addresses. Local attractions include galleries, monuments, playgrounds and museums. You can also order a free guide.
e-mail: Explore@gov.ns.ca

Go Las Vegas

www.golasvegas.com
Where to stay, where to eat and what to do in Las Vegas. You can book online and if you've seen enough casinos, there are lists of local sights, amusement parks and venues, shops and night clubs to keep you busy.
e-mail: via online form

Greater Philadelphia Tourism

www.gophila.com
If you have a RealTime player you can go on a guided tour on this web site. If not you can download it free. Accommodation and restaurants are listed by area and price range. There are links to music clubs and other entertainment venues, cultural events and theatres.
e-mail: via online form

In Vancouver

www.vancouver-bc.com
The site lists travel services and city attractions. Most hotels, restaurants and clubs have links to their own web pages.
e-mail: Info@vancouver-bc.com

LA.com

www.la.com
The guide to local attractions and tourist services includes local beaches, Hollywood studios, museums and Disneyland. There are search engines for comedy clubs, music and night venues, shows and movie reviews, accommodation and restaurants.
e-mail: not available

New Mexico Reservations

www.taoswebb.com
A visitors guide to northern New Mexico. From skiing to white water rafting to

chamber music, they have it all. Follow the community links to customise your vacation or take an all-inclusive package.
e-mail: res@VisitNewMexico.com

New York

www.newyork.com
New York provides information on tours, hotels, restaurants, shopping, entertainment, games, news and weather in the Big Apple.
e-mail: not available

New York City Guide

www.newyorktoday.com
The New York Times runs this excellent web site with an up-to-date guide to all tourist events, attractions and services. Each subject has a search engine that delivers lots of information and links to other pages.
e-mail: Nytoday.help@nytimes.com

Newfoundland and Labrador Tourism

www.gov.nf.ca/tourism/
There are lots of ways to enjoy yourself in this part of Canada. Each region has links to clubs and resorts, scenic tours with great natural beauty and a range of package tours. You can e-mail the hotel reservation centre and order a brochure online.
e-mail: via online form

Official Guide to Houston

www.houston-guide.com
There is a lot to satisfy the cultural palette with ballet, theatres, museums, operas and the concert hall. Historical and natural attractions, sports clubs, guided tours and a calendar of events add to what there is to do. Travel essentials come in full measure.
e-mail: not available

Out There

www.out-there.com
Adventure sport in Canada is covered

regionally in this guide. Each sport is identified with the best places to go, equipment rental companies, links to manufacturers' web pages, instructors and guides, accommodation, books, magazines and weather. A very good web site.

e-mail: Info@out-there.com

Parks Canada

parkscanada.pch.gc.ca
For every historical site, national park or reserve in Canada you will find pictures and information on how to get there, local events, entrance fees, services and opening hours.

e-mail: not available

Passover in the Islands and the American Southwest

www.passovervacations.com
Details about a number of resort hotels that provide accommodation and food under Orthodox rabbinic supervision in the USA and some Caribbean islands. In addition to normal holiday activities, there is an emphasis on Kosher cuisine.

e-mail: info@passovervacations.com

San Francisco Convention & Visitors Bureau

www.sfvisitor.org
Leisure and business travellers will find all they need to plan their trip.

e-mail: via online form

Ski Guide

www.ski-guide.com
This is a complete guide to ski resorts in the USA and Canada. Pick out the resort by name or off the maps. Search engines will help you choose not just location but terrain difficulty, summit height and services. Each resort has lodging, dining and shopping guides, trail maps and links to official web sites.

e-mail: not available

The New England Ski Guide

home.earthlink.net/~nortonc/ski/
This site incorporates all the skiing locations in New England - Vermont, New Hampshire, Maine, Massachusetts, Connecticut and Rhode Island - with up-to-date prices, special deals and events. Links connect you to resort pages and details of ski trails, schools and passes, snow reports, lodging and special offers.

e-mail: nortonc@earthlink.net

The Nunavut Handbook

www.arctic-travel.com
This is the traveller's guide to the northernmost regions of Canada. The web site helps you plan your journey with vital information on weather and the correct clothing to wear. Guides tell you where to stay, what to see and how to get around.

e-mail: Kristat@nortext.com

The Official New Brunswick Website

www.tourismnbcanada.com/web/
A guided tour of the best attractions and some amusing facts about the province. Hotels and restaurants are listed regionally.

e-mail: via online form

Touring Texas

www.touringtexas.com
This is a general link page for tourists and business travellers in Texas. Links take you to official city web sites, real estate agents, a hotel reservation centre, wildlife and sports operators, car rentals, airlines, galleries, restaurants and shops.

e-mail: Halb@bigfoot.com

TourOttawa

www.tourottawa.org
The site has a general information page and search engines for local activities and tourist services. Each engine has external links with more details.

e-mail: via online form

Travel Alaska

www.travelalaska.com
If you have a RealTime Player you can watch four virtual tours. If not, you can download it free. You will find links to hotels in four cities and local travel agents.
e-mail: Travelalaska@digital-sherpas.com

US National Parks

www.us-national-parks.net/
There are guides to over fifty American National Parks. Each park is located, with advice on how to get there and what to expect. Maps show special features. Park regulations, weather, a guide for campers and hikers, a list of hotels and a calendar of events are linked.
e-mail: Info@us-national-parks.net

VisitDetroit.com

www.visitdetroit.com
As home to Ford and Chrysler, Detroit has several memorials and museums dedicated to motor industry pioneers. There are other attractions, nightlife venues, restaurants and hotels. You can order a complete visitors' guide online.
e-mail: not available

www.quebecweb.com

www.quebecweb.com
The most popular local outdoor activities in Quebec Province are dog-sledding, fishing, golf and skiing. Or you might want to visit the cities and see what they offer. Either way, all the information is well presented and wonderfully illustrated.
e-mail: not available

World wide

About.com

home.about.com/travel/index.html
This is an omnibus guide to different continents, countries and several US cities. Apart from general information, there are links to hotels, restaurants and tours, as well as cultural guides with lots of information.
e-mail: not available

Backpack Traveller

bptravel.tripod.com
News, hints and tips, medical guidance and equipment advice for the backpacker. The Country Database has useful information about bank opening hours.
e-mail: inquire@thebackpacktraveler.com

Country Digest

web3.asia1.com.sg/tnp/journey/travel
This is a guide to Southeast Asia, northern Australia and Turkey. The site contains lists of hotels with price ranges and contacts, shopping and tour guides and practical advice about visas, climate, money and cuisine.
e-mail: not available

Events Worldwide

www.eventsworldwide.com
Choose the location, event category and time within the next five years and the up-to-date database provides a list of scheduled events with brief descriptions.
e-mail: via online form

Expert Travel, Vacations and Tours Guide

spectravel.com
The site is organised into sections, so that the Places To Go link contains a list of recommended destinations around the world, each of which is briefly described. The Things To Do link has lots of activities, with a link to each which tells you where you can do it. You will also find information on business travel, fun trips, travel discounts and tips, exotic vacations and bargain airline tickets.
e-mail: admin@spectravel.com

Foreign Languages for Travellers

www.travlang.com/languages

Going some place where the language is foreign? Simply click on the country you're visiting, for a choice of basic words, numbers, shopping, dining, time and dates, places, directions and general travel words. And what's more, there are links to country information and maps.

e-mail: not available

Globewalker's City Guide

www.globewalker.com

This ambitious site intends to cover major world cities, but so far has only completed Budapest, London, Toronto and Montreal. It is an excellent guide to the each city, with information specific to travellers from the UK, USA and Canada. There are links to travelcompanies, airlines, domestic railways and a European Railway Server; hotels, local transport, maps and tourist attractions. Your browser has to be Java enabled to access the pull down menus on the site.

e-mail: not available

GoSki Travel Center

www.goski.com

The main ski resorts world wide. There are maps of ski trails, details of facilities, an online shop to buy gear, with a wealth of information on equipment, manufacturers and user reviews. Links take you to package deals, hotels, resorts, airline tickets and car rental.

e-mail: not available

Jewish Travel

jewishtravel.com

Information about resorts and restaurants world wide for Jewish travellers, including business, family and singles trips. There are many links on the community page, including

travel tips, a bulletin board, guest book and bookstore.

e-mail: not available

Lycos Destination Guide

travel.lycos.com/Destinations/

A very useful guide to most destinations world wide, listed by region, then country. Each country has information about passports and visas, money, transportation, accommodation, resorts, social and business profiles, climate, history and government. You can even make your own contribution to their database by filling in an update form.

e-mail: not available

MyTravelGuide.com

www.mytravelguide.com

An attractive site packed with information and links. The home page shows an atlas of the world; click on the area you are interested in, or chose from the countries listed. There is also a distance calculation facility as well as currency converter, driving directions, miles manager, interactive atlas, world clock, flight tracker, language guide as well as dozens of other links.

e-mail: via online form

Travel Source

www.travelsource.com

This is the ultimate travel web site. There are free links to travel related businesses around the globe with pages for each country, each State in the USA and Province in Canada, as well as listings under headings for accommodation, airlines, vehicle rental and more.

You can explore destinations using the Go Location link, by country, continent, region or place to stay; purchase travel publications online and chat using the Chat Room facility. And if that isn't enough, Hot Deals, Best Cruise Deals and Lowest Airfares bring you up to date before you book online.

e-mail: info@wwtravelsource.com

Diplomatic Missions

World wide

British Foreign & Commonwealth Office
www.fco.gov.uk
A good, easy to navigate site with information on visas, foreign policy issues and links to News, Travel, Trade, and Directory. For example, the Travel link gives advice on Do's and Don'ts, British Consular Services and related subjects.
e-mail: not available

EmbassyWeb.com
www.embpage.org
Embassies and foreign representations from all over the world. Links take you to alphabetically listed international sites, world news, up-to-date breaking news and its own search facility.
e-mail: via online form

Foreign Affairs & Trade - Australia - Travel Advice
www.dfat.gov.au/consular/advice/advices_mnu.html
Advice from the Australian Authorities for travellers, listed by country including health, safety and immigration matters. Other links give embassies and more.
e-mail: via online form

Luxembourg
www.luxembourg.co.uk
Click on Luxembourg Embassies Abroad for a list of Embassy addresses world wide. At the bottom of the page further links take you to the Tourist Office, Requirements to live in Luxembourg, Visas and an Embassy directory.
e-mail: via online form

New Zealand High Commission
www.newzealandhc.org.uk/index2.html
For travellers to and from New Zealand. Click on Immigration for the New Zealand Immigration page, which offers links to choices of visas available. Click on any of these for further details.
e-mail: via online form

Norway
www.norway.org.uk
The home page has a tab menu running along the top giving details of Consulates, Embassies, Tourism and more. There are links to visa information and news headlines.
e-mail: via online form

Republic of Angola site
www.angola.org/index.htm
Scroll down the home page and type Visas in the search box, then click on Visa Information for details. Internet Directory will give you a list of Angolan Embassies and Government sites. Visitors' Favourites and Basic Facts are worth looking at.
e-mail: not available

Tagish - Embassies World Wide
www2.tagish.co.uk/Links/embassy1b.nsf/
You will find Embassies and Government Web Sites by Continent and Country simply by clicking on the appropriate link. Then you get contact details and links to other web sites.
e-mail: via online form

The Electronic Embassy
www.embassy.org
This site has information on all Foreign
Embassies in Washington D.C. The
FAQ section is particularly helpful;
it tells you how to renew a foreign
passport, how to e-mail any embassy
in the world and anything you need to
know about travel documents. There
are other links well worth looking at.
e-mail: via online form

US State Department -
Travel Warnings
travel.state.gov/travel_warnings.html
US government information about
travel problems world wide. Offers
advice on trouble hotspots, details
on crime, medical facilities, health
information, traffic safety, aviation
safety and more, with links to other
related sites.
e-mail: not available

Equipment Suppliers

Africa

South African Spearfishing Supplies

www.spearfishing.co.za
They are distributors and exporters of
South African products, particularly Rob
Allan spear fishing and free diving
equipment. The spear guns are regarded
among the finest on the market and are
exported around the world. For trade
enquiries click the enquiry link.
e-mail: info@spearfishing.co.za

Europe

Ski Surf 2000

www.skisurf.co.uk
Windsurfing and winter sports
equipment for all levels of competence.
They stock most major brands, advise
on equipment and run a mail order
service. The Special Offers and Used
Kit pages have some of the best
bargains.
e-mail: howard@skisurf.co.uk

Typhoon Cyclone

www.typhoon-int.co.uk
Clothing for in or out of water and water
sports products sold around the world.
Products include diving dry suits and
equipment, thermals, commercial and
military dry suits, aviation immersion

suits and more in an excellent range,
all well illustrated.
e-mail: sales@typhoon-int.co.uk

North America

Berry Scuba

www.berryscuba.com
The ultimate diving outfitters from
goggles to underwater cameras and
everything between. The homepage
lists their stores, training sessions,
special offers and an informative
online catalogue.
e-mail: orders@berryscuba.com

Campmor

www.campmor.com
Online outdoor and camping gear
superstore. You can browse for
products by category or brand name.
Orders can by made by online form
or telephone; shipping to addresses
in the USA only.
e-mail: customer-service@campmor.com

Ski Closeouts

www.skistop.com/skclose.htm
One of the largest ski shops on the
east coast of the USA, with everything
you could possibly need on the ski
slope. Their winter wear comes from
popular manufacturers, and their ski
equipment caters for everyone from
beginners to Olympic champs.
Ordering online is not yet available.
e-mail: skistop@pagelinx.com

World wide

Above Ground Designs

www.adventuresports.com/shops/
aerialchair/welcome.htm
They make the Aerial Chair - the
newest and coolest way to lounge
wherever you go. The Photo Gallery
shows you all the ways to use it.
Take a look, you may be intrigued.
e-mail: cloud@aerialchair.com

Academy Sports and Outdoors

www.academy.com/academy.nsf

A wide selection of travel gear and clothing together with sports and fitness training equipment, all on one web site. To find the store nearest you, click on the Store Location Finder button.

e-mail: Academy@academy.com

Action Direct

www.action-direct.com

Gear for hunters, campers and the outdoor person. The online catalogue lists the full range with many items not available in stores and you can take advantage of special offers. You can order online, with most items being shipped within 48 hours.

e-mail: info@action-direct.com

Adventure DooDads

www.adv-doodads.com

Secure online shopping for outdoor gear and equipment. If you are looking for hiking, camping and climbing equipment, in fact anything for outdoor holidays, they seem to have it. Books, nature CDs and a range of travel accessories add to their inventory.

e-mail: Cust-serv@adv-doodads.com

Adventure Sports Online

www.adventuresports.com/new/
shopdir.htm

The products and shops section of this outdoor activity guide. All manner of great gear is available from a variety of suppliers, including winter sports, biking gear, climbing gear, tents, sleeping bags, backpacks, footwear and so on. You can also carry out an Outfitter Search or a Product Search by country or activity using the pull down menus.

e-mail: via online form

Appalachian Mountain Supply

www.adventuresports.com/product/ams

Outdoor adventure gear with equipment of a type taken on several Himalayan

expeditions. For a free catalogue, call or fill out the request form. You can transact online.

e-mail: amsupply@flash.net

Aqua Flite

aquaflite.com

Wetsuits and diving gear in a complete selection of standard sizes, which can be personalised to suit you. It will be difficult to find a bigger range of styles, colours and accessories and as if that's not enough, they will tailor suits to your dimensions and specifications. Most credit cards are accepted.

e-mail: not available

Aquatic Outfitters.com

www.aquatrec.com

Water sports equipment store offering a complete line of swimming, fitness and travel equipment and accessories. Search the catalogue for particular equipment or click on a category for a wide selection. Credit card transactions are welcome.

e-mail: sales@aquaticoutfitters.com

Backpackgear.com

www.backpackgear.com

Footwear is their speciality but they also run a backpackers' emporium with everything from tents to tea bags, all items illustrated and priced.

e-mail: backpack@backpackgear.com

Backpacking Gear Community

shop.affinia.com/travelexperiences/store

You can view the products by Merchant, Brand or Category, or use the search engine if you know what you want. The home page features a range of must-have products.

e-mail: not available

Baldas USA

www.adventuresports.com/
product/baldas

High quality, high tech snowshoes in all sizes for men, women and children,

designed for the worst snow and ice conditions. All models are made of space age materials and ordering from the drop down list cannot be easier.
e-mail: vanmgmt@aol.com

Bargain Travel Center

www.bargain-travel.com
Travel goods and accessories with immediate despatch to home or holiday destination. Browse through a great selection of luggage, books, converters, clocks, binoculars, videos and electronics. If you know what you want, type it in the search box and find it immediately.
e-mail: not available

Bass Pro Shops Outdoor World Online

www.basspro-shops.com/index.cfm
A full range of travel products from automotive accessories to fishing hooks. Select a main category and a list of all gear on offer is displayed. Shop by dropping your choices in the Cart.
e-mail: not available

Bavarian Village

www.skigolf.com
This consortium of shops sells ski and golf equipment and travel services. You can browse each separately. Equipment is also available for hire and you can buy discount lift tickets.
e-mail: not available

Cencal

www.cencal.com
Travel accessories originally designed for the aviation industry, using materials many times stronger than normally available and durable enough for the top of Mount Everest. So if you plan on going there you know where to get your gear.
e-mail: cencal@c-zone.net

Cumberland Transit

www.ctransit.com
Practically everything you will need to travel confidently, including a good selection of sports equipment. Each product category features a number of brands, so click on the logo. There is a Warranty & Factory Repair link for some items.
e-mail: info@ctransit.com

Discount Luggage

www.luggageman.com
Major brand luggage at a discount. The durability rating 1 to 10, taken from warranty and damage records, gives you an idea of what to expect from your luggage. The Top 10 Sellers also gives an indication of what to buy.
e-mail: smluggage@fix.net

Eagle Creek

www.eaglecreek.com
Everything for the traveller to pack a bag and go. Travel gear, backpacks, wheelie bags, duffle bags, Pack It systems and accessories. Each link has a selection of products and a search engine helps you find exactly what you are looking for. You can purchase online.
e-mail: not available

Footprint Designs

www.adventuresports.com/product/footprint
End-of-line and surplus stock travel items at discounts. Click on the picture for details and use the secure link for ordering online.
e-mail: not available

Footsloggers

www.footsloggers.com
Hiking, backpacking, climbing, camping and outdoor equipment and then some more. All major brands are available with online icon for current specials. To get quotes, use the Request page.
e-mail: footsloggers@helicon.net

Gear Addict

www.web-dzine.com/gearaddict/
You can purchase travel goods from Gear Store; post and respond to questions on Gear Forum; read or write opinions in Gear Reviews. The Soapbox Forum is the place to voice your opinion on outdoor topics; and you can advertise what you want to buy or sell.
e-mail: contact@gearpro.com

GearHead

www.gearhd.com
Aimed at the beginner preparing for his first adventure without much of a clue or no time to shop around. You will get a complete gear list from which to make your purchases for which you pay the cost plus a small service fee to Gearhead. Major credit cards are accepted.
e-mail: Wct1359@aol.com

Gearoom.com

www.gearoom.com
Outdoor enthusiasts who love equipment and have a mission to help others get a feel for gear. Reviews are product-based and in-depth. The Book Store page and Gear Auction section are very useful.
e-mail: not available

Golf Warehouse

www.thegolfwarehouse.com
They say they are dedicated to providing the largest and broadest selection of golf products in the world. The online catalogue contains literally thousands of items covering every aspect of the sport, with items specifically for women, children and beginners. You can order by e-mail, phone or fax.
e-mail: customerservice@tgw.com

Gordon Griffiths Fishing Tackle

www.gordon-griffiths.co.uk
Fishing equipment suppliers to dealers and distributors world wide. With what they offer, fish don't have much of a chance. For more information, click on the product.
e-mail: fishingtackle@gordon_griffiths.co.uk

Gorp

www.gorp.com
Gear for hiking, camping, boating, fishing, winter sports, kids, gear repair and general travel. Each category has a product guide and tips on choosing the right gear. There is a boutique section, a women's corner, books and maps, video and CD pages and Gear Discussion to share tips on buying, using and swapping gear.
e-mail: sales@gorp.com

Great Outdoor Emporium Mall

www.tgoemall.com
This is probably the largest, most visited service for shoppers of outdoor recreation gear. There are more than 2000 departments and outdoor enthusiasts will find everything for all sports and outdoor activities.
e-mail: help@tgoemall.com

Huntingtons on the Web

www.jcn.com/huntingtons
As luggage and leather goods merchants they go back several generations and they will personalise your purchases for free. Click on the items on the home page for pictures and details of products. Order by fax or e-mail.
e-mail: hunthelp@huntweb.com

Jagged Edge Mountain Gear

www.jagged-edge.com
Clothing for winter camping and mountaineering. The online catalogue gives the full range. Navigate the store by clicking the category you want to browse; when you find something you want to buy, click the Add Item button beneath. To complete your order, click the Check Out button.
e-mail: jemg@jagged-edge.com

Le Travel Store

www.letravelstore.com
Everything you need in travel gear
and accessories from locks and tags
to clocks and bags. Check the Travel
Gear On Sale page for bargains.
e-mail: gear@letravelstore.com

Learn2.com

www.learn2.com/corporate/
Before you buy your next pair of hiking
boots be sure to read the instructions
on this site. Apart from footwear there
is a large range of other travel and
sports equipment. To start shopping
click on the Buy it Here link, then follow
the instructions until you are ready to
check out.
e-mail: Learn2@Learn2.com

Leki USA

www.leki.com
US-based with hiking, trekking, skiing
and fitness products. Click on the
category on the navigation bar, use the
search engine or the Find It index page.
Fill out the online form, or e-mail for
more information.
e-mail: service@leki.com

Lightweight Backpacker

www.backpacking.net/gearshop.html
Everything on this site has been
designed to reduce the backpacker's
load. Products from shelters to cutlery
are manufactured in lightweight and
ultra-light materials. Browse around
the Gear shop and visit Gear Reviews
for opinions.
e-mail: Associates@backpacking.net

Long Road Travel Supplies

www.longroad.com
Quality mosquito nets for travel, camping
and home use designed for maximum
possible protection against biting insects
under almost any condition. See for
yourself and order by e-mail or phone.
e-mail: sales@longroad.com

Luggage Land

www.luggageland.com.au
This Australian travel luggage store
has online product information and
an ordering facility. They offer
international brands, fine quality
Australian-made leather goods and
a wide range of travel accessories.
They also offer tax-free shopping, free
delivery and other valuable services.
e-mail: luggage@luggageland.com.au

Macabi Skirt

www.macabiskirt.com
Original adventure travel skirts for
cool comfort and an attractive alternative
to shorts and pants. The quick
drying fabric is durable and adjusts
easily to changes in weather and activity.
Prices are marked and you can order
online or by mail.
e-mail: sales@macabiskirt.com

Mountain Woman

www.mountainwoman.com
A wide selection of branded clothing
and equipment for adventurous women.
You can clad yourself from head to foot
and then some. Order online, e-mail or
call for advice or suggestions. They ship
world wide at cost.
e-mail: info@mountainwoman.com

MPI Outdoors

www.adventuresports.com
They manufacture and distribute a
range of unique comfort and protection
products for outdoor use specialising
in all-weather blankets. There are
online instructions on how to deal
with emergencies and develop
survival skills.
e-mail: outdoor@ix.netcom.com

Nomad Outdoor
& Travel Equipment

www.nomad.nl/f-com.asp
Functional outdoor gear and wear from
tents to boots. For more details click on

the product picture. The site has an expeditions page and a travel guide.
e-mail: not available

Northwest River Supplies
www.nrscatalog.com
One-stop shop for branded boating equipment for men, women and children. Other lines include boats, kayaks and accessories and camping equipment. All products are priced and you can buy online.
e-mail: nrs@nrsweb.com

Out in Style
www.adventuresports.com/shops/out-in-style/welcome.htm
A large inventory of camping, hunting, law enforcement supplies and military surplus goods. When you're done browsing you can order online, with shipping generally within 48 hours.
e-mail: sales@outinstyle.com

OutdoorReview.com
www.outdoorreview.com
This is a forum for outdoor enthusiasts to exchange opinions, ideas and experiences related to travel gear; to find new campsites and post reviews of those you've visited; to get and give advice in the Tech Talk section. There are trail reviews, a photo gallery and message boards. If you want to get rid of old gear or get a good deal on quality products visit the Marketplace.
e-mail: Mikel@outdoorreview.com

Overtons.com
www.overtons.com
Online boating supplies, with everything you might ever need for your water craft. You can request a full catalogue or place an order online, major credit cards are accepted, deliveries possible apparently world wide.
e-mail: service@overtons.com

Savanna Jones
www.savannajones.com
Travel equipment and goods with highly functional and stylish luggage a speciality. They also market a wide range of accessories, suitable for several manufacturers' models, to turn your town car into a tourer.
e-mail: info@savannajones.com

Seattle Fabrics
www.seattlefabrics.com
Fabrics and hardware for outdoor and recreational activity. They have everything you need to make your own equipment down to the thread to put it all together. You can order in person, by phone, fax, e-mail, or post with payment by credit card, personal cheque or money order.
e-mail: Seatlefabrics@msn.com

Sportif USA
www.sportif.com
Quality performance clothing for outdoor activities from backcountry to beachfront and every place between. Check out the products by category or use the search engine if you know what are you looking for. You can order online.
e-mail: not available

The Education Source
www.edusource.com
Products for families travelling with children from car seats to onboard entertainment. An award-winning interactive globe-computer atlas is featured online. Check out the Top Ten link for the best in educational material.
e-mail: editor@edusource.com

The Luggage Shop
www.the-luggage-shop.com
They carry a wide selection of luggage, leather goods and travel accessories from leading manufacturers. Click on the label to view products.
e-mail: inquiry@the-luggage-shop.com

Tilley Endurables

www.tilley.com
Manufacturers of adventure and travel clothing. The store locations finder will tell you where they are. Their web site has a testimonial board, clothing profile Q&A and more. Their products will cover you from top to toe and their accessories make welcome gifts.
e-mail: not available

Totally Outdoors

www.adventuresports.com/shops/ totally/welcome.htm
Women's outdoor clothing and equipment made from hard wearing performance fabrics in flattering feminine fashions size XS - XXL. The online store departments have the products and educational resources to help women better enjoy the outdoors.
e-mail: info@totallyoutdoors.com

Tough Traveller

www.travelsource.com/travelstore/tough traveler/toughtraveler.html
Travel gear with the emphasis on toughness. The full range is displayed and if you want a complete catalogue, contact the agent. Order online by using the form.
e-mail: not available

Travel Products

www.travel-accessories.com
A wide range of practical, proven travel accessories for bikers and motorists from maps to meals on the go. All products are shipped within 48 hours with a one-year guarantee. The site has a search engine and useful travel links.
e-mail: delblau@msn.com

Travel Smith

www.travelsmith.com
Versatile, easy care and easy to pack travel wear. Select the Free Catalogue link and you get clothes covering the whole spectrum, from daytime touring to nights on the town, from jungle treks to ocean cruises. This versatile web site beats the High Street shop window.
e-mail: service@travelsmith.com

Travel-news.org

www.travel-news.org/equipe.html
Travel equipment, gadgets, guides, essentials and non-essentials for the traveller. They have way-out products like a device that controls your washing machine from your laptop via the Internet. Or would you prefer a device that plugs into your telephone and routes calls through the Internet, so you make calls anywhere in the world at local rates? Take a look, you'll be amazed.
e-mail: not available

Travelsuppliers.com

www.travelsupplies.com
Travel luggage, organisers, outdoor accessories, guides, equipment and appliances for travellers. Browse by category, brand, or innovative items or use the search engine. Press the On Sale button for current bargains.
e-mail: not available

Food

Africa

Franschhoek - Guide to the Valley of the Huguenots

www.exinet.co.za/wine2/frshoek/index.htm
This picturesque valley is a premier destination in the World of Wine with some of South Africa's most acclaimed restaurants. Cuisine ranges from Cape Country fare to sublime French.
e-mail: via online form

Tunisian Cuisine

www.tourismtunisia.com/eatingout/cuisine.html
This page highlights Tunisian restaurants on a map. Click on any and the address, phone number and what they serve come up, some with photos. There are also links to pages about the culture, attractions and shopping in Tunisia.
e-mail: info@tourismtunisia.com

Asia

Coca International Restaurant

www.coca-inter.com
A chain of Thai restaurants in Asia and Australia. The home page shows you what they look like and then you can browse menus and pick up other details.

Text is in English and Thai.
e-mail: via online form

DiningAsia.com

www.diningasia.com
A guide to dining in the Asia Pacific Region. Links take you to pages of Chinese, French, American and Filipino food in a range of restaurant types. Presently the site covers some of the countries in the region and is being expanded to include the whole area.
e-mail: via online form

PHOOD.COM

www.phood.com
This simple and easy to use restaurant guide covers fifteen areas around Manila, capital of the Philippines, from fast food to fine cuisine, giving you plenty to feast on.
e-mail: via online form

Restaurantsweb.com

www.restaurantsweb.com
A guide to the very best in Singapore wining, dining and entertainment. There are many sophisticated venues for an evening out, but more exciting are the hawker areas with superb food at low cost where the locals go to eat. Check out the Promotions page for short-term specials. You can book by direct e-mail link.
e-mail: ellen@pace-advtg.com

Singapore Unofficial Food Page - Makan Time

www.sintercom.org/makan/index.htm
Food is one of Singapore's claims to fame. This guide is like an Asian food directory classifying information under a variety of titles including Places to Eat after 12. There are links to Food and Entertainment, an official Singapore Tourism Board guide and a wonderful picture gallery.
e-mail: via online form

Taipei Restaurant Review

www.geocities.com/TheTropics/Cabana/
7031/dining/dine_index.html
Restaurants in Taipei, Taiwan sorted into
eighteen cuisine styles. Click on one and
you get a list, fully detailed with rating,
price, contact information and menus.
e-mail: via online form

The Essential Asian Bar Guide

www.asianbarguide.com
Some 250 bars in eleven Asian countries
are covered by this guide. Information for
each city is organised by district. Contact
details, food, drink and ratings are all there.
e-mail: not available

The Ultimate Bangkok Dining Guide

www.v-media.co.th/dining/
On the home page you will find listings
of vegetarian restaurants and shops,
all kinds of ethnic dining and cyber cafés
in Bangkok. Most listings are garnished
with contact details and photos. Some
restaurants have their own home page
where cuisine, menus and prices are
set out.
e-mail: via online form

Tokyo Food Page

www.bento.com/tf-rest.html
More than a thousand restaurants,
cheese shops, wine bars, bakeries and
pubs in Tokyo are listed on this web site.
You can search the restaurant database
by name, location, cuisine or use the
links to neighbourhood guides. A useful
feature is the list of recently opened
restaurants, with directions on how to
find them.
e-mail: via online form

Tung Lok Group

www.tunglok2.com/index2.htm
This Singaporean company runs a
chain of restaurants. All contact details,
menus, special occasions and pictures
are on the site.
e-mail: GM@tunglok.com

Turkish Turquoise Coast Guide

www.turkuaz-guide.net/index.html
Part of the guide to the turquoise coast
of Turkey is a restaurant directory worth
looking at if you plan to go there.
e-mail: via online form

Australasia and Oceania

Auckland's Dining Inspirations

www.auckland-dining.co.nz
The guide covers restaurants, night
clubs and cafés within Auckland, New
Zealand. Use the navigation bars and
index to search this well-designed site.
You can vote for your favourite
restaurant, add a link and try your
luck in a free dinner draw.
e-mail: via online form

Best Restaurants of Australia

www.bestrestaurants.com.au
Everything you need to know about
food, wine and beer in Australia. The
home page has links to dining in all its
forms and a monthly list of the very
best. For something out of the ordinary,
visit the Best Venue page.
e-mail: admin@bestrestaurants.com.au

Maui Menus - Island Dining Information

www.mauimenusonline.com
Reviews, feature articles and menus
from some of Maui's top restaurants,
from five star hotels to sports bars,
with a monthly recommendation.
Use the restaurant finder navigator
bar on the home page.
e-mail: via online form

Restaurants in Sydney - Australia

ausbiz.com/sydney
Restaurants in Sydney, Australia
listed alphabetically or regionally with
addresses and numbers. There are
links to travel, transport and leisure
in Sydney.
e-mail: not available

Sushinet
Sushinet.com.au
A network of Japanese restaurants in Melbourne, Australia listed alphabetically, by location and rating. You will find contact details and ratings. If you are a sushi lover, check out the other related sites.
e-mail: Sushi@jb2.com.au

Caribbean

Bob Green's Anguilla Restaurant Guide
menus.ai
The cuisine of Anguilla in the Caribbean Islands is representative of the region. From the home page you can access individual restaurants, some of which are good reads. Before heading off there to dine, make sure online that the restaurant will be open, as many close during the low season.
e-mail: via online form

Caymans
www.caymans.com/~caymans/ Restaurants.html
The Cayman Islands web site has a general guide to restaurants. Clicking on a name gives you a picture, a brief introduction to the cuisine, the menu and contact details. You can book online.
e-mail: via online form

Europe

Bradford Curry Guide
dialspace.dial.pipex.com/town/park/ yfr60/
Bradford is the curry capital of Britain. This friendly web site reviews and grades curry houses and locates them on a city street map.
e-mail: via online form

Budapest Week Online Restaurant Guide
www.budapestweek.com/restaurants. html
A guide to major restaurants in Budapest, Hungary classified by cuisine. Each restaurant is briefly sketched with contact details.
e-mail: via online form

Chef Moz Dining Guide
chefmoz.dmoz.org
Restaurants mainly in Sweden and other European countries. Select a city to get a list of restaurants or find the restaurant using the quick search engine. In addition to the usual information, there is a brief review of cuisine, price range, service and ambience. If inclined, you can add your own favourite restaurant to the site.
e-mail: via online form

Curry Central
www.currycentral.co.uk
There are more than 800 curry restaurants in London, England listed by district. Selecting an area gets a list of restaurants with contact details. Items of current news and restaurant reviews make interesting reading. If you want to try out your cooking skills check the recipes, or invest in one of the books recommended.
e-mail: via online form

Eat Germany
www.eat-germany.net
A restaurant guide to Germany with the ten best listed on the home page. The power-find search engine will help you locate restaurants under more than twenty categories, all of which carry details like facilities for the disabled, live music, children specials, outdoor seating and more. Text is in English and German.
e-mail: via online form

Eating out in Greenwich & Blackheath

info.greenwich2000.com/local/ restaurants/eating.htm
Greenwich, England, where east meets west, has numerous restaurants catering to all pockets and palates. Search the web site under style of cuisine. There are links to local entertainment, pubs & bars, accommodation and travel tips.
e-mail: webdirector@greenwich2000.com

La Tasca

www.latasca.co.uk
La Tasca is a chain of Spanish restaurants in the UK. The home page tells you where they are, what they serve and who famously ate there. There is also a link to the San Miguel home page.
e-mail: via online form

Little Chef

www.little-chef.co.uk
This is the UK's premier roadside restaurant chain, of which there are over four hundred in Britain and Ireland. Click on a city and a list of restaurants with locations and contact numbers will appear. Additionally, using the search engine you can locate a restaurant relative to a Travelodge, Burger King, petrol station or disabled access.
e-mail: via online form

Pierre Victoire - Bonjour

www.pierrevictoire.co.uk/home/ default.shtml
To get Pierre Victoire's view of France in the UK, check out this site with more than 25 of his restaurants all over the country. His web site is very informative, with individual pages devoted to his restaurants, menus and food talk.
e-mail: via online form

Resto.be

www.Resto.be
This is the most complete restaurant guide to Belgium with more than 3,000 restaurants indexed by price range, cuisine, city and name. Critics' reviews and culinary contests are recorded on site. You can book online.
e-mail: via online form

The Best World Restaurants Index

www.marlin.co.uk/marnet/restaura.htm
The best restaurants in the Caribbean, Europe, the UK and the US. Clicking on these regions gives a number of choices like reviews, cuisine specialities and others. To recommend a restaurant you like, send an e-mail to the web provider. There are other links worth investigating.
e-mail: via online form

The Dining Guide for Travellers and Food Lovers

citiestodinefor.com
Wonderful eating suggestions at the world's favourite places. There is a choice of seven types of cuisine and a Wild Card. Each city has its unique food featured and each month a new City to Dine is highlighted with its exciting restaurants.
e-mail: via online form

Where to Eat

www.where-to-eat.co.uk/home.htm
A directory of more than 3,500 London restaurants. Four navigation bars at the top of the home page help you find your way around the site. Presently you search by cuisine but in future there will be other search methods.
e-mail: info@where-to-eat.co.uk

World Table

www.worldtable.com
World Table is devoted to travel, food and wine, particularly in France and New York. There is a wealth of information on restaurants, why they are good and details of cookery schools. Two external links take you Digital Hors d'oeuvres and Gourmet Food magazine.
e-mail: Bux@worldtable.com

Latin America

Cancun Menus

www.cancunmenus.com
Overhung with a view of lovely Cancun are a map of the downtown area of the Mexican island and the Restaurant Association. An index guides you to the best restaurants in Cancun. Click on the name and you get contact details and cuisine. Guide books of the island are for sale online.
e-mail: via online form

Puerto Rico - Let's Dine

www.letsdine.com
To complement this restaurant guide in Puerto Rico you get reviews in English and Spanish and a collection of great menus. Add your favourite restaurant if you have one.
e-mail: via online form

Middle East

Restaurant Guide in Lebanon

www.cedarweb.com
A food and entertainment guide to Lebanon which you can search by restaurant name, cuisine, region or budget.
e-mail: via online form

Restaurant@Lebanon.com

www.lebanon.com/restaurants
Two long lists of restaurants in Lebanon, one with local, the other international, cuisine.
e-mail: Info@lebanon.com

North America

Canada's Restaurant Guide

www.restaurant.ca
This beautifully designed web site provides a fine guide to good food in Canada's major cities. Click first on the city link on the home page then select your preferences from the drop down menus. You can also search by alphabetical listing. All restaurants are rated according to quality.
e-mail: cochrane@cuisine.ca

CuisineNet-Menus Online

www.menusonline.com
Here you have a guide to dining out in sixteen major US cities. On the home page, click on a city and a list of restaurants will appear. Each restaurant is given a brief review with an online menu, some accompanied by appetising pictures.
e-mail: via online form

DineBC.com

www.dinebc.com
This is a searchable database of virtually all restaurants in British Columbia, Canada. Present listings exceed 4,700 with daily updates. Search by location, view the menu and take contact details. Submit an unlisted restaurant and you join a free dinner for two monthly prize draw.
e-mail: via online form

Diner City

www.dinercity.com
Go to the map of the USA, click on a State and you get a list of classic diners, roadside restaurants and a photo gallery. You will also find links to cafés and coffee shops, classic motels and gas stations.
e-mail: via online form

DineSite

www.dinesite.com
This guide has information on restaurants in just about every US city. Searching on this site is fun, easy and intuitive. Once you have clicked on a city, you may choose to search under a variety of categories to see how many times a restaurant comes up. A list of most requested restaurants appears for each city daily. There are online

contacts to most of the restaurants listed.

e-mail: via online form

Dining Edge.Com

www.diningedge.com

Dining in all styles in and around Cleveland, Ohio USA. You get a feel of the atmosphere, details of cuisine and entertainment and a lot of books to buy about food and wine.

e-mail: via online form

Dining Metro Restaurant Guide

www.diningmetro.com

Dining in and around Washington DC, USA. Enter any feature of a restaurant, name, cuisine, city and the search engine does the rest.

e-mail: via online form

Eat Here

www.eathere.com

A colourful and informative guide to 550 roadside diners and restaurants in the USA and Canada. You search for the restaurant by state, highway, type of food or keyword.

e-mail: garyandkathy@eathere.com

Hudson Valley Network

www.hvnet.com/TOUR/or/eat/
mexico.htm

Large site, packed with information on travel, drink and cuisine. There are many links to Hudson Valley subjects and a list of Mexican restaurants in the area.

e-mail: hvnet@warwick.net

Kerry's Restaurant World

www.kerrymenu.com

New restaurants, party facilities, wine and special events in some ten major US cities can be searched on this site by clicking either the navigation bars on the home page or the name of city on the map.

e-mail: feedback@kerrymenu.com

Maryland Restaurants Online

www.marylandrestaurants.org

To find a restaurant in Maryland with news and views about dining, gift certificates and discounts follow the simple instructions on the home page.

e-mail: via online form

Menuz

menuz.com

This comprehensive guide of US restaurants has a premier online menu service. By using the quick search engine you get great menus, cuisine, food links, recipes, pictures and more. The reviews help you choose a restaurant.

e-mail: via online form

Metro Milwaukee Dining

www.metromilwaukeedining.com

Over 2,000 restaurants in the Milwaukee region of Wisconsin, USA. The home page has three search engines to find a restaurant by location, cuisine or alphabetically.

e-mail: via online form

Minnesota Monthly

www.minnesotamonthly.com/Dining/
Dining.html

A complete guide to restaurants in and around the metropolitan area of Minnesota, USA, classified by cuisine. Click on a cuisine listing and restaurants appear, each with brief details.

e-mail: via online form

New Jersey's Premier Restaurant and Dining Guide

www.njdiningguide.com

Some of the best restaurants in New Jersey, USA. Reviews are updated weekly with news of weddings and banquets. You can even win a dinner for two.

e-mail: staff@njdiningguide.com

Ohio Dining

www.ohiodining.com

Restaurants in Ohio, USA. You can

search by County, City, Cuisine, Name and Price. Each restaurant is listed with contact details, specialities and menus.
e-mail: via online form

Palm Desert Restaurants

www.palmdesertrestaurants.com
This guide gives what it regards as the favourite restaurants and night-spots in Palm Springs and its environs in the USA. You can check out prices and what you can expect at these places. There are links to the home pages of some restaurants.
e-mail: via online form

Phoenix Linksee.com

phoenix.linksee.com/Dining/
A complete guide to restaurants in Phoenix, USA with more than 150 restaurants and fifteen cuisine styles. Click on the category and you enter the restaurant web page. There are restaurant reviews and links to other dining guides.
e-mail: via online form

Ray's Waterfront

alaska-online.com/waterfront/index.htm
Ray's Waterfront offers innovative Alaskan cuisine, fresh local seafood, in a waterfront setting. External links connect you to other Alaskan subjects worth checking out.
e-mail: not available

Restaurant & Dining Guide

www.mdining.com
Pictures, maps and full menus of restaurants in and around Los Angeles, California. To search, simply click on Restaurants on the home page and lists will appear by location.
e-mail: midining@globalm.com

Restauranteur - An Interactive Dining Guide

www.restauranteur.com
Restaurants in California and Colorado USA. Click on a region and you get a

map of the State. Each restaurant has contact details, menus, dinner give-aways and other enticements.
e-mail: gait@restauranteur.com

Restaurants America

www.restaurantsamerica.com
This web site provides a complete guide to US restaurants nation-wide. In addition to listing restaurants, there are online menus, links to other restaurant guides, restaurant jokes and more.
e-mail: via online form

Richmond Restaurant Guide

www.gatewayva.com/restaurant/
Guide to dining in the Richmond area of Virginia, USA. In addition to a list of great restaurants you get reviews and restaurant links. If you know a good restaurant, add it online.
e-mail: via online form

Steven Shaw's New York Restaurant Review

www.shaw-review.com
Steven Shaw reviews the top restaurants and food stores in New York. He adds cuisine guides to other countries and writes culinary essays, which make enjoyable reading.
e-mail: via online form

The Boston Restaurant Guide

www.bostondine.com
You can search this guide to restaurants in Boston USA alphabetically, by cuisine style or locality. There are lots of good pictures and you can join the site club to receive regular updates.
e-mail: via online form

Toronto.com

www.toronto.com/Toronto/Restaurants_Bars/
A complete guide to restaurants and bars in Toronto, Canada including smoke-free dining and 24-hour eating directories with some good reviews.
e-mail: via online form

Washingtonian Online - Restaurants & Dining

www.washingtonian.com
This wonderful site tells you where to eat well in the American States of Washington DC, Maryland and Virginia. You can search alphabetically, by cuisine, location, price or rating. It lists the hundred best restaurants, food and wine events, where fresh fish is available and lots of other food related information.
e-mail: via online form

Welcome to Applebees.com

www.applebees.com
Casual dining at more than one thousand restaurants in forty-eight US States and eight other countries. Use the Restaurant Locator on the navigation bar to get details of your nearest branch.
e-mail: via online form

Welcome to The Restaurant Guide

www.the-restaurant-guide.com
This vast guide lists almost 300,000 restaurants in the USA. There are menus and entertainment guides and you can add your favourite restaurant to the list.
e-mail: via online form

World wide

Eat There

www.eatthere.com
With the ambition to be the best Internet guide to restaurants world wide, this site lets you search for your choice based on price range, type of cuisine, standard of service and location.
e-mail: via online form

Eat-Out.com

www.eat-out.com
World wide guide to restaurants and cafés easily accessed from lists on the home page. Many have their own links, enabling you to visit them online and

read their menus. You can add to the lists, get free recipes and news.
e-mail: via online form

Ginkgopress

ginkgopress.com
This is an "eat smart" cuisine guide aimed at all travellers. The site sells books about eating abroad, which you can order online.
e-mail: not available

McDonald's

www.mcdonalds.com
McDonald's is synonymous with fast food and this is where it's at. The home page has all the information about the Group and its new franchises. Click on the appropriate region and soon you will cover the world with their outlets.
e-mail: via online form

Myanmar Restaurant Worldwide

www.myanmars.net/people/ restaurants.htm
Information about Burmese restaurants and cuisine in New York, San Francisco, Washington, Hong Kong and Malaysia. There is also some travel information about Burma.
e-mail: via online form

Restaurantrow.com

www.restaurantrow.com
100,000 restaurants in 47 countries and the list grows daily. There are more than five ways to seek out a restaurant, all of which are fully explained. If you register online you will receive e-mail newsletters about the newest restaurants in your town and can book for free at participating restaurants.
e-mail: via online form

Restaurants.Net

www.restaurants.net
This world wide network of restaurants has two search systems, one of which is for the restaurant hunter.

Choose location from the city list,
then cuisine and all is revealed.
e-mail: via online form

Shamash: The Jewish Internet Consortium
shamash.org/kosher/
Kosher Restaurant Database covers
Kosher restaurants world wide and
provides three different search
methods: search for a restaurant,
update information, add new
restaurant. To search for a restaurant,
fill in the blanks in the boxes and
click on Begin Search.
e-mail: kosher@shamash.org

The Sushi World Guide
www.sushi.inforgate.de/
World wide guide to eating sushi.
Together with a new web site at
http://sushi.to. you get a forum for
sushi lovers and Japanese food fans
around the globe. You will find a list of
favourite restaurants, useful expressions
for Japanese meals, a sushi photo
gallery and links to other Japanese
resources.
e-mail: via online form

The Ultimate Restaurant Directory
www.orbweavers.com/ULTIMATE/
Use the search engine on the home
page to find a restaurant world wide.
There are links to specific dining guides
in different cities. You can even remove
a listing, add a guide link or alter
comments about a restaurant.
e-mail: urd@orbweavers.com

VegDining.com
www.vegdining.com
A guide to 700 strictly vegetarian
restaurants around the world. You can
add your favourite restaurant to the
list and join VegDining Discussion
Lists for culinary news.
e-mail: feedback@VegDining.com

Vegetarian Pages
www.veg.org/veg/
The definitive Internet guide for
vegetarians and vegans. The home
page has encyclopaedic information on
food, recipes, nutrition and so on. There
is a useful World Guide to vegetarian
restaurants and resources. You are
welcome to add to the lists.
e-mail: via online form

Zagat.com
www.zagat.com
This friendly guide has more than
20,000 reviews and ratings of restaurants
world wide. First choose a location on
the home page, then search using any
combination of Zagat rating, cuisine,
cost, location and special features.
Registering as a member gets you
special discounts, maps and driving
directions to listed restaurants.
e-mail: via online form

Health

Asia

Bali: The online Travel Guide - Health

home.mira.net/~wreid/bali_p2h.html
The attractive home page lists a guide
to remaining safe and healthy whilst
visiting Bali. All of the major health
risks and diseases are covered, and
where appropriate, advice on treatment
and drugs.
e-mail: not available

World wide

ACEP online - The Traveller's First Aid Kit

www.acep.org/PUBLIC/PI000400.HTM
You need Adobe Acrobat Reader, as the
document is downloadable in PDF. The
helpful two-page guide tells you what to
take when travelling abroad. There is
some information about common diseases.
e-mail: via online form

CDC Travel Information

www.cdc.gov/travel/
This well-designed site has general
health information for the traveller.
Each country has its own health tips
and advice, all of which should be
given due regard.
e-mail: not available

Coping with Jet Lag

travelassist.com/mag/a81.html
One-page practical guide for the
frequent air traveller to cope with,
and hopefully avoid, jet lag.
e-mail: via online form

Diving Medicine Online

www.gulftel.com/~scubadoc/ndxtree.htm
For those going on a diving holiday.
Lots of health advice and information to
keep divers healthy and avoid problems,
from ear infections to biting insects.
e-mail: via online form

Doctor Trish - Travel Health

www.travelinglite.com/health.html
Doctor Trish gives helpful travel health
advice to the discerning traveller. Lots of
tips from food hazards to her top ten
list. Further links give more information
on each subject.
e-mail: not available

Flyana.com

www.flyana.com
This colourful site advises on flight health
issues. Diana Fairchild discusses the hazards
of air travel and offers tips on how to
survive flying, covering subjects like ear
pain, fear of flying, air rage, radiation, jet
lag and more. Other links give passenger
advice, consultations and so on.
e-mail: diana@flyana.com

GORP Great Outdoor Recreation Pages

www.gorp.com/gorp/health/main.htm
Stay Healthy While You Travel is the aim
of this site. Using information from
wilderness survival to dealing with snake
bites, will help the intrepid traveller to
do so anywhere on the planet.
e-mail: via online form

Health Information for Canadian Travellers

www.csih.org/trav_inf.html#top
Although this web site is aimed at

Canadians travelling abroad, the information applies to all travellers. There are tips for before you leave, what to take with you, advice on what to do while away, and when you return home.
e-mail: not available

IAMAT
www.sentex.net/~iamat/mb.html
This web site explains the benefits of becoming a member of IAMAT if you are a regular traveller. Membership entitles you to medical services world wide with charges fixed by IAMAT. The home page has several links - with pictures of creepy crawlies - including geographical areas of risk, maps of malaria risk, where it is unsafe to swim and advice on protection against malaria.
e-mail: via online form

International Travel Healthline
www.travelhealthline.com
Everything you need to know before travelling abroad. Click on Medical Information on the home page to obtain a list of the main health concerns when travelling. Though it does not list health issues specific to countries, it does suggest treatment and medication.
e-mail: not available

Internet Health library
www.internethealthlibrary.com
As the title says, a library of all manner of health resources, with up-to-date health news, information and research. Use the Search facility to find your specific enquiry.
e-mail: not available

ISTM News Service
www.istm.org/news.html
Up-to-the-minute health reports from danger areas around the world, with lists of travel clinics and clinic web sites by country.
e-mail: via online form

Lonely Planet Guide - Health Check
www.lonelyplanet.com/health/
A good health guide for the traveller before, during and after the trip.
e-mail: via online form

MASTA - Medical Advisory Services for Travellers Abroad
www.medicalonline.com.au/medical/masta/index.html
The user-friendly home page has several headings: Travel Diseases, Disease Status Map, General Travel Health, Online Travel Brief and Product Catalogue. Lots of help and information for the traveller with health concerns, and advice on prevention and treatment of the main diseases likely to be caught whilst abroad.
e-mail: via online form

MCW HealthLink
healthlink.mcw.edu/travel-medicine/
If you aren't hypochondriac by nature you should visit this site. If you are, there is a lot of useful information on signs and symptoms, prevention, treatment, and so on.
e-mail: via online form

Outdoor Action Guide to High Altitude: Acclimatisation & Illnesses
www.princeton.edu/~oa/safety/altitude.html
Aimed at travellers going climbing. Help and advice on all aspects of problems related to high altitudes including prevention, treatment and medicines, with links to related topics.
e-mail: not available

Sea Letter - Travel Health Tips by Noel Noren
www.sealetter.com/ Oct-96/tips.html
Specifically for sea travellers, this one-page fact sheet gives onboard health advice and tips.
e-mail: Sharon@sealetter.com

SHC Medical Library - Travel Health & Immunisations

www.byu.edu/stlife/health/library/travel/travel.html
Though aimed at student travellers, the web site is appropriate for anyone. Links take you to Disease Outbreak Updates, Immunisations, Illnesses/Infections, and Medications to Take when Travelling. An e-mail service is available to Ask the Doctor.
e-mail: health-web@byu.edu

Staying Healthy in Asia, Africa & Latin America

www.moon.com/staying_healthy/index.html
This clear, well designed web site has lots of helpful links listed under three main headings - Before you go, Arrival & Preventing Illness, Diagnosis & Treatment.
e-mail: via online form

The International Travel Medicine Clinic

www.hsc.unt.edu/clinics/itmc/contents.htm
Though the home page is uninspiring, there is a lot of useful information and advice on Health Hazards According to Destination, Infectious Diseases, Malaria & Its Prevention, and a whole lot more.
e-mail: jlicciar@hsc.unt.edu

Third World Traveller - Travel Health

www.thirdworldtraveler.com/Travel/TravelHealth.html
Three main links - diseases, health alerts, disease risks and precautions. Take each in turn, then click on the country you intend to visit for a comprehensive list of potential risks and precautions.
e-mail: steve@thirdworldtraveler.com

Travel Health Information Service

www.travelhealth.com
You need Real Player to enjoy this very colourful web site. To see the potential health risks in the country you are visiting, click on the Risk Assessment by Destination link. Further links under General Prevention Guidelines should not be viewed by arachnophobes! Links to world health organisations update you on tropical diseases.
e-mail: via online form

Travel Health Online

www.tripprep.com/index.html
This is a guide to health and safety in more than 220 countries.
e-mail: via online form

Travelhealth - Site Map

www.travelhealth.co.nz/SiteMap.htm
The helpful map-style menu is well designed and easy to use. Click on your choice to find all you need to know before travelling abroad. Diseases are listed alphabetically, as are vaccines, health services and advice. Further links to other related sites.
e-mail: via online form

Travelwise - Travel Health Newsletter

ihtm.11net.com/tw.htm
For the air traveller there are links to Jet Lag Solutions, Staying Healthy in the Sky, Are you safe from Hepatitis A? and Cabin Air Quality for the frequent flyer. Lots of hints and sound advice.
e-mail: burkeyb@mciworld.com

Tropical Medical Bureau

www.tmb.ie/
Travel health information world wide with advice on vaccinations, malaria protection, travellers' diarrhoea, insect bites, survival tips, travel kits, etc. Ask Travel Doctor is an e-mail link for your health query online.
e-mail: via online form

Virtual Hospital

www.vh.org/Providers/Textbooks/TravelMedicine/TravelMedHP.html
Emporiatrics, or the study of travel-related diseases, contains vital

information for travellers. The Travellers With Special Conditions section offers advice to pregnant women, those with disabilities, diabetes, and so on. There are lots of links to other helpful information.
e-mail: librarian@vh.org

WHO - World Health Organisation
www.who.int
WHO is the main authority on world health issues, and also provides information for travellers. The colourful home page has a menu and links. Click on Health Topics for information on diseases and other health issues.
e-mail: via online form

Insurance & Money

Asia

Finance India
www.finance.indiamart.com
This web site is mainly for travellers to and from India. There is a currency converter for rupees.
e-mail: Sales@indiamart.com

Stockk Foreign Exchange Rates
www.stockk.com/forex
Currency exchange rates, updated every 3 minutes, for major Asian countries. There is a menu for other financial information.
e-mail: via online form

Australasia and Oceania

Uni-Care Educational Travel Insurance
www.uni-care.org
Uni-Care specialise in travel insurance for those in education world wide, going to study in Australia and New Zealand. Clicking appropriately takes you to links for Premium Rates, Online Application Form, Policy Features, Rates, Benefits and more.
e-mail: not available

Europe

Bradford & Bingley
www.bradford-bingley.co.uk/homehelp.htm
The Help section on the home page of this UK-based company opens a list of insurance options. Click on the travel insurance button and links will then provide graphs of basic travel insurance costs world wide. There are no online quotes, so try the helpline.
e-mail: bbbs@bradford-bingley.co.uk

Columbus Direct
www.columbusdirect.co.uk
The home page of this attractive, user-friendly site has links to up-to-date news on world wide trouble spots. These specialist travel insurers offer single trip or annual multi-trip quotations with well laid-out jargon explained policies, a help menu and index. Links take you to helpful organisations like the Youth Hostel Association and Expatnetwork.
e-mail: not available

Insuranceontheweb.co.uk
www.insuranceontheweb.co.uk/index.htm
If you complete the online application form they will submit it to an insurer who will then contact you with a quotation.
e-mail: not available

Kingfisher
www.whiteley-insurance.co.uk
Just choose which type of holiday insurance you require from the opening menu - Winter Sports, Single Trip or Annual Trip cover and enquire by dialling the freephone number quoted.
e-mail: not available

Ourway Travel Insurance
www.ourway.co.uk
Travel insurance specialist aimed at the UK traveller. Links offer information and online application forms for travel and

holiday insurance, long or short stay travel insurance, expatriate insurance, working abroad insurance and lots more.
e-mail: admin@ourway.co.uk

Travel Insurance Network

www.travelinsurancenetwork.com
This is a free UK service for requesting travel-related insurance advice. It explains various policies and where to buy them. You can apply online.
e-mail: not available

TSB

www.lloydstsb.co.uk
This site has its own search facility. By typing in travel on the Homepage, you get a list of travel money choices such as ordering travellers cheques, foreign currency and popular destinations. Clicking on Travel, gives you hints on travelling abroad, travel services and insurance, a help line and more. Information on credit cards is also available.
e-mail: not available

North America

Baum Insurance Services

www.healthinsuranceca.com
Travel and other insurance for the American traveller. When you get to the travel insurance page you will find an online form to complete.
e-mail: via online form

Direct FX Online Foreign Currency Exchange

www.foreign-currency.com
This site enables you to order foreign currency over the web from this US-based company. Pay with a major credit card and the cash will be delivered by US registered mail. The main menu contains information on reselling currency, requesting quotes, travel insurance, testimonials,

and more. There are a few travel links.
e-mail: admin@ foreign-currency.com

Laurus Travel Group

www.canada-travel-insurance.bc.ca
They specialise in travel insurance for Canadians and those wishing to visit Canada. The site has an application form and useful links for the traveller looking for an overview of insurance cover.
e-mail: info@laurustravel.bc.ca

World wide

4 Exchange Rates

www.4exchangerates.com
Up-to-the-minute world wide exchange rates with links to a currency converter. This site has its own search facility - select a topic, then enter it in the box at the bottom of the page.
e-mail: not available

All Aboard Benefits

www.allaboardbenefits.com
International short or long-term travel insurance for individuals, families, groups, students, expatriates and immigrants. You can apply online to this US-based company. Click the left menu for a list of user-friendly benefit choices.
e-mail: info@allaboardbenefits.com

Alliance & Leicester

www.allianceandleicester.co.uk/info/index.asp
This UK-based company offers financial services world wide. The Travel Services link on their web site takes you to an Exchange Rate Calculator, Visa Travel Money Card, Money Transfer Checker and Travel Insurance. You will not get online quotes, so try the freephone number.
e-mail: not available

American Express
www.americanexpress.com
Select the Travel option under the Personal menu bar and click the Go button on the home page for information world wide on travellers cheques, flight insurance, how to use your card abroad and book your holiday. There are links to a currency converter, travel tips and advice.
e-mail: via online form

Art Of Travel
www.artoftravel.com
If you want to travel Europe and the world on just $25 a day take a look at this site. There are travel tips, lots of links and help on travellers cheques, credit cards, currency exchange, how to save money on accommodation, flights, food, transport and how to spend your money wisely.
e-mail: not available

ASA
www.asaincor.com
US travel insurance company operating world wide. The home page welcomes you orally. Clicking on International Medical/Health Insurance gives you a list of benefits and an online form which will be automatically e-mailed to ASA.
e-mail: asaincor@aol.com

Bank of Scotland
www.bankofscotland.co.uk/personal/
Go to the dedicated holiday travel page of this UK-based bank, click on Personal on the home page and up come exchange rates, currency calculator, travel insurance, travellers cheques, credit cards, a holiday handbook and more.
e-mail: via online form

Barclays Bank
www.barclays.co.uk/personal.html
By choosing the Travel option in the Service and Site index on this page, you are given several options - Access Your Money Abroad, Travel Money, Travel

Insurance, Service Information, Special Offers and Travel Information. Clicking on appropriate subjects will give you a wealth of information on Barclays' rates for their cards, travellers cheques, foreign exchange and other money matters.
e-mail: not available

Benefit Concepts
www.benefit-concepts.com
These US-based insurers provide travel insurance world wide. There is a lot of information online but if you need more, use the Ask A Question link and the answer will be e-mailed to you. Quotations are available online.
e-mail: sales@benefit-concepts.com

Black Fox International
www.black-fox.com
Instant online quotes and applications for short-term, long-term and group travel insurance world wide. The home page has information on airlines, hotels, car hire and general travel needs. Several links lead you to helpful insurance advice.
e-mail: jc@black-fox.com

Budget Travel Resources
www3.sympatico.ca/donna.mcsherry/
Insightful guide into how to save money when travelling. On the home page, click on The Cheap Like Me Travel Society to find dozens of ways to save money. There are links to Guide To Being Cheap offers with suggestions on how to save on transport, lodging, eating and currency exchange worldwide.
e-mail: not available

CGU Direct
www.cgudirect.co.uk
This UK company offers travel and other insurance. Choose Travel from the left menu or click on one of the links for a single or annual online quote. Forms are simply laid out and easy to complete.
e-mail: not available

Champion Insurance
www.champion-ins.org
Short and long-term insurance for
travellers to the USA. Links lead you
to specific menus with online forms,
tell you how to contact their agents
and request further information.
Some forms can be downloaded.
e-mail: info@champion-ins.com

CIBC Insurance
www.cibcinsurance.com
They provide travel medical insurance
for travellers from Canada. The home
page details the cover and a box to click
for an online application form or quote.
e-mail: not available

City Insurance
www.city-ins.com/travel.htm
When you click on Travel Insurance on
this futuristic style Canadian web site,
you can submit an online application
form. A broker will contact you by fax,
e-mail or telephone and assist you.
e-mail: not available

Cityman Travel
www.citymain-insurance.co.uk
The home page of the UK-based
company is divided into three categories
- Long-Term Travel Insurance, Annual
Multi-Trip Travel Insurance and Single
Trip Travel Insurance. Choose any link
for information and instant quotes.
e-mail: not available

Club Direct
www.clubdirect.co.uk
The UK-based company offer world
wide travel Insurance for backpackers,
winter sports, long-term travellers,
single trip, annual multi-trip, holiday
car rental insurance and European
breakdown insurance. Online quotes
are promised, so for now dial the
freephone number.
e-mail: not available

Co-Op Bank
www.co-operativebank.co.uk
This site has its own navigator and a
table of contents. Click on the Visa icon
and you get a list of Visa options, one of
which is Holiday Club. This shows you
how to save up to 12% on various holiday
costs by using your Visa card, how to use
your card abroad and offers a search
facility for the best available prices. Click
on Personal Banking and you get details
about Travellers Cheques and more.
e-mail: not available

CSA Travel Protection
www.travelsecure.com
US-based world wide travel insurers
with a friendly site offering free travel
information and advice. You can apply
for and receive quotes online.
e-mail: via online form

Currency Converter
**womenswire.com./bloomberg/
currency.html**
Exchange rates from over 200 countries.
It has an easy to use currency converter
a small section on holiday budgets with
question and answer pages.
e-mail: not available

Downunder Travel Insurance
www.downunderinsurance.co.uk
A UK company operating world wide, sets
out travel insurance options. A link takes
you to a map showing where their offices
are with the nearest subway stations. There
is a freephone number. You have several
different travel insurance policies to choose
from, including Adventure Travel,
Backpacker Travel, Comprehensive Travel
and more. There are lots of links and travel
information in this well designed site.
e-mail: not available

Endsleigh Insurance
www.endsleigh.co.uk/main.html
The excellent home page offers a choice
of travel insurance. Choose from

World-wide Traveller, Group Travel, Study Abroad, and Annual Multi-Trip Travel and you will get an immediate online quote.
e-mail: not available

eTravel.org

www.etravel.org
This UK web site has lots of useful information, tips and advice for the world wide budget traveller. There are links to other money matters.
e-mail: via online form

Euro Symbolic Site & Calculator

195583.com
This web site really wants to help you convert the Euro but it will tell you the value of any currency in terms of any other world wide.
e-mail: laurent@pele.org

Exchange Rates

www.x-rates.com
This well presented web site gives currency exchange rates, time-based charts, conversion tables, foreign currency calculator and photos of paper money so you know what you are paying for. Data are gathered from the Federal Reserve Bank of New York daily. You can buy currency online by clicking on the link.
e-mail: via online form

Exchange Rates Central

www.econofinance.com/xrate.htm
This currency converter gives 36 exchange rates world wide. It is easy to use and contains links to other money matters.
e-mail: via online form

Finance Yahoo

finance.yahoo.com
The currency conversion chart is easy to use. Choose the currency of your departure country by scrolling in the left-hand box and your destination country in the right-hand box, then click on Convert and you get today's

exchange rate. There are links to market guides, questions, daily updates and historical charts.
e-mail: not available

HSBC

www.banking.hsbc.co.uk
HSBC, the UK-based bank, offer travel insurance, currency exchange, travellers' cheques and credit cards world wide. Click Holiday Help and Tips and the menu opens; click Holiday Insurance and you get an instant quotation and application form.
e-mail: via online form

International Health Insurance

www.intlhealthinsurance.com
Health insurance designed for the traveller world-wide. You are offered a fast quote facility and online application choosing from three length-of-stay categories.
e-mail: insurance@imglobal.com

Journey Wise Travel Insurance

www.journeywise.co.uk
They cover insurance for all types of travel world wide. The main menu guides you through the following options - Description of Cover, FAQ, online quotes, help information, hints and tips on how to have a safe journey.
e-mail: not available

Kitt Travel Insurance

www.kitt-travel.com/insure.htm
This well designed US web site has links to the full range of travel insurance world wide. You get quotes and can transact online. Clicking on Travel Insurance navigates you through a variety of helpful advice.
e-mail: kitt@kitt-insurance.com

Leading Edge Travel Insurance

www.leadedge.co.uk
The home page gives you a choice of three types of travel insurance world

wide - Backpackers, Annual, or single-trip. However, they cater only for the younger traveller, who must be no more than 39 years old when travelling.
You get online forms and quotes.
e-mail: enquiry@leadedge.co.uk

Moneyworld

www.moneyworld.co.uk
The home page contains a menu of services including Currency Converter, Currency Powersearch, which shows the best performing currencies, foreign exchange rates and tourist rates. By clicking on Guides you get information about travel insurance and credit cards.
e-mail: feedback@moneyworld.co.uk

National Westminster Bank

www.natwest.com
This site has a well laid out home page. In the Personal category, choose Going on Holiday from the scroll bar. This opens a presentation page with options. Either click play or choose an option. Apart from the usual services available - currency converter, holiday insurance, credit cards, travellers cheques - this site provides a holiday calculator which helps you calculate how much your entire trip will cost, holiday money matters and reminders - cash to take with you, making final holiday payments, holiday loans and so on. There is also a choice of tools to calculate air miles, compare credit cards and more. This is a thoroughly useful site.
e-mail: not available

Oanda

www.oanda.com
Offers up-to-the-minute exchange rates on currency world wide. Enter your destination country in the left-hand box and up come today's exchange rates. Type in any date you wish and a helpful Historical Currency Table will show how rates have fluctuated since then. This site also provides foreign currency forecasts,

pricing plans and a timing service.
e-mail: not available

Patrick Leigh Travel Insurance Agency

www.pat-leigh.co.uk
This UK-based company sells world wide insurance cover to anyone ticketed on a scheduled flight to any destination in Australia, New Zealand or Japan. You must apply by e-mail, phone or fax.
e-mail: post@pat-leigh.co.uk

Preferential Worldtrekker Insurance

www.worldtrekker.com/trekhome.html
Under the PDF heading there is a downloadable Document Format which is ideal for viewing documents clearly. Click on the Quote/Buy button for an online quote or transaction. There are links to travel tips, summaries and details of insurance plans available to UK residents only.
e-mail: not available

Priceline

www.priceline.com
This user friendly site helps you save money on hotel rooms and airline tickets by working on a Name Your Price basis. Click on this link and you are taken to a page where you enter the amount you are willing to pay, destination and length of stay, using the calendar supplied. Priceline will supply a list of hotels and other requirements within an hour.
e-mail: not available

Royal Sun Alliance

www.royalsunalliance.co.uk
They offer UK, European and world wide cover with clear geographical definitions, exclusions and an extensive list of options for all your holiday insurance requirements. Their option menus and FAQ are well laid out and you can get quotations online.
e-mail: not available

Sri International & Travel Medical Insurance

www.specialtyrisk.com
These US insurers provide medical insurance to travellers and almost everyone else with instant quotes, which can be transacted online by credit card. There are many useful links: Travel Advisor, Frequent Traveller, Help Desk and others.
e-mail: info@specialtyrisk.com

The Universal Currency Converter

www.xe.net/currency
Small currency converter offering conversion to and from any currency world wide. Click on the link Full Universal Currency Converter for larger amounts. The site is easy to use and instructions are clear.
e-mail: via online form

Tranters

www.ttravelinsurance.com
This well-designed site of UK-based insurers offers a choice of nine travel insurance plans world wide. Prices are tabled but no quotes or application forms are available online.
e-mail: c.tranter@advsys.co.uk

Travel & Holiday Insurance Shopper

www.shopper.ukf.net
This easy to use UK web site offers what it considers the best value travel insurance from those available world wide. Choose your destination on the home page, click and you get an online quote. Other links give you a currency converter, travel tips and advice.
e-mail: not available

Travel Insurance Club

www.travelinsuranceclub.co.uk
UK-based travel insurers world wide, with various policies from backpacking to winter sports. You can download policy documents. Online application forms, premium lists and other

literature are simple and user-friendly.
e-mail: admin@ticltd.co.uk

Travel Insurance Direct

www.travel-insurance.net/index.html
US-based insurers providing travel insurance for those departing from the UK and Eire. Premiums are listed but there is no online form. The Travel Advice option takes you to helpful sites.
e-mail: d.direct@dial.pipex.com

Travel Protect

www.travelprotect.com
This US web site offers to save you 70% on your travel insurance and other transactions world wide. Policy details and premiums are listed through links, but online quotes are not available. Click on Secure Enrolment Form to submit your enquiry.
e-mail: via online form

Tripod

www.members.tripod.com
Clicking the Travel link takes you to a main travel page. Enter Currency Converter in the search box then choose from dozens of currency converters.
e-mail: not available

TTT Foreign Exchange

www.ttt.co.uk
This web site offers Tourist Exchange Rates and Currency Converters as well as Wholesale Note Rates. It also has daily special offers on some currencies.
e-mail: enquiries@ttt.co.uk

UAE Pages

www.uae-pages.com
Click Currency Exchange at the top of the home page and you get a converter for all currency world wide.
e-mail: via online form

Visa Travel Money

www.trwl.com/visa.html
The well-designed web site is part of the

UK-based Thomas Cook Travel Money Services. Click the Services link to take you to further links for Money grams, Foreign Currency, Foreign Cheque Collection, Travellers Cheques and Currency Guides.
e-mail: not available

Worldwide Travel Insurance
www.wwtis.co.uk
This well-presented site is easy to navigate. The home page contains a large choice of travel insurance options world wide, shown with pictures and links. They have options such as Winter Sports Cover, USA Cover, International Cover and more. You get a lot of help and information on this site.
e-mail: not available

Maps

Asia

Free maps of Asia & The Pacific

darkwing.uoregon.edu/~caps/maps.html
Clicking on links on the home page
will take you to maps of countries and
major cities in Asia and the Pacific.
Now click on a city and you get a colour
street map.
e-mail: caps@darkwing.uoregon.edu

Japan Maps

SunSITE.sut.ac.jp/asia/japan/maps/
There is every type of map available for
travellers to Japan from physical features
of the whole country to the Tokyo
Subway. Tourist maps have zoom-in
boxes giving street maps of city centres.
e-mail: not available

Maps of India

209.240.23.10/maps/delhi/index.html
View India with a variety of maps
providing a range of information.
e-mail: not available

Maps of Indonesia

users.powernet.co.uk/mkmarina/
The home page of this well designed
and attractive site presents an atlas of
Indonesia with a list of countries below
in the form of links. You can view a
digital map of the world by clicking

on the right hand link. Diving maps
and sea charts are also available.
e-mail: via online form

Australasia and Oceania

Ausway

www.ausway.com.au
This user-friendly site provides local and
regional maps for Australia, with online
examples for Melbourne and Sydney.
Just enter the street name and suburb
for an online map. Further editions are
available via the online order form.
e-mail: via online form

South Pacific Island Web Atlas

www.usp.ac.fj/~gisunit/pacatlas/atlas.htm
An attractive home page with
photographs and information about
the atlas. Click on Start The Atlas link
to receive a colour atlas of the South
Pacific Region. Click on Region/Island
to receive a more specific atlas.
e-mail: via online form

Europe

European Home Page

s700.uminho.pt/europa.html
Click on any of the European countries
or flags for a map of that country.
Please note that the language will be
of the country you have chosen. The
maps are large and vary in detail.
e-mail: pinj@di.uminho.pt

French Travel Gallery

www.europe-france.com/France/
welcome.shtml
Choose any region of France on this
colourful, user-friendly site by clicking
on the link on the home page.
Alternatively, you can use the keyword
search. There are also plenty of helpful
links for the tourist to museums,
sightseeing and Metro information.
e-mail: via online form

is map
www.ismap.com/geo/adefault.htm
This site is designed for travellers to France. The home page gives you a small map of France showing the different regions. Enter an address in the search box or just choose a city from the scroll menu. There is also a mini overview of the city and a zoom facility. Lots of links for related travel topics, including hotels and shops.
e-mail: info@isweb.com

msn.atlas
maps.atlas.cz
Maps of the Czech Republic and plans of 138 towns. Chose Prague Castle, and you are shown a clear, colour map of the castle. If you want a more detailed street map, enter the name of the street in the boxes provided and press Search.
e-mail: not available

Multimap
uk.multimap.com/map/places.cgi/
Detailed and colourful online maps of the UK. Lists of local hotels, tourist attractions, pubs and restaurants are also given. Choose by place name, postcode, street or grid reference. World maps are also available - just enter the place name and country.
e-mail: not available

National Atlas of Sweden
www.sna.se/e_index.html
Click on Web Atlas on the home page to receive a choice of 4 types of map. Choose Map of Sweden and you are given three locations that you can zoom into for regional maps showing major routes, towns, and cities. Further tourist links are also available.
e-mail: info@sna.se.

Ordnance Survey
www.ordsvy.gov.uk/home/index.html
Ordnance Survey is a long established government body that has mapped the whole UK. There are sections to help you find a specific map, sites for education, products and services, news and events, jobs and more. Type in the postcode and Get a Map gives you a chart of the area. You can order by phone or purchase at retailers, all of whom are listed.
e-mail: custinfo@ordsvy.gov.uk

Streetmaps UK
www.streetmap.co.uk
UK based street map service. Search by London Street, Postcode, UK Place, Ordinance Survey Grid, Latitude, Longitude, Telephone Code or Landranger Code. Maps are detailed and clear, showing landmarks, railway stations and hospitals.
e-mail: streetfeedback@btex.co.uk

Middle East
www.inisrael.com
www.inisrael.com/maps/
If you are planning to visit Israel, you can download maps of the main cities on this site, provided by Israel's Tourism Guide. You need to complete an online form before downloading any of the maps. There are links at the bottom of the page to accommodation, travel agents and car rental.
e-mail: via online form

North America
Free Trip
www.freetrip.com
Use this fun site to design a custom road route within the USA. Want to take the scenic route? Skip the tolls? Accurate results with distances and driving times are given. There is also an online form to request further information if you need it.
e-mail: not available

MapBlast

www.mapblast.com/mblast/index.mb
US based web site providing maps and
step-by-step driving directions to your
chosen destination. Enter the addresses
in the boxes provided to show a local
map. A zoom-in facility shows you the
details of side streets.
e-mail: via online form

Maps On Us

www.mapsonus.com
Maps of the USA. The home page offers
a choice of Plan Route where you enter
your departure and destination. You can
then choose a map for the fastest route
or best motorway route. The Draw Map
option asks you to enter your destination
to obtain a local map of the area. Zoom
in or out for more detail. Click on the
What's Nearby option for a helpful list
of tourist attractions, restaurants and
shops. Plenty of other helpful links are
available.
e-mail: MapMaster@switchboard.com

The National Atlas of Canada

atlas.gc.ca/english/index.html
Atlas style maps of Canada showing
the major cities and regions. Click on
National Atlas and choose from General
Maps, Economic Maps, or Human
Maps.
e-mail: via online form

The Trip.com

www.thetrip.com/content/airport/index/
Maps of the USA. Choose a state from
the scroll menu. You then have a choice
of three maps - Airport Map, Regional
Map or Terminal View. Regional Maps
show major routes and surrounding
towns.
e-mail: via online form

www.nycsubway.org

www.nycsubway.org/maps/
Maps of the New York Subway. Click on
the links for various suburbs or areas.

You will find lists of all the stations
on any particular line.
e-mail: brakeman@nycsubway.org

Yahoo Maps

maps.yahoo.com/py/maps.py#Search
A simple, no frills site. Just type in the
address and city in the USA and Yahoo
will provide you with a local map
pinpointing the address given. Links for
local hotels, railway stations, restaurants
and traffic information are available.
e-mail: not available

Zip2.com

**www.zip2.com/scripts/staticpage.dll?ep
=9002&ck=&adrVer=-1&ver=d3.0**
Click on the links for directions and
maps of the USA. When you have found
your desired map, you can request
directions on how to get from point A
to point B, choosing between the fastest
or shortest route. Clear directions are
given, including another map showing
the suggested route.
e-mail: not available

World wide

Altapedia online

www.atlapedia.com
Full colour physical and political maps
of the world including lots of information
about the country you are visiting on
this attractive, easy to use site.
A search facility and regional maps
are available.
e-mail: via online form

ArcData Online

**www.esri.com/data/online/
quickmap.html**
For the USA, enter the addresses in the
boxes provided for a local map of each
area. For international destinations,
enter the name of the country to obtain
a less detailed atlas-style map showing
its major cities.
e-mail: aoteam@esri.com

De LORME

www.delorme.com/CyberMaps/
De LORME Cybermaps provide a Cyber
Atlas which gives you online maps, and
CyberRouter for route planning and
driving directions in the USA. Click on
each button to give a sample of route
and travel maps. This site also offers
special holiday deals.
e-mail: not available

Elstead Maps

www.elstead.co.uk
You can purchase practically any kind of
map online from this user-friendly web
site. Despatch is promised with 48
hours of ordering. If in doubt e-mail,
Stephen at Elstead and he will help you
find your way around the site.
e-mail: enquiry@elstead.co.uk/

EnviroMapper

**www.epa.gov/ceisweb1/ceishome/atlas/
enviromapper/**
This site is designed for travellers to the
USA. The home page contains a colourful
picture of America. Just click on the
state you are visiting to obtain a state
map. Then choose the town or city and
zoom in for more detail.
e-mail: not available

Euroshell.com

www.shell.com/euroshell/routeplanner/
Route planner for those travelling
abroad by car. Enter departure and
destination, choose whether you want a
normal route description or detailed,
fastest or shortest routes. You are then
shown a map with a table showing road
names and locations. Total distance and
travel time is also calculated for you.
e-mail: not available

Excite Maps

maps.excite.com/world
Type in any address anywhere in the world
and you are initially given a country map
showing the city you have entered.

By selecting the chosen city you can
continue to zoom in until you have a
very localised map with street names.
e-mail: not available

Expedia

maps.expedia.com/quickmaps.asp
Simply enter the name of the city or
town and country to obtain an online
map showing the major routes. Driving
directions are also available, as well as
helpful travel links.
e-mail: via online form

Mapquest

www.mapquest.com
USA online map service which provides
driving directions, maps, local city
guides, travel reports and even travel
deals on cheap hotel bookings. Enter
the destination and choose from Quick
Map or Map Search.
e-mail: via online form

Maps.com

www.maps.com
This site has links for Digital Maps. A
Map Store will sell you securely online a
variety of maps for most of the world -
satellite maps, international travel
guides, atlases and globes, large scale
digital maps, driving and route maps,
gift ideas, antique maps and lots more.
e-mail: info@maps.com

Maps in the News

www.map.lib.umn.edu/news.html
Maps of places that have attracted
recent news stories, good or bad. Find
out where not to ski by checking maps
of European avalanche areas. Areas are
listed by country as links.
e-mail: not available

Maps of the World - University of Texas

**www.lib.utexas.edu/Libs/PCL/
Map_collection/world_maps.html**
Basic, no frills site supplied by The

University of Texas providing world wide maps of islands, oceans, countries and continents. The home page has lists of links with helpful download figures in brackets.
e-mail: not available

MetroPlanet

www.metropla.net/
This site provides maps and pictures of subway networks all over the world. More than 120 cities are grouped by continent. Each continent has a map and by clicking on a city you will obtain a map of the underground system with pictures of stations and trains. Most city pages include links to official or unofficial pages. This site is worth exploring if you ever need to use the metro in a foreign city.
e-mail: robert.schwandl@unforgettable.com

National Geographic

www.nationalgeographic.com/maps/
Attractive atlas style colour maps pinpointing the capital of each country. Enter city in the Find a Place box for more detail, then click to zoom-in.
e-mail: not available

Quick Maps

www.theodora.com/maps/ abc_world_maps.html
Quickmaps' home page lists countries of the world in handy links. Click on each link to show a map of the country. Further links give information on geography, economy and transportation.
e-mail: not available

ReliefWeb

www.reliefweb.int/mapc/
This user-friendly, clear and concise site provides online regional, reference, thematic and country maps world wide.
e-mail: via online form

SkiMaps.com

www.skimaps.com/Archive/us.html
Information for skiers in the USA. Click

on the bar menu to choose which State you wish to visit. You are then given a list of links to ski resorts in the area. The map gives information on the layout of the resort and ski runs. There are also links to snow reports, travel and lodging reservations and resort information.
e-mail: via online form

Streetmap.com

www.streetmap.com
Click on the Streetmaps link on the home page, then the country, the city and you will have a large, clear, coloured street map with lots of detail.
e-mail: info@encyberpedia.com

Subway Navigator

www.subwaynavigator.com/bin/cities/ english
Route finder to help you plan your journey via the subway in over 60 major cities world wide. Simply click on the desired link under the country heading. You then get a visualisation of your route, together with a description of your journey and the best route to take.
e-mail: not available

University of Texas Map Collection

www.lib.utexas.edu/Libs/PCL/ Map_collection/islands_oceans_poles/
Basic, no frills site supplied by The University of Texas providing world wide maps of islands, oceans, countries and continents. The home page has lists of links with helpful download figures in brackets.
e-mail: not available

Virtual Tourist

www.vtourist.com
An excellent site for those travelling anywhere in the world. Lots of travel links and information on the home page. Click on Example for Build Your Travel Page, and you are shown some striking photographs of Capetown, together with all the information you

need for a visit, including Accommodation, Food and Must See Activities. For maps, click on the left-hand links, listed as countries. When the country map appears, you can then click on a region or area for further detail.
e-mail: via online form

World Atlas

cliffie.nosc.mil/~NATLAS/
Maps of countries and islands of the world supplied by NATO. Choose your desired area by clicking on the left-hand links. You are then given a further choice of separate country maps or overview maps. Excellent quality with further links to Images and Cities.
e-mail: not available

World Collection of Railroad, Subway & Tram Maps

pavel.physics.sunysb.edu/RR/maps.html
Alphabetical list of countries containing links to public transport maps. Clear, colourful, well-designed maps with a smaller overview of where you are in the country and further links to take you to regional rail maps.
e-mail: not available

World Timezone Map

aa.usno.navy.mil/AA/faq/docs/ world_tzones.html
Find out the time in the country you are visiting. World Timezone Map allows you to find out the time of any country in the world. It shows a world atlas with a graph giving the number of hours to add or subtract.
e-mail: not available

WorldAtlas.com

www.worldatlas.com/aatlas/world.htm
World Atlas supplies online maps for around the world. Choose from Detailed Maps or Locator Maps. Choosing Detailed Maps gives you a further choice of Continent Map, Country Map or Fact. Atlases, guides and further helpful links are available.
e-mail: not available

Planes

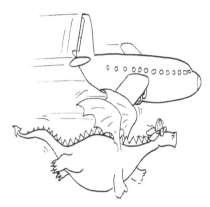

Africa

Air Madagascar

www.air-mad.com
The web site combines booking access to the airline with a travel guide to Madagascar, giving a sketch of the island's history, geography, languages, and climate. The home page has links to travel information, history, cuisine, weather, a list of offices and contact details.
e-mail: info@cortez-usa.com

Air Malawi

www.africaonline.co.ke/airmalawi/
Air Malawi operate a few flights on the eastern coast of Africa and their web site has all the information you need. Flight schedules, special package deals for flights and hotel accommodation and booking form come online. Cargo service costs are also listed.
e-mail: airmalawi@africaonline.co.ke

Asia

Dragon Air

www.dragonair.com
Dragon Air operates a domestic service in China and a small international service to a few Asian countries. The web site has a route map with each city viewable separately. A search facility will take you to flight schedules, fares, holiday packages, cargo services and Frequent Flyer Programme. The airline is based in Hong Kong and all fares are listed as single journeys in Hong Kong Dollars.
e-mail: not available

Druk Air - Royal Bhutan Airlines

www.drukair.com
Royal Bhutan Airways flies between five Asian destinations and claims to be the only airline that flies to Paro in the Himalayas. The whole flight schedule is displayed in one table and reservations can only be made at an office listed on the site. If you want to fly over the Himalayas around Paro be sure to book well in advance.
e-mail: via online form

GMG Airlines

www.gmggroup.com
GMG Airlines flies between six cities in Bangladesh. The flight schedule is tabulated with stopovers en route. Fares are also stated in US Dollars with discounts for children. The Golden Deer Club is their Frequent Flyer Club.
e-mail: via online form

Mongolian Airlines

www.miat.com.mn
Miat, Mongolian airlines operate domestic and a few international flights to Japan, Korea, Germany and Russia. The site contains flight schedules and services, a guide for hotels and e-mail addresses for booking. There are links to tourist information about Mongolia.
e-mail: via online form

Australasia and Oceania

Air Fiji

airfiji.net/
Air Fiji is a domestic carrier operating small aircraft between most of the islands in the archipelago. A map of all

destinations with a timetable is provided. You can book your ticket online but make sure you use the secure payment form as an unsecured form also exists. Groups of 12 or more have a separate web page all to themselves.
e-mail: via online form

Air Nauru

www.airnauru.com.au
The airline of Nauru in the Pacific ocean flies to Australia, New Zealand and several Pacific islands. The web site tells you all you need to know about their operations, lists accommodation on the island and gives an extensive guide to the history of the Republic.
e-mail: via online form

Harris Mountains Heli-ski

www.heliski.co.nz
They operate helicopters in the Harris Mountains in New Zealand, providing skiers with some 400 runs off 200 peaks. The web site has comprehensive guides to skiing, flights, weather and safety. All flights can be booked online by completing a form.
e-mail: hmh@heliski.co.nz

Kendell Airlines

www.kendell.com.au
Kendell are regional carriers for south-east Australia, flying between the states of South Australia, New South Wales and Victoria. It is part of Ansett Australia and you can book online as the link provided transfers you to the Ansett travel desk. The Kendell web site has a route map, a schedule of flights and a page offering a choice of Australian theme holidays such as cruising, wildlife and nature tours, which can also be booked online.
e-mail: kendell@kendell.com.au

Koala Air Safaris Australia

www.koalaair.com.au
On offer are six safari tours in and around Australia and Tasmania. Each tour is fully described with its itinerary and what there is to see. Text is in English and German.
e-mail: moreinfo@koalaair.com.au

Polynesian Airlines

www.polynesianairlines.co.nz
Major destinations across the Pacific Ocean between Australia, New Zealand, Samoa and Fiji are connected by Polynesian Airlines. Details of all destinations and flight schedules are provided but booking must be made through agents or one of their listed offices. There are pages with holiday specials, customer services and destinations, with travel times and fares.
e-mail: enquiries@polynesianairlines.co.nz

Caribbean

Air ALM

www.airalm.com
This small airline serves the Caribbean and a few American cities. In alliance with several other small airlines in the region they run frequent daily inter-island services. Their schedule is online but booking is via agents or one of the listed offices. They also carry cargo and mail and the web site has a guide to beauty spots in the Caribbean.
e-mail: via online form

Fly-BVI

www.fly-bvi.com
This charter service operates a range of aircraft in the Caribbean. There are details of rates, a guide to sightseeing and special interest flights and FAQ section. There is an online availability and request form for booking and a guide to some of the best anchorages in the Caribbean. Fly-BVI is the only airline in the Caribbean to fly to the island of Virgin Gorda, which has several resorts.
e-mail: info@fly-bvi.com

Island Air - Cayman Islands

cayman.com.ky/com/iair/index.htm

They are very small, operating only between the Cayman Islands. In addition to scheduled flights they offer courier and charter services, sightseeing tours and rent hanger space. For contact use the e-mail link or the phone and fax numbers listed.

e-mail: via online form

Nevis Express

www.nevisexpress.com

Day trip shuttle and charter services between the Caribbean islands of Nevis and St. Kitts. There are also sightseeing flights over the volcano on Monserrat. A flight schedule and booking facility are online with contact information.

e-mail: via online form

Europe

Aer Lingus

www.aerlingus.ie

The Aer Lingus web site provides information about their routes with flight schedules, reservations and a frequent flyer program. Information for business and leisure travellers and travel insurance is shown separately. Online booking is not possible but all their offices world wide are listed. Some of these accept e-mail reservations.

e-mail: not available

British Midland

www.iflybritishmidland.com

British Midland operate throughout the UK and fly to many cities in Europe. The online route map tells you exactly where they go. All flights are detailed and can be booked online separately for the UK and Europe, for which links are provided on all pages.

e-mail: not available

Buzz

www.buzzaway.com

Low cost site from the low cost airline with optional extras. Select your destination from the pull down menu and brief details are given about it. You are asked to read the terms and conditions before making an online booking.

e-mail: not available

Go

www.go-fly.com

A low cost subsidiary of British Airways with flights to popular European destinations. There are eight pages of news, special offers, online booking, hotels, insurance, car hire, destinations, route map, flights, why fly Go and travel agents. An e-mail service will inform you of all current offers. Text is in several languages.

e-mail: via online form

Ryanair

www.ryanair.com

They provide budget no frills flights to the UK, Ireland and Europe. A simple site with flight schedules, route map and current Hot Deals. Booking is by telephone.

e-mail: not available

Spanair

www.spanair.com/uk/index.asp

Spanair operate mainly within Spain, the Balearic and Canary Isles. To book online you must apply for a PIN to access this service. The site has flight schedules and destination guides, route maps and links to sites of interest at each destination. Text is in English and Spanish.

e-mail: not available

Latin America

Copa Airlines

www.copaair.com

Based in Panama, Copa Airlines operate between thirty major destinations in twenty countries in the Americas. There

is a route map, flight schedule and seating plans. Bookings can be made through agents or one of the listed offices. They offer package holidays, as well as cargo and courier services.
e-mail: via online form

Maya Airways

www.mayaairways.com
The domestic carrier for Belize operates between seven destinations in the country. The flight schedule, details of each airport and a booking facility come online. You also get information and a home page about Belize by natural light.
e-mail: mayaair@btl.net

Travel Air

www.centralamerica.com/cr/tran/travlair.htm
This page is part of the Costa Rica web site. Travel Air fly domestic services only and the site has a route map and flight schedules for high and low seasons. Booking and further information are available via e-mail from their San Jose office.
e-mail: travelair@centralamerica.com

North America

Air North

www.airnorth.yk.net
Passenger, charter and cargo services throughout the Yukon, Alaska and North West Territory. All flight, service and destination information is provided with seasonal variations. Their Klondike Explorer Pass allows travel anywhere within the network for twenty-one days at a fixed low fare.
e-mail: airnorth@yknet.yk.ca

Airline toll free numbers

www.princeton.edu/Main/air800.html
This university site, probably constructed as a project, has very useful information. Airlines are listed alphabetically with onsite links to many and a US toll free

number. Other links connect with Internet 800 Directory, Airlines of the Web and discount airfares.
e-mail: airlines@princeton.edu

Alaska Airlines and Horizon Air

www.alaskaair.com
The destinations of these two companies are mainly on the West Coast of the USA, Canada and Mexico. The home page has search facilities for flights, fares, flight status and mileage plans, all on drop down menus. Online information includes destination guides with maps and weather reports, a long list of deals offered by each company including trips to Disneyland, ski packages and California sunshine holidays. You can download flight schedules, as well as book and check in online to speed up the process at the airport.
e-mail: via online form

Colgan Air

www.colganair.com
US domestic carrier operating around New York, Washington DC and Boston. The route map shows their destinations; clicking them gets flight information, car rental, hotels, major attractions, airport details and local links. To book call your travel agent or the toll free number on the site.
e-mail: colganair@aol.com

Mesa Air Group

www.mesa-air.com
They operate in Colorado and New Mexico and by links with other US domestic carriers cover other States. Contact is through a US free phone. Their flight school and company store are described online.
e-mail: Jonathan.Omstein@mesa-air.com

Mexicana Airlines

www.mexicana.com.mx/mx2/english/home.asp
Mexicana Airlines fly mainly within the Americas but alliances with other

airlines take passengers further afield. A search facility helps you check flight schedules by inputting departure and arrival cities and you can book online. The home page has a Mexican City Guide and a booking service for Mexseasun package holidays in Mexico. Text is in English and Spanish.
e-mail: helpus@mexicana.com

Scenic Airways
www.scenic.com
See the great US national parks from the air, or be transported there by plane. A tour map shows their operations in south-western USA. Several other web pages include links, discounts, and shopping. All contact numbers are provided. You can book online. Text is in English and Japanese.
e-mail: res@scenic.com

South West Airlines
www.iflyswa.com
Southwest Airlines is a domestic carrier that flies to most south-western US destinations. The web site is clearly laid out and easy to use with various online services listed across the top of the home page. These include flight reservations and schedules, fares, special deals and details of their frequent flyer club. Booking online is possible. A link takes you to their vacation company.
e-mail: not available

World wide

Aeroflot
www.aeroflot.com
Aeroflot's new web site has a lot more information than destinations and flight schedules. They list their offices in Russia and the USA, advise on obtaining visas for Russia, provide links to features about the country and explain their connections with Air France.
e-mail: info@aeroflot.com

Air Afrique Airlines
www.airafrique-airlines.com
Eleven African states operate Air Afrique Airlines. Most flights are in western Africa with a few to west European destinations. Drop down menus on the site give you flight schedules, tourist, visa and health guides to the eleven states. You can book through their offices world wide or travel agents and the site tells you how.
e-mail: not available

Air France
www.airfrance.co.uk
The Air France web site has a status page that tracks departure and arrival times of their flights world wide. Their alliances with Delta Airlines in the US and other airlines around the world are linked on the home page. The Frequent Flyer Club has a facility to check your account and a guide to your benefits. Another link takes you to Air France sites around the world with an extensive list of countries and languages.
e-mail: not available

Air India
www.airindia.com
The Maharajah symbol of Air India guides you through the large web site. Flight schedules, advanced reservations, aircraft seating plans, seat availability, Frequent Flyer Program, FAQ, destination guides, cargo transportation, in-flight services and a directory of Air India offices all come courteously online. There is a link to their US web site.
e-mail: via online form

Air Jamaica
www.airjamaica.com
Air Jamaica serves the Caribbean islands and several major US cities. The web site has flight schedules and guides to the Caribbean with travel tips and special offers for travellers wishing to island hop. They also offer vacation packages

and sponsor special events.
e-mail: via online form

Air Mauritius
www.airmauritius.com
Air Mauritius claims to operate one of
the best intercontinental flight services
out of Africa. One link on the home
page gives you the weather, their offices
and a destination search. The other
provides flight schedules and online
booking which requires a traveller ID
and password obtainable from the
airline. They operate a loyalty scheme
and cargo services.
e-mail: via online form

Air Nemo
www.geocities.com/CapeCanaveral/4285/
A guide to the airline industry with links
to other sites of interest, such as all the
major airline web sites, airport codes,
related manufacturers and news. Its Air
Bulletin is a weekly newsletter of events.
e-mail: airnemo@geocities.com

Air New Zealand
www.airnz.co.uk
Air New Zealand is a global carrier. On
their well-designed web site you will find
maps showing international and domestic
routes and all their flight schedules.
Bookings cannot be made online but
the site supplies contact details of the
office nearest to you. There are web
pages for all their services, a frequent
flyer program, special offers and cargo
transportation.
e-mail: via online form

Air Seychelles
www.airseychelles.net
The web site reflects the pride the
airline take in their part of the world.
The islands are promoted as a paradise
waiting to be visited. Fares and airline
schedules are available online but you
must book through your local travel
agent or Air Seychelles office. There is

an online guide to airline services and
an excellent guide to the islands with
lots of useful tips.
e-mail: airseychelles@aviareps.co.uk

Airlines of the Web
flyaow.com
A database of air travel world wide with
links to almost 500 airline sites divided
regionally. A Cyberfare search service
finds cheap Internet fares, has travellers'
tips, frequent flyer guide, car rental,
hotels and all-inclusive vacation packages.
You can register and get yourself a
password or just access the site as a
guest. The Faremail service sends you
fare information.
e-mail: not available

Airsafe.com
airsafe.com
Over thirty web pages containing safety
information for airline passengers. The
guides cover subjects from better travel
to safety records of airlines and aircraft
types and books about air disasters with
pages devoted to the airline deaths of
celebrities.
e-mail: not available

All Nippon Airways
svc.ana.co.jp/eng/index.html
The Recreation Room on the web site
has trivia quizzes and downloads for
screen savers. The large site tells you
everything you need to know about flight
schedules, seat availability, in-flight
services, destination and airport guides,
Frequent Flyer Club and a host of tourist
information about Japan. Booking must
be done through their offices or agents.
e-mail: via online form

American Air
www.americanair.com
The AA web site home page gives
immediate access to all services through
five pull down menus including flight
schedules, travel planning, special fares

and corporate information. To book online join the AAadvantage Club free. Booking on the Internet brings benefits along with special fares and complete holiday packages.
e-mail: not available

Ansett Australia

www.ansett.com.au
Ansett Australia run both domestic services and international flights between Australia, New Zealand, Japan and Fiji. Drop down menus list their services and the Travel desk will help you check flight details and book online. As an additional service Ansett offer holidays, airport transfers, valet parking and a frequent flyers club. The home page has links to special offers, flights and an arrangement with the new Disney studio in Australia.
e-mail: via online form

Austrian Airlines

www.aua.com
Use the drop down menus and search engine for flight schedules and planner, weather, special offers, a travel guide and online booking. A Jetshop, FAQ and list of their offices world wide take up other pages.
e-mail: not available

British Airways

www.british-airways.com
British Airways is one of the largest airlines in operation and their web site is suitably matched in size. Information includes flight schedules, arrival and departure times, airport details and world offers from the UK. There are pages for their frequent flyer club, Concorde, travel Q and A, holiday booking services, travel insurance for UK residents, a virtual tour of their new terrace lounges using Quicktime, city guides and a list of their web sites around the world. My Travelspace is the online booking service; to use it you must register for a log-in

name and password.
e-mail: not available

BWIA International Airways

www.bwee.com
BWIA link all the Caribbean islands with a few gateway cities like Miami, New York, Toronto and London. The site has a route map, flight schedule, destination guides and details of three membership clubs with benefits for the traveller.
e-mail: via online form

Canadian Airlines

www.cdnair.ca
Canadian Airlines offer a full online booking service. You can also download their software. You get special rates for booking online and earn points. The site has destination profiles and downloadable route maps to help plan your trip. If you don't have an Adobe Acrobat reader, a link is provided. Text is in English, French, Chinese and Japanese.
e-mail: comments@CdnAir.CA

Cathay Pacific Airways

www.cathaypacific.com
The Cathay Pacific web site is easily navigated with shortcuts to all flight information, schedules, fares and online booking. "Mr Sun" will help you find holiday details and cargo services. Details of in-flight services, a currency converter and destination guides come online. The Frequent Flyer Club, The Marco Polo, allows members to check their accounts online. Links to other Cathay Pacific sites around the world take you to special deals and more information.
e-mail: not available

Cayman Airways

www.caymanairways.com
They fly between the Cayman Islands and link them with Jamaica and a few US cities. A flight schedule and a form requesting fare quotations come online.

You get to join the frequent flyer program on your first flight.
e-mail: not available

Cubana
www.cubana.cu
Based in Cuba they have offices world wide. The web site has an online flight schedule, a guide to the fleet of aircraft, details of their cargo service and a few pages about Cuba. Text is in English, Spanish and French.
e-mail: ecadcom@iacc3.get.cma.net

Czech Airlines
www.csa.cz
This is a vast web site crammed with information. Flight schedules, frequent flyer programs, destination maps, fares and contact numbers for all its offices are listed and you can book online. They help you to book car hire, hotels and entertainment and full vacations through their offices.
e-mail: via online form

Delta Airlines - Skylinks
www.delta-air.com
Their home page has links to all Delta services including online booking, route planning, destination guides, fares and flight schedules on a pull down menu and a Quick flight reservation box for instant fares and flights information. The Frequent Flyer Club is also linked and a special offers service can be e-mailed to you if you wish. The link to their Air France alliance takes you world wide.
e-mail: not available

Easyjet
www.easyjet.co.uk
The Easyjet web site has all the information you need to book any of their many European flights online. There are schedules, fare guides, maps and destination guides. The site has two special links to other services. The first

is Travel Extras, a booking service for car hire, accommodation, car parking and travel insurance, the other, Easyeverything.com is an Internet shop not specifically travel oriented.
e-mail: stelios@easyjet.com

Emirates
www.emirates.com
Based in Dubai, they fly to 47 destinations around this tourist hub. A simple search facility will pick out your flight when you key in your departure and destination. Their special meals, young travellers, group travel and chauffeur drive services are all detailed.
e-mail: via online form

Ethiopian Airlines
www.ethiopianairlines.com
Ethiopian Airways operate within continental Africa and to some destinations in Europe and the Middle East. While the web site is informative about travel in Ethiopia, details of aircraft flown, duty-free goods and special offers, it does not say enough about airline services and routes.
e-mail: via online form

Ghana Airways
www.ghana-airways.com
Ghana Airways operate routes on the west coast of Africa but with alliances offer a world wide service. The web site has details of all flights, fares and information about Kotaka International airport, special deals, tips about travelling in Ghana, communications, visas, local transport, currency and customs and their in-flight magazine.
e-mail: not available

Gulf Air
www.gulfairco.com
Gulf Air operates several world wide routes. Online you will find flight schedules and booking, a guide to in-flight services and route maps with additional

information for each destination. There is a photo gallery and a page with links to cities and travel information.
e-mail: via online form

Iceland Air

www.icelandair.co.uk

World wide services with a trans-Atlantic focus. You can book your flight, car hire and hotels online. Flight schedules, destination guide, special offers and frequent flyer program are detailed. There are guides to Iceland and excursions in Reykjavik.
e-mail: london@icelandair.is

KLM UK

www.klmuk.com

This is the UK division of KLM for people travelling from the UK to the rest of the world. The flight information page has flight schedules and fares and links to Webworld, their online booking service. You can leave a voice message on the phone and they will call back and assist with booking. Details of the frequent flyer program, The Flying Dutchman, are on a separate page as are their own hotel and car booking service and airport directory with check-in guides.
e-mail: via online form

Korean Air

www.koreanair.com

There is an introductory multimedia section, downloadable if your PC is of recent design. The main page has a lot of visually interesting information. The site is split into directories of destinations, flight details and FAQ. Bookit is the online booking service where you find special Internet offers. Skypass is their Frequent Flyer Program; if you register, their web page will be personalised to you each time you log in.
e-mail: via online form

LOT Polish Airlines

www.lot.com/english/

The LOT web site offers passenger and cargo transportation. The travel centre has flight schedules, route maps, online ticket and hotel booking and car hire facilities. You can plan your trip with the destination guide. GOPoland and a link to an Air tours Poland Travel catalogue are useful reading for those travelling to and within Poland. The Frequent Flyer Club gives air mile incentives for booking online. Text is in English and Polish.
e-mail: lot@lot.com

Lufthansa

www.lufthansa.co.uk

Lufthansa have different web sites for each country. This is the UK version and contains flight details of the routes they operate from the UK with some special offers. The schedules which can be downloaded are subdivided into European, International and German domestic flights. The Infoflyway service, for which you must be registered, helps you book online. There is also a frequent flyer program and a travel shop selling Lufthansa merchandise.
e-mail: not available

Malaysia Airlines

www.malaysia-airlines.com

Malaysia Airlines flies to most major world cities where they also have offices. These are listed with a search facility to help you make your travel arrangements as no flight information is available on the web. Apart from giving details of the company and its services the site offers, through a subsidiary, package golfing holidays within and outside Malaysia.
e-mail: via online form

Middle Eastern Airways

www.mea.com.lb

Based in Lebanon, they highlight tourism in the region with special offers for Lebanon appearing on the home

page. A route guide, flight schedules and details of their own holiday company take up other pages on the site.
e-mail: via online form

Northwest Airlines Worldweb

www.nwa.com
You get immediate access to search facilities on this well-designed web site. You can book online, check flight status and download the Northwest schedule if you wish. Their cargo service can be tracked online and the alliance with KLM Dutch Airlines extends their operations around the world. The home page contains promotions, a fast search service for flight booking and trip planning, Frequent Flyer Club and country-specific sites.
e-mail: not available

Olympic Airways

www.olympic-airways.gr
The Greek flag carrier operates world wide and the maps show their extensive routes. A search facility helps you with flight schedules, fares, and special offers. You can access the frequent flyer club by clicking on the distinctive logo. Their in-flight service guide lists entertainment and on board shopping.
e-mail: olyair10@otenet.gr

Philippine Airlines

www.philippineair.com
The web tells you all you need to know about their extensive flight schedules, fares and promotions, route maps with distance and journey times and in-flight services. Other features include a Frequent Flyer Club, cargo services, in-flight magazine, their own tour company and travel tips. You can book at any of their offices but not online. They offer courses in flying and also help if you are afraid to fly!
e-mail: via online form

Qantas Airlines

www.qantas.com
The Qantas web site is packed with airline information and holidays in Australia. Quantim, their Travel Itinerary Manager, contains all their flight information downloadable, at present, only on a PC. Most flights are bookable online except some domestic flights for which you must call the local Qantas office; all their offices are listed with a search facility. Package holidays in Australia are described on a separate page.
e-mail: not available

Royal Air Maroc

www.royalairmaroc.com
Royal Air Maroc have a fairly extensive network of flights from Casablanca. Maps have links to further information on each flight destination. You can book online, get flight information, a guide to business and leisure travel with tips about Morocco, cargo transportation and Safar, a Frequent Flyer Program. Text is in English and French.
e-mail: info@royalairmaroc.co.ma

Royal Brunei

www.bruneiair.com
Royal Brunei Airlines operate in Southeast Asia, Europe and Australia. The site route map shows all destinations. Drag the mouse across the screen and you get the flight frequency to that destination. In-flight services, special deals, the company's own holiday offers and tourism in Brunei come online. An alliance with British Midland extends their routes in Europe.
e-mail: not available

SAS

www.scandinavian.net/
Scandinavian Airways operate world wide. The web site has all the passenger flight and service information you require but the online booking service

is accessible only in Scandinavia. The home page links you to all their services - onboard shopping, flight tracking system and a directory of offices outside Scandinavia with phone and fax numbers. A students' page offers special fares and details of a Travel Pass system.
e-mail: not available

Singapore Airlines
www.singaporeair.com
The colourful Singapore Airlines web site has route maps for all destinations including those of Silk Air, a subsidiary company. Between them they fly all over the world. Flight schedules, online booking and shopping from their own catalogue and Frequent Flyer Club are all accessible on the home page. Other features located in a drop down menu include in-flight dining and entertainment, a guide for Stopover holidays organised through the company and details of alliances with other airlines around the world. For information not immediately accessible a search facility is provided.
e-mail: not available

South African Airways
www.saa.co.za
Online booking is not available but this web site is full of information. Fares and flight schedules, seating plans, a guide to onboard services, Voyager, the Frequent Flyer Club and special deals are all provided. There is a request form for weather details, language and general guidance about local destinations. A map shows their offices world wide.
e-mail: via online form

Sri Lankan Airlines
www.airlanka.com
The Sri Lankan Airlines web site is the home of the renamed Air Lanka. They fly to Asian, Middle Eastern and a few European and Australian destinations. Details of all flights are given on the site

with a directory of offices world wide. Online you will find a Sri Lanka holiday booking service, a guide to in-flight and cargo services.
e-mail: via online form

Swissair
www.swissair.com
The well-designed Swissair web site is full of useful flight information and provides links to several more sites. The two most significant menus provided are their online booking service and travel planner pages. With the first you can book either through the timetables or by budget. The travel planner has pages with flight schedules, price guides, route maps, exchange rates, destination guides and helpful travel links. Additionally there is a page with special deals, a frequent flyer program, a service guide for different travel classes and a travel experience online which streams live onto your computer.
e-mail: via online form

The Air Traveller's Handbook
www.cs.cmu.edu/afs/cs.cmu.edu/user/ mkant/public/travel/airfare.html
This is an online equivalent to a travel handbook. It contains a vast amount of information and direct links to a whole range of other web sites. Each aspect of travel is featured in this guide, with useful extras for travellers handy with a mouse. The site is well laid out and you can add information online if you feel something is missing.
e-mail: mkant@cs.cmu.edu

The Trip
www.thetrip.com
An online booking service and guide for flights, car hire and hotels world wide. It has destination guides, US State and city maps, airport maps, a currency converter and a travel news page. Its engines will search multiple sites to find the best deals with all transactions

possible online. It also has a flight tracker and vacations page for booking complete holidays; you can earn air miles and bonuses by booking online.
e-mail: via online form

Trans World Airlines
www.twa.com
TWA operate routes mainly within North America but through alliances with other airlines they offer flights to many more destinations. You can view their flight information with the option of booking online or just to check availability. Trans World Access is their online booking system for which you require a log-in name and password. Registration is free; all you have to do is fill a short form. The airline also has its own vacation booking service covering North America, Europe and The Ancient World. They also transport cargo.
e-mail: via online form

US Airways
www.usairways.com
US Airways serve the USA, Canada and Mexico extensively and transatlantic routes between these countries and many European destinations. The web site describes all services with fares and schedules, their flight club, which provides facilities in 21 US cities for business travellers and their Air Miles program. You can access the online booking site as a guest but they prefer you to join their Personal Travelworks service; answering a few simple questions gets you a log-in name and password. You can also book car hire and accommodation with special Internet deals.
e-mail: not available

Virgin Atlantic
www.fly.virgin.com
This well-designed site has a home page which lists various regions around the world and asks you to click on your home area. This brings you details about their local services. The information pages include flight schedules, route networks, airport details, arrangements with other airlines, a frequent flyer program, in-flight entertainment, vacations and guides to special offers, weather and currency. You can book online.
e-mail: via online form

Webflyer
www.webflyer.com
This online guide for frequent flyers examines the best ways of earning and using air miles. Incentive programs offered by all the airlines are rated so you can compare their merits. In addition there are fare finder and flight tracking services, chat rooms for frequent flyer discussions, passengers' opinion polls and lots of links to other air-related sites.
e-mail: not available

Trains

PLATFORM 3

Africa

Africa Online - Kenya: News & Information

www.africaonline.co.ke/AfricaOnline/
diary/transport/railway.html
Africa Online is a web site maintained jointly by Kenya, Tanzania, Zimbabwe, the Ivory Coast and Ghana. Railway information is limited to two domestic lines and one international line to Uganda.
e-mail: info@africaonline.co.ke

Blue Train

www.bluetrain.co.za
Blue Train run trains with two classes, luxury and deluxe, on two South African routes: Pretoria-Cape Town and Pretoria-Victoria Falls. The interiors of the trains are displayed, with details of all the services available. The routes and their attractions are amply described with the fares you can expect to pay. Online reservation is possible. A Practical Traveller's Guide to South Africa is full of useful information.
e-mail: bluetrain@transnet.co.za

National Railways of Zimbabwe

www.sunshinecity.net/nrz/railinfo.html
This site has timetables, fares and

telephone numbers for the whole railways system of Zimbabwe.
e-mail: not available

Spoornet

www.spoornet.co.za
Spoornet runs freight and passenger rail transport in South Africa as part of the government owned Transnet company. The site provides train timetables on main line routes but no fares information.
e-mail: not available

Asia

Central Railway (Indian Railways)

www.cr-mumbai.com/menu.html
Indian State Railways site is designed especially for tourists and offers a wide range of services including luxury trains. India's major tourist attractions are listed and clicking on any of them will give you brief information and train timetables to get there. The site contains a map of India and there are timetables for most major Indian cities.
e-mail: not available

China Rail Timetable Index

minyos.its.rmit.edu.au/~tbmlc/btchina/tt/
This page forms part of a web site called Budget Travel China, which provides omnibus tourist information about the country. There are train timetables for major routes in China with a map but not much more about the railway system.
e-mail: not available

JREast (Japanese Railways - East)

www.jreast.co.jp/e/index.html
JREast run the super-express Shinkansen trains in eastern Japan and services between Tokyo and Narita airport. The English language page is designed for tourists. There are no timetables, which suggests that the trains are frequent. Route fares are

clearly stated and each station has its own city sightseeing information. The site has links to European railways, Japanese Ministry of Transport and Japanese National Tourist Organisation. You can download a PDF file with a map of the Greater Tokyo Area showing every JR line and station.
e-mail: not available

Kereta Api Indonesia - Indonesian Railroad
members.tripod.com/~keretapi/
This is an unofficial web site and only the main routes are mentioned. There are timetables and fares, and the e-mail address of Indonesian Railways.
e-mail: indra.krishna@hotmail.com

Quetta - Pakistan Information Gateway
www.geocities.com/Athens/Forum/6182/
This site contains general information about Pakistan. The train section has a timetable for express trains from Karachi to Peshawer.
e-mail: info@anjum.cjb.net

Taiwan Railway Administration
www.railway.gov.tw
The site has train timetables and fares for routes throughout Taiwan. You can order your ticket online but not by credit card. They also offer package tours, each of which is described with prices and itineraries. There is also some information on other services.
e-mail: railway@railway.gov.tw

Unofficial Malaysian Railways Website
members.tripod.com/~KTMB
This unofficial web site provides lots of useful information. You will find timetables, ticket prices, links to the official Malaysian rail sites and useful e-mail addresses. It also links you to Tourism Malaysia, the Malaysian Transport Web Site and the Malaysian

web site search engine. Additional features include maps, pictures of trains and of Malaysia itself, and several travel suggestions.
e-mail: darkcurves@yahoo.com

Australasia and Oceania
CityRail
www.cityrail.nsw.gov.au
Cityrail run the local train services in Sydney Australia and surrounding areas. The site has a map of the regional transport system, timetables and fares for all suburban railways. There are special tourist routes covering major attractions in the area.
e-mail: infodir@ozemail.com.au

Countrylink
www.countrylink.nsw.gov.au
Countrylink run local rail services in New South Wales, Australia. The site has train timetables, fares and lots of information about on-board services. Package holidays are offered with plenty of hotel links. You can book by e-mail.
e-mail: customers@countrylink.nsw.gov.au

Great Southern Railway
www.gsr.com.au
The Great Southern Railway is an interstate Australian organisation combining The Overland, Indian Pacific and The Ghan systems. The site advertises timetables and fares with a currency converter. You can book by e-mail. You have links to maps, souvenir shops, discount offers and media articles concerning GSR.
e-mail: saleagent@gsr.com.au

Puffing Billy
www.pbr.org.au/gembrook/
A simple site giving basic information about this Australian rail company that offers package deals for leisurely group travel and week end breaks along an historic railway line, the "Puffing Billy".
e-mail: gtt@net2000.com.au

Queensland Rail Traveltrain

qroti.bit.net.au/traveltrain/
This site has a railway map of Queensland, timetables and fares for major routes, several rail passes and an Australian version of the Orient Express.
e-mail: qroti@bit.net.au

Tranz Rail (New Zealand Railways)

www.tranzrail.co.nz
Tranz Rail is New Zealand's leading multi-modal transport company, offering an integrated national network of rail, bus and ferry services. The well-designed site offers detailed rail, bus and boat timetables and fares, with a credit card booking option and complete travel packages.
e-mail: news@tranzrail.co.nz

V/line

www.vline.vic.gov.au
V/line run train services in Victoria State, Australia. The site includes timetables and fares for regional and interstate trains from Melbourne, a network map, booking information and a link to VicTrip - a page about transportation in Victoria. They offer interesting holiday packages.
e-mail: not available

Westrail

www.westrail.wa.gov.au
This site gives you timetables and fares for train and bus travel in Western Australia. There is a link to TransPerth Journey Planner, which provides information about Perth Urban transport.
e-mail: westrail@westrail.wa.gov.au

Caribbean

Cuban Escorted Rail Tours

www.amigainternational.on.ca/ CubanRailTours/index.html
A Canadian travel agent and two friends collaborate in this venture which offers rail tours around Cuba's major tourist attractions. The site explains the Cuban rail system, lists timetables, fares and generally informs you about local tourism. Their tours are well described with a photo gallery.
e-mail: cubaman@multiboard.com

Europe

Belgian Railways

www.b-rail.be
The Belgian National Railways (NMBS/SNCB) provide domestic and international rail services. Their timetables include the high-speed trans-European trains like TGV, Thalys or Eurostar, all of which can be booked online. You will find information about all their services and domestic fares, facilities for the disabled and a network map. Text is in English, German, Dutch and French.
e-mail: doccenter@b-rail.be

CFR - Romanian State Railways

www.cfr.ro
CFR is a state company that operates the rail services throughout Romania. The site does not provide any links useful for tourists or online booking but it has a simple search engine with many filters and options. These will take you to domestic and international connections and current ticket prices. This information is hard to come by elsewhere. Text is available in Romanian and English.
e-mail: admin@cfr.ro

Czech Railways

www.cdrail.cz
This is a limited site with little information. But if you specify your route and travel date you will receive full details of trains, connections, fares, journey times and distances.
e-mail: black@datis.cdrail.cz

Eurail

www.eurail.com
The Eurail Pass offers discount tickets and passes valid on the railway systems of most European countries. As the site is still being assembled, little information is available, but you will find a list of participating countries and details about the passes.
e-mail: info@bnl.nl

European Railway Server

mercurio.iet.unipi.it
Although this site is unofficial it is extremely useful to anybody wanting to travel in Europe by rail. It has links to every available railway web site in Europe, most of which are in English, railway timetables and "railfan" pages where you will find pictures of old, modern and high-speed trains.
e-mail: m.van.uden@worldonline.nl

Eurostar

www.eurostar.com
Eurostar is a high-speed train service run jointly by British, French and Belgian railways. The site gives you timetables, fares and explains booking procedures in Britain, Belgium, France and abroad with special offers for frequent travellers. There is a facility to order brochures by e-mail.
e-mail: new.comments@eurostar.co.uk

Ferrovie dello Stato (Italian State Railways)

www.fs-on-line.com
This site is in Italian, English, German, French and Spanish. There is very little station information and few links to web sites in other countries, but you will find some rail connection details.
e-mail: not available

HZ - Hrvatske Zeleznice (Croatian Railways)

www.tel.hr/hz
The official site of Croatian Railways is part of the Telecommunication web site. As a result there is very little information about railways. A map will help you plan your route and train timetables are listed. No fares are quoted. Text is in Croatian, English and German.
e-mail: hz-webmaster@hz.tel.hr

Iarnrod Eireann (Irish Railways)

www.irishrail.ie
The CIE Group of Companies runs the Irish Railways, Dublin Bus and Irish Bus networks. The site provides inter city and suburban train timetables and freight transport information. The Schools page contains general information about the company's services. Other links take you to sites with coach tours, ferry services, government information, the Irish Tourist Board, media, airline and railway services in Northern Ireland and Europe. The site is in Irish and English.
e-mail: INFO@irishrail.ie

MAV - Hungarian Railways

elvira.mavinformatika.hu
Anyone wanting to travel to Eastern Europe by rail from the west must go through Hungary. MAV provides both domestic connections and international links to the Balkans and the former Soviet Union. The site has a search engine with a "no extra fare" option for budget travellers. This allows you to make every possible journey between any two stations on a given day. Clicking a station name or train number will reveal the station timetables or route itinerary. Text is in Hungarian, English and German.
e-mail: mavinformatika@ mavinformatika.hu

NS - Dutch Railways

www.ns.nl/reisplan2.asp
The home page of this site is in Dutch with no links to English pages. However, this URL takes you to a search engine in English from which you can find

information on both domestic and international routes from Holland. All fares are quoted in Dutch Guilders.
e-mail: nsbeheer@twinspark.nl

NSB BAN (Norwegian Railways)
www.nsb.no/persont/index_en.html
As the official web site is in Norwegian without links in English, this URL takes you directly to an English language page. The page has a journey planner with fares and a booking facility may be introduced in due course. Tourists get special offers and railway travel tips.
e-mail: via online form

Portuguese Railways
www.cp.pt
Portuguese State Railways have an official web site, which offers a simple search engine to find you prices and suburban rail connections in all the major cities in Portugal. There are many links to tourist information, accommodation, entertainment, places of interest and bus timetables. A map is provided to help you plan your journey.
e-mail: not available

Railtrack
www.railtrack.co.uk
A timetable for all trains in Britain, covering all the separate train operators, but without prices. You will also find information on fifteen of the major British railway stations.
e-mail: via online form

Renfe (Spanish Railways)
www.renfe.es/ingles/index.html
On this site you can plan your journey in Spain noting any connections necessary between cities. Fares in pesetas and rail services are clearly stated. Timetables come separately for Commuter, Regional, Express and high-speed AVE trains.
e-mail: tcombi@renfe.es

SBB Online (Swiss Railways)
www.sbb.ch
In addition to train and ticket information, SBB Online offers a wide range of e-mail services including addresses for job and house hunting in Switzerland. The home page has links to other Swiss railways, shipping companies and municipal transport as well as current cultural events. Online credit card purchasing is available for domestic and international journeys. Information is provided in English, German, French and Italian.
e-mail: railinfo@sbb.ch

ScotRail
www.scotrail.co.uk
ScotRail operate two Scottish railway systems: North Highland and West Highland. They publish their timetables and fares on this site with a link to the National railway timetable provided by Railtrack. You can book by Credit card or on the phone and take advantage of special offers and City breaks which combine rail travel with accommodation and touring.
e-mail: meenanf.scotrail@ems.rail.co.uk

SNCF French State Railways
www.sncf.fr
The English language part of the site applies only to the section France and Abroad; everything else is in French. Click the tiny British flag at the upper right of the screen and you will find all relevant information and can book your seat, but credit card transactions are not possible. There is information about refunds and discounts, general travel, on-board services for the disabled and children and addresses of travel bureaux abroad that represent them.
e-mail: webcom@sncf.fr

TagplusGuiden
www.samtrafiken.com
The official Swedish railways site is in Swedish. TagplusGuiden is in English

and combines travel and connections by rail, bus and ferry in Sweden.
e-mail: redaktion@samtrafiken.se

Thalys®

www.thalys.com

Thalys® is a super express train service run jointly by the German, Dutch, Belgian and French Railways. The site contains ThalysÆ timetables and fares but online booking is available only to Dutch, Belgian and French passengers. Additional features include special offers for travel to Euro Disney or Alpine ski resorts.
e-mail: not available

Thames Trains

www.thamestrains.co.uk

Thames Trains run rail services west and north west of London. The site has a route map and planner via the Railtrack site and online booking is possible. There are links to London Information including a Theatre Guide, British Airways, Heathrow Express and Great Days Out, which makes tour suggestions along their routes.
e-mail: customer.thames@ems.rail.co.uk

Trainline

www.thetrainline.com

Register on this site and henceforth you can buy all your railway tickets for any route in Britain. Tickets come by post in two days so make sure you allow enough time before your trip. All credit card transactions are secure.
e-mail: not available

TravelService

bahn.hafas.de/bin/query.exe/es

This is probably the best site for European railway users. The search engine provides connections to most European countries with an option to choose between luxury and budget travel. Because the German Railways official web site is only in German, this is a

bonus for English speaking travellers; you can check prices and discount possibilities and buy your tickets online by credit card.
e-mail: support@db-fahrplan.de

TTD - Russian Railway Timetables

gamayun.physics.sunysb.edu:8080/5/

This unofficial web site covers most rail connections not only in present-day Russia but also in the whole of the former Soviet Union. The site gives you train timetables for direct travel between stations. Timetables for indirect connections are still being worked out. Because the site is unofficial and inflation in Russia is high, fares are not quoted.
e-mail: dmitry@gamayun.physics.sunysb.edu

Virgin Trains

www.virgintrains.co.uk

Virgin Trains run two rail companies in Britain: West Coast Trains and Cross Country Trains. They offer discounts on all their routes and discounts for booking online through a secure system. The timetable covers connections with all train companies in the UK and a daily weather forecast is provided.
e-mail: via online form

VR - Finnish Railways

www.vr.fi

This is a reasonably good web site with a map of the rail network and information about Finland. There are 30 domestic and international routes, each with an itinerary and timetable, so you have lots of choice. To calculate your fares just type in departure and destination stations. Make sure you take into account all discounts and supplements.
e-mail: not available

ZSR - Slovak State Railways

www.zsr.sk/english/index.html

ZSR is the state-owned company that runs the railways in Slovakia. The

English language section of this web site has a map with links to other European railways. The search engine will help you find rail connections, distances and price information in Slovak Korona. The timetables include all major Slovak stations and mountain trains.
e-mail: gro120@zsr.sk

Middle East

Iranian Railways
www.msedv.com/rai/index_e.thml
This is an unofficial page providing information on domestic and international passenger rail services in Iran. Clicking a city on the site map will list all train traffic to and from and fares payable. There is also some information about Iranian Railways, the Persian calendar and Tehran metro.
e-mail: zenobia@aconet.it

Israel Railways
www.israrail.org.il/english/
Israel has a small but convenient railway system that once followed the coast from Syria in the north to Egypt in the south. The home page is in Hebrew, but this is a link to English pages. There is a railway map and clicking on a station brings up brief information. A route planner provides connection details and fares are given in Israeli Shekels.
e-mail: yariva@israrail.org.il/

North America

Amtrak
www.amtrak.com
This well laid out site has a route planner with connection details and fares. There are national route maps of the West, Central and East sectors of the USA. The whole timetable can be downloaded in PDF format. You are also informed about onboard services, facilities for disabled passengers, travel packages, discounts and travel agents

selling Amtrak services world wide. To book you must first register online.
e-mail: service@sale.amtrak.com

Grand Canyon Railways
www.thetrain.com
Grand Canyon Railways offer tours along the Grand Canyon. There is a guided tour along the route which you can follow on a map, as well as timetables and fares. There is also a link to Farwest Airlines, which operate domestic flights. The railway company has sales agents internationally.
e-mail: info@thetrain.com

MTA
www.mtamaryland.com
MTA run the transportation services in Maryland, USA. They publish timetables and fares for Light Trains, Subway Trains, Buses and the Maryland County Rail service. There are special facilities and fare reductions for disabled passengers.
e-mail: not available

Rocky Mountaineer Tours
www.rkymtnrail.com
On offer are spectacular rail tours in the Canadian Rocky Mountains. All the tours are described with photographs. Booking is not possible online but you will find addresses of their agents world wide.
e-mail: ericb@rockymountaineer.com

The Alaska Railroad
www.akrr.com
The Alaska Railroad company offer passenger services and guided tours. The site contains train timetables and passenger fares. You can download their brochure, covering all services, in PDF format. There is a rail map and an impressive photo gallery.
e-mail: not available

VIA Rail Canada

www.viarail.ca

VIA operate trains throughout Canada from the Atlantic to the Pacific. The web site has a route planner showing connections and fares. Timetables can be downloaded and you can book online by credit card. VIA offer discounts to frequent users. There is a link to Discover Canada, a travel guide to the country. Text is in English and French.
e-mail: via online form

World wide

Trains Unlimited Tours

www.trainweb.com/trainsunlimitedtours/products.htm

Rail adventures with 600 trains on 115 rail systems in 26 countries around the world. Choose from North, Central and South America, Russia and Africa. Tours can be as extensive as you wish. Check the home page to view the trains, choose the tours and note the prices.
e-mail: info@trainsunltdtours.com

Travel Operators

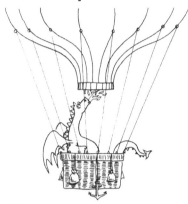

Africa

Abseil Africa

www.millennia.co.za/abseilafrica/
Abseil off the cliffs of South Africa's Cape region. Four major areas cater to this fast growing sport with qualified instructors teaching you the tricks. Check out details, itineraries and prices.
e-mail: Abseil@iafrica.com

Africa Travel net

www.africatravelnet.com
This excellent web site has all the information you can conceivably require to travel to South Africa and other countries in that continent. Everything is easily accessible from links on the home page; follow the links and use the maps and all will be revealed. You can book online.
e-mail: staff@staff.co.za

African Bush Breaks

www.africanbushbreaks.com
They take care of the smallest details of your African vacation, from tours and safaris in the famous games reserves of South Africa to scenic safaris in Kruger National Park. Take your pick from an armful of wonderful trips; online photos show you what they promise. Use the enquiry form for further information.
e-mail: enquiries@africanbushbreaks.com

African Horizons

www.africanhorizons.com/page27.html
Safaris and tours to Eastern and Southern Africa for leisure, incentive, adventure and business travellers with destinations in Tanzania, Uganda, Zimbabwe, Botswana, Namibia and South Africa. All guides are professional with a vast knowledge of local fauna and flora; vehicles are safe and comfortable. Choose accommodation from 5-star hotels to tents.
e-mail: info@africanhorizons.com

Big Five

www.bigfive.com
Luxury mobile camping safaris and elephant safaris in Zimbabwe's top wildlife reserves. Accommodation is in spacious, insect proof, walk-in tents. View wildlife on foot, horse or elephant, by boat or land cruiser with professional guides. There are bushman caves and paintings, the grave of Cecil Rhodes, black eagles, black and white rhinoceroses.
e-mail: info@bigfive.com

Cape to Cairo

www.capecairo.com
A safari specialist for Southern and East Africa. Their tours have delightful names like Okavango, Ngorongro and Mala Mala, which is probably the world's top safari camp.
e-mail: Capcairo@erols.com

Conservation Corporation Africa

www.sandibe.com
The spectacular Okavango Delta with some of Africa's most breathtaking locations, wildlife, exquisite safari lodges, personal service and pan-African cuisine. Tours take you to Victoria Falls, the Serengeti plains, the great Ngorongoro Crater and the southern savannahs. You can book online.
e-mail: not available

DreamWeaver Travel

www.dreamweavertravel.net
Community-based culture and
adventure holidays in West Africa.
Groups are kept small to ensure better
quality experience and preserve local
communities. Tours range from 5-day
whale-watching to 2-week camel treks
among the Tuareg people.
e-mail: Dudley@dreamweavertravel.net

Egypt Tours & Travel

visitegypt.net
Mediterranean cruises and land
tours in the Middle East with a choice
of single and combined country tours.
If you want a special package call
or e-mail. You can book online.
e-mail: info@visitegypt.net

Egypt Tours & Travel Office

123easy.com/gcn/egypttours
You can browse a whole range of tours,
each with a link to detailed description.
Most are in Egypt but some take you to
Israel, Jordan, Syria and Turkey. You can
book online.
e-mail: Egypt@starnetinc.com

Egyptian Connection

www.egyptontheweb.com
Travel services across Egypt. Follow
the links to a range of tours, packages
and travel tips or tailor your tour from
the Custom Packaged Tours Generator
form online. Other links lead to external
pages about Egypt.
e-mail: questions@egyptontheweb.com

Fish Eagle Safaris

www.gorp.com/fisheagle/
More than a hundred guaranteed
departures a year of packaged fly-in
safaris in Botswana, Namibia, South
Africa and Zimbabwe. Groups are small
and the pace is leisurely. You can get
yourself on the mailing list for free
newsletters.
e-mail: exafrica@aol.com

Geosafaris

users.erols.com/pmnet/geo/safari.htm
Small and separate well-appointed
safari camps in the Masai Mara Game
Reserve and Nakuru National Park.
You can safari on foot or ride a camel
to see wildlife found only in northern
Kenya. Trained guides keep you informed
about fauna, flora, and regional culture.
e-mail: geosafaris@iconnect.co.ke

Green Madagascar Tours

www.greenmadagascartours.com
Eco-tourism across Madagascar,
the 4th largest island in the world.
Some brilliant graphics accompany
tour descriptions. Use e-mail for
enquiries and bookings.
e-mail: greenmadagascartours@
simicro.mg

Karell's African Dream Vacations

www.karell.com
Karell do South Africa. The home
page has links to safari destinations,
safari lodges, resorts, package holidays,
information, news and a safari map.
Click on the map and you get a list of
all the destinations in that area, each
with a short description and photographs.
e-mail: eat@sf-escapes.com

Kenya Travel

www.kenya-travels.com
Safaris apparently are not always jeep
mounted. This wonderful Kenyan web
site shows you how else it can be done,
with mountains to climb and coasts to
dive. These are full package holidays
and you can book online.
e-mail: info@kenya-travels.com

Lets Go Safari!

www.letsgosafari.com
African tour operator based in Nairobi
with branches in Tanzania and Uganda
and numerous agents across Africa.
They offer air, road, and camel safaris,
walking tours, mountain trekking,

cycling, horse riding, ballooning,
boating, deep sea fishing, scuba diving,
archaeological and ornithological tours
and beach holidays. Useful links help
you book your hotel and enquire about
restaurants in the area.
e-mail: info@letsgosafari.com

Lotus Travel
www.lotustravel.com
US-based with tours across Egypt.
The menu on the main page lists tours,
each of which has links to detailed
information. You can choose the hotel
or cruise ship and book online.
e-mail: mailto:tours@lotustravel.com

Maridadi MSL Safari
www.africaonline.co.ke/AfricaOnline/
maridadi/maa.html
The Nairobi travel company specialises
in East African air travel, wildlife and
lodge safaris, adventure camping
and beach holidays. There is some
information about Kenya and links
to African sites.
e-mail: maridadi@users.africaonline.co.ke

Motorcycle Tours Southern Africa
comm.lia.net/mctoursa/default.htm
Leisurely motorcycle rides through
South Africa on BMW R100 and
R100RS bikes followed by a support
vehicle with trailer and spare bike.
All accommodation is in comfortable
hotels. The home page has maps of
routes and general maps of South
Africa.
e-mail: mctoursa@pmb.lia.net

MTTB
www.mttb.com/mttb/english/index.htm
Tour operators in Mauritius providing
full travel services and a wide range of
excursions and cruises. They also run
tours to the islands of the Indian Ocean,
Australia, Africa, Asia, Europe and
America.
e-mail: mttb@intnet.mu

Nomade Voyage
www.nomads-of-mali.com
On offer are regular or customised tours
across Mali and Mauritania in West
Africa. Some of the tours are illustrated
on the home page. External links tell you
about visas and vaccinations. Online
tour booking is possible by filling in the
form. Text is in English and German.
e-mail: nomade@cefib.com

Ocean Adventures
www.oceanadventures.co.za
Whale and dolphin encounters on board
a tour boat off the coast of South Africa,
listening to their underwater songs.
These are short tours of two to three
hours; longer trips go further along the
coast for a champagne beach picnic.
These give you the time to look out for
fish eagles, have a walk or a swim.
e-mail: info@oceanadventures.co.za

Orchids' Safari Club
www.ila-chateau.com/orchids/
Probably the finest gorilla watching in
Central Africa. You start your journey in
the family run waterside hotels with
spectacular views over Lake Kivu, then
raft on the Luhoho River, visiting a tea
plantation and pygmy families or
trekking through the dense rain forest of
Kahuzi-Biega in search of lowland gorillas.
e-mail: orchids@ila-chateau.com

RCJM Travel & Tours
www.rcjm.co.za
One stop safari shop for the whole of
Southern Africa, Botswana, Zimbabwe and
Namibia. Select a country link on the home
page for an overview of tours, overland
safari packages and big game fly-in safaris
or choose to have your tour customised.
e-mail: info@rcjm.co.za

South Africa Tours
www.capetours.co.uk
UK tour company with more than 25
years experience in South Africa.

The easy to navigate web site has sections on accommodation, safaris and sports holidays. You can customise your trip if you prefer.
e-mail: CapeTours@aol.com

South African Adventures
www.otc-travel.co.za
Take a look at this South African playground with links to every tour from safaris to mountain hideaways. You can book online with a currency converter to help you.
e-mail: Nasier@iafrica.com

Sunway Safaris
www.icon.co.za/~sunway/
Camping safaris and lodge tours for small groups in South Africa, Mozambique, Zimbabwe, Botswana and Namibia. Links on the home page explain their style of travel and what to expect in Africa. Tours include all equipment, transport and meals.
e-mail: sunway@icon.co.za

Swain Africa Tours
www.swainafrica.com
African lodges, walking safaris, luxury trains and adventure tours anywhere in South and East Africa. Their offices in Africa open round the clock to assist in emergencies. Tell them what you want and they will fax or e-mail you within 24 hours.
e-mail: info@swainafrica.com

Tandem Tours
www.tantours.co.za
Personalised tailor-made tours to Southern Africa for eco-tourism, sightseeing, golfing, 4 X 4 trailing, fly-fishing and hunting. Choose any combination or any other tour and they make the arrangements. Suggested programs are on the home page.
e-mail: tandem@mweb.co.za

The Bosman Safari Company
www.safaris.bw
Big game viewing in Botswana and South Africa in a well appointed private thatched lodge with commanding views of the reserve. Or you can choose mobile safari camping in traditional East African safari tents and hot water showers.
e-mail: safaris@mega.bw

Travel Options
www.traveloptions.com.na
One stop travel shop to Southern Africa and the Indian Ocean Islands for individuals and groups. Home page itineraries are suggested for guidance only. Design your holiday with their advice.
e-mail: via online form

Unique Safaris
www.uniquesafaris.com
Tanzanian wildlife, photo and bird safaris of any type you wish, from luxury to adventure, from lodges to camping, with a dash of cultural and educational experience.
e-mail: uniquesaf@sybernet.co.tz

United Paradise
www.united-paradise.com
They promote holidays and luxury resorts in Tenerife - Island of Eternal Spring. Currently they are marketing three resorts, and services to travellers are inclusive. A visit to the individual resort pages will keep you informed. The Come for Free link invites twenty couples a week to enjoy a holiday in one of the resorts at no charge. To participate in the free draw, complete the form.
e-mail: not available

West African Journey
www.westafricanjourney.com
Immerse yourself in the culture of West Africa in a guided tour with four to ten people. You will see traditional healing

arts, use of medicinal plants and shamanism; music and dance with live concerts, drum expositions and dance lessons; flora and fauna and travel through all three of Senegal's climatic zones - savannah, desert and forest.
e-mail: wwaj@westafricanjourney.com

Asia

AAA India Tours and Travels
www.aaaindia.com
The home page lists their travel services with a range of tours across India. Each tour is detailed with photos and daily programs. All their services are listed in the About Us section.
e-mail: mailto:aaaindiatour@hotmail.com

ABC Travels
www.ABCTRAVELS.com
ABC Travels, with offices in Bombay, Delhi, London and Houston, specialise in Indian holiday resorts. The home page has links to information on airlines, car rental and accommodation. They offer complete tour packages and cruises. You can book online, take advantage of special offers and download a visa application form on the home page.
e-mail: Holidaylinks.India@ elnet.ems.vsnl.net.in

Absorbtours
www.absorbtours.com
Southeast Asia the way you want to see it with an emphasis on arts, crafts and culture from hand weaving to longhouse habitation. Choose your numbers and the tour will be designed to suit.
e-mail: info@absorbtours.com

Adventure Tours Pakistan
www.atp.com.pk/atp
Adventure tours in Pakistan and other Asian countries. Mountaineering, trekking, jeep, camel and horse safaris, geological exploration and other tours

with full travel support.
e-mail: enquiry@atp.com.pk

Akshaya India Tours & Travels
www.akshayaindia.com
They offer individual, group leisure, incentive tours and corporate travel services, which include conventions, conferences and exhibitions. Their special interest tours take you around the temples, the Buddhist circuit, wildlife safaris, river rafting, yoga and nature cures and more. For more information, use the Contact Form button.
e-mail: Akshind@vsnl.com

Ameriasa Tours
www4.jaring.my/iad/ameriasa/
Apart from full travel services, they offer tours to major tourist areas in Malaysia and outbound tours to South East Asia and the Far East.
e-mail: ameri@po.jaring.my

Asya Tur
www.asyatur.com.tr/turkey/homepage.htm
Turkey's main sites and attractions with a touch of culture and cuisine. Beside escorted tours, they provide services to holiday and business travellers. There is general information about Turkey, its cities and historic sites, immigration formalities, and a bit about the language.
e-mail: incoming@asyatur.com.tr

AT-Philippines
www.atphilippines.com
Travel company with full services for visitors to the Philippines and other major destinations in Asia. The home page has information on places of interest, food, entertainment, transportation, visas and customs information.
e-mail: tess@asiatravel.com

Attalia Travel Agency
www.attalia.com.tr
Based in Istanbul, they cover all aspects of travel in Turkey. Package and customised

holidays, accommodation, city and country tours, yacht charter, car rental and airline ticketing.
e-mail: info@atalia.com.tr

Avarayr Tours

www.avarayr.am

Excursions in Armenia through historical and archaeological sites; hiking, alpine and rock climbing and camping with all equipment provided. They also arrange tickets to the opera, concerts, ballet, museums and festivals
e-mail: Avarayr@arminco.com

Bayazit Tours and Travel

hometown.aol.com/bayazit

Customised tours, yacht cruises and vacation rentals in Turkey. Their package tours are featured on the site with full itineraries. You can book online.
e-mail: bayazit@aol.com

Beltop Travel Service

www.beltop.com

A travel service catering to the non-Japanese speaking community in Tokyo for business and leisure travellers.
e-mail: sales@beltop.com

Borneo Eco Tours

www.borneoecotours.com

Eco tourism at its best in Borneo with jungle and mountain trekking, white water rafting, botanical visits, bird watching, wildlife safari cruises and photography. They are well equipped with land and water transportation. You can order books and videos about Borneo on the home page.
e-mail: Kk2000@srikom.com.my

Burma Expeditions

www.burmaexpeditions.com

This London based company offers tours across Burma, or Myanmar, as it is now known. The site is well organised so start with the virtual tour, then work through the itineraries section, which

has details, prices and maps. The About Burma section leads to external pages with political and travel information.
e-mail: burma@netcomuk.co.uk

China Focus Travel

www.chinafocustravel.com

US company with many tours throughout China. The tours section has links to full details. You can book online and take advantage of special promotions advertised in the new window on site.
e-mail: info@chinafocustravel.com

China Travel Service

chinatravelservice.com

This excellent site specialises in vacations to China and Hong Kong with stop-overs in other parts of the Far East. Services include visa handling, hotel reservations, package tours, business and special interest travel. Their China tours cover the most interesting aspects of the country.
e-mail: info@chinatravelservice.com

China Travel Tibet Tour

www.chinatoursite.com

The China Travel web site offers a wide range of tours across China and Tibet through its Beijing and California offices. Among them are the Silkroad, Ecotours, Chinese cities, Cruises, Tibet tours, and many others including the possibility of designing your own tour. You have more than 30 hotels to choose from. There is an information section that answers every question you may have from dress code to visa applications, with a list of helpful Chinese words and phrases. All bookings can be made online.
e-mail: info@tibettour.com

Columbus Travels

www.indianwonders.com

You tell them where you want to go, what you want to see, how much or little you want to spend and they will tailor your vacation to suit, with a

large measure of the romance and mystery of India.
e-mail: Columbus@bom5.vsnl.net.in

Crystal Holidays
www.crystalholidays.com
Way out adventure and cultural tours in India including a variety of safaris, temples, monasteries and meditation tours plus a host of tours in time for the major festivals.
e-mail: crystal@nda.vsnl.net.in

East Greets West Travel
www.eastgreetswesttravel.com
This is a good China travel web site, offering both package and customised group tours designed to impart Chinese culture and history and to explore its natural wonders at affordable prices. A full travel service takes care of everything.
e-mail: info@eastgreetswesttravel.com

East-End Travels and Tours
www.adventureindia.com
Elephant safaris in Nepal, white water rafting on the upper Ganges, camel safaris in the Rajastan desert, palaces, forts and exotic shopping trips. Every tour package includes airport transfers, good hotels and meals. Trained guides escort you on most tours.
e-mail: eastend@del2.vsnl.net.in

Espirit Du Temps
www.naytov.com/links/esprit/
Fascinating tours in Central Asia - Uzbekistan, Kazakstan, Tadjikistan, Kirgizistan and Turkmenistan. Ancient cities, country cuisine, folk concerts, national costume displays and busy oriental markets come in the packages. Accommodation in the best hotels or a family home if you prefer.
e-mail: espirit@samuni.silk.org

Ever Sun Travel
www.eversun.com.hk
They confirm hotel bookings in the Far East, generally within 24 hours but no

later than three days, consolidate airline tickets, sell tour packages and rent mobile phones.
e-mail: eversun@eversun.com.hk

Everett Travel
www.angelfire.com/biz/everett
Escorted tours in the Buddhist circuit with language guides all over India. They provide all the services of a travel agent.
e-mail: not available

Festival of Asia
www.asiafest.com
Multi-cultured Asia has lots of festivals. Choose your festival travel package either by time of year or destination. Prices and conditions appear in the How to Buy section. You can request a brochure and newsletter online.
e-mail: tour@festivalofasia.com

Friends in High Places
www.fihp.com/index2.html
Trek in Nepal along the teahouses or go on a major expedition. Working with other organisations they offer other adventures in Nepal listed on the home page. Combine your trek with rafting, jungle safaris, balloon rides or spend a night or two on a bare mountain.
e-mail: info@fihp.com

Golden Hill Travel
www.goldenhilltravel.co.uk
Small groups with customised tours in Nepal, India and Tibet. Their treks take you to places you are only likely to see on screen. Take a look at the pictures, itineraries and be tempted.
e-mail: not available

Golf Orient
www.golforient.com
The site says a lot about golf in Thailand. They arrange individual and group vacations for golfers. Select the Vacations page for more about golfing events throughout Thailand. There are

corporate competitions and golf events linked to conferences and exhibitions.
e-mail: golfo@samart.co.th

Himalaya Expeditions

www.himalayas.org
Some of the most challenging treks and expeditions in the Himalayas, Tibet and India. They offer first class equipment, excellent food and professional guides. There is a lot to choose from including orchid & rhododendron tours.
e-mail: not available

Himalayas Treasure & Travel

www.himtrek.com
Whether you take one of their packages or elect to run your own vacation you will experience all the charm and wonder of the Indian subcontinent and beyond. The Trek and Expedition menu gives full details of what to expect. Very impressive photo gallery
e-mail: Govindsh@himtrek.com

Holiday World Tours

www.hwtour.com
The site, which immediately sets the oriental tone, has its main menu divided into four sections, of which Destinations leads to country links across South East Asia. These in turn give information about tours, accommodation and online booking forms.
e-mail: info@hwtour.com

Holly Chase

www.igc.apc.org/hollychase/
Learn to cook in Istanbul and while you're doing so, get a taste of Turkish cosmopolitan cuisine, history, culture, arts and crafts.
e-mail: rumney@uconnvm.uconn.edu

Ilkay Travel Agency

www.ilkaytravel.com
Helicopter cruises, hotel bookings, car rentals and excursions in Marmaris and around Turkey. The excursions offer

contains tours to various places and adventure trips including diving, jeep safaris and white water rafting. All excursions include transfers to and from hotels, guides, all entrance fees, lunch and transport in air-conditioned buses. Descriptions and pictures of each excursion are available.
e-mail: excursion@ilkaytravel.com

Indebo

www.indebo.com/home/index.htm
Special interest groups with a taste for the exotic, educational tours, weddings and fashion shows will all find something exciting in India. In addition their tours in the Himalayas put you where you can look down upon the world.
e-mail: Indebo.India@gems.vsnl.net.in

Indica Travels

www.indicatravels.com
Indian travel agency offering ticketing, ground transportation, inbound and outbound tours, conferences-cum-exhibitions, handling of foreign exchange and passport/visa services. There are seven selected tours to discover India under the Travel Plans page, or you can plan your own itinerary.
e-mail: indtrav@del3.vsnl.net.in

Indodaman Travel

www.indodaman.com
Group travel, package tours, eco-tourism, herbal health, culture, history and archaeology and leisurely adventure in Thailand. The home page contains information about cities and hotels.
e-mail: travel@indodaman.com

Irkutsk-Baikal

www.irkutsk-baikal.com
Several former Soviet Republics are banded together offering a wide range of tours. On the other hand you may prefer to visit the USA, in which case they can help as well.
e-mail: baikalsea@pp.irkutsk.ru

Islands Private Limited

islands-pvt.com
They plan and arrange affordable holidays in the Maldives for honeymooners and water sportsmen at resort islands. Live-aboard diving safaris and game fishing offshore are specialities. You get full travel services and assistance with reception and transfers.
e-mail: islands@dhivehinet.net.mv

Jaltour Online

www.jaltour.co.uk
The home page has links to tours, accommodation and general travel information. Tours are regionally divided; flight details and fares appear in the Flights section. More information and a brochure can be requested online.
e-mail: via online form

Kim's World Travel

www.orientvacations.com
The Great Wall of China or a jungle adventure in Borneo come within the ambit of their Asian tours. Join an escorted tour or take a custom designed individual adventure. Select the Plan Your Vacation page and fill in the information requested.
e-mail: info@orientvacations.com

Kintetsu International

www.kintetsu.com
A great way to visit Japan at budget prices with even better deals for students. Stay with the packages and you'll be all right. You can book online.
e-mail: not available

Maharani Voyages

www.maharanivoyages.com
From culture to bird watching in India, Nepal and Bhutan on a budget. You can book online on this very attractive web site.
e-mail: maharani@nda.vsnl.net.in

Malaysia Travel

www.mta-tvl.com
Discount airfares and complete travel packages to Southeast Asia with each destination page linked to lots on offer. You can book online.
e-mail: not available

Mangga Travel

www4.jaring.my/iad/mtt/
Guided agricultural, adventure and eco-tours in Malaysia including fishing, trekking, diving, mountain biking, climbing and white water rafting.
e-mail: mangga@pd.jaring.my

Mansion Travel

www.mansiontravel.com
Though they offer tours, cruises and airline tickets world wide their speciality is China and South East Asia. Use the hypertext links to check out their tours.
e-mail: info@mansiontravel.com

Mason's Travel

www.masonstravel.com
Full service travel agents and tour operators for the Seychelles. Excursions are mainly sea-based, fishing, diving, yachting and making the most of fabulous beaches.
e-mail: rohit@seychelles.net

Mesra Tours & Travel

www.mesra.com/tour/
Indonesian adventure and eco-tours including rain forest treks, river boating, orang utan watching, bamboo rafting, wild life at Kutai Park, and so much more. All tours have detailed itineraries.
e-mail: mesratours@smd.meda.net.id

Minar Travels

www.minartravels.com
Touring indoors, playing outdoors or a little yoga and meditation in the Indian subcontinent with money saving programs. The web site has a lot to excite you and you can book online.
e-mail: resv@minartravels.com

Modetour

www.modetour.com
All-inclusive package tours and cruises in South Korea. Prices are quoted for the two main groups, City Tours and Korean Tour Packages. You can book online.
e-mail: jkim@modetour.co.kr

Nemekh Tour

www.mongol.net/nh/index.htm
Eco-tours for vacationers, students and researchers. Itineraries cover central and western regions of Mongolia and include hiking, animal watching, mountaineering, horse riding, fishing, hot springs, cross country drives and bird watching.
e-mail: not available

Nepal's Nature Trail Trekking

www.allnepal.com
Treks in Nepal, Tibet, Bhutan and India. The home page has links to tour options, FAQ and travel tips. Use e-mail to get their newsletter. If you need convincing, take a look at the picture gallery.
e-mail: nature@mos.com.np

One Stop Travel Center of Thailand

www.onestop-thailand.com
This large site can be browsed by either choosing a region or an activity. Each regional page has links to hotels, a photo gallery, activities and maps. You can book online. Following the other route takes you to those areas of Thailand most recommended for a particular activity. Links to external pages give you general information about the country.
e-mail: postmaster@onestop-thailand.com

Opus Travel Philippines

opustravel.8m.com
Select a destination in the Philippines, check out what is on offer, type in your enquiries to the agent and click Submit.
e-mail: xan@hotmai.l.com

Pacific Bestour

bestour.smarter.net/index.html
US-based with travel offers across Asia. This excellent site advertises special offers and last minute bargains from a range of tours that can be booked online. There is some useful information about travelling in Asia.
e-mail: not available

Rajjas Tours & Travels

www.rajjas.com
Rajastan has some of the most historic forts, palaces and cities in India. You can see them with professional guides, ride an elephant, eat sumptuously in the manner of the moghuls, all as part of a package. To savour what is on offer take a good look at this elegant web site.
e-mail: rajas@jp1.dot.net.in

Siam PGA Holidays

www.thailandgolf.com
Golf vacations in Thailand with tours as customised as you wish. Packages, all-inclusive with specified rounds of golf on weekdays, can be combined with breaks at locations like the River Kwai, Phuket and Pattaya.
e-mail: contact@thailandgolf.com

Sights of India

www.sightsofindia.com
This is a wonderfully designed web site with beautifully illustrated tours all over India. Information is plentiful and one section gives a general round-up of the country. Book online using the form.
e-mail: sights@ndf.vsnl.net.in

Silk Steps

www.silksteps.co.uk
Tailor made trips throughout South East Asia with a price guide. Tell them what you want, complete the booking form and they will get back to you.
e-mail: Info@silksteps.co.uk

Snow Lion Expeditions
www.snowlion.com
Those with a taste for adventure may want to explore the lesser-known regions of the Himalayas, Central Asia, Mongolia, Indochina and Indonesia. The FAQ section may have some answers for you. Special offers with opportunities to win a free trip are advertised online. The booking form can be downloaded in PDF format.
e-mail: info@snowlion.com

Sovereign Tours
www.sovereigntours.com
Package tours to Southeast Asia and the Far East to suit any budget. They are agents for Thai Airways, Cathay Pacific Airways, Orient Express Trains and Cruises.
e-mail: info@sovereigntours.com

Suma Terra Holidays
www.sumaterra.com
A very informative site about Sumatra, the largest Indonesian island. Adventure travel and eco-tourism encompass a large number of activities. The site's many sections are easy to navigate and you can book tours and accommodation online. Links to external pages are filled with useful information.
e-mail: info@sumaterra.com

Thai Marine Leisure
www.thaimarine.com
They claim to be the largest and most experienced yacht charter agent in Thailand, operating from Phuket. Services include marine brokerage, yacht charter and management. Check out specials of the month and listings of motor and sailing yachts.
e-mail: Info@thaimarine.com

The Savile Turkish Collection
www.saviletours.com
Luxury hotels, private villas with pools, air-conditioned mini-cruises, escorted tours and holidays in Turkey. If you want a treat take a look at this site.
e-mail: info@saviletours.com

The Sitara Group of Companies
www.sitara.com
Small groups along the Silk Route in Central Asia, Iran and Pakistan with a range of cultural, adventure and special interest tours. The Marco Polo Adventures tour goes on jeep and camel safaris.
e-mail: sitarapk@silk.org

The Travel Company
www.phuket.com/tours/travelco.htm
Apart from package tours and hotel reservations in Thailand and Southeast Asia, they offer safaris, elephant trekking, champagne cruises and sea kayaking. Tours take you to national parks, islands, mountains, beaches and villages by a variety of vehicles and occasionally on foot.
e-mail: Travelco@loxinfo.co.th

Tourrs Travels
www.welcometoursandtravels.com
There are more than 250 package tours on offer all over India. You are promised a full travel service including organising conferences and exhibitions. All information, enquiry and reservation forms are accessible from the home page. Take a look at the Photo Gallery and the About India links while you're there.
e-mail: Welcome@md2.vsnl.net.in

Travel Borneo
www.travelborneo.com
You start with an overview of Borneo then the home page shows the tours on offer. There is an online enquiry form, as well as links to external pages for places of interest, hotels and airlines.
e-mail: ikchin@pd.jaring.my

Travel Indochina Online
www.travelindochina.com.au
Off the tourist route in Vietnam, China, Thailand, Laos, and Cambodia. Itineraries are well-paced with professional tour leaders. Groups are limited to fifteen for good tour management.
e-mail: travindo@travelindochina.com.au

Tri Jaya Tour & Travel
www.trijaya-travel.com
They cover all the main tourist areas of Sumatra. Choose your location and the duration of your vacation then book online or ask for more information. You get very attractive rates for hotels in Bali.
e-mail: trijaya@attglobal.net

Turkish Wine Tours
www.turkishwinetours.com
Tour the wine regions of Turkey. There are detailed and well-organised tours listed on this site, with an introduction to Turkish wines.
e-mail: behcet@superonline.com

Uno Tours and Travels
www.unotoursntravels.com
This is a wonderful site for travellers to India. Services are provided for leisure, adventure, nature and health seekers. Possibilities are wide ranging - heritage, temple and pilgrimage tours, beaches and back waters, cruises, forest campsites with wild life safaris, coral reefs, catamaran safaris, nature cures and mud-baths. All the information is online and you can use the Holiday Planner link to tailor your vacation to your needs.
e-mail: mail@unotoursntravels.com

Vacations Tours
www.vacationsindia.com
This excellent web site offers so vast a range of exciting tours and services to the Indian subcontinent, packaged or customised, it seems there is nothing

else you could want to do. There are links to help you explore India and its major cities.
e-mail: Rajive.wahie@gems.vsnl.net.in

Vantage Travel
www.asiaairfare.com
For a cheap ticket to some Asian and European cities, take a look at this web site. Also on offer are package holidays to all major cities in Asia with current specials featured on the home page.
e-mail: sales@AsiaAirfare.com

White Nights
www.concourse.net/bus/wnights/
There are several unusual and exciting tour packages to Siberia, Mongolia and the Golden Ring of Russia, including St Petersburg and Moscow - archaeological expeditions to Siberia, life in a Russian village, cruises to islands in Lake Ladoga and Onega and kayaking in the fjords of Lake Ladoga. Prices are listed for everything on offer including travel from Moscow to Beijing. Information about visas, customs, money, health and safety are accessible from the home page.
e-mail: wnights@concourse.net

World Connections Travel
www.Mindspring.com
As wholesalers of international travel, they consolidate sales for several major world airlines specialising in Asia and domestic travel in the US. Their current offers are listed under the Airfare Special link on the home page.
e-mail: wctravel@mindspring.com

Yuki Tours
www.yukitour.com
Excursions throughout Cappadocia and Turkey with historical, archaeological and biblical tours. Special interest tours include trekking, ballooning and a whole lot more.
e-mail: yukitours@superonline.com

Australasia and Oceania

Activity Warehouse

travelhawaii.com
There are more than two hundred different activities to choose from in Hawaii - sedate dinner cruises to up-in-the-air paragliding. All the major islands have their list of most popular activities offered at discounts, so you would do well to study them. For more information, use the Request Mailouts link.
e-mail: seana@aloha.net

Activity World

www.hawaiiactivityworld.com
A booking service for Hawaiian activities, tours, excursions and attractions day and night. You are advised to review all the options each island offers then make a tentative itinerary so you won't criss-cross between islands.
e-mail: info@hawaiiactivityworld.com

Advance Tours & Travel

www.advancetravel.com.au
Australia and the South Pacific with emphasis on bowling, music and dancing. The other activities include diving, surfing, skiing and sailing. You can join Free Travel Club to receive weekly specials by e-mail. Use the Travel Enquiries link for your questions.
e-mail: Reservations@advancetravel. com.au

Adventure Quest Club Of Australia

www.acay.com.au/~aqca/
Australian holidays out of the ordinary. Small groups explore nature, dive, fish, tour world heritage conservation areas, national parks and the Great Barrier Reef. Key words on the home page highlight all of their activities. You can book online.
e-mail: not available

Aussie Outback Safaris

www.aussiesafaris.co.nz
Safaris and tours for small groups across Australia and New Zealand. They market a range of vacations but encourage you to fashion your own. There is enough information about local tourism and several maps to help you make your plans online.
e-mail: doug@aussiesafaris.co.nz

Australian Splash Down

www.ozsplashdown.com
Action Galore in Australia. The range of activity and experience reflects Australia's sports culture. Services can be as inclusive as you like. Simply complete the information form and consultants will customise a holiday in Australia or Fiji.
e-mail: not available

✗ Austravel

www.austravel.com
Austravel run tours to Australia and New Zealand. They arrange flights, accommodation and car hire and offer discount packages for group travel. You can obtain brochures, visa and travel insurance advice online and phone free for information.
e-mail: ukinfo@austravel.com

austravelinfo @ btinternet.com

Biodiversity Ecology Tours of New Zealand

www.forento.co.nz
Eco-tours for ornithologists, botanists, entomologists and naturalists. If you are of the fellowship or just interested, these tours may have something for you. Field trips take you face to face with conservation, the bio-diversity of New Zealand's coastal, forest and alpine environments, as well as traditional Maori use of plants. Itineraries are flexible and you can see as much of New Zealand as you wish.
e-mail: enquiries@forento.co.nz

Blue Hawaii Vacations

www.blue-hawaii.com
They cover more than a hundred of the most popular resorts on the main

Hawaiian Islands, which are well described on the site. Their expertise is in arranging flights, accommodation and car rental bookings.
e-mail: see@blue-hawaii.com

Classic Voyage

www.classicvoyage.com
The destinations are Hawaii, Tahiti, and the Pacific and clicking on one of three pictures on the home page tells you what's on offer. Packages come by type, duration and price so take your pick. For more information click on the package. There are links to car rental, general information and reservations.
e-mail: info@voyagepacifictours.com

Discover West Holidays

www.discoverwest.com.au
From cars to cruises in West Australia with music to greet you to this excellent web site. Explore your holiday by region, choosing a destination and all will be revealed.
e-mail: web@discoverwest.com.au

Dive Adventure

www.diveadventures.com/png.htm
Australia's leading diving holiday specialist with offices in Sydney and Melbourne. They look after any number of travellers to any destination in the world at competitive rates. Though the South Pacific is their pond they operate world wide. Select your destination from the featured islands on the home page map. Each island link has a list of favoured spots, description of underwater life, temperatures and diving conditions and helpful travel information.
e-mail: Advnture@magna.com.au

Down Under Endeavours

www.downunderendeavors.com
Easy to navigate Australian site with lots of information about travel destinations and tours on offer. The itineraries section deals separately with Australia,

New Zealand and Fiji. There are photo thumbnails which expand when clicked. You can book online in the Ask Us section.
e-mail: DUEndeavor@aol.com

Exotic Paradise Islands

www.hideawayholidays.com.au
Paradise, or the nearest you can get to it on earth, lies scattered all over the Pacific. This Australian-based company offers all-inclusive holidays to the Pacific islands from an Australian departure city or stop-over packages for international travellers.
e-mail: sales@hideawayholidays.com.au

Gondwana Travel ✗

www.gondwanatravel.com.au
Charter and personalised itineraries throughout Australia for holidaymakers and special interest groups. They cater to train enthusiasts and bird watchers, organise educational and eco-trips.
e-mail: info@gondwanatravel.com.au

Haba Great Barrier Reef Adventure

www.habadive.com.au
Snorkelling and Scuba Diving in the Great Barrier Reef, Australia. You can visit two unique reefs daily and get diving tuition if you wish. Contact by e-mail for further information.
e-mail: enquiries@habadive.com.au

Hideaway Holidays ✗

www.hideawayholidays.com.au
Using any Australian gateway city you can take advantage of air-land packages to several Pacific islands at competitive prices. Some of their special deals are exclusive to Internet users. The site has good travel information and package prices.
e-mail: Sales@hideawayholidays.com.au

INTA-Aussie

www.inta-oz.com
Organised tours in Australia and Oceania for all from schoolchildren to

senior citizens. Click on the map of Australia to see what is available in each State. There is also a Gay Line you can contact to speak to a specialist travel consultant.
e-mail: info@inta-aussie.com

Island Hoppers Hawaii Aerial Tours

www.fly-hawaii.com/above/
See the most picturesque places of the Hawaiian Islands by air. The web site describes panoramic flights over the coasts and volcanoes. Prices cover regular, customised and charter flights. If you book in advance, you get a free video of Hawaii's best. You can book online with all major credit cards. The FAQ link is very helpful.
e-mail: flyhawaii@fly-hawaii.com

Island Style Vacations

www.island-style-vacations.com
Honeymoon, dive, snorkel, whale watch or just plain lie on the beach, it seems like the Hawaiian islands were made to measure. The pictures tell you the rest.
e-mail: info@island-style-vacations.com

Kauai's West Side Activities

www.hawaiian.net
A personalised activity planning service for adventures on Kauai. You can choose from helicopter tours, boat tours, hiking, kayaking, scuba diving, snorkelling, whale watching and horseback riding. Fill out the e-mail questionnaire to make a reservation.
e-mail: kauaifun@hawaiian.net

Kiwiland Holiday

www.kiwiland.co.nz
Holidays in New Zealand with the full package of services and an emphasis on doing it by road or rail to enjoy the scenic beauty of the country. Contact the agent for anything you especially want or book online.
e-mail: kiwiland@kiwiland.co.nz

MudMaps Australia

www.mudmaps.com
Explore the Australian outback between Sydney, Canberra and Melbourne in comfort in the company of experts. There are several tours to choose from including Australia's largest National Park, highest mountains, a diversity of landscapes and eco-systems.
e-mail: mudmaps@mudmaps.com

Northern Territory Adventure

www.probemedia.com.au/AyersRock/ ayersrock.htm
Camping safaris and bus tours in Australia for independent travellers and backpackers. Lots to choose from, with some tours accompanied by experienced guides.
e-mail: not available

Overland 4WD Safaris

www.overland.com.au
Trevor and Denise Booth run overland 4-WD safaris across Australia as you have never experienced them before. They take you to all the regular tourist areas, then take off to isolated outback settlements, abandoned gold-mining towns, remote sheep stations and wildlife.
e-mail: Info@overland.com.au

✗ Premier Travel Online

www.premiumgroup.co.nz
Online booking of travel services in Australia, New Zealand and the Pacific. Booking flights, cars and hotels online will be confirmed within 24 hours. Other services include global business travel in all its forms, conference management and freighter cruising world wide.
e-mail: not available

South Seas Adventures

south-seas-adventures.com
They provide adventure tours to many destinations in the South Pacific and live-aboard diving to wrecks and reefs in Fiji and the Solomon Islands. They also

organise weddings and honeymoon vacations. You can book online.
e-mail: Info@South-Seas-Adventures.com

Taka Dive

www.taka.com.au
There is a photo gallery accessible from the main page that will make you want to dive right in. The Australian Taka Dive company specialise in scuba diving tours to the Northern Great Barrier Reef and the Coral Sea. Links from the home page take you to internal pages explaining their day and night diving packages and equipment rental services. You can book online, stating your particular requirements. The web site is also available in Japanese.
e-mail: takadive@taka.com.au

Trans Niugini Tours

www.pngtours.com
Leading inbound tour operators in Papua New Guinea, operating a series of world famous Wilderness Lodges. They are fully equipped with coaches, boats and aircraft linking the lodges. Tours take you all over the country and show you just about everything. They have international offices in the USA, Australia, Japan, Europe and UK. You can book online.
e-mail: Bookings@pngtours.com

Tropical Inspirations

www.tropicalinspirations.com
Inspirational vacations in the South Pacific include a full scuba diving service and other ecology-related vacations. Links on the home page take you to special offers, marine charters, resorts, a photo gallery, weather, currency and lots more.
e-mail: Tropical.Inspirations@juno.com

Caribbean

4allinclusives.com

www.4allinclusives.com
They specialise in Caribbean holidays. Complete the Quote Request form and they will suggest the ideal package for you, or you can do it yourself, searching by Resort or Island. Booking online is not available.
e-mail: service@4allinclusive.com

Best of the Tropics

www.best-tropics.com
Caribbean tours staying in the best hotels, apartments or villas in Turks & Caicos, Dominican Republic, Aruba, Bonaire and the British Virgin Islands. Each island link has descriptions, pictures and a list of resorts. You get full travel services and excursions.
e-mail: info@best-tropics.com

Caribbean Adventure Tours

www.tourcarib.com
Outdoor and eco tours to St. Croix in the US Virgin Islands. Kayaking, photographic and hiking tours are all priced with a list of programs to suit beginners and experts. Instructions and equipment are provided and you can book online.
e-mail: not available

Caribbean Adventures Reservation Service

www.reservations.ky/
Diving in the Cayman Islands with an experienced organisation to guide you. Use the booking form on the home page.
e-mail: reservationky@worlddive.com

Caribbean Yacht Charters

www.caribbean-charters.com
Select your vessel type, crewed or bareboat and cruise the Caribbean. There are packages combining five days ashore with five days sailing on a luxurious yacht.
e-mail: Howya@sprynet.com

Cruz Bay Watersports

www.cbw-stjohn.com
If you are travelling to the Virgin Islands this web site is a unique source of

information. You will find lists of activities, accommodation, maps, travel tips, restaurants, weather reports and a great deal more. The site is well illustrated and practically every beach is described. The accommodation link contains hotels and inns together with private homes, villas and condos for rent, which you can book online.
e-mail: info@cbw-stjohn.com

Cuba Travel

www.cubatravel.com.mx
They say Cuba is in a time warp, where everything stopped with the revolution. There are good diving sites and theme tours that show you the architecture, culture, music and dance of the country.
e-mail: info@cubatravel.com.mx

Grand Bahama Vacations

www.princess-vacations.com
They offer package vacations and outdoor adventure holidays with a good deal of water sports in the Bahamas. You will find all the information you need on the site.
e-mail: not available

Honeymoon Travel

www.honeymoontravel.com
Tying the knot in the Caribbean gets a new twist on this web site. You are offered all-inclusive wedding and honeymoon packages at discounted prices. This also applies to the well-known resorts on the islands. There is a lot of information and you can get an online quote for what you have in mind.
e-mail: not available

Horizon Tours

www.horizontours.com
Horizon Tours specialise in Caribbean vacations, all-inclusive resorts, island weddings and small Caribbean inns. You can browse island packages for Antigua, Aruba, Bahamas, Barbados, Curacao, Grand Cayman, Jamaica,

Puerto Rico, St.Lucia and Turks & Caicos. To make a booking, check availability or request additional information, complete the online form or e-mail.
e-mail: elloyd@horizontours.com

Jamaica & Caribbean Vacations

www.jamaicavacation.com
Fifty fabulous vacations from hundreds of departure cities are on offer in budget Sandals and deluxe Super Club resorts. The home page has links to information about the Caribbean, with a particularly useful Before You Go section containing maps and places of interest. Logging in on the Get a Quote Now and Low Price Quote will get you a response within 48 hours.
e-mail: zoom@ecis.com

Lator Gator Travel

www.latorgator.com
They specialise in Jamaican vacations with an abundance of choice. If you want to venture further you can cruise to Mexico and the Caribbean.
e-mail: info@latorgator.com

Tropical Destinations Travel

www.tdtravel.com
Special offers for the Caribbean. The Diving Index link on the homepage is full of information for those wanting a diving holiday.
e-mail: not available

Uneeda Vacation

www.uneedavacation.com
On offer are package holidays for budget and luxury travel in the Caribbean. Part of the site is still under construction but the Cruise link is fairly informative. Online booking is not yet available.
e-mail: RESERVATIONS@ uneedavacation.com

Europe

À Paris

www.halcyon.com/aparis/
Groups are limited to fifteen on
trips around Paris, Paris-Provence,
Provence-French Riviera and
Paris-Normandy tours. Check the
Future Trips link for information on
forthcoming tours.
e-mail: aparis@halcyon.com

Accent Travel Services

www.travelaccent.com
Specialist holidays world wide with
activities pinpointed to where they can
be done best. The web site is divided
into sections according to activity, with
each having links to tours. One section
is devoted to travelling through Italy,
the company's special interest. Online
booking and a chat line are under
construction.
e-mail: info@travelaccent.com

Acorn International Travel

www.king-creation.co.uk/acorn/
They specialise in travel to Poland and
in particular a year-round fully equipped
luxury coach services to and from the
UK. Their coaches also travel to Russia,
Belo-Russia and Ukraine. If you prefer
to fly they arrange flights, hotels and
travel insurance.
e-mail: acomeuropa@btinternet.com

Agri Tours Ireland

www.agritours.ie
The home page sets out agricultural
tours as part of getting to know the
country. Each tour draws a balance
between study, enjoying the culture of
the people and the scenic beauty of
Ireland. Browse a whole range of tours
and look at some truly charming
pictures. You can specify any special
needs on the online booking form.
e-mail: agrirtoursirl@tinet.ie

All Prague Reservation Bureau

www.aprb.cz
They cater to tourists coming into the
Czech Republic. Their accommodation
database has more than 300 hotels in
Prague, 1200 in the country and more in
castles and fortresses. Within the country,
they take care of all touring, cultural
programs, cruises on the river Vltava,
wine tasting and lots more.
e-mail: Aprb@ctg.cz

Architectour, a Roman Holiday

www.architectour.com
Music and wonderful pictures enhance
this unusual holiday site. You get to
enjoy the architecture and archaeological
heritage of Rome. Itineraries give a
little history and mention forthcoming
events. The accommodation section
helps you find a place to stay and for
additional information, fill the online
form.
e-mail: info@architectour.com

Auto Europe

www.autoeurope.com
Though they specialise in world wide car
rentals with an online booking service,
they also offer discounted airfares and
hotel packages world wide. Check out
the Travel Specials for exclusive online
deals. You can plan your vacation online
or order a brochure. There is a 24 hour
toll free line with a Call Now feature.
e-mail: not available

Balkan Air Tour

www.travel-bulgaria.com/balkanairtour/
index.html
Mountain and sea holidays and tours
with all the necessary equipment are on
offer in Bulgaria. The photographs are
beautiful and the views of the sea coasts
and mountains are stunning. Booking
accommodation is simple and you get
assistance with airports and flight
tickets.
e-mail: bat@travel-bulgaria.com

Battlefield Tours

typenet.com
Sites of battles, mainly in Northern
France. Small groups are taken around
World War battlefields, war graves,
fortifications, museums and sites of
earlier European wars.
e-mail: typenet@europemail.com

Bella Italia

www.bellaitalia.com
The home page is in all major European
languages with all services and tours in
Italy briefly described. There are lists of
restaurants, links to travel agents and a
section on Italian wines. Tours can be
booked by e-mail.
e-mail: info@bellaitalia.com

Bennett Tours

www.bennett-tours.com
Tour through Scandinavia and Russia.
Information is well organised and the
site easy to navigate. In addition to
regular tours you are asked to plan your
own tour. You can request a brochure,
check tour availability and book online.
e-mail: info@bennett-tours.com

Blue Bear Travels

bluebeartravels.com
Leisure walking holidays in the Spanish
Pyrenees for those wanting to enjoy good
local cuisine and to relax in quaint
accommodation after the day's exertions.
Whether the tour is guided or you go it
alone, they offer you the full package with
a variety of walks. Check details online.
e-mail: info@bluebeartravels.com

Brit Tours

www.brittours.com
Small, quality regional tours of Britain
and Ireland. Keeping groups small
allows variation in itinerary.
Accommodation ranges from B & B and
country cottages to elegant town houses.
Check programs on the home page.
e-mail: tours@brittours.com

British Tours

www.britishtours.com
Guided tours of Britain from day-trips
to and out of London, to 14-day themed
tours, Shakespeare Remembered,
Highlands and Islands, the Magic of
Wales and more. They also book
accommodation if you wish.
e-mail: info@britishtours.com

Celestial Tours

www.spiritualtours.co.uk
Spiritual tours of the sacred sites of
Scotland, England and Ireland through
ancient stone circles, fairy mounds,
castles and mystical glens. Tour agenda
are left open so that you participate
in ceremonies, meditations, healing,
channelling sessions and whatever else
which might appear. Check the home
page for itineraries and information
about guides.
e-mail: info@spiritualtours.co.uk

Chronotours

www.chronotours.com
Seminars, congresses and incentive
travel in France for individuals and
groups from 10 to 600. They rent
vintage cars, organise hot air balloon
rides over the Musketeers region,
scooter and bicycle rides or angling
in the Pyrenees with instructors,
all of which are detailed on site.
e-mail: chronotours@chronotours.com

Coast to Coast Packhorse

www.cumbria.com/packhorse
An adventure holiday in Britain,
walking from St. Bees on the Cumbrian
Coast across the magnificent Lakes
and Dales to Robin Hood's Bay on
the Yorkshire coast. Links provide
information on accommodation,
transport, timetables and prices,
whilst a map shows the routes.
An online booking form completes
the package.
e-mail: not available

Corsican Places

www.corsica.co.uk
Corsica solo. Villas with swimming
pools, period village homes, villas by
the sea, apartments and studios in
popular resorts, hotels and auberges.
Programs include water sports, scuba
diving, canyoning, paragliding and horse
riding. All staff speak French and
English.
e-mail: info@corsica.co.uk

Cosmos Holidays

www.cosmos-holidays.co.uk
Cosmos has been offering package
holidays to the British public for over 40
years. The options available are summer
and winter packages and late deals
world wide. Submit your UK post code
and you will be informed where your
nearest Cosmos dealer is. You can
order a series of brochures online.
e-mail: not available

Creative Travel

www.creative.com.cy
Short breaks, theme trips and seminars
in Cyprus with an extensive range of
services. Oenology or wine appreciation,
archaeology, agriculture and a host of
others. Or you can combine Cyprus
with a cruise to Israel, Jordan, Egypt
or the Greek Islands.
e-mail: creative@spidernet.com.cy

CustomWalks

www.customwalks.com
Customised walking and biking trips
for private groups in Italy, France and
Turkey. You go where you want, with
whom you want and when you want
with the finest hotels and cuisine or
budget facilities. You can stay on well
beaten tracks if you check itineraries
on the home page. Use the Contact Us
page to book online.
e-mail: Info@customwalks.com

Dilos - Holiday World

www.dilos.com
Many wonderful holidays are promised
in Greece and the Aegean Archipelago
with accommodation as you like it.
There are cruises in the Mediterranean
and archaeological tours in the region.
Though Greece is the centrepiece, this
site also covers other European countries.
e-mail: reservations@dilos.com

Discover France

www.discoverfrance.com
Tourist services across France, especially
biking tours and France Getaways.
There is an e-mail newsletter you can
obtain by subscription; this keeps you
up-to-date and advertises special offers.
You can also buy the best guidebooks
on France and book tours and hotels
online. There is a link to France Hotels
with information about accommodation.
e-mail: info@discoverfrance.com

DiVine Tours

www.divinetours.com
Tours across Italy from package holidays
to customised tours. Travel information
is well organised and you can book
online. There is a special tour section
for food and wine lovers, with lots of
information about wine and vineyards.
e-mail: info@divinetours.com

Domani

www.domani-usa.com
Italian vacation and car rentals and
Eurail Passes for American, Canadian
and Mexican travellers. Some featured
destinations are in the nicest parts of
Italy.
e-mail: Go.italy@domani-usa.com

Dr. Thomson's Tours of Historic Canterbury

www.drttours.u-net.com
Dr Thomson guides tours around
this historic English city and offers
trips to France and Belgium via the

Channel Tunnel. All tours have
professional guides.
e-mail: not available

Dracula Tours Transylvania

**www.draculatour.com/Transylvania/
Dracula.htm**
Skilled local guides who know the
region well enough to separate fact from
fiction. The Californian company run
tours to Transylvania, exploring territory
evoked by Bram Stoker's novel. They
offer a complete service with quality
transportation, first class accommodation,
translators and knowledgeable guides.
e-mail: not available

E-Tours

www.etours.cz
Bird watching, bear watching and
agricultural tours in Eastern Europe or
combine Birds with Music, Birds with
Bats, Birds with Wind or Birds with Beer.
Cultural tours to Prague take in parks
and gardens, the Jewish Heritage, music
and folklore and photographic tours.
e-mail: info@etours.cz

European Travel Partners

www.europeanhotels.co.uk
Quality group travel in western Europe
specialising in Short Breaks of two to
three nights in main cities and Longer
Stays of one to two weeks in Spain.
e-mail: info@europeanhotels.co.uk

Festival Ireland

www.festival-ireland.ie
Cultural and special interest holidays in
Ireland with emphasis on Festival Holidays.
Festival tickets are guaranteed and come
with accommodation, excursions and
transportation. Special events in Ireland
include World Cup matches, quaffing
oysters in Galway, dancing the
Charleston in Killarney and more. The
home page lists forthcoming events and
a search engine helps you find them.
e-mail: festival@omara-travel.com

French Adventures

www.frenchadventures.com
Private tours of Paris and the surrounding
areas by limousine, helicopter and
hot-air balloon. You stay at chateaux
and unique hotels. Tours can be private
or scheduled with walks, museum visits
and mini-bus excursions.
e-mail: info@frenchadventures.com

Geographic Bureau

www.geographicbureau.com
One of the oldest private Russian
adventure travel companies specialising
in expeditions to the remote areas of
Russia and former USSR Republics.
Some of their tours take you where
foreigners were excluded for decades.
Check out the itineraries on the home
page.
e-mail: gb@geographicbureau.com

Gloria Tours

www.webgate.bg/gloriatours
Bulgaria, skiing and touring. The home
page has the itineraries and though
excursions start in Sofia, they can be
modified at will. Tours can be combined
with other countries like Greece and
Turkey. Programs include guides and
other nice touches, so check them out.
e-mail: gloriagroup@bitex.com

Grand European Tours

www.getours.com/2000/index.shtml
Explore Europe on a cruise liner or
by train visiting some of the continent's
best known castles, palaces, museums
and cathedrals. Or cruise the
Mediterranean with stops in Egypt,
Israel and Portugal. The ultimate in
leisure touring comes in the Super
Leisure package.
e-mail: not available

Greek Tour & Cruise Center

www.greektouristcenter.com
There is much to enjoy on this web site
which offers a whole range of good

packages in the Mediterranean that you can enlarge at will. The countries included are clearly nominated and all their services detailed. Cruises can be arranged on all major lines sailing the Mediterranean or you can privately charter from the substantial fleet.
e-mail: aegeanvision@msn.com

Holidays in the UK

www.holidayuk.co.uk
Hike it, bike it or float with it if you like that better, all over the UK. If that's not enough, look up boating in France, Italy, Germany and Holland, something is bound to catch your fancy.
e-mail: booking@holidayuk.co.uk

Horses North

www.horsesnorth.com
Horse riding tours in Iceland on gentle and smooth-gaited Icelandic horses. Tours of varying distance and duration take you to otherwise inaccessible beautiful and rugged areas. Most tours are all-inclusive.
e-mail: horsesnorth@taconic.net

IntelService Center

www.intelservice.ru
If you travel to Russia or the former Soviet Union, you may need assistance with the paperwork. They will help you sort out your visa, together with all the other arrangements, especially when you want to set your own itinerary.
e-mail: info@intelservice.ru

InterTours

www.acer-intertours.com
Travel in Norway and from Norway to the rest of the world. They offer several programs, independent or escorted, including Norwegian safaris, winter vacations, fishing and hunting tours with all equipment supplied.
e-mail: not available

Just Your Own European Travel

www.justyourown.com
Escorted customised tours to Europe. Choose your itinerary, set your pace and leave the rest to them. The choice is great, from intense city tours to Alpine expeditions.
e-mail: jodan@montana.com

Key Tours

www.keytours.com
On the home page you will find details of tours in the East Mediterranean. You can browse the destinations either from the map or menu list for tour details, schedules and prices. An FAQ section and online order form help with more information.
e-mail: keytours@mnsinc.com

Krueger Travel

www.kruegertravel.com
If you want to celebrate your wedding in a Scottish castle, check this one out. Lots of wonderful holiday suggestions all over the UK with a Travel Planning button to help you decide.
e-mail: scotsmaster@kruegertravel.com

Les Liaisons Délicieuses

www.cookfrance.com
If you want a gourmet tour of France with a dash of culture, take a look at this site. You get French wine and food, some of which you can cook yourself under the guidance of a master chef. The tours are fully organised with accommodation and enjoyable excursions. There are 20 useful links and a booking form online.
e-mail: info@CookFrance.com

London Sport

www.londonsport.com
London Sport offers soccer lovers the opportunity to watch Premier and European matches live. Their holidays include accommodation and transportation. The site links take you

to the latest sports news and an online sport bookstore. You get hotel details, maps and a schedule of matches.
e-mail: sales@londonsport.com

MiForr
www.failte.com/miforr
Highlighting Ireland's culture, legends and folklore with abbeys and castles, music and dance. Then for fresh air walk up a hill or what you will. There's a lot on offer here.
e-mail: miforr@tinet.ie

MIR Corporation
www.mircorp.com
A journey on the Trans-Siberian Railway or a European brewery crawl are just two travel packages on offer in Russia and the independent States of the old USSR.
e-mail: mir@igc.apc.org

MUSART
www.musart.com
Tours in Italy for opera and art-lovers. Four main sections list art tours, opera houses, accommodation and forthcoming events. Each section has links to detailed information and photos. The booking form online can be faxed.
e-mail: dan75@musart.com

Nonstop Travel
www.la-supermall.com/nonstoptravel/
The USA to Europe and back with the full package of services. They also arrange European, Canadian and US rail passes.
e-mail: nonstoptravel@la-supermall.com

O'Connors Fairways Travel
www.oconnors.com
Each week you get special offers and bargain fares to Ireland with online schedules for the main serving airlines. As a bonus you can fly to Ireland and get to London for free.
e-mail: trvlirish@aol.com

Opa Tours Greece
www.greecetravel.com/opa/
Art, archaeology and fun in Greece with must-see sights and places of unique interest seldom offered elsewhere. Tours are all-inclusive, hotels are first class and you can book online.
e-mail: not available

Oralia Travel & Tours
www.oralia.com.cy/index.html
Special interest tours with a difference in and around Cyprus for beginners and the initiated. The discovery expeditions can also be exciting. You can book online.
e-mail: oralia@spidernet.com.cy

Pandion-D
www.birdwatchingholidays.com/index.shtml
Following your hobbies on tour in Bulgaria. Birds, botany, butterflies, love of nature, national customs, folklore, history, archaeology all with good helpings of Bulgarian cuisine. Prices and dates for all programs are online. The home page has a photo gallery.
e-mail: pandion@einet.bg

Paris International Guided Tours
www.paris-tours-guides.com
The home page is in several European languages. Though tours in Paris are the centrepiece of the site, several other European cities are included. Graphics are poor but the site can be used to book tours online, pay for them by secure credit card transaction and keep abreast of special offers and forthcoming events.
e-mail: info@paris-tours-guides.com

Paris Vision
www.parisvision.com
See Paris and environs by day or night. Take your pick of transportation and guide-interpreter. All Our Excursions is

the page; Type, Theme, Comfort and Keywords select your excursion, then click the search button.
e-mail: not available

Passage Tours of Scandinavia

www.passagetours.com
More than a hundred escorted tours from May to September in Scandinavia and Northern Europe. Check out the site for some truly marvellous tours of fjords, old capitals, the North Cape Cliff and escorted voyages on famous Coastal Steamers. There are weekly coach departures to St. Petersburg, Moscow and Nordic regions.
e-mail: info@passagetours.com

Plus Ultra Tours

www.spaintours.com
Tours to Spain and Portugal from the USA. Explore their escorted coach tours and see why they are so popular. Off-season vacations offer savings from November to March. They give full travel services to those wishing to go it alone. You can book online.
e-mail: mail@spaintours.com

Polarex Travel Agency

www.polarex.cz
Special interest tours, congresses, conventions and meetings in Central Europe. Programs include culture and art, wine tasting and spas. Check out the country style restaurants, cultural and sports events.
e-mail: info@polarex.cz

Polish Travel Centre

www.polishtravel.com
In addition to full travel services in Poland they offer money transfer and package delivery services to East European countries. They are also agents for a number of cruise lines. You can book online.
e-mail: sales@polishtravel.com

Pony Express

user.tninet.se/~tri375u/eng_index.htm
Six-day guided trail riding in Sweden on healthy Nordic pack horses. Families get wagons and draft horses. Tours are adapted to experience and you can rent a horse and live in a lodge or a ranch. Other activities include fishing, mountain biking, walking and canoeing.
e-mail: Pony.express@beta.telenordia.se

Prime Tours

www.primetours.co.uk
Group tours all over the UK and Ireland. They market UK rail and Eurostar tickets, ferry and tour tickets, theatre and concert tickets and a whole lot of London and Surrounds sightseeing tours.
e-mail: Kathryn@primetours.co.uk

Profil Rejser

www.profil-rejser.dk/commerical/commerical.htm
They market tours to Eastern Europe and the former Soviet Union through more than 700 travel agents in Scandinavia. They also offer a youth and student exchange scheme. The site only provides a list of contact details.
e-mail: profil@profil-rejser.dk

Puppentours

www.puppentour.com
Annual tours to the finest Doll and Toy Museums in Europe combined with historic doll making towns and factories, sightseeing and shopping. Professional guides accompany groups limited to twenty-five.
e-mail: liebling@puppentour.com

Quo Vadis Travel

www.qvts.com
Golf in Portugal, or Portugal for its own sake. They arrange everything including the courses, some with discounts. If golf is not your scene

they'll show you the real Portugal.
You can book online, by fax or post.
e-mail: sales@qvts.com

QXL.com

www.qxl.com
Buy a holiday package in Europe at an
auction. There are loads of bargains in
all categories with lists of bids.
e-mail: via online form

Renaissance Travel

www.yutravel.com
Travel to Eastern Europe and China
from the USA with air fares and value
discounts. Prices vary with the season
and there are some real bargains, so
keep looking. You can book online.
e-mail: reneissance@yutravel.com

Rhapsody Tours

www.rhapsodytours.com
North American tour operator with
premium packaged tours to Central
Europe and especially Budapest, Vienna,
Prague and Bratislava. Scheduled
itineraries run from 6 to 27 relaxing
days exploring the countryside, villages
and historic sites.
e-mail: info@rhapsodytours.com

Rhenia Tours

www.rhenia.gr
Travel services in Greece and Turkey
by coach, bus or car. They also manage
hotels on Samos with lots of
accommodation on the island.
e-mail: vorsprun@gemini.diavlos.gr

Romantic Czech Tours

www.czechtours.com/romantic/
Biking and hiking tours across the
Czech Republic. Several sections on
the home page detail their services.
For more information about the tours
use the online form. There are links to
other tour companies.
e-mail: romantic@czechtours.com

Saranjan Tours

saranjan.com
Unusual tours to Spain and Portugal for
discriminating travellers to absorb the
food, wine, history and culture. Groups are
restricted to fifteen. You can also choose
an all-inclusive customised package.
e-mail: info@saranjan.com

Scantours

www.scantours.com
Scandinavia, Russia, the Baltic States,
Iceland and Greenland on a theme tour
or a great city package. If you prefer
more personal arrangements, visit the
Design Your Own section and blend
your ideas with their suggestions.
e-mail: info@scantours.com

SeaEurope Holidays

www.seaeurope.com
Inexpensive tours and cruises to
Scandinavia and northern Europe
including the UK and Russia. Stay in a
city or cruise overnight between capital
cities. All tours allow you to extend your
stay at favourite destinations.
e-mail: not available

Simply Travel

www.simplytravel.co.uk
A UK-based company, offers holidays
in Greece, Turkey, Corsica, Portugal,
Tuscany and Spain, as well as a range of
ski holidays. There is ample information
on all aspects, including childcare.
Tailor-made holidays are part of their
service, you can request brochures and
book online.
e-mail: ski@simply-travel.com

Sunbizz Travel

www.snowbizz.co.uk
Family run ski holidays in the high altitude
French resort of Puy St. Vincent. They
cater for the whole family with a crèche,
ski school and children's club. The site
has a lot of information and late deals.
e-mail: not available

Tartan Tours

www.tartan-tours.com
US company offers unique cycle, golf and castle vacations in Scotland. Each type is detailed with prices. You can book online.
e-mail: STEVEBEEDIE@YAHOO.COM

Thalassa Travel & Tourism

www.travel.com.cy/main.shtml
Full service travel in Cyprus with everything on tap including fun and games and short boat trips to Israel, Egypt and the Greek Islands. You can book online.
e-mail: Thalassa@travel.com.cy

The Northerner

www.northerner.com/travel.html
World's largest shop for travel to Scandinavia. The home page has a selection of personalised services, seasonal programs, weddings and honeymoons, dog-sledding, snow mobile or reindeer safaris, Ice Hotel, the world's largest igloo, whale safari and cruises.
e-mail: info@northerner.com

The Untravelled Moors

www.untravelledmoors.co.uk
Discover Spain's fascinating Moorish past and its present through its art, architecture and culture. Three guided tours take you to Andalusian Melting Pot, In Sephardic Footsteps and Old Castille.
e-mail: info@untravelledmoors.co.uk

Time Travel

timetravel.virtualave.net
They offer travel services anywhere in Russia with quality guided tours in Moscow and St Petersburg. Visa support, tours and special packages, conferences, professional and study tours, all at the click of a mouse.
e-mail: not available

Tours of Tuscany

www.tuscanytours.com
All-inclusive art history and culture tours to Tuscany and Umbria. Tours are designed for travellers interested in renaissance history, art and religion, with a taste for fine food, a sense of humour and love of adventure. Groups are limited to twelve.
e-mail: info@tuscanytours.com

Towne & Country Tours

www.towneandcountrytours.com
Luxurious accommodation and world-class cuisine. Equestrian Tours in Hungary, Gourmet Food & Wine in Switzerland and Hungary, Culture and Opera in Prague Budapest and Vienna and more. Tell them what you are looking for by e-mail or complete the form.
e-mail: logan@tez.net

Trans Europe Tours

www.destinationseurope.com
Everything you could want for a wedding, honeymoon, customised holiday or group tour of the UK and Europe. There are several travel options and a list of recommended hotels divided by country. Online booking is available from every internal page. There is a newsletter facility and FAQ section.
e-mail: holidays@destinationseurope.com

Unipress Travel Department

www.odessa-ua.com
There are several tour options on offer for the Ukraine. Links take you to hotel lists and you get assistance with visas, transfers, guides, air and rail ticket reservations. Students have special programs with discounts. Lots of pictures of Odessa and other parts of the country. You can book online.
e-mail: info@odessa-ua.com

Villa Vacation Travel

www.italyvilla.com
Villas, apartments, farmhouses, two castles and two towers, many with pools, are listed on this web site. They are all over Italy, with several on the islands. Download the online form,

complete and mail it and you will receive a catalogue.
e-mail: info@italyvilla.com

Village Travel Service
www.venturablvd.com/lao/
village-travel-service
Anywhere you want to go at any price level you choose. Use the online travel inquiry form, mentioning any special reason for your trip if you have one and allow at least 24 hours for a faxed response. On the home page you can choose from a wide range of holidays and destinations.
e-mail: villagetravel@venturablvd.com

Virtually There
www.virtually-there.com
Rail passes and car rentals all around Europe. There is a lot of information about railways and fares for major European cities. The Car Rental link has weekly rates for seven European cities. The web site has links to all things French and tells you a lot about the country. Other links give the weather anywhere in Europe, currency and metric converters.
e-mail: info@virtually-there.com

Vision Travel
www.visiontravelinc.com
Teddy Bear Tours of the World for Collectors is just one of many unique programs for special interest groups. There are so many wonderful holiday plans and ideas, so many distinct services and so much information on this web site that it deserves a visit. Their association with Carlson Wagonit Travel, gives them access to the latest travel news. As booking online is not yet available, contact them by e-mail, fax or phone.
e-mail: nina@visiontravelinc.com

Vista Tours
www.vistatours.com
You get an all-inclusive cruise service from all the German seaports and rivers,

including the before and after land arrangements. The Discover link helps you find your way around Germany. On offer are also special holidays in other parts of Europe. As booking online is not available, contact them for assistance.
e-mail: info@vistatours.com

Voyage Europe
www.voyageeurope.com
If your destination is Europe and you need help to organise your travel, click on the trip-planning link and you will be assisted with creating an itinerary and working out details. There are some great tips for accommodation and getaway options for alpine skiing.
e-mail: not available

Zeus Tours
www.zeustours.com
They offer tours, cruises and holiday packages in the Greek islands. The well-designed home page gives access to their range of holidays with prices and schedules. You can book online or contact your nearest travel agent.
e-mail: info@zeustours.com

Latin America

AAA Tours and Travel
www.aaatours.net
Full service travel company with very exciting adventure tours to Costa Rica. Package holidays are clearly set out with choices of volcanoes, rafting, fishing and lots more. They organise meetings, conferences, special events and private tours.
e-mail: Info@aaatours.net

Aerosaab Airplane Tours
www.aerosaab.com
Aerosaab Airplane Tours offer unique aerial tours across the most picturesque parts of Mexico. The home page contains route maps, descriptions and photos of panoramic flights. You can

choose a standard flight tour or rent the plane for a customised flight. Prices and online booking are provided. An external link takes you to a worthwhile Mexican travel guide.
e-mail: info@aerosaab.com

Alternative Farm Tourism

latinwide.com/farm-tour/
Adventure through Bolivia with alternative travel possibilities and a bias toward ecology, society and agriculture. Villages and farms, cocoa, coffee and nut plantations are on the itinerary. You can book online.
e-mail: Tca.yuri@latinwide.com

Amazon Travel Experts

www.amazontravelcenter.com
Tours designed to take you to the remoter parts of Latin America. Wherever you click on the map of the continent you get details of tours on offer. The graphics could be better, but information is ample. Check out the last minute specials and packages for small-budget travellers. You can book online.
e-mail: info@amazontravelcenter.com

Andes Adventures

www.andesadventures.com
Trekking adventures or running along the Inca Trail could be a way to work up a sweat. These are vacations with a difference and you can see what's ahead of you from the pictures.
e-mail: info@andesadventures.com

Aqua Tours Adventures

www.aquatours.net
All you can do in Cancun, especially the water sports, are described with prices in the Services section. Use the Contact Us link for reservations. Text is in English and Spanish.
e-mail: aquatours@aquatours.net

Arassari Trek

www.arassari.com
Adventure tours in Venezuela from trekking and white water rafting to paragliding. Check out the photographs and use the contact details to book.
e-mail: info@arassari.com

Austral Tours

www.australtours.com
Tour packages to South America exploring the Amazon, visiting Iguazu Falls, Lake Titikaka, the Galapagos Islands, Easter Island, Macchu Picchu, cruising the Amazon river and trekking in the Andes. City Stopovers package together two nights accommodation, return fares and a half-day tour.
e-mail: sales@australtours.com

Aventrip

www.aventrip.com.ar/index2.htm
Adventurous excursions all over Patagonia in Argentina, to lakes and mountains, lodging at hostels and camp sites. Raft, trek, rappel, ski, hike and snow walk around the mountains. The home page has maps and information about services.
e-mail: informes@aventrip.com.ar

Bike-Hike Adventures

www.bikehike.com
Adventure through South and Central America. Take your pick from or combine mountain biking, white water rafting, rock climbing, horse riding, inner tubing, tree canopy tours and trekking.
e-mail: info@bikehike.com

Blumar Turismo

www.blumar.com.br
From offices in Rio de Janeiro and Naples, Florida, they offer tours throughout Brazil. The famous Rio Carnival is featured among several special interest tours. Links on the home page give you access to hotel rates, photo galleries and online

reservations. Text is in English and Portuguese.

e-mail: blumar@blumar.com.br

Bolivian 4 X 4 Safaris

members.xoom.com/_XOOM/jbx/ index.html

All inclusive two-week Bolivian expeditions driving through some of the most outstanding scenery in the world, visiting ancient Indian sites and experiencing modern day Aymara and Quecha cultures at first hand. The wild life you will see is the stuff of TV documentaries. Tours are limited to twelve and accommodation in the larger cities is in the 5-star category. You can book online.

e-mail: Jackson@zuper.net

BR Online Travel

www.brol.com

Great package tours to Rio de Janeiro and other Brazilian cities and exciting excursions into the tropical forests along the Amazon. Take a look at their air travel offers and Brazilian notes.

e-mail: brol@brol.com

Carmoar Tours

www.carmoar.com

Adventure and eco-tourism in Bolivia with tours from relaxed walking and study trips to unforgettable adventures and expeditions. They provide specialist guides and all appropriate transportation for the changing terrain. Most trips visit the major attractions of Bolivia, like Los Yungas, Copacabana, Tiawanaku and Chacaltaya.

e-mail: info@caromoar.com

Costa Rica Golf Adventures

www.golfcr.com

One-stop golf travel shop for Costa Rica. The home page gives details of golf packages, courses, hotels and tours for non-golfers. Or you may wish to consider fishing and night-life packages. You can book online.

e-mail: golf@centralamerica.com

De Luxe Destinations

www.come-to-brazil.com

Argentina, Brazil and Chile are covered separately on this web site. Click on one and up come links to tour descriptions, prices and accommodation. You can book your trip and hotel online.

e-mail: sales@come-to-brazil.com

Diplomatic Tours

www.boliviabiz.com/tourism/company/ diplomat.htm

A full travel service in Bolivia with guides into Inca country if you wish. Skiing, adventure and eco-holidays are all part of the portfolio.

e-mail: diplomatic@boliviabiz.com

Elena's Ecotour Safaris

www.rainforestsafari.com/emerald.htm

Eco-safari programs in Puerto Rico with a choice between all-inclusive camp safaris and do-it-yourself parador safaris. They rent you the car, give you the maps and make the arrangements. You can also sail, hike, fish, kayak and snorkel, visit the rainforest, hot springs and volcanic rifts.

e-mail: elenaharley@hotmail.com

Escape

www.delphis.dm/escape/

Sports tours in Dominica from November to April. Most activities are aquatic, rafting, tubing, swimming under waterfalls, in pools and cascades. Groups are limited to eight for beginners, intermediate and advanced participants.

e-mail: not available

Explorama Lodges

www.explorama.com

Five lodges in a quarter million acres of protected primary Amazon rainforest. Wildlife, pink dolphins and exotic birds make this part of Peru irresistible. Professional and multilingual guides work with each small group. The home

page has general information, maps and itineraries.
e-mail: amazon@explorama.com

Explore Bolivia

www.explorebolivia.com
Fishing, hiking, bird-watching and photographic vacations throughout Bolivia, or trips with some of each. You really get to grips with the country on foot, mountain bike, 4-wheel drive, raft or kayak. Check out details on altitudes, equipment, vaccinations and suggested reading before your trip.
e-mail: wplorbol@ix.netcom.com

Explore Earth

www.exploreearth.com
Exploring, conserving and restoring our natural world. Expeditions go to Peru and Costa Rica. You journey through the Amazon rainforest, visit the world's longest canopy walkway system and participate in ongoing research projects. Less adventurous travellers can explore the jungles of Costa Rica.
e-mail: questions@exploreearth.com

Galapagos dive land.com

www.galapagosdiveland.com/html/ dive.html
Diving in the Galapagos, either land-based or aboard the Daphne. The Ecuador side of the tours has trips to some of the best spots in the Amazon Basin and high Andes of Ecuador.
e-mail: info@galapagosdiveland.com

Galapagos Tours

www.discovergalapagos.com
Canadian company running tours to the Galapagos. There is a wonderful picture gallery and you can download the videos with the software link online. Use the tour planner and the virtual tour to help choose your trip. You can book online.
e-mail: inti@agt.net

Galasam International

www.ipse.net/galapagossenio
Tours for senior citizens to the Galapagos. Their vessels carry 16 passengers between Ecuador and the Islands. The home page has information about the boats, the Islands, fares, Internet promotions and travel tips. There is a lot to do at both ends of the voyage.
e-mail: Galapagos@galapagos-senior.com

Global Travel Club

www.global-travel.co.uk
Fabulous eco-adventure, island tours and the highlights of Belize. You get dense emerald rainforests and the crystal clear waters of the Barrier Reef. Between them there is a whole range of adventure, wildlife, caving, horse riding, boating, diving and cruising holidays, or just relaxing on a Caribbean beach.
e-mail: info@global-travel.co.uk

Gold Coast Travels and Expeditions

www.homestead.com/panamagold coasttravels/MountainsandValleys.html
Tours and Expeditions for small groups in Panama. Among their locations are: La Posada, near the headwaters of nine rivers; Sierra Llorona; a tropical rain forest reserve overlooking the Caribbean Sea; Cristobal harbour and El Valle, an extinct volcano crater with its botanical gardens.
e-mail: Gold-coast@cwp.net.pa

Great Trips

www.travelsource.com/ecotours/ greattrips.html
Hassle-free and exceptional adventure tours to Central and South America. Diving among coral reefs, horse riding on jungle trails, hiking the rainforest or canoeing rivers and exploring Mayan ruins are all part of their portfolio.
e-mail: greattrips@isd.net

Guatours

www.guatours.com
Guided tours in Guatemala and the Mayan World. Jungle trips by boat and raft, horse riding, volcano climbing, golf, sailing, fishing and diving come in packages with a whole lot more. Guides speak English, Spanish, German, French, Italian, Dutch and other languages.
e-mail: info@guatours.com

Holiday Tours

www.holidaytours.com
Tour operators and airfare consolidators for South America, particularly Argentina, Brazil, Chile and Peru with especially good rates from the US. They have a good range of European holidays and world cruises.
e-mail: Travel@holidaytours.com

Inkaways Tour Operator

www.inkaways.com
Inkaways offer a wide range of tours in the Sacred Valley and the surrounding areas in Peru. The featured destinations are Iquitos, Cusco, Maldonado, Puno, Arequipa, and Lima. Inkaways also organise customised tours. An online reservation form is available on the home page.
e-mail: qoyzueta@bestweb.net

Inti Travel and Tours

www.discovergalapagos.com/intitravel/
Rainforest and jungle tours, lodges, cruises, treks and hikes in Amazonian parts of Brazil, Ecuador and Peru. Check out the site for truly wonderful locations. Licensed guides intimately familiar with the environment and people lead the tours. You can book online.
e-mail: inti@agt.net

Island Connections

www.islandconn.com
Good travel services with bargain fares to Central America. Their focus is Honduras, where they offer water sports in all its forms from river rafting to ocean sailing. This site has links with good text and wonderful pictures.
e-mail: Islandconn@travelattitudes.com

Journey Latin America

www.journeylatinamerica.co.uk
Escorted group tours, customised itineraries and flights to Central and South America. Information with flight fares and hotel ratings is in table format and easy to scan.
e-mail: tours@journeylatinamerica.co.uk

Kallpa Tours

www.kallpatour.com
Customised tours to Argentina, from high adventure to tango dancing. If you prefer to choose your holiday by region, use the map on the main page. All tours are fully detailed, some with photo thumbnails. Enquire and book by e-mail.
e-mail: info@kallpatour.com

Korzo Tours

www.ascinsa.com/KORZO
The coast, highlands and jungle of Peru provide between them enough to satisfy every taste. Machu Picchu, the mysterious and beautiful city of stone in the highlands, is very much the jewel in the crown. Text is in English, Spanish, German and Japanese.
e-mail: Korzo@ibm.net

Maya Exotic Travel

www.mayaexotic.guate.com
Several tour packages to Guatemala are slanted toward traditions, culture and spirituality. Others are for eco-tourism where you enjoy the wonders of the rainforest, the Mayan heritage, the sun and beaches.
e-mail: not available

Maya Mountain/Lodge & Tours

www.belize.com/mayamountain.html
Eco-travel vacations to the Belize rainforest, Mayan ruins, reefs and

other options come together with educational workshops, study programs and conferences.
e-mail: online@mayamountain.com

Pam Tours

www.pamtour.com.ec
Starting in Ecuador you can cruise, tour the beaches, the Andes or the Amazon. All tours are priced with itinerary and dates; links lead to external pages of interest. Use the drop-down menus to collect information and book online if you wish.
e-mail: mailto:pamtour@pi.pro.ec

Patagonia Travel Adventures

www.patagoniaadventures.com
Small group tours in Argentina and more specifically, Patagonia. There are three packages that immerse the traveller in a timeless landscape, visiting places normally out of reach.
e-mail: patadvr@aol.com

Payachatas Adventure Travel

www.chile-travel.com/payachts.htm
Tour operators in North Chile with trips to Santiago, Easter Island, Arica and Calama. There is some information on what to see in Chile, car rental, travel agents, accommodation, food and restaurants. Text is brief so fax for more details.
e-mail: not available

Peru Adventure Travel

www.grasmick.com
Based in Colorado they provide general travel services and specialise in holidays in Colorado, Mexico's Copper Canyon, and Peru. Their adventure tours cater for most activities and archaeological expeditions. You will find a good bibliography and lots of unpublished information.
e-mail: Adventur@rmii.com

Puerto Rico Tours

www.puertorico-tours.com
George Lopez conducts private sightseeing tours for visitors to Puerto Rico. He escorts you to all the popular locations like the national rain forest, Luquillo Beach, caves of Camuy, Old San Juan, colonial city of Ponce and the restored Taino Indian Village. Ask nicely and he'll take you on a horse racing or golf tour.
e-mail: george@puertorico-tours.com

Rain Forest Tours

www.costaricabureau.com/rainforest/diving.htm
Costa Rican Eco-adventures and tours with a few packages to Cuba. Diving, rain forest tours, rafting, sport fishing and bird watching give you plenty of choice, then add canals, volcanoes, beaches and a National Park.
e-mail: rainforest@costaricabureau.com

Safari Ecuador

www.safari.com.ec/birds_of_ecuador.html
Ecuador is one of the world's premier bird watching countries. Groups are limited to eight and all guides are well experienced in the field.
e-mail: admin@safari.com.ec

South American Expeditions

www.southamericaexp.com
Swimming with pink dolphins, meeting shamans and travelling off the tourist circuit in South America in groups limited to fifteen. Some expeditions are available only to women.
e-mail: weekly@packbell.net

Sunshine Services

suntourpa.home.att.net
Customised travel for corporate events in the Dominican Republic or Costa Rica. Meetings, sales incentive, executive key account and group travel fall within their portfolio. These vacations can include golf and scuba

diving with lessons, local dining, theme parties, sport fishing, cigar rolling, land and sea excursions.
e-mail: suntourpa@worldnet.att.net

Tsanza Adventures

www.amazonrainforest.com
Adventure holidays in Peru, sea kayaking, flat water canoeing, trekking, hiking, bird watching, freshwater angling, mountain biking, llama trekking and whatever else catches your fancy. All guides are Peruvian and well experienced.
e-mail: tsanza@amazonrainforest.com

Turismo Cocha

www.cocha.com
Travel packages for Patagonia, Easter Island, the Atacama Desert, lakes and fjords in Chile. Each destination has a list of corresponding tours from which you select and complete a form. Flight schedules, accommodation and other information is accessible online. To book click on the reservations button.
e-mail: webadmin@cocha.com

Untamed Path

www.angelfire.com/ca3/untamedpath/ index.html
Small groups adventuring to the back corners of South America. No more than eight together allow for more interaction with local people and their culture. All programs are described online.
e-mail: info@unthamedpath.com

World Reservations Centre

www.mexicohotels.com
You search this friendly web site accompanied by Mexican music. Choose your destination in Mexico from the map on the home page and you get pictures and packages with prices and other details.
e-mail: mexicohotels@mexis.com

Middle East

AtlasTours.Net

www.atlastours.net
They want to make your visit to Jordan, Syria, Lebanon and Israel enjoyable and unforgettable. The home page tells you about sites and cities, hotels, entertainment and excursions. For more details complete the inquiry form.
e-mail: info@atlastours.net

Caravanserai Tours

www.caravanserai-tours.com
Libya and Iran by camel and 4x4 safari. The site has information about both countries and what to see there. Booking online is not available.
e-mail: info@caravanserai-tours.com

Darna Travel

www.darnatravel.com
They specialise in pilgrimage tours to the Holy Land for Christian and Muslim travellers from the Far East, Europe and USA. You can choose a regular tour or have one tailored for you. The pictures will tempt you.
e-mail: sales@darnatravel.com

Dead Sea Beach Tours

www.dsbt.com
Tour the Jordanian side of the Dead Sea, the lowest place on earth. You can choose from biblical, educational and adventure excursions camping in the desert and travelling by camel. Check out the pictures, itineraries and maps.
e-mail: wael@dsbt.com

Gold Carpet Touring

www.goldcarpet.co.il
You can choose from a range of sightseeing and religious tours across the Land of the Bible. Each tour is listed with details, photos and price. There are several very useful links on the main page. Enquiries can be made on the form online.
e-mail: gct0001@ibm.net

Holy Land Pilgrimages

www.galilee.com
Pilgrimages to the Holy Land with
the opportunity to meet and worship
with local Christians in their churches.
Journeys include full educational and
spiritual programs at affordable prices.
There are tours to other Mediterranean
countries.
e-mail: samra@galilee.com

InTourNet

www.intournet.co.il
Services and links for travellers to Israel
and the Mediterranean, with information
on hotels, yachting and pilgrimages.
For further information, quotes and
booking online click the Online Travel
Consultant button.
e-mail: yaakov@intournet.co.il

Israel Travel Discounters

www.israelnow.com
Discounts and an all-round travel
service to Israel with some very good
tours and a pilgrimage to Jerusalem.
If that's not enough hit the information
request button on the main menu.
e-mail: itex@israelnow.com

Keli Tours

www.keli-tours.co.il
Keli Tours operate across Israel and
the Middle East serving people with
physical handicaps. Their services are
very special and include medical treatment
in the Dead Sea area, agricultural and
archaeological tours and seminars,
biking tours, scuba diving, and lots
more, all of which are fully described.
The home page comes in English,
Spanish and Portuguese. Bookings can
be made online.
e-mail: info@keli-tours.co.il

Mediterranean Tours Specialists

www.medtours.com
Eastern Mediterranean with specially
designed tours to Egypt and Israel.

Itineraries include treks, cruises,
safaris and more.
e-mail: info@medtours.com

Universal Group of Companies

www.universalyemen.com
Travel services in the Yemen.
Accommodation ranges from deluxe
hotels to guest-houses; excursions,
package tours, trekking and camping
with all equipment provided are
accompanied by multi-lingual Yemeni
guides. The home page has notes on the
history, geography, climate and cuisine
of the country. Take a good look at the
terms and conditions section in the
Company Profile link. Booking online
is not available.
e-mail: tourinq.company@
universalyemen.com

North America

Academic Travel Services

www.academictravel.com
They offer Performance Tours and
Educational Tours, among others.
This informative web site lets you feed
in your requirements then suggests
suitable holidays as a package with
all-in prices. Follow the hypertext
links for more information.
e-mail: not available

Ace Travel House

www.acetravel.com
If you are new to them click the
New User button and get yourself a
password. Then you can access the
sports travel packages and tickets on
offer. Other offers take you to
Nashville for music and Jacksonville.
e-mail: not available

Advantage Charleston

www.advantagecharleston.com
Three package tours of Charleston,
South Carolina - getaways, history
and golf. If you don't fancy any, concoct

your own, picking out the elements from the menu.
e-mail: info@advantagecharleston.com

Alaska 2 Wheel Tours

www.alaskamtbike.com
Whether you want to mountain bike, kayak, hike, raft or ski in Alaska, winter or summer, take a look at this well-designed web site where pictures zoom and tours come alive at a click. You can book online, stating your preferences.
e-mail: info@alaskamtbike.com

Alaska Connection

www.alaskaconnect.com
Alaska on a plate with every conceivable type of vacation, all with complete travel services, yacht and motor home rentals. Their Sportsman's air fares to Alaska are probably the lowest you will find.
e-mail: alaskaod@alaska.net

American Auto Tours

www.americanautotours.com/index.html
Planned self-drive tours in the USA and Canada with travel packages that include hotel accommodation. You are equipped with a personalised travel book that details where you stay and what you visit with directions, photos and maps for every part of the route. They offer up to four-week itineraries with driving distances limited to four or five hours each day. Hotels have favourable locations and include National Park lodges.
e-mail: info@americanautotours.com

American Tours & Travel

www.travelgroups.com
Student group travel to Orlando, Washington DC, Los Angeles, New York, Hawaii, Europe or a cruise with an opportunity to perform on the high seas. There are special deals for youth groups at Orlando theme parks.
e-mail: info@bandfest.com

Apache Trail Tours

www.apachetrailtours.com
Guided jeep tours into the Superstition Mountain Foothills to pan for gold, hiking, horse and hay rides, barge excursions, backpacking treks and outdoor adventures on the Apache Trail in Arizona.
e-mail: not available

Arctic Ladies

arcticladies.com
Unique experience travelling the wilderness of Alaska and Yukon for adventurous women. Explore in a small group of like-minded individuals or follow your own itinerary. Equipment is up-to-date and satisfies the most rigorous safety requirements; accommodation is first class and carefully selected.
e-mail: info@arcticladies.com

Aspen Ski Tours

www.skitours.com
Ski holidays in the Rocky Mountains of North America. Their packages are truly all-inclusive down to last-minute cancellations. You select to your requirements and budget and they do the rest. The home page tells you what you can expect.
e-mail: agents@skitours.com

ATV Action Tours

www.actiontours.com
Thirty-four scenic land tours, some combined with plane and helicopter rides, in Southwest Nevada, Arizona and California. Most tours are by comfortable, air-conditioned vehicles originating in Las Vegas. There are exciting packages with well-trained tour guides. Check all their tours; they are well-designed and presented. For those with their own transport, they offer U-Drive and U-Rent programs.
e-mail: atvtours@aol.com

Away to Travel

www.away2travel.com

Located in Florida, they specialise in Central America. There are monthly special offers to nominated destinations worth looking at. Click the contact button on the home page to get in touch.
e-mail: not available

Bayonne Travel Centre

www.bayonnetrv.com

Atlantic City has casinos by the number with lavish entertainment and plush accommodation in all leading hotels. Additionally the site has detailed information on domestic and international travel services.
e-mail: Bayonne2@bayonnetrv.com

Bird Island Boat Tours

fox.nstn.ca/~birdisld/

Bird life by boat in North America and Nova Scotia. You follow the scenic coast to two rock islands to see a variety of birds, the colourful Atlantic Puffin, grey seals, seabirds and bald eagles. Groups from 15 to 51 get special rates.
e-mail: birdisld@fox.nstn.ca

Canada Outdoors

www.canada-outdoors.com

Use the map with its links on the home page to simplify surfing this site. There are two vacations on offer, Canadian Heritage Expeditions and white water rafting on Ottawa River. One section of the site gets you connected and two others deal specifically with tours. There are charming pictures and several useful links.
e-mail: team@canada-outdoors.com

Caravelle Travel Management

www.caravelle-travel.com

Mainly US domestic travel management with a little international trade. Big on corporate travel, meetings, conferences backed by full travel support. For the leisure traveller they provide adventure travel and alternative lifestyle vacations. You can book online.
e-mail: vacations@caravelle-travel.com

Casino Airlink

www.casinoairlink.com

Largest US tour operator to the Mississippi Gulf Coast. Vacation packages include airfares, transfers, baggage handling and casino/hotel accommodation. Each casino link gives ample description and photographs. They also offer Mississippi, New Orleans, Florida and Golf packages.
e-mail: general@casinoairlink.com

Discount USA Travel

www.discountusatravel.com

This is a general reservation page on which you can book airline tickets, cars, hotels, holiday packages and last minute deals for the USA. You can compare their offers with others and save up to 50%. All online credit card transactions are secure.
e-mail: not available

Dynasty Vacations

www.dynastyvacations1.com

Ten Bahamian cruises and vacations, each with a brief description and price. The cruise liners are among the largest operating in the Caribbean.
e-mail: not available

East Town Travel

www.easttowntravel.com

Their customised tours take you to the theatre, galleries, architecturally interesting buildings and sports centres of various US cities and a few more outside the country.
e-mail: easttown@execpc.com

ElderTreks

www.eldertreks.com

A Canadian company offering travel services for those aged over 50. Rate your physical fitness then check their

listing to choose the most suitable tour for yourself. Trips are amply described with dates, prices and region. You can book online and read plaudits from past travellers.
e-mail: eldertreks@eldertreks.com

Escape Artist Tours
www.sf-escapes.com/index.shtml
This wonderful web site offers you an escape from the usual in San Francisco, the Napa Valley, Lake Tahoe and surrounding Bay Area. They arrange parties, special events, romantic getaways and a long list of outdoor activities including yachting, hot air ballooning, treasure hunts and more. Links from their home page take you to specific regions and services. It's all there, just click your mouse. Booking online is not yet available.
e-mail: eat@sf-escapes.com

Florida Festival Tours
www.floridafestivaltours.com
Student group travel to Orlando, Atlanta, New York and Washington DC. If you are a musical or dance group and want to participate in a festival, check out the site. There are performance opportunities at Disney, Universal, Sea World and Busch Gardens in Florida. Those who don't want to perform can opt for just plain fun trips.
e-mail: fftours@worldramp.net

Go For the Gold - Adventure Tours
www.nuggethunters.com
Gold, gem and relic prospecting tours in Georgia, Arizona and Tennessee. Apart from prospecting, you have the fun of the campsite, excursions, barbecues and more. You can book online.
e-mail: not available

Gray Wolf Adventures
www.graywolfadventures.com/home/index.html
Guided Native American tours with one-of-a-kind adventure vacations throughout the White Mountain Apache, Hualapai and Navajo nations. This is an opportunity to befriend these people, learn their customs, explore rarely visited tribal sites and witness sacred ceremonies. You must be in good health and be prepared for moderate physical exertion. Special deals take care of club and family getaways.
e-mail: info@graywolfadventures.com

Holiday Travel International
www.holidaytvl.com
Discount airfares and tours to Las Vegas, Reno and other US cities. And families need not feel left out in these fast moving cities as accommodation and tours can be arranged in theme parks.
e-mail: not available

Jeep Destinations
www.jeepdestinations.com
Jeep travel with your own guide in all 54 US National Parks. Use the Travel Directory link on the home page for a map, overview, history, and a stack of information on each park; select your jeep on the top bar of the page. Other holidays include fishing and women outdoors.
e-mail: not available

Kingdom Magic Travel
www.kingdommagictravel.com
Disney World online. Where to stay and what to do while eating. Apparently you can do it all on a budget.
e-mail: admin@vacationwithus.com

Kodiak Adventure
www.kodiakadventure.com
All-inclusive packages between Anchorage and Kodiak 250 miles away, lodging at Buskin River Inn. Activities include fishing, bear watching, river rafting, horse riding, 4-wheeler treks, kayaking and more. Declare your

preferences and they will customise
a package for you.
e-mail: Info@kodiakadventure.com

Las Vegas Golf Adventures

www.lasvegasgolfadventures.com
One call does it all golf vacation service
in Las Vegas. They book golf tee-off
times, hotel accommodation and
transportation for individuals and
groups of all sizes. Trained staff assist
you from the planning stage onward.
e-mail: jsmith@lasvegasgolf
adventures.com

Latitude Travel Company

www.latitudetravel.com
Holidays and accommodation in
Florida and the Bahamas. If you register
you are eligible for a discount vacation.
e-mail: info@latitudetravel.com

Maple Ki Forest Retreat

www.ecoville.com/maple-ki/
Maple Ki Forest in Ontario, Canada,
provides "space for the soul to breathe",
a sanctuary for people to take a break,
with vegetarian macrobiotic cuisine
and yoga therapies. The home has a
maximum capacity of seven.
e-mail: not available

Marlin Baker Travel

www.marlintravel.com
If you're bound for north-west British
Columbia and south-east Alaska take
a look at this very good web site.
It's all there with loads of tempting
options.
e-mail: Mbtravel@citytel.net

Maxxim Vacations

www.maxximvacations.com
You can peek at birds and bergs doing
their thing in Newfoundland and Nova
Scotia. And for a lot else click on the
tour name.
e-mail: not available

MCO Travel & Tours

www.mcotravel.com
Tours of all types across the USA.
Start from the site map and follow
links to the kind of holiday you want.
The number and range of hotels are
enormous but selection is simplified by
a good search system. To book online
you need to obtain a password. Text is
in English and Spanish.
e-mail: info@mcotravel.com

Northwest Voyageurs

www.voyageurs.com
Small, owner-operated business
offering intimate, quality trips to the
wildest places in Oregon and Idaho.
There are brief itineraries, trip details
and departure dates. You may wish to
visit the mountain biking, hiking and
fishing pages. For more details, maps
and trip notes, contact the company.
e-mail: Nwvoyage@voyageurs.com

Pro Musica Tours

www.promusicatours.com
Pro Musica Tours package exciting
tours for opera-lovers in North America.
Their friendly web site has an up-to-date
list of specialised tours on offer. Every
tour program has a link which gives you
very detailed information about opera
events, accommodation and prices.
These tours can be designed to suit
your special needs and interests.
Charming photographs of opera stars
and fine art masterpieces come with
the information. Online reservations
are possible.
e-mail: not available

Pro Sports

www.pro-sports.net
Round the clock tickets and travel
packages to major sporting events in
the USA. They claim that they can
arrange tickets to international sporting
events even if they are sold out, with
free delivery. The site is full of Pro-Sport

chat and pages for hundreds of teams. Fan Central has news and photos for fans.
e-mail: Sales@pro-sports.net

Puffin Travel

www.puffintravel.com
Nature in the raw in Glacier Bay, Alaska. Their packages fix your flight, accommodation and tours. To these you can add kayaking, sea lion and whale watching and fishing, checking out the best seasons online. Don't forget to pack your gloves.
e-mail: sandy@puffintravel.com

Raptim

www.raptimusa.com
Their mission is solely to facilitate and co-ordinate travel arrangements for missionaries. Their mission-related services cater for the needs of individuals, groups, families and other travel agents in North America. There is an online Travel Quote Form.
e-mail: Raptim@raptimusa.com

RealSouth Tours

www.realsouthtours.com
Unique tours of historical, archaeological and nature sites in Florida, coastal Georgia and South Carolina. Guides are professional and know the territory well. You visit prairies, natural springs, gardens, coastal islands, native American mounds, quaint villages and historic homes. Tours vary in length and can be customised to include fishing, canoeing, biking, hiking and diving and a host of other expeditions.
e-mail: realso@gnv.fdt.net

Rescenter

www.skijacksonreservations.com
Full travel services for ski resorts in Utah, Lake Tahoe, and Jackson Hole. There is a lot of useful information on this web site about flights, ski facilities and lodges with seasonal price

variations. For more details complete the online form.
e-mail: travel@skijacksonreservations.com

Shouppe Travel

www.amextravelrep.com
Florida is their territory and using Amadeus, the largest reservation system in the world and the American Express Worldwide Select hotel program, you can be sure of discounts.
e-mail: info@anextravelrep.com

Sky Island Tours

www.angelfire.com/az/skyisland/ skyisltors.html
Mexico's famous Copper Canyon and south-eastern Arizona's marvels. Photo Tours & Workshops cater for beginners and advanced amateurs or anyone who wants to take pictures. Natural History Tours take you to destinations to enjoy the unique environment and wildlife.
e-mail: csrsarc@vtc.net

Spectrum Golf

www.spectrum-golf.com
One stop shop for golf vacations and events in North America with guaranteed tee-off times in premiere clubs like Phoenix, Scottsdale, Palm Springs, Las Vegas and Los Cabos, Mexico. They also arrange golf vacations in any region of the world. You can book online.
e-mail: Msgolf1122@aol.com

Super Holiday Tours

www.superholiday.com
Group travel packages all over the USA. The destination section has links to local information and tour programs. There are links to affiliated companies. You can request information and book online.
e-mail: shtours@aol.com

Teen Tours of America

www.teentoursofamerica.com
Three to six-week vacations for teenagers in North America. Programs

ensure safe environments and meaningful activities supervised by mature and caring adult staff. Check out the itineraries.
e-mail: tourtta@teentoursofamerica.com

Tour Resources International

www.touresourc.com
All aspects of planning tours in the USA for the performing arts, with full travel services. They book your venue, hotels, coaches, airlines and everything else.
e-mail: touresourc@aol.com

Travel USA

www.travelusa-mds.com
You get instant online pricing for air travel from most US cities to popular vacation destinations. Five major links on the home page deal with hot-spot destinations, casino cities, discount travel and special offers, corporate and group travel, speciality and sports tours, with tickets for the events included.
e-mail: bookings@travelusa-mds.com

Trump Travel

www.trumptravel.com
You will find all the travel services you may need and a good variety of interesting and exciting holidays - a one-stop shop for travel in the US. Travellers are assisted with planning their trip and getting the best prices.
e-mail: info@trumptravel.com

Twin Travel and Cruises

www.twin-travel.com
A variety of package and customised holidays are on offer - weddings and honeymoons, golfing packages, spa vacations and cruises. Single travellers get special deals. The Specials link has a wide range of offers in many parts of the world. Booking online is not available.
e-mail: rsvp@twin-travel.com

Universal Southport Travel

www.universal-travel.com
These US agents offer the full range of

services to both corporate and leisure travellers including travel reports, 24-hour emergency travel assistance, world wide customer care, airline, hotel and car rental discounts and a host of others. Contact is by telephone, e-mail or completing the inquiry form.
e-mail: donna@universal-travel.com

Universal Travel Services

junior.apk.net/~funtrip/
There are travel offers to a few parts of the world for corporate clients. Follow the links to Trips and Themes for details. To book you will have to use the phone.
e-mail: funtrip@apk.net

Utah Ski Vacations

www.travelsource.com/ski/skiutah.html
On offer are customised packages to seven Utah ski resorts with a choice of accommodation. There is a link to Delta Vacations Promotions with a different range of holidays to resorts in Europe and north America, with several interesting Internet deals. Contact is by telephone.
e-mail: not available

Vacation.com

www.vacation.com
This is a database of almost ten thousand US Travel Agents, providing the full range of travel services. To find an agent, enter your zip code and use Agency Finder to locate a nearby office. The Vacation Finder has drop-down menus to help you plan all aspects of your holiday including budget. There are several featured tour destinations all over the world.
e-mail: customer-mail@vacation.com

Vacationsinc.com

www.vacationsinc.com
On offer are holidays in north America from white water rafting to skiing. Get your details from the Services link.

The Ski Resorts link covers everything to get you there and back. Complete the Vacation Bid Request for prices. You can book online from the home page or the Destinations link.
e-mail: res@vacationsinc.com

Valley Travel

www.valleytravel.com
Cruise holidays, group and customised vacations are their speciality. They arrange world wide ticketing, car rentals and hotel reservations. Dream Vacations cover honeymoons and family reunions, while tours and cruises come as regular and themed including jazz bands, food and wine festivals, fishing, music and opera, National Geographic and more. To book just complete the form.
e-mail: Jolley ent@earthlink.net

Wildwest Travel

www.webcom.com/~wildwest/
This is strictly adventure travel with horse-mounted or snowmobile tours and Alaskan Cruises. The home page has a very useful Travel link with information on airlines, accommodation, regional details, dining, weather and lots more. You can purchase travel accessories and book online using the Worldspan Dates and Destinations system, which gives you real-time availability of all your travel needs.
e-mail: Wildwest@webcom.com

Woodlake Travel Services

www.woodlaketravel.com
Although they specialise in US destinations, they also organise Golf and Ski vacations to Europe. The map tells you where they operate and clicking on a location will produce a mine of information. The Leisure Travel link lets you choose from a range of adventure holidays, cruises, family vacations and more, with links to search those destinations. You can request information and book online.
e-mail: not available

www.IneedaVacation.com

www.ineedavacation.com
You get to all the California-based Disney attractions on this web site. Use the drop down menu at the bottom of the home page for information, then book online.
e-mail: sales@ineedaVacation.com

Yankee Holidays

www.yankee-holidays.com
On the homepage you can browse six US and five Canadian cities, all with holiday packages. The link for each city provides a brief description, a list of tour packages, and other links to order brochures or book on-line. Yankee Holidays specialise in theatre packages, sending thousands of theatre-goers every year to the best shows with guarantees of the best seats. They offer discounted airfares and special peak-season packages; they accept late reservations and operate a cancellation charge waiver scheme.
e-mail: info@yankee-holidays.com

Polar

Adventure Network International

www.adventure-network.com
If you want to tour Antarctica, make sure you are ready for the experience. Check out the maps and pre-tour sections; the base camp section describes the arrival and departure points and tour programs tell you everything else you need to know. There is an online enquiry form.
e-mail: adventurenetwork@com-puserve

Polarcircle.com

www.polarcircle.com/index.htm
The North and South poles are tailor-made for ski expeditions, dog-sledding, helicopter trips, skydiving and ballooning. Guides are professional, experienced and helpful and escort you on all tours.
e-mail: info@polarcircle.com

Wildlife Worldwide - Polar Regions

wildlife-ww.co.uk/ploar.htm

The polar regions, the Arctic and Antarctic, the sub-Arctic and the Falkland Islands provide exceptional tour locations. You may have seen them on TV but seeing shoals of basking whales, seals, penguins and seabirds for real can be breathtaking. In the north you get walrus, polar and brown bears, Arctic foxes and flocks of unusual waders and seabirds. The destinations are diverse and tours generally last two to three weeks.

e-mail: sales@wildlife-ww.co.uk

World wide

4th Dimension Tours

www.4thdimension.com

US travel wholesalers specialising in group and individual air and land packages to Latin America and Europe. Click on the region and further menus for that area will appear. You can request brochures and book online.

e-mail: mis@4thdimension.com

4U2-Travel Services

www.focusmm.com/4u2

Internet-based travel agents. The home page is a delight with very good animations and pictures. 4U2 organise all your travel requirements world wide with a range of special deals and package tours to many world destinations. There is a map link, a world time link and an international direct dialling index, DDI, for anywhere in the world, on the home page. The Search facility is not yet in operation but most of the links on the home page are set up so that you can choose your travel according to budget and destination.

e-mail: 4u2trave@4u2travel.com.au

Aaeros Travel

www.aaeros.com

While they specialise in Latin American and Caribbean destinations, they also offer discounted international air fares, vacations and cruises world wide. The Travel Information link is full of tips to help you plan your journey. There is an FAQ section and a How to Prepare for a Trip link, particularly useful if you are new to finding your dream holiday on the Internet. Take a look at their descriptions of the Mexican State of Oaxaca and Costa Rica. You may also find their Specials interesting.

e-mail: aaeros@ix.netcom.com

Abercrombie & Kent

www.abercrombiekent.com

US-based and industry leaders, they organise travel to more than a hundred countries from Antarctica to Zimbabwe. The home page has links to Destinations, Activities, About our Trips, Marco Polo Club and more. You can request a brochure online and download video clips with the software link provided. Newsletter subscription and online booking form are linked from the main page.

e-mail: via online form

Above the Clouds

www.aboveclouds.com

American travel company specialising in eco-tourism and adventure in high places with a focus on the Himalayas, Europe and Patagonia. You can take a scheduled tour or have one designed for you. They serve numerous academic and well-known private institutions.

e-mail: info@aboveclouds.com

Access Travel

www.accesstravel.com

An online booking service for world wide travel. Their range is very large and if you cannot find what you are looking for, complete the form on any destination link.

e-mail: Qts1@ix.netcom.com

Access Worldwide

www.accessworldwide.com

Apart from regular travel services, they offer European rail tours, online hotel reservation with an emphasis on India and a whole flotilla of cruises anywhere in the world. You can book online.
e-mail: sales@accessworldwide.com

Acruise Best Buys

www.buyacruise.com

As leading high volume discount cruise agents they aim to provide the lowest available cruise prices. They offer family and corporate cruises world wide with additional senior citizen discount, extra perks for incentive groups and their employees and more. Apart from cruises they provide a variety of travel services to international travellers.
e-mail: info@buyacruise.com

Adam Travel

www.adam-travel.com

A US company specialising in Greece, Egypt, Israel and Italy and discounted domestic and international airfares, hotels and car rentals. Each package is linked to price and content information; itineraries have their own button.
e-mail: fly@adamtravel.com

Advanced Travel Management

www.advancedtravel.com

Corporate flight, hotel and car reservation system world wide. They use the ResMail flight information system, which provides flight options and fares. Instructions online tell you how to choose your flight and make a booking including ordering your in-flight meal. Online you can also use Sabre TripReview to view your travel plans via the web and Mileage Minder which keeps track of travel awards for flights, car rentals, hotels, affinity cards and more.
e-mail: not available

Advantage Prime Travel

www.prime-travel.com

Broad-based assistance with travel planning, especially sports-related tours and services in Western Canada and packages to the finest ski towns and resorts in Switzerland, France and Austria.
e-mail: info@prime-travel.com

Adventure Associates

www.adventureassociates.com

Australia-based with services across the world, particularly polar expedition cruises to Antarctica and the High Arctic, Latin America and Australasia. Easily navigated, the site has many useful facilities - newsletter subscription, online booking, photo gallery, search facility and links to informative external pages.
e-mail: mail@adventureassociates.com

Adventure Quest.com

www.adventurequest.com

More than 1,300 adventure trips for families, groups and independent travellers from luxury safaris and gourmet cycling tours to mountain treks and cultural journeys in remote regions. The home page lists them and if you can't find something you like, ask for assistance.
e-mail: not available

Adventure Travel Society

www.adventuretravel.com

The aim of this Society is clearly stated on the web site. To that end its vacations are adventure oriented for the sheer pleasure of enjoying the environment. To explore what you can do use Adventure Search. The site is well designed, with lots of information at your fingertips. You can join in the cause and obtain membership benefits, which include savings on all aspects of travel.
e-mail: not available

Adventure Women

www.adventurewomen.com
Active women, 30-something, can adventure tour all year round on four continents. Excursions are graded from easy through moderate to high energy. Grade yourself then select from a very wide variety of exciting tours in Asia, Africa, Europe and North America.
e-mail: Advwomen@aol.com

Adventures Abroad

www.adventures-abroad.com
Operating from US and European offices, they organise tours for small groups across the world. You have a selection of tours to choose from with wonderful pictures to excite your interest and links to maps, magazines, travel agents, FAQ and tours of special interest. Newsletters and brochures can be ordered online.
e-mail: info@adventures-abroad.com

Adventures in Good Company

www.goodadventure.com
Outdoor and wilderness trips for adult women of all ages, backgrounds and life experience. Trips range from weekend backpacking to international hiking and biking, exploring Anasazi ruins in New Mexico, trekking in Nepal or rock climbing in Joshua Tree National Park. The site also contains the recipe of the month, useful links, outdoor tips and topics.
e-mail: trips@goodadventure.com

Agent Green Travel

agent-greene.com
Agent Green, together with international affiliations, organise your special occasions, private and public. Links from the home page lead you to hot travel deals world wide. Large discounts are offered on group cruises with the group leader qualifying for a free cruise. Use the Tell Agent Green what you want form and he will fix you up with a special deal.
e-mail: khaf@erols.com

Air Discounters International

airdiscounters.com
They offer discounted travel to most major destinations on the planet and travel packages to some locations. Special links take you to current deals. You can make enquiries but cannot book online.
e-mail: griff@airdiscounters.com

Air Treks.com

www.highadv.com
This one-stop shop will take you around the world and you can use the Trip Builder to create your own itinerary. Twelve thousand flights and hundreds of destinations should give you millions of routes. If that's too much to handle they will help you or you can opt for one of their Roof of the World tours or African safaris.
e-mail: airtreks@highadv.com

AJ Travel

www.ajtravel.com
Corporate travel is their game, especially organising all aspects of meetings and conferences from the venue to the speaker's water jug. Their main location is San Antonio but they can replicate the services elsewhere in the world. As members of ASTA they obtain lower rates with leading travel providers.
e-mail: info@AJTravel.com

Alameda Travel

www.alamedatravel.com
Selected destinations world wide for any occasion, or just having a break. Select a destination link and follow it to heaps of vacations, or take the Tours link to a multitude of packages on every continent. Some links on this friendly site keep you going with music.
e-mail: info@alamedatravel.com

All Horizons Rancho Travel

www.allhorizonstvl.com
They offer a full travel service to several parts of the world, from car hire to luxury

cruises. Their expertise is in planning customised leisure travel, but can help with a variety of package and guided tours.
e-mail: Allhorizonstvl@worldnet.att.net

All Wanderlands Travel

www.allwanderlandstravel.com
They want to help you make informed decisions about your vacation or business trip. If you have an idea, let them know and an agent will get back to you with helpful information. They feature several vacations, all worth a good look.
e-mail: info@allwanderlandstravel.com

Alladin Travel

www.aladdin-travel.com
Affordable family vacations to a variety of destinations world wide. The Best Buys in Vacations, Tours and Cruises give you the most you can get from your holiday budget. There is so much choice you are bound to find something suitable. If not, complete the online forms for assistance.
e-mail: sales@aladin-travel.com

Andiamo Adventours

www.andiamoadventours.com
Small groups make these hiking and biking tours in Italy, Switzerland and California friendly and personal. Or you can customise your trip to include kayaking, golfing, fly-fishing, bird watching, skiing and surfing with other options like wine tasting, landmarks, parks and art.
e-mail: Mike_gomes@andiamo adventours.com

Aquatic Adventure Tours

www.divetours.com
Aquatic tours to the best diving destinations, combined with underwater fun, golf, kayaking, tennis and other sports. They operate more or less around the world so check the destinations online. Instructors will assist you and

accompany the tours if you wish.
e-mail: not available

Archers Direct

www.archersdirect.co.uk
The UK company offers great value holidays on a marvellous web site. Choose between world wide or summer sun holidays or both if so inclined, then follow the links for full details, special offers and a brochure request facility. Booking must be made by phone until an online facility has been added.
e-mail: enquiries@archersdirect.co.uk

Archetours

www.archetours.com
Architectural tours world wide. Itineraries are built around architectural themes, historical periods, specific architects, movements or regional architectural phenomena. Their groups include professionals in the business, so you never know who you may meet.
e-mail: archetours@aol.com

Aristotle Travel

www.aristotle.gr
Christian, biblical, classical, educational and theological study tours; archaeology, art and history are all part of their portfolio. They operate mainly in Greece, Israel, Turkey and Egypt but include other destinations in Jordan, Russia, Italy and the UK.
e-mail: aaristotle@hol.gr

Aroma Tours

www.aroma-tours.com
Aromatic journeys world wide. Tours for aroma therapy enthusiasts and garden lovers, all the way to delightfully decadent gourmet tours in France, Turkey, Bali and Australia.
e-mail: info@aroma-tours.com

Around The World Travel

www.discounttravelhawaii.com
Though they offer travel services world

wide, they specialise in discount air travel and prepaid tours to and within the Hawaiian Islands. These tours include Polynesian culture, volcanoes, helicopter flights, luaus, and Pearl Harbour.
e-mail: aloha@atwt.agencymail.com

Art Connections
www.art-connections.com
Art History and Cultural excursions in Europe and the USA. Tours led by an art historian, may include cooking classes, wine tasting, trips to archaeological sites and visits to private galleries and gardens.
e-mail: info@art-connections.com

Asia Travel
asiatravel.com
Asia Travel has offices in the Middle East and Asia, providing hotel and resort reservation services across the world. The home page links you to hotels they represent, categorised according to room rate. You can book online easily, special discounts are offered for this facility. Internal pages with country links take you to airports, travel information and touring. An additional feature allows you to send electronic postcards to your family and friends.
e-mail: asiatrav@asiatravel.com

Avanti Dimensions
www.avantidimensions.com
Their territory is Europe and Latin America. European vacation packages include intimate hotels, paradors in Spain and pousadas in Portugal; the tours are slanted toward activities like walking and biking, cooking schools and so on. Central American travellers go to beach resorts, eco-lodges, Mayan ruins, national parks and more. South American packages take in capital cities, beach resorts, jungle lodges, Machu Picchu, Galapagos and Chile cruises and much more. You can book online.
e-mail: info@avantidimensions.com

Azure Travel Bureau
www.azuretravel.com
World wide cruises and the Indian subcontinent from Tibet to the Maldives with a full travel service, including escorted tours.
e-mail: not available

Bales Worldwide Holidays
www.balesworldwide.com
The exceptional navigation system of this site makes searching easy and interesting. UK-based, Bales offer a full range of travel services world wide. Select a region on the world map and you enter a more detailed map, then follow the links to your holiday. The online booking facility confirms prices and dates even while you are booking. Tailor-made vacations have their own section.
e-mail: enquiries@balesworldwide.com

Bargainholidays.com
www.bargainholidays.com
Lots of bargains world wide, listed by price ceilings in the Bargain Basement. You never know what you might pick up in a last minute deal.
e-mail: via online form

Best Fares Online
www.bestfares.com/travel_center/desks/ top25desk.asp
This US-based discount club offers members discounted US internal flights, international flights and holidays. Links tell you how to become a member, give travel information and e-mail deals.
e-mail: via online form

Birdwatching Tours from Wings
tucson.com/wings/Birdwatching_Tours. html
Bird watching in sixty countries on seven continents. Tour leaders are competent professionals catering to beginners and experts alike. The catalogue has itineraries and

descriptions of more than two hundred events.
e-mail: wings@wingsbirds.com

Black Sea Travel Services
www.black-sea.com
They offer travel services to Mexico, Hawaii and Europe. Their European section offers individual or bus escorted tours; car rentals anywhere on the continent and Eurail passes. Cruises are world wide with premier lines.
e-mail: not available

Blaney's Travel
www.blaneystravel.com
Lively tours to exotic places like Bali, Petra, Taj Mahal and the pyramids and camping holidays in Asia, Africa and America. Additionally they package holidays with sporting events world wide. Check out the discount travel by e-mail.
e-mail: blaneys@BlaneysTravel.com

Bridge the World.com
www.bridgetheworld.com
A wonderful site that helps you sort out travel needs from insurance to hotels and flights. You can chat online to an agent, view special offers and create your own round-the-world itinerary. Links to ABTA, FCO, and Lonely Planet.
e-mail: not available

Bridgewater Travel
www.bridgewater-travel.co.uk
This UK-based company organises travel to Central Europe and the USA. On this well-designed site you can explore a country before deciding or, using the search page facility, choose a holiday to suit your taste and budget. A Special Offers link tells you about current deals.
e-mail: usa@bridgewater-travel.co.uk

Broadreach
www.gobroadreach.com
Summer adventures for teenagers with scuba diving, sailing, paddling, back country marine biology and wilderness programs in the Caribbean, Australia, the Middle East, Central and South America. Check the programs featuring particular activities.
e-mail: questions@gobroadreach.com

Cabo Kurt Adventures
www.royalafricansafaris.com
African safaris, Costa Rican Eco-Tours, Tahiti or Great Barrier Reef diving, you can take your pick. The home page has internal links to tour descriptions and a remarkable photo gallery. Other links in the text lead you to lots more to keep you interested. Make your enquiries by e-mail, phone or fax.
e-mail: cabokurt@cabokurt.com

Calgary National Travel
www.cnts.ab.ca
Full travel services in Greece, Turkey, Egypt, Israel and Jordan. They offer villas, hotels, apartments, a range of tours, yacht charters, discovery cruises and more. Their cruise fares are probably the lowest in Canada.
e-mail: vlahosc@cadvision.com

Call of the Wild
www.callwild.com
For women only. The large selection of tours and destinations world wide can be searched from the down-drop menu. Other sections have FAQ, press releases about the company, the guides they use and a tour calendar. You can book online or by e-mail.
e-mail: trips@callwild.com

Carlson Wagonit Travel
www.carlsontravel.com
There is a selection of hotel and resort offers around the world, with a list of accommodation available, plus a short description at each location with a few pictures. There are also links to travel guides and maps and some games.
e-mail: via online form

CARP Travel

www.carptravel.com

One stop travel shop for Canadians over 50. Enter region, category and price range in Plan Your Vacations and take your pick of what comes up, or find a package to suit. The choice covers just about everything.

e-mail: carptravel@justvac.com

Casino Tours

www.casinotours.com

Casino Tours represent several gambling establishments across the world. Online you can shop for books, videos and gambling paraphernalia. You will find last minute special offers in their Junket Trips section. You can book online.

e-mail: casino@mindspring.com

Cheapflights.com

www.cheapflights.co.uk

This no-frills site gives you bargain travel world wide. Choose your destination from the alphabetic menu.

e-mail: not available

Club Med

www.clubmed.com

Club Med has a wonderful web site with a vast amount of easily accessible information. Start at the map and follow links to internal pages where you will find everything you are looking for. Several online services are available in addition to booking; you can order a brochure, send an electronic postcard, get the latest news and good deals and tell them what you think about them. A Village Directory link makes choosing your destination very simple.

e-mail: not available

Club Senior Sports

www.clubseniorsports.com

If you are a senior citizen and have a sport you enjoy, the club has groups of like-minded who combine sport with their holidays all over the Americas. Bike through a rain forest, hike on a basalt beach, kayak with spinner dolphins or snorkel with fish.

e-mail: Clubnews3@aol.com

Cobblestone Tours

www.cobblestonetours.com

Culture and history in the Basque and Catalan regions of Northern Spain and Maya country in Guatemala. Groups are kept small and all programs show prices, itineraries and departure dates.

e-mail: info@cobblestonetours.com

Concierge.com

www.concierge.com

Site with travel deals, quick fare finder, airfare bargains, airport guides, currency converter, B & B, maps, advice and would you believe it's world wide?

e-mail: not available

Contiki Holidays

www.contiki.com

Contiki offer a variety of holiday possibilities. They serve both travellers and travel agents. The web site itself offers a whole range of Internet features, many of which can be downloaded. You can search for your perfect trip, send a postcard to a friend and exchange ideas with others on the travellers' community page.

e-mail: contiki@contiki.com

Costco Travel

www.pricecostcotravel.com

Price Costco Travel offer discounted vacation packages to Europe, Hawaii, Orlando and the Caribbean, discounted airfares, hotels and car rentals if you have a Costco Travel ID. World wide cruises on the best liners and affiliated hotels in the USA, London and Paris are other features. You can book online.

e-mail: Travel2@psmt.usa.com

Creative Leisure

www.creativeleisure.com/vacation/
hawaiigolf/golf.html
Hawaiian golf vacations. The home
page lists condos with great golf nearby
where they arrange a round or two of
golf. They do the same in the UK,
Caribbean, Mexico, Singapore and Bali.
Prices are not listed.
e-mail: not available

Crossroads Adventures

www.xroadsusa.com
Small group travel with a multilingual
tour guide and driver, more than fifty
itineraries in North America and several
in Australia. Accommodation is mainly
camping with hotel stays in cities. Tour
routes, pictures, guides and contact
details are well presented.
e-mail: info@xroadsusa.com

Crystal Blue Vacations

www.cbvonline.com
These are the resorts of a variety of
holiday clubs scattered around the
world. Each club has its features page
with details of facilities and every
conceivable holiday activity.
e-mail: info@crystalbluevacations.com

Custom Spa Vacations

www.spatours.com
Change your shape, look and lifestyle
with a Spa Vacation in North America.
If you prefer a ranch vacation in Arizona
or Massachusetts, follow the links as the
site has interesting vacations on offer.
Prices are listed.
e-mail: not available

Cyclevents Tour Worldwide

www.cyclevents.com
Affordable fun tours in selected
countries world wide for cycling
enthusiasts. Most rides are designed
for experienced riders, but energetic
beginners by conditioning themselves
pre-ride, may conquer the routes with
a little effort and a smile.
e-mail: not available

Dance Holidays

www.danceholidays.com
If you want to dance your way around
the world take a look at the web site of
this UK based company and listen to the
wonderful music online. Whether your
preference is salsa, tango, flamenco,
belly-dancing, jive or line-dancing, they
have a trip for you. Each dance style has
a selection of holidays, which include
accommodation, dancing and language
classes, touring and lots of nightlife.
Online booking is still to be installed;
meantime register on the form provided
and you will receive news by e-mail.
e-mail: enquiries@danceholidays.com

David's Trips and Tours

www.davidtours.com
Leading providers of luxury travel to the
Gay community and Friends. All tours
are designed for casual sophistication
and affordable luxury. They operate in
South Africa, Central Europe and
Morocco and run plush weekend trips
to New Orleans. The web site gives a
feel of what to expect.
e-mail: Info@davidtours.com

Deckchair.com

www.deckchair.com/defaultie4loot.htm
Type in your holiday destination,
departure and return dates, with the
number of adults and children travelling,
and you will be given details of flights
available from the UK.
e-mail: not available

Dimensions in Travel

www.dimensionsintravel.com
Outdoor activities are the central feature
of these excellent tours world wide.
Other offers include Hawaiian travel
packages and instant ticketing for
European destinations.
e-mail: Info@dimensionsintravel.com

Disney Vacations

disney.go.com/DisneyVacations/
As expected, this is an exciting, fully animated web site, better seen than described. You are taken right into the fantastic world Disney has created, with virtual tours across the site. You can do everything online with the click of a mouse and that's as much as need be said.
e-mail: via online form

Dive Discovery

www.divediscovery.com
World wide diving and adventure travel to exotic places. Photographic safaris in Africa, trekking and sea kayaking everywhere, with visits to stone-age communities in Irian Jaya and Papua New Guinea.
e-mail: divetrips@divediscovery.com

Earth River Expeditions

www.earthriver.com
If you enjoy rafting be sure to visit this web site. Expeditions are offered in Peru, China, the USA, Canada and Ecuador. You are given details of each tour with marvellous photos of the region and its inhabitants. A chart puts all the information together and lets you choose. There is a section about guides, safety and river ranking worth reading. You can book by e-mail.
e-mail: earthriv@ulster.net

ebookers.com

www.ebookers.com
Online travel service for flights, car hire, hotels, holiday deals, insurance and a Flight Watch service. The home page has a handy Find a Flight table, and an auction page to bid on international flights. Other menus include Specialist Travel and Special Offers while Tools has a world clock and tells you about weather, currency and UK airports.
e-mail: via online form

EF Performing Arts Tours

www.efperform.com
Give your group the chance to perform at venues in Europe, North America, the South Pacific and Australia and project them into the international spotlight. All participants get the opportunity to discover new places, cultures, and languages on group travel adventures. Programs are designed to balance rehearsal and performance time with sightseeing and free activities.
e-mail: not available

EF Religious Tours

www.efreligion.com
Catholic youth groups and schools throughout North America get to discover first hand the religious sites of Lourdes and Fatima, the Holy land, as well as Europe's churches, synagogues and cathedrals.
e-mail: Religious.tours@ef.com

Ellie Gahan Travel and Cruise Centre

www.elliestravel.com
Romance in Hawaii, Mexico, Tahiti or Belize by cruising with the best companies. You choose, they say they do the rest.
e-mail: aspire@elliestravel.com

Enchanted Vacations

www.enchantedvacations.com
For more than a decade, this family-owned company has been organising vacations and honeymoons to three main destinations - Hawaii, Mexico and the Caribbean, each with its own link. Use the Fast Response Form for a quotation and within 24 hours you will receive a complete customised travel package.
e-mail: Mexico@enchantedvacations.com

Envoy Travel Online

www.envoytravel.com
This is an online full-service travel agency located in Chicago, specialising in good quality vacations world wide, with special expertise in listed countries.

They deal with major cruise lines and give you lots of information on their web site.
e-mail: goenvoy@ix.netcom.com

Equator-Net

www.equator-net.co.uk
Aimed at the business traveller, Equator Net offers to dispense with the middle man. Register online and you will be able to book your travel, accommodation, chauffeur service or car hire, rent a mobile telephone, buy your foreign currency and travel insurance. There are also travel tips and advice. No e-mail address, but there is a UK freephone number if you need help.
e-mail: not available

Equinox Travel

www.equinoxtravel.co.uk
On offer are tailor made itineraries and group tours in Europe and Southern Asia. Navigation is easy and you quickly get at the information you need. The photo gallery is delightful. You can book online.
e-mail: reese@equinoxtravel.co.uk

Equitour Horseback Riding Holidays

www.ridingtours.com
Horse riding with more than one hundred tested circuits on six continents. They suit the ride to your ability, taste and budget. Click on the world map to select from dressage in Portugal to a cattle roundup in the Rockies and more elsewhere. You may enjoy exploring the Instructional Programs.
e-mail: Equitour@wyoming.com

Eurotrip.COM

www.eurotrip.com
Information and advice on cheap tickets and budget travel in Europe aimed mainly at students. This site has a chat room and links to other helpful web sites. The colourful and user-friendly home page has icons and pictures to help you find your way around. A free travel newsletter is available.
e-mail: andrew@eurotrip.com

Explorations in Travel

www.exploretravel.com
Outdoor and cultural adventures world wide for women over 40. Itineraries include long walks in New England, cross-country skiing or canoeing, biking, whale watching in Alaska, snorkelling in the Caribbean.
e-mail: women@exploretravel.com

Explore Worldwide

www.explore.co.uk
Possibly the largest range of adventure tours, treks, safaris and expeditions. They invite you to travel to new and unusual destinations with over 200 original adventures in 96 countries spending anything from eight days to six weeks as an individual or part of a group. You travel as the terrain requires; accommodation at small friendly lodgings emphasises comfort rather than luxury. Take a look at this wonderful site just for the pleasure.
e-mail: info@adventureworld.com.au

Explorers

www.explorers.co.uk
World wide scuba diving, visits to Europe for school groups and total solar eclipses. Diving holidays go from the clear waters of the Red Sea to the remote Ghost Fleet of Truk Lagoon. To set you off there are diving instructions online.
e-mail: dive@explorers.co.uk

Far Horizons Archaeological and Cultural Trips

www.farhorizon.com
Archaeological and Cultural Tours in Mexico, Central and South America, Easter Island, Syria, Jordan, Iran and Thailand. They offer adventure, education and a new understanding of world culture, with lectures and dinner parties

to cultivate friendship.
e-mail: journey@farhorizon.com

Farebase

www.farebase.net

This is a search facility world wide for charter and scheduled flights, late availability holidays and bargains within price brackets.
e-mail: via online form

Footprint Adventures

www.birding-tours.co.uk

UK company with travel packages and customised tours around the world. You can search the site according to where you want to go or what you want to do. There is a site map, online holiday and flight booking and external links to information on travel insurance, guides, books and maps.
e-mail: sales@footventure.co.uk

Franceline's Cultural Tours

www.franceline-tours.com

Customised travel in East and West Europe, Tunisia, Russia and the Far East. Check the Featured Tours section for details or design your trip. All services can be paid for online.
e-mail: Franceline@franceline-tours.com

FreeGate Tourism

www.freegatetours.com

Tours to Europe, the Mediterranean and Latin America. Destinations are listed and tours described with prices and dates. FAQ, contact details, special offers and online booking are available.
e-mail: mail@freegatetours.com

Freewheeling Adventures

www.freewheeling.ca

Adventure travel in several countries in North America, Europe and Israel. View Adventure Index for prices, dates and destinations. The Freewheeling Experience link on the home page

gives all the other details.
e-mail: bicycle@freewheeling.ca

Gay and Lesbian Active Vacations

www.alysonadventures.com

Alyson Adventures specialise in active and adventure travel for gays and lesbians. Information is abundant with an up-to-date news link and FAQ section. Booking and catalogue requests can be made either by e-mail or phone. The trip schedule is conveniently divided alphabetically or by date, activity and destination.
e-mail: info@alysonadventures.com

Genie Travel Online

www.genie-travel.com

Genie Travel Online brings together about 1700 travel agents providing quality services world wide. Their excellent web site has huge amounts of information and is well worth a visit. Hot Deal lets you choose holidays to suit yourself; newly married couples have a variety of honeymoon venues on offer and at the Fun Stuff link you can buy brochures, books, games, recipes and Travel Trivia. Other interesting links include weather forecasts, maps, online reservations, 24-hour world wide emergency services, access to a range of financial services and lots more.
e-mail: info@genie.travel.com

Glacier Valley Wilderness Adventures

www.glaciervalley.com

They offer out-door recreational adventure for individuals and groups in the Americas. Kayaking, mountain biking, scuba diving and dog-sledding are just a few of their vacations.
e-mail: glaciervial@baraboo.com

Gotta Go Discount Travel

www.gottago.com

You get a complete travel package in addition to discounted airfares to Europe and Asia. There are links to

cruises in the Gulf of Mexico, Alaska, the Caribbean and Mediterranean and online contact information if you wish to sail elsewhere. Similarly if their package tours do not appeal, just ask for what you want.
e-mail: info@gottago.com

Great Expeditions

www.greatexpeditionstravel.com
Great Expeditions, based in Colorado, organise adventure travel in Africa, Mexico, the Caribbean, Australia, New Zealand and the South Pacific. They specialise in scuba diving, biking and nature tours, horse-riding safaris and other outdoor activities, with special deals for group travel. You can book online with the form provided.
e-mail: ge@greatexpeditionstravel.com

Hidden Trails International Riding Vacation

ridingtours.net/index.htm
Riding tours world wide. Choose from more than 100 riding tours, guest ranches and outdoor vacations. Each link has overviews, information on cities, history, education, and a list of related books.
e-mail: hiddentrails@hiddentrails.com

Hole in Sky Tours

www.holeinthesky.com
Solar eclipse expeditions combining good vacation value with optimum eclipse viewing. The home page has pictures of past eclipses and projected Eclipse Safari tours to Africa in 2001 and 2002.
e-mail: Eclipse98@earthlink.net

Holiday House

www.holiday-house.com
Wholesalers with customised vacations here, there and everywhere. Shop online with the Trip Planner, adding each product to your basket until you think you have all you want, then save it for future reference.
e-mail: not available

Holidays Afloat

www.holidaysafloat.com
An unbeatable range of world wide cruises from barges to tall ships to state of the art cruise liners. There are four categories to choose from so that you are bound to find something to please you. Alternatively you may wish to have your cruise tailored to suit. This is a good site to start looking for a cruise.
e-mail: not available

IGLU.COM

www.iglu.com
This specialist in winter-sport holidays offers discounted accommodation and holiday packages. There is a search facility for accommodation and links to downloadable 3-d maps of the area you are visiting. Lots of useful links worth investigating.
e-mail: enquiries@iglu.com

International Expeditions

www.ietravel.com
Wonderful graphics and pictures illuminate this site, which offers travel services world wide. The Destination section has lots of information and links to external sites. You can request a brochure and book online.
e-mail: nature@ietravel.com

Internet Travel Services

www.internet-travel.com
Leading all-inclusive resorts and cruises in and around the Gulf of Mexico. Check the database for hot deals.
e-mail: mt@internet-travel.com

Island Dreams Tours & Travel

www.islandream.com
If water sports are your game, take a look at this site to dive and snorkel world wide. The photos set you going, the stories are intriguing and you can book online from the home page.
e-mail: info@islandream.com

Island Honeymoons

www.islandhoneymoons.com
Pick your tropical island on the globe for an all-inclusive wedding and honeymoon customised and to a budget.
e-mail: not available

JMB Travel 2000

www.jmb-travel.co.uk
Opera for opera lovers in 40 cities world wide with more than 100 productions in season. Choose a city and you get the itinerary, programmes and prices. There are escorted tours to festivals in Krakow, Warsaw, Helsinki, St. Petersburg, Verona and Wexford.
e-mail: info@jmb-travel.co.uk

KE Adventure Travel

www.adventuresports.com/travel/ke_adventure/welcome.htm
Trekking, climbing, mountaineering, mountain biking, cultural journeys and safaris for all ability levels in the mountain regions of the world. They say that all their expedition leaders are professional and highly experienced.
e-mail: Keadventure@enterprise.net

Kollander World Travel

www.kollander-travel.com
They have a department for every type of travel and provide the whole array of services. There is something for everyone. Make sure you register so you can book online.
e-mail: kwtravel@kollander-travel.com

Lastminute.com

www.lastminute.com
Everything is discounted - hotels, holidays, flights, even restaurants and entertainment. The home page has links to all these and a list of the warmest destinations at each time of year. There is an auction facility so you can decide what you want to bid.
e-mail: via online form

Lone Wolf Adventure

www.lonewolfadventureco.com
You are invited to have The Ride of Your Life. On offer is an unforgettable cycling experience through the mountains of Colorado and rainforests of New Zealand. All tours come with comfortable accommodation, meals, daily ride maps detailing routes and elevations, a fully equipped support vehicle and knowledgeable local guides.
e-mail: info@lonewolfadventureco.com

Lowestfare.com

www.lowestfare.com
Specials, Hot Deals, Great Vacations and Cruises from this online holiday travel agent. Select your destination from the drop down menus. All prices are quoted in US Dollars. There are links to a low fare finder, currency converter, travel news, weather reports and maps. You can also check out the Coolest Place on Earth each day.
e-mail: support@lowestfare.com

Mountain Adventures

www.mountainadventures.com
Experience the magic and mystery of remote, exotic regions. Trips include Kilimanjaro in Africa, Aconcagua in the Argentinean Andes, Himalayas in Nepal and Illimani in the Bolivian Andes. They offer rock and ice climbing and expedition training.
e-mail: mtnadv@netshel.net

Mountain Travel.Sobek

www.mtsobek.com
Adventure travel with more than 100 trips to 60 countries on six continents. You can trek in Nepal, walk in Africa, raft on uncharted rivers and ski cross-country to the South Pole. Visit Ethiopia, Yemen, Corsica, Alaska, Peru, and other countries off the tourist track. Groups are limited to fifteen, guides are fully trained and equipment is the best available.
e-mail: info@mtsobek.com

My Travel Site

www.mytravelsite.com

The stated aim of this internationally
affiliated company is to provide reliable,
professional and personal services to
travellers. Focusing on casinos, cruises
and adult vacations, they sell complete
travel packages. This excellent web site
helps you plan your dream holiday and
when you're done choosing, book using
the online form and you'll get a discount.
e-mail: Adventure@ytravelsite.com

Nomad Travel

www.nomad-travel.com

Exotic adventures world wide for individuals
and small groups. Itineraries, prices and
dates are downloadable and there are
special deals for net surfers advertised
on the home page. You can book online
by secure credit card payment.
e-mail: info@nomad-travel.com

Olivia Cruises and Resorts

www.oliviatravel.com

Olivia Cruises and Resorts are only
for women. The home page carries
information about their cruises, resorts
and tours world wide. Each of these is
fully described with links to prices, ports
of call, ship layout and more. A contest
online offers a prize of a 7-night
Caribbean cruise. There are several
ways to make contact.
e-mail: info@oliviatravel.com

Orient Canada Travel

www.octravel.com

Canada and South East Asia may be
very different but each region has its
own attractions and both are equally well
presented on this site. There is a lot on
offer and the discounts are worth looking at.
e-mail: info@octravel.com

Orient-Express Trains and Cruises

www.orient-expresstrains.com

The famous Orient Express offers luxury
train tours across Southeast Asia,
Europe and Australia. This wonderfully
designed web site is a treat in itself.
It has lots of information with online
booking, an image library and many
special offers. Links take you to cruises
on offer.
e-mail: not available

OutWest Global Adventures

www.outwestadventures.com

Year-round tours for gays and lesbians
throughout North America and the
world. Vacations are mainly out-of-doors
listed by season, dates and activities or
you can check out particular trips for
details.
e-mail: dheinzen@outwestadventures.com

Pilgrim Tours

www.pilgrimtours.com

Wholesale tour operator offering land
and cruise programs to Europe and
Africa in modern coaches with a variety
of accommodation and discounts for
work teams and study groups.
e-mail: res@pilgrimtours.com

PlanetRider Travel Directory

www.planetrider.com

This is an online travel resource
with links to bargain holidays, airfares,
car rental and cruises. You get maps,
currency conversion, reservations, and
other services. Choose from Destinations,
Landscapes or Activities on the menu at
the top of the home page.
e-mail: not available

Points of Interest

eztn.teamtrams.com/points/

They help you tie the knot in Hawaii
or wherever else you choose, making
all the arrangements; you just have
to be there on time. Other travel services
include cruises world wide and vacations
in the Caribbean, Disney World and
European capitals, fixing theatre tickets
and rail passes.
e-mail: poire@ibm.net

Poltours

www.poltours.co.uk
Good prices for flights, inclusive
holidays and city breaks in Poland,
Eastern Europe and world wide. They
offer the full range of transportation
with coach travel high on the list. Short
break programs take you to cities all
over the world.
e-mail: sales@poltours.co.uk

Posh Journeys

www.poshjourneys.com
A pot-pourri of escorted tours to unusual
locations all over the world. They keep
groups small, usually not more than
fifteen and select locations for charm,
atmosphere, history, and quality service.
e-mail: contact@poshjourneys.com

Practical Traveler

www.practicaltraveler.com
Full travel services and customised
holidays - spas, diving, white water rafting,
skiing, biblical tours and lots more.
Cruises, yacht charters and Caribbean
villas are another branch of their business.
There is a lot on offer at this site.
e-mail: practicl@ix.netcom.com

Premier Travel & Cruise

www.premiertravel.com
They are part of a network of 1700
American Express Offices in 130 countries
offering a vast range of tour packages
from the basic to the most elaborate.
Tell them your preferences and they do
the rest, including very specialised trips.
You can book online.
e-mail: travel@premiertravel.com

Prestonwood Travel

www.ptravel.com
You name it in the field of world travel
and they do it. This is a big web site with
a lot on offer, from a weekend package to
a customised minutely planned vacation
from their Luxury Collection.
e-mail: tours@ptravel.com

Princetravel

www.princetravel.com
Prince Travel specialise in holidays to
Japan and Hong Kong, tours, conventions
and group holidays, with links to airline
ticket reservations and cruises.
e-mail: info@princetravel.com

Prism Holidays

www.prismholidays.com
US company with world wide destinations.
You can pick and choose accommodation,
cruises and tours, all of which are amply
detailed. You can request a brochure
online.
e-mail: via online form

Protravel International

www.protravelinc.com
The Caribbean is their playground.
Every island link has a map, tour data,
where to stay and what to do there.
Their European experience will give you
fully guided tours or simple packages
from golf in Scotland and Ireland to
historic tours in Italy and Greece. They
also market discounted cruise holidays.
e-mail: info@protravelinc.com

Quality Christian Travel Programs

www.eo.travelwithus.com
Christian travel programs at an
affordable price, travelling in the
footsteps of Jesus in the Holy Land
and St. Paul in Turkey and Greece.
Nine itineraries cover Israel with
extensions to Egypt, Jordan, and Italy.
Catholic Pilgrimages include eleven
tours; the Other Travel Programs link
has eight itineraries to England, Italy,
Scandinavia and much more.
e-mail: eo@travelwithus.com

Quest Global Angling Adventures

www.fishquest.com
If you are an angler take a good look at
this web site. You can choose your holiday,
plan your trip and shop online for
fishing gear, books, videos and apparel.

Make reservations on the form provided and send it by e-mail. Sign the guest book and you will receive newsletters from the company.
e-mail: questhook@aol.com

QuinWell Travel Service

www.quinwell.com
On offer is the full range of travel services for lots of destinations world wide. Take your pick of their vacations as they cover all types from honeymoons to families travelling with pets. You can book online.
e-mail: rbeech@quinwell.com

Rancho Mirage Travel

www.ranchomiragetravel.com
On the home page of this web site for gay and lesbian travellers, there are links to destinations world wide, special deals and packages, cruises, tours and more. Another link goes to a lesbian travel centre with venues and events of interest.
e-mail: info@ranchomiragetravel.com

Randall International Services

www.randalltravel.com
Before you access information on this web site you must register, as most of the links on the home page require a password. Services are of a highly personalised and exclusive nature for business travellers in some of the most elegant and luxurious locations around the world. Corporate functions and unique excursions are individually planned.
e-mail: wrandall@randalltravel.com

Rascals in Paradise

www.rascalsinparadise.com
Rascals in Paradise specialise in family holidays world wide. To find out what they offer, visit their charmingly animated web site. Every internal page is linked to online reservation and enquiry facilities.
e-mail: trips@RascalsInParadise.com

Red Sea and Worldwide Holidays

www.regal-diving.co.uk
Scuba diving and outdoor activities world wide. To browse all the information, start from the site map. Destinations are described in great detail with accompanying photos. If you already know where you want to go, check out the travel tips, special offers and activity selector facility. You can order a brochure and book online.
e-mail: andy@regal-diving.co.uk

Renshaw Travel

www.renshawtravel.com
As part of the world wide network of travel operators they have literally thousands of travel offers. To find the holiday you want just select from the drop down menus for Sea and Land Vacations.
e-mail: sales@renshawtravel.com

Resort Reservation

www.resortres.com
Accommodation in condos, villas and resorts in Mexico, the Caribbean and the USA. You can home in on exact locations on the destinations page. Each link has enough detail to decide and book online.
e-mail: friends@resortres.com

Rex Travel

www.rextravel.com
This is specialist travel with the emphasis on special. For openers you get European Balloon Adventures, Botswana Wing Safari, Around the World by Private Jet, Great Rail Journeys of the World. Everything is laid on, just pay up and turn up.
e-mail: vacation@rextravel.com

Robin's Travel

www.robinstravel.com
They are a full service travel agency with lead specials changing every Monday. Keep looking because you never know which destinations are on

offer until they are posted.
You can book online.
e-mail: robins@wspan.com

Robinson Travel Services
www.robinsontravel.com
They offer the whole range of vacations
including Club Med resorts. Many of
their packages include frequent flyer
miles. They specialise in European
and Hawaiian destinations, which can
be customised if you prefer, as well as
a range of cruises. Contact them by
telephone or e-mail.
e-mail: info@robinsontravel.co

Sacred Journeys
www.sacredjourneys.com
Women travelling to sacred sites
where goddesses have been honoured
for millennia. There are tours and
pilgrimages to the UK, Ireland, Israel,
Hawaii and 3-day spiritual retreats in
North California. Enjoy the experience,
healing and companionship.
e-mail: alaura@wco.com

Saga Holidays
www.sagaholidays.com
US-based travel company catering
to the over 50's. They operate world
wide offering travel packages listed
by continent. All tours are detailed
with maps and photos. You can order
a brochure online and bookings can
be made by e-mail or phone.
e-mail: Sales_info@sagaholidays.com

STA Travel
www.statravel.co.uk
On offer are discounted airfares,
holidays and accommodation - Beds
on a Budget. Click on the List of Routes
link for a table of airfares. Alternatively,
there is a helpful fare calculator at the
bottom of the home page. Lots of other
useful links and information.
e-mail: not available

Sue Brown Travel Consultants
www.snft.com
Full service travel company based in
Huston, Texas specialising in corporate,
group and incentive packages.
Destinations feature Disneyworld,
leading resorts, tourist islands, spas
and Hawaii. Sign up for the Singles
Club and receive a monthly newsletter
and invitation to gatherings in Houston.
e-mail: staff@snft.com

Sunbusters Travel
www.sunbusters.com
Full travel services for leisure and
corporate travel world wide. They offer
discounted domestic and international
air fares, corporate travel and meeting
planning, cruise specials, tour packages
everywhere, family vacations, gift
certificates, romantic getaways,
weddings and honeymoons, corporate
discounts and much more.
e-mail: info@sunbusters.com

Sunfinder Vacations
www.sunfinder.com
Personalised travel services to the
Caribbean, Mexico and Hawaii. Golf,
scuba diving and snorkelling, shopping,
beautiful beaches and honeymoons
are the reasons to go. Check out the
discussion boards, useful travel links
and recommended reading.
e-mail: info@sunfinder.com

Sunsations Travel
www.sunsations.com
Corporate and business travel services,
special interest vacations, activity holidays,
eco-tours, group tours, dream holidays
and conventions world wide. Each holiday
type is detailed on separate pages.
e-mail: mlach@sunsations.com

Tailor Made Travel
www.tailor-made.co.uk
UK company offering customised travel
and holiday packages across Australia,

New Zealand, Canada, Fiji and Africa. The home page has links to each region, travel tips about visas, currency, weather and more. Online booking and brochure request facilities are provided.
e-mail: sales@tailor-made.co.uk

Telme Global Traveller
www.telme.com
Online travel broker offering competitive prices on hotels, flights and travel insurance. They claim to offer the Internet's first e-miles reward scheme. Enter your details in the online form and click Search. The main menu has useful travel information.
e-mail: via online form

The Great Canadian Travel Company
www.greatcanadiantravel.com
Unusual destinations and exciting holidays in Canada and world wide from polar bear tours in the Arctic to zebra and elephant safaris in Africa, wines of the world, archaeological tours or mountain climbing anywhere there are mountains. Just looking at the Extreme Adventure pages is a lot of fun.
e-mail: sales@gctc-mst.com

The Northwest Passage Adventure Travel Outfitters
www.nwpassage.com
Outdoor adventures in many parts of the world for anyone, beginners to the experienced. You will find details from the Trip Information link on the home page.
e-mail: info@NWPassage.com

The Tripmaker - Outdoor Adventures & Ecotours
www.thetripmaker.com
World wide outdoor adventures and eco-tours for all ages, budgets and experience levels. Four main links on the home page give details of so many wonderful tours you are bound to

find one to excite you. Use the form or e-mail to request more information.
e-mail: tripmaker@bellsouth.net

The Vacation Store
www.takeoff.com/cs/
They offer cruises and other travel packages world wide. On the home page you can use the cruise search to locate the perfect cruise or the vacation search for a holiday of your preference, then use the listed phone number for prices and booking.
e-mail: not available

Thomson Holidays
www.thomson-holidays.com
You get the full spectrum of travel world wide services and a web site with vast amounts of information. Use the search facility on the main page and by following links to internal pages, go step-by-step to online booking facilities. Just choosing your holiday fills you in on what you can expect at every destination. You are kept abreast of ticket availability and the latest hot deals.
e-mail: comments@thomson.co.uk

Top Deck Adventures
www.topdecktravel.co.uk/index.html
Discounted flights and holidays for the 18 - 30's age group. This attractive, user-friendly site has lots of links and a helpful scroll menu on each page to help you navigate.
e-mail: res@topdecktravel.co.uk

Transworld Travel
travel.prometeus.net
A variety of travel services world wide, with good short-stay packages being a speciality. They also have special deals on airline tickets, accommodation and car rentals, each of which apply to a group of countries listed online.
e-mail: tour@euro.kharkov.ua

Travel Bids

www.travelbids.com

Save money on your travelling from
room reservations to airline tickets by
entering an online auction. Information
is clearly laid out for beginners, with
various links to guide you through to
making your first bid. The service is
available world wide.

e-mail: questions@TravelBids.com

Travel Channel

www.travelchannel.com

One stop travel shop where all your world
wide travel questions are answered, from
planning a trip By Idea or Destination, to
booking hotels, flights or cars, with some
cut price deals. Tools & Tips advise you
on weather, currency conversion, travel
health and tips. The site is packed with
helpful links and is also very easy to use.

e-mail: not available

Travel Class

www.travelclass.co.uk

Holidays for schools, skiing and snow-
boarding in Europe and USA and residential
adventure holidays in the UK. Details of
all programs, adult accompaniment and
student instruction are online.

e-mail: alastair@travelclass.co.uk

Travel Consolidators.com

www.travelconsolidators.com

Discount airfares to three main
destinations - Europe, Africa and the
Middle East. The Travel Request link
gives you two forms. Use the Travel
Request form to find out about pricing
for airfares, cruises and tour packages,
and the Traveller Profile form to receive
special offers by e-mail.

e-mail: Europe-for-less@worldnet.att.net

Travel Cuts

www.travelcuts.com

Discount holiday brokers selling flights,
accommodation, tours, travel insurance,
and air, rail and coach passes for

students and budget travellers. There
are links to tariff tables and an online
enquiry form.

e-mail: via online form

Travel Experts

www.prairienet.org/business/travex/
homepage.html

UK and Caribbean resorts with lots of
help from the agents, with planning to
a budget. You can book online.

e-mail: not available

Travelbag

www.travelbag.co.uk

This site claims to offer some of the
best deals on airfares, accommodation
and holiday specials. Destinations
are mainly long-haul and flights are
business class. Travel insurance is
available, with links to several policy
types and an online quotation service.

e-mail: not available

Travelocity

www.travelocity.co.uk

This online travel agent gives you access
to bookings for flights, car hire, hotels
and holiday packages. There are also
special weekend deals and a guide to
destinations, all available on the home
page. Other links take you to a currency
converter and a theatre guide.

e-mail: not available

Travelport

travel-port.com

Three travel agents combine to give you
wide ranging holidays world wide with
cruises, adventure and just plain leisure
to choose from, with the best value for
your travel dollar.

e-mail: not available

Travelsavers UK

www.travelsavers-uk.com

A budget travel broker offers cheap
deals on hotels, flights and holidays.
The site has links to a currency

converter, lonely planet guides, weather information, airlines and so on down to sleeping in airports! The online enquiry form will get you a response by telephone or e-mail.
e-mail: fares@travelsavers-uk.com/ index.htm

Travelshoppe.com
www.Travelshoppe.com
One-stop travel shop offering everything on discount world wide.
e-mail: via online form

Travelzone
www.travelzone.xtcom.com
Honeymoons, spas, skiing, cruises, family adventure are all here. Phone, e-mail or complete the form and you are in touch.
e-mail: Nancy simon@hotmail.com

Travex
travexnet.com
On offer are travel packages and customised tours with a vast range of possibilities in Southeast Asia, Australia, New Zealand and some European destinations. You can book online.
e-mail: info@travexnet.com

Tread Lightly
www.treadlightly.com
Eco-excursions to many parts of the world, mainly Mexico, Central and South America and Asia. Mountains, deserts and tropical forests are equally their scene. They also offer discounted airfares and assist with car and van hire. Browse through their expeditions or e-mail for a customised trip.
e-mail: info@treadlightly.com

Trip Web
www.tripweb.com
You can book flights and get lots of travel information from passports to vaccinations. They guarantee lowest available airfares and arrange car and

hotel reservations. To book click the Reservations button on the home page. Under the Specials link you will find Cruises to the Caribbean.
e-mail: not available

Tripmakers.com
www.clubtripmakers.com
Discount travel agents who organise trips to Mexico and airfares world wide, with special offers to Dublin and Tel Aviv from the USA. Registration with the Club entitles you to discounts.
e-mail: not available

Tripquote.com
www.tripquote.com
This is a free service to travellers in the USA and Canada, presently being extended. You easily find your way around the site and get a travel quote within 24 - 48 hours. The travel library and FAQ pages are very helpful.
e-mail: staff@tripquote.com

Tropical Travel Agency
www.tropicaltravel.net
Various travel packages are on offer including cruises, tropical islands and ski holidays; take your time, as there is a lot to choose from. To book, complete the Reservation Inquiry Form
e-mail: sales@tropicaltravel.net

Tropical Treasures
www.tropicaltreasures.com
Tropical Treasures specialise in all-inclusive resort holidays in the Caribbean, Mexico, and Fiji. They plan special and group events with a discount system. To book, scroll down the home page and click the Reservations button.
e-mail: svoak@tropicaltreasures.com

Trrravel Company
www.trrravel.com
You can register online to receive a free country guide and take part in a holiday auction with prices starting at almost

nothing. The web site shows travel services and information separately. A multiplicity of links helps you choose a tour to suit, while online guides and travel magazines suggest unusual travel ideas. A flight directory will pick out your most suitable flights.
e-mail: not available

Turquoise Travel
www.findthegems.com
Turquoise Travel arrange golf vacations, cruises and specialist tours including exceptional food & wine vacations in California and elsewhere, garden tours in Holland and Ireland, chateaux and gardens in France, gardens and villas in Italy, art and educational tours. For more information, complete the online form.
e-mail: not available

U wood Travel
www.uwoodtravel.com
They offer cruises to the most popular coasts world wide and special interest European tours. These are accessed separately. For additional information prices and travel brochures, complete the form available from the Sign Out guest book link.
e-mail: scu@uwoodtravel.com

Ultima Travel
www.ultima-travel.com
Disneyworld, beach vacations, and Europe are on offer. The home page has several links with lots of useful information for business and leisure travellers. Online booking is not available
e-mail: uti@ix.netcom.com

Ultra Adventure Tours
uati.com/students.htm
The student tour possibilities offered are almost endless, itineraries are designed to suit budgets with transportation in luxury coaches, good accommodation, meals and student parties as part of the package.
e-mail: Karen@uati.com

Uncommon Adventures
www.uncommonadventures.com
Diving, surfing and adventure travel to remote parts of the world. You can search by destination, where you will find sample itineraries with details, or you can go direct to the Itineraries page, or ask for a customised tour.
e-mail: theworld@uncommon adventures.com

UNI - Travel
www.unitrvl.com
There are several links on this site to Specials and Discounts for airline weekend fares and hotels and other travel companies for special interest groups. A whole variety of vacations are on offer in the Package Tours link. You can book online from the home page.
e-mail: bwood@unitrvl.com

Uniglobe.com
www.uniglobe.com
They offer one-stop shopping for airline tickets, cruises, car rentals, hotels and vacation packages, as well as access to travel information and merchandise. Their toll-free round-the-clock services are reputed to be award winning. Their vacations cover a lot of ground and sea, all of which you will find on site. You can book online.
e-mail: not available

Uniglobe Passport Travel
www.uniglobepassport.com
Whether you travel for business, recreation or the unusual, you may find something of interest on this site. To book or request information, click on the link at the bottom of each page.
e-mail: not available

United Ventures Touring Company

www.kalemegdan.com
On the home page, select your destination on the world map or use the inquiry form. The travel information link provides general information and visa and customs regulations for Yugoslavia, New Zealand and the USA. To book click on the Sabre icon on the homepage.
e-mail: uvt@kalemegdan.com

University Travel

www.univtravel.com
University Travel specialises in discounted airfares and tour packages to selected locations around the globe. From the home page you can get to package tours on several continents and a fares link with low international and domestic airfares around the world. Complete the information request form and your questions will be answered.
e-mail: utravel@univtravel.com

Upscale Travel

www.upscaletravel.com
For a little pampering and a vacation with personal service in exotic and unusual places, take a look at this web site. There are many wonderful locations and great ideas you are unlikely to come across elsewhere.
e-mail: info@upscaletravel.com

UTAG Travel

www.utag.com.au
Log in your departure and destination cities world wide, what you want to do, click on the Plan your Trip button and they will do the rest. They have a vast database of over 5,000 hotels and are the Australian part of Woodside Travel Trust, reputed to be the largest travel management company in the world. There is a lot of useful information on weather, health, currency, maps and travellers' tips. A special facility will help you find your nearest UTAG Travel agent.
e-mail: not available

Vacation Getaways

www.vacation-getaways.com
Vacations to selected US destinations with a large choice of things to do, places to stay and eat, special deals and specialist holidays by the number. For prices and reservations, make contact by e-mail or telephone.
e-mail: getaways@vacation-getaways.com

Vacation Outlet

www.vacationoutlet.com
If you want a flight and hotel vacation or a cruise getaway, check the Vacation Package Specials for the best discounted prices. Destinations are mainly in Europe and the Americas. There is also a link to ski holidays. For prices and more information, call the listed number.
e-mail: not available

Vacation Reservation

www.vacationreservations.com
These travel agents help you with holiday plans more or less world wide. They offer a whole range of accommodation from campsites to luxury hotels, holidays you can select by hypertext link, adventure trips, cruises, health & culture getaways, weddings and honeymoons, sports and family vacations. To book, contact them by e-mail.
e-mail: info@vacationreservation.com

Valerie Wilson Travel

www.vwti.com
As one of the largest travel consultants in New York they provide a full range of services to corporate clients, promising the lowest rates and hassle-free arrangements. They also specialise in cruises world wide which you can select from a range of options to suit a budget. You can book online.
e-mail: info@cruisesofvalue.com

Value Holidays

www.valhol.com
If you are travelling in a group and you

want your tour customised, take a look at this excellent web site. There are Music Appreciation Tours with a full program of opera and concerts; Pilgrimage & Religious Tours; Cultural Tours with visits to museums, galleries and places of special interest. Student & Performance Tours give you an opportunity to perform with bands of all types; Family Reunions; European Ski, Golf & Adventure Tours with lots of outdoor activities. Booking online is not yet available.
e-mail: sales@valhol.com

VegiVentures

www.vegiventures.com
Vegetarians and vegans on holiday need not feel left out. VegiVentures offer holidays in Britain, Turkey, and Peru. Information is fairly inclusive and the food section has sample menus. You can subscribe to a newsletter and keep yourself informed.
e-mail: holidays@vegiventures.com

Venture Travel

www.venturetravel.com
You can suit yourself as to how you select your holiday - by destination, type or price point, or search the whole database geographically. Then complete the Quote Request form and when you're satisfied, book online for all your travel requirements.
e-mail: info@venturetravel.com

Victor Emanuel Nature Tours

www.ventbird.com
They claim more than twenty years experience in adventure and nature tours from the Amazon to Zimbabwe. Guides escort you on 140 tours to over 100 land-based destinations. Browse through the catalogue and visit the 2000 Schedule of Tours by Month. Unique among bird watching tours are cruises that take you to bird sanctuaries otherwise inaccessible.
e-mail: info@ventbird.com

Victoria Travel

www.victoriatravel.com
You get a variety of travel services including bargain world wide airline tickets, hotel and car rental reservations, a full range of vacation packages, flights to Russia and the Ukraine, visa and other services. Vacation packages include Europe, USA, Caribbean Islands, Asia and the Pacific, ski trips and cruises. The Prices link on the home page will tell you the cost and you can book online.
e-mail: tickets@victoriatravel.com

Village Travel

www.villagetravel.com
This is an all inclusive travel web site crammed with special deals, customised vacations, full services to business and leisure travellers and lots more. Clicking the Information button on the home page links to the Carlson Wagonit home page, with more holidays and travel information.
e-mail: connieb@villagetravel.com

Voyagers International

www.voyagers.com
You can shoot the world with a camera, but before doing so visit this highly photographic web site with lots of useful information. Schedules, prices and booking come online.
e-mail: info@voyagers.com

VTS Travel Direct

www.vtstraveldirect.com
Their speciality is Corporate Travel. The exclusive VTS Travel Direct Program saves business travellers up to 50% off when booking as a package rather than in components. They provide several other useful services such as Management Reports, 24-hour emergency booking and processing of passports and visas. The Leisure Traveller link on the home page has information on resort discounts,

cruise specials, vacation getaways and world wide Spas; a Traveller's Toolset with weather, calendar, world time and currency and a list of 1800 US hotels.
e-mail: connieb@villagetravel.com

White Star Tours

www.whitestartours.com
Tours, cruises and vacation packages for everyone, particularly senior citizens. The Our Tours link gives a list of exciting tours throughout the USA, Canada and elsewhere. Click on any of the hyper-linked tours and you get an itinerary, pictures and prices.
e-mail: not available

Whiteside Travel Online

www.whitesideww.freeserve.co.uk
On offer are Scottish vacations and holidays world wide. The latter are table formatted with all relevant details. Use the search link to find the most suitable vacation then fill in the form. An agent will respond within two days.
e-mail: Maria@whitesideww.freeserve.co.uk

Windward Travel

www.windwardtravel.com
As an American Express Travel Representative Office they have access to a wide selection of resorts, cruises and getaway packages to suit all pockets and taste. You can book online.
e-mail: travel@windwardtravel.com

World of Travel Online

www.worldoftravel.com
Links on the home page set out the regions and types of holiday offered. African Safaris, Alaskan Cruises, Concord Flights, Luxury Travel and European Value Tours are detailed with itineraries and pricing. Group travel and professional meetings of any size can be customised.
e-mail: staff@worldoftravel.com

World Travel Masters

www.worldtravelmasters.com
The home page has six links; Special of the Week, Domestic Fares, International Fares, Cruises, Travel Packages and Travel News, with a small number of offers.
e-mail: wtm@worldtravelmasters.com

World Travel Partners

www.worldtravel.com
You are offered an opportunity to join the philosophy of this third largest travel company in the USA, which combines all aspects of world travel. Links from the home page take you to company organisation more than products. The Terraquest link gives you several virtual expeditions on the web, one of which won the Best of the Web Invision Award in 1996.
e-mail: info@worldtravel.com

World Travel Vacations

1stoptravelshop.com
With over 1700 Travel offices, they cover the globe with their services. You get current prices from the Free Travel Quote Form. A whole range of holidays is on offer with many worthwhile up-to-minute deals. You can book online.
e-mail: Ronald@interpoint.net

World Ventures Tours and Travel

www.wvtt.com
You can buy travel accessories on the Boutique link and Travel Tips reminds you to lock your door before you leave. If you require information on the other links fill the Information Form, accessible on the Profile link.
e-mail: knox@wvtt.com

World Wide Travel

www.worldwide.co.za
They offer complete travel services to South Africans travelling at home and abroad, or for foreigners visiting South Africa. Additionally they specialise in

conferences, co-ordinating travel arrangements for delegates, arranging facilities, function rooms and banqueting services. Information is well organised and bookings can be made online.
e-mail: info@worldwide.co.za

World Wide Travel Service

www.wwts.com
On offer are Adventure Travel, Cruises, Dream Vacations and Only The Best holidays world wide. There are several links to information on this excellent web site that will help you choose your trip and plan it, including health, visas and a currency converter.
e-mail: not available

World Wide Vacations

www.worldwidevacations.com
A superb web site packed with information about all types of holidays anywhere in the world. A large number of links take you to world destinations or types of vacation with more links to check locations, request tickets, accommodation, travel and cruise packages and lots more. You can book online.
e-mail: reserve@worldwidevacations.com

Worldview Tours

www.worldviewtours.com
Although India and Nepal are the main attractions, there are more than fifty tours on six continents in this colourful web site. Choose the best season to visit India and Nepal through the Useful Information link then select your holiday. You can book online.
e-mail: nino@worldviewtours.com

Worldview Travel

www.101travel.com
World View take you primarily to Hawaii and Mexico, but also organise cruises and spa excursions around the globe. There are also a few Hot Cruises Deals you might want to look into.
e-mail: info@worldviewtravel.com

Worldwide Escapes

www.wwescapes.com
This wonderful web site gives business travellers in Asia customised weekend breaks and short vacations. And you don't have to strain yourself if you don't want to, since the trips are graded from Easy to Strenuous Activity. City and Country links are a good source of information. You can book online.
e-mail: info@wwescapes.com

Worldwide Tour and Cruise Programs

www.vancouvair-services.com
There is a mine of information for travellers in several world centres through links on the home page. If you are looking for a winter holiday, an escorted bus tour in Europe or train timetables of major railways world wide you are likely to find it here. The International and the Others links give you a lot more useful travel information.
e-mail: holiday@vancouvair-services.com

www.Traveltrust.com

www.traveltrust.com
Corporate and leisure travel world wide. Leisure travellers get all the help they need and corporate travellers even get their conferences organised down to post trip billing reconciliation and program evaluation.
e-mail: travel@traveltrust.com

Young's Worldwide

www.youngstravel.com
Based in New England, with more than 1,700 offices around the world. They specialise in Caribbean destinations and as American Express Travel Services representatives have access to the whole range of travel service suppliers. They operate two travel clubs, Mercury and the more luxurious Century Club. They claim to offer the lowest airfares available on this first rate web site.
e-mail: not available

Travelogues & Journals

Africa

A Journey Through Ethiopia

www.casema.net/~spaansen/
The author has turned his trip to Ethiopia into a travel guide. He ably describes where he went, what he saw and makes suggestions for other travellers. There are pictures and comments on the country's landscape, people, flora and fauna and links to Ethiopia-related pages.
e-mail: Spaansen@casema.com

Africa in the Beetle

www.stoessel.ch/beetle_africa.htm
Marcel Stoessel drove 11,000 km through southern and western Africa in his 1974 VW and took a lot of pictures. He also travelled to Vietnam, Cambodia and Bosnia and shares his adventures on this interesting site.
e-mail: Marcel@stoessel

Souvenir

www.swimmingduck.com/souvenir/
index.html
A trip to the Ivory Coast turned into advice on how to get along there - do's and don'ts of behaviour, customs regulations, local money and how not to get cheated, a photo album and links to other travelogues and pages.
e-mail: via online form

Tunisia Travel Story

www.geocities.com:80/Athens/Troy/
8725/Tunisia/tunisia.htm
A group of Finnish students visited the ancient ruins of Tunisia. They describe the monuments and provide a collection of enjoyable pictures. Their travel tips and recommendations of places to visit are worth noting. There are links to Tunisian web sites.
e-mail: Haha@lib.hel.fi

Asia

A Travelogue by Erik Futtrup

infoLanka.com/org/srilanka/travel/
trip3.html
Erik Futtrup gives useful tips to travellers planning a trip to Sri Lanka. There are sample prices of accommodation, transport and dining services and suggestions of where to go and what to do. This server has three other travelogues with lots of information and pictures.
e-mail: not available

David and Bill's daily travel diary North Korea

www.ozemail.com.au/~davidf/
homepage/nk_1994.htm
This is a very detailed and personal diary from the trip David and Billy organised to North Korea. It contains no pictures but you will find a lot to interest you, especially on the reality of life in the country.
e-mail: not available

Greg's Mongolian Journal

www.oz.net/~guerrero/
This is Greg's diary of one-and-a-half months in Mongolia. There is a lot about the people and environment, supported by many pictures and a word or two of advice, with links to

Mongolia-related web pages.
e-mail: Guerrero@oz.net

Indonesia - A Travelogue by Charles Cremers

utopica.com/charles/
Charles Cremers' Indonesian travelogue is well designed, has many pictures and is easy to navigate. It is unusual in that it is divided into chapters, each with memoirs about individual islands and regions. There are several maps and links to other travelogues and Indonesia-related web sites.
e-mail: Ccremors@yahoo.com

Phil Aylword's India Photo Essay & Travelogue

phil.savory.org/phil/index.htm
Phil Aylword kept a diary during his month-long trip to India. He visited more than ten places which he discusses with photos and includes some useful tips and typical prices. The map of India shows what attracted him particularly. He advises on how to prepare yourself before going to India and recommends a list of books to read.
e-mail: Aylward@onramp.net

Australasia and Oceania

David's Trip to Micronesia

micronesia.freeservers.com
Each of the five parts of the travelogue refers to an island in Micronesia and Nauru. David gives his personal impressions and adds advice for intending travellers. There are links to other travel pages and a picture gallery.
e-mail: Djwilson25@hotmail.com

New Zealand Trip Report

www.webfoot.com/travel/trip/trip.nz.html
A personal travel guide to New Zealand with sound information and good advice. A picture gallery is supported by notes on flora and fauna. There are links to local guides, travelogues and hostels.
e-mail: not available

Caribbean

Caribbean Travel Roundup Newsletter

www.caribtravelnews.com
This is a huge collection of about five hundred personal travelogues, reports and news releases from the Caribbean, listed by time of release, island or keyword. Although there are no pictures, you will find reviews of resorts, islands and restaurants with comments and warnings not ordinarily found in travel guides.
e-mail: Editor@caribtravelnews.com

Europe

Beer Travel in Germany

www.teleport.com/~dgs1300/ reise96971.html
An employee of a US brewery made several journeys to southern and eastern Germany to taste its most famous beers. This is his diary. He describes the finest breweries, beer inns and best beers of each city he visited. A good read for beer lovers.
e-mail: not available

Brama Travel

www.brama.com/travel/
Brama is a Ukrainian business directory. Its travel section has four travelogues the best of which is Kathy and Bill Clark's 1997 Ukrainian Vacation. It is more concerned with passing on useful tips than recording personal impressions. Each town is accorded a brief history and photo gallery.
e-mail: not available

Itineria Spitsbergensia

latinitas.org/phototheca/ spitsbergensia_en.html
This is a very exciting travelogue of the Svalbard archipelago, which contains the island of Spitsbergen. There are numerous photos of extraordinary

quality, taken in spectacular conditions - arctic nights, sunsets, sunrises and other wonderful light conditions. You can enlarge the pictures and view them in full screen size. The author is well acquainted with the archipelago and knows where and when to point his camera.
e-mail: Sm@tandberg.no

Lynn and Steve's trip to Switzerland
www.geocities.com/TheTropics/Resort/6822/
A personal diary of their trip to Switzerland logs their itinerary, mileage, where they stayed and what they saw and did. Out of this come good advice, a price guide and some very good pictures.
e-mail: not available

Stephen's Trip to Romania
www.primenet.com/~srdrake/romania.htm
Stephen's memoirs of a trip he made to Romania may guide you on where to stay and what to eat there. There are maps, notes on ethnic groups and links to other travelogues and Romania-related sites. Though the diary is in plain text it has links to pictures.
e-mail: Srdrake@primenet.com

TheTravelzine.com
thetravelzine.com
This is a collection of travelogues of western or southern Europe. Each is a diary with pictures and useful travel tips with links to cities mentioned. New diaries are welcome.
e-mail: Donlin@thetravelzine.com

Travels In Russia '95
www.webcom.com/whills/Russia/Russia95a.html
This is the diary of a trip from Finland to Japan through Russia. The cities the author passes through and his adventures aboard the Trans-Siberian train are described with pictures taken in various parts of the world.
e-mail: Whills@webcom.com

Latin America

Central American Sea Kayak and Jungle Expedition
www.caske2000.org/
Two independent journals describing three-year-long kayak expeditions from Baja in California to Panama. There are several adventure and people stories, local cuisine and a guide on getting food in the jungle and surviving at sea.
e-mail: Caske@yahoo.com

Costa Rica Journal
members.aol.com/chris21172/costarica/front.htm
A trip journal, a slide show of Costa Rica and travel related links make up this site. The journal describes the journey in detail, with an explanation of local terms and customs, advice on what to do and where to go.
e-mail: Chris12272@aol.com

Huka.com
www.huka.com
This entertaining site is a diary of a trip to Ecuador and the Galapagos Islands. Each day records what was visited with an explanation of terms and historical notes. Throughout the text you will see highlighted place names; clicking on them will take you to one of five hundred photos on the site.
e-mail: Dave@huka.com

Isla Margarita Vacation Page
www.geocities.com/TheTropics/Cabana/6858/
Isla Margarita is a beautiful island off the Venezuelan coast. A packed picture gallery and personal notes on weather, people, beaches, restaurants and transport should give you a pretty good idea. There are links to tourism

and maps of the island.
e-mail: Nicholsonj@halifax.crosswinds.net

La Ruta Maya
**www.euronet.nl/~jeroen_k/
la_ruta_maya.htm**
On this well illustrated site the author
traces Mayan civilisation through Mexico,
Guatemala and Honduras. He describes
their monuments, gives useful tips about
what to take, health and money matters,
customs and immigration. There are
links to weather data and maps.
e-mail: Jeroen_k@euronet.nl

Latin America Travel Journal
**www.cris.com/~Elpolvo/latina/
index.htm**
Personal impressions of a trip along
the Pacific coast from Mexico to Chile.
The author's diary gives lots of detail
down to her packing list, advises on
where to go, what to do, what to
avoid and a guide to prices.
e-mail: Cher7@sprynet.com

Middle East

Diary of Trip to the Middle East
www.mdb.ku.dk/tarvin/diary/
A Danish medical student records
his trips to Lebanon, Syria and Jordan.
He includes with his diary useful travel
information not likely to be found
elsewhere like getting there, when to
go, sample prices and a short Arabic
phrasebook.
e-mail: Tarvin@mdb.kn.dk

North America

Big Adventures
www.bigadventures.com
The author describes his 1,800-mile
trip along the Pacific coast from Mexico
to Canada. He adds picture stories from
other parts of the USA and Hawaii and
links to other travel pages.
e-mail: not available

Glenn Lindgren's Off the Wall Travel
**www.lindgren-group.com/
travels-in-mexico/**
The travelogue has a picture gallery
and many links to Mexican web sites,
the journal has personal advice,
suggests where to stay, places to visit
and guidance prices. There is a large
photo gallery, recipe book, FAQ and
links to travel-related web sites.
e-mail: not available

Tailwinds '96
**www.voyager.net/tailwinds/general/
index.html**
Ed Norman's 6,000-mile bicycle journey
from Alaska to Florida took ninety-eight
cycling days. Each day he tells you
where he went with amazing pictures.
He adds a list of necessary books,
facts about food, equipment, packing
and his sponsors.
e-mail: not available

Polar

Skiing in the Arctic
**cuiwww.unige.ch/~masselot/trips/
index.html**
The author crossed Iceland, Spitsbergen
and Greenland on skis. The journey is
described in detail, as are the specifications
of equipment and a list of sponsors.
Most important are the tips on how to
find a sponsor and prepare for such a
journey.
e-mail: Masselot@cui.unige.com

Tony Hansen's Antarctic Journal
www.mageesci.com/Antarctic/
Travel guides to the Antarctic are rare.
This somehow fills the gap. After three
trips and reaching the South Pole Tony
Hansen must be an expert. His pictures
capture extraordinary spectacles of light
and his notes describe life, nature and
the weather. There are links to other
expeditions to the continent.
e-mail: TontHansen@megeesci.com

World wide

A Travel and Wildlife Page
www.rjpreston.freeserve.co.uk
Travel pages with personal impressions and beautiful pictures from exotic countries. Each country has a gallery of thumbnails which when clicked enlarge to half-screen size. There are links to other travel pages.
e-mail: Rjpreston@rjpreston.freeserve.co.uk

Around the world on a bicycle
ourworld.compuserve.com/homepages/ianburns/
A British traveller, Ian Burns, spent a year cycling across the world. Starting in France he went through Italy, Greece, Turkey, Iran, Pakistan, India, Thailand, the USA and Ireland. His diary describes what interested him most, his adventures, the pictures he took, his bicycle and the equipment he used on his journey. He includes some useful travel tips.
e-mail: Ianburns@compuserve.com

Chuck Anderson
Bicycle Travel Stories
home.earthlink.net/~chuckanderso/
If you are thinking about a cycling trip, take a look at this site. There are stories and pictures from some of the countries Chuck visited, a list of recommended books, advice on packing and equipment and links to cycling associations around the world.
e-mail: Chuckanderso@earthlink.net

Doug Burnett's Travelogues
home.msen.com/~burnett/index.html
Doug Burnett travelled through Europe, the Middle East, Iran, Turkey, Greece, India, China, Mexico, Jamaica and Brazil to seek out the local people and their countries. Information on visas, hotels and travel arrangements are worth noting.
e-mail: Burnett@home.msen.com

Gone Walkabout
www.gonewalkabout.com
One day an American computer programmer decided he was losing contact with himself. So he went off for a year-long break to find himself again. Now he travels every year, recording his diaries and pictures on this site, to share his experiences with others. For good measure, he has added maps and links to travel related subjects.
e-mail: Nomad@gonewalkabout.com

Jim's Travel Page - Going Places
members.aol.com/_ht_a/jims1999/travelpage.htm
The site is designed for those who have read about particular countries and want to hear of personal experiences there. Diaries, in plain text without pictures, relate to countries around the world.
e-mail: not available

John, Mary and Kathy's Travel Page
ourworld.compuserve.com/homepages/johnliu/homepage.htm
These extracts come from a year-long journey from New Zealand to Europe through Oceania. You will enjoy the adventures, people and animals and pick up a few hints on preparing for such a long trip.
e-mail: 101670.2635@compuserve.com

Life After Tyranny
www.ourfounder.com/bone
A German student from Frankfurt relates his trips to places off the travel agents' track. He describes, with lots of pictures, his trips to North Korea, Belarus, Bosnia and Herzegovina and cities on the Polish-German border. Scratching below the surface, he finds wonderful people in the places generally considered as scorched earth.
e-mail: Kudos@bone.8m.com

Matt's Travel Journal
www.qantm.com.au/ext/mclarkson/
When Matt toured Europe, the Middle
East and South America, he kept a diary
in which he recorded what he did and
saw and where he slept. He added his
impressions and advice on what to take,
what to leave, how to prepare and a
large picture gallery.
e-mail: TravelJournal@excite.com

Max @ School - Living an Adventure Novel
www.solomax.com
This site describes an extraordinary
kayak journey taken by the author from
western Canada along the Pacific coast,
through Nicaragua and then along the
Atlantic coast to East Canada. It contains
a detailed diary divided by region, for
each region you can choose to see a part
of his journey from the map provided.
You can also see the wonderful pictures
he took along the way.
e-mail: Max@solomax.com

Nomadic Tales
weecheng.simplenet.com
Tan Wee Cheng from Singapore travelled
extensively through the European part of
the former Soviet Union, Eastern
Europe, Ireland, Denmark, Morocco,
Central Asia and China. There is a store
of information for backpackers, good
pictures, price guides and links to
travel-related sites.
e-mail: Weecheng@postone.com

Our Trip around the World
www.ourtrip.com
The author wishes to encourage people
to travel the world in vans by sharing his
experiences with them. There are several
travelogues, a detailed description of his
van with interior plans, facilities and
equipment; budget tips, packing and
equipment advice and keeping trip diaries.
There are links to similar sites and maps.
e-mail: Joencara@excite.com

Pierre Flener's Travel Page
www.dis.uu.se/~pierref/travel/
Pierre Flener records his trips to Egypt,
Jordan, Iran, Uzbekistan, Turkmenistan
and Nepal and writes a travel guide
to Turkey, Iran, Uzbekistan and
Luxembourg. Though his diaries have
no pictures they make interesting
reading, not least for tips on how to
behave, what to visit, where and what
to eat. A Diary of a Foreigner living in
Turkey is his recollections of three years
spent in that country.
e-mail: Pierre.Flenner@dis.uu.se

Rec. Travel Library
www.travel-library.com
This is an extraordinary collection of
links and home pages to numerous
personal travelogues listed by country.
Each has further links to travel guides,
local transport, travel agents and culture
pages. The travelogues themselves
are in turn listed by year. Some of them
have links to authors' home pages.
As the site is continuously updated the
number of pages grows, covering the
whole world.
e-mail: not available

Salmon Pond
www.cco.caltech.edu/~salmon/
This travelogue tells the story of Lynn
Salmon's trips to China, Argentina,
Australia and the Pitcairn Islands.
Her detailed diaries have links to the
attractions she records with pictures
and travel tips. She includes a few
interesting recipes she picked up along
the route.
e-mail: Salmon@cco.caltech.edu

Salon Travel
www.salon.com/travel
One of the most comprehensive
collections of travel writing on the Web,
witty, intelligent and entertaining. Well
worth a visit.
e-mail: not available

Travel Diaries

www.infomatch.com/~denysm/
This collection of travelogues describes trips to India, Bangladesh, Nepal, Indonesia, Vietnam, the Philippines and Mexico. You will find some very interesting information, useful tips and a record of daily expenses and mileage covered.
e-mail: Denysm@infomatch.com

Travel Experiences Community for Backpackers

www.t-e.co.uk
If you are a backpacker, this is your site - personal travelogues, messages, discussion groups, photo albums, packing advice and travel guides from around the world. You can read about the experiences of others, present yours or discuss your adventures with other backpackers.
e-mail: not available

Travelogues

www.ksheard.freeserve.co.uk/travel/travelogues.html
The common feature of these illustrated travel diaries is that they describe destinations not among the most popular with travellers - the least known of the Canary Isles, Greenland, Iceland, the Himalayas, Bulgaria and more. You can mine them for useful information, not available in travel guides.
e-mail: Kevin@ksheard.freeserve.co.uk

Weather

Asia

BMG Homepage
www.cbn.net.id/commerce/bmg/
This web site gives up-to-date meteorological and geophysical information about Indonesia. Daily updated weather forecasts and historical weather data are also available. There are links to the home pages of its five regional offices.
e-mail: bmg@cbn.net.id

Japan Meteorological Agency
www.kishou.go.jp/english/index.html
The web site of the Japan Meteorological Agency is partially in English. Daily updated weather forecasts cover all major Japanese cities over 24-hour periods.
e-mail: pro@hq.kishou.go.jp

Korea Meteorological Administration
www.kma.go.kr/index.htm
The Korean Meteorological Administration gives 24-hour predictions and 4-day outlooks for the main South Korean cities. The home page carries information on current weather, numerical prediction, satellite imaging, aviation weather and lots more. Text is in English and Korean.
e-mail: jeonso@kma.go.kr

MSS - Meteorological Services Singapore
www.gov.sg/metsin/
The Singapore Meteorological Services update their 24-hour weather forecasts every four hours. On its home page you will find several subjects of interest and shower and thunderstorm warnings. Information provided under Marine Wx Intranet is available to MSS subscribers only.
e-mail: MSS_Operations@mss.gov.sg

PMD-Pakistan Meteorological Department
www.met.gov.pk
The Pakistan Meteorological Department updates national weather forecasts daily. The web site provides both 24-hour and 48-hour forecasts with current humidity readings. You will find 4-day forecasts for all major cities and flood reports.
e-mail: pmdep@paknet2.ptc.pk

Thai Meteorological Department
www.thaimet.tmd.go.th/met-tmd/ eng/menueng.asp
The Thai Meteorological Department provide 24-hour weather forecasts for land and sea areas and weather charts, all updated daily. Text is in English and Thai.
e-mail: tmd@metnet.tmd.go.th

The China Meteorological Administration
www.cma.gov.cn
Most topics on this web site of the China Meteorological Administration appear in English. 24-hour and 7-day forecasts apply to all Chinese provincial capitals while many major world cities get 24-hour forecasts. China Weather Online gives quick weather reports of selected cities.
e-mail: wi@www.cma.gov.cn

Europe

Deutscher Setterdienst -DWD
www.dwd.de/e_dwd_home.html
Current weather and forecasts for the week ahead in Germany with satellite pictures. There are world wide meteorological links. Text is in English and German.
e-mail: via online form

European Centre for Medium-Range Weather Forecasts -ECMWF
www.ecmwf.int/
Twenty-one European States collaborate in this web site, forecasting medium-term weather for the whole continent. There is more detailed information of member States.
e-mail: via online form

Finnish Meteorological Institute
www.fmi.fi/ENG/
Current weather in five major Finnish cities with forecasts for five-day periods and weather reports for shipping. Satellite pictures of the current weather bring it all to life. Text is in English and Finnish.
e-mail: via online form

Hungarian Meteorological Service
www.met.hu/index-e.html
Specifically for Budapest and Hungary and generally for Europe. Current weather with short and medium-term forecasts.
e-mail: mets@met.hu

MeteOnline
www.meteonline.ch/en/start.shtml
Swiss site giving reports of current weather conditions and 5-day forecasts for Europe. Refer to regional forecasts for local weather. Text is in English, German, French and Italian.
e-mail: via online form

Norwegian Meteorological Service
www.dnmi.no/varsel/ verkart/ eng_verkart.html
Daily weather information in great meteorological detail for all major Norwegian cities is updated hourly. Text is in English and Norwegian.
e-mail: mets@met.hu

Royal Meteorological Institute of Belgium
www.meteo.oma.be/IRM-KMI/
Current weather in major Belgian cities with 5-day forecasts, climatic and ozone data. Text is in English, Dutch and French.
e-mail: not available

SMHI
www.smhi.se/egmain/index.htm
Daily weather forecasts and warnings of sudden changes in Sweden. There are several weather databases for research. Text is in English and Swedish.
e-mail: via online form

The Icelandic Meteorological Office
www.vedur.is/english/megin_eng.html
Land, sea and air weather information for Iceland, with warnings of possible avalanches, coastal flooding, earthquake, sea ice and other aspects of Nature's unfriendliness.
e-mail: office@vedur.is

North America

British Columbia Weather News
www.bchighway.com/weather/
Weather news for British Columbia, Canada. For the latest forecasts click on the province.
e-mail: Info@bchighway.com

Rain Or Shine
www.rainorshine.com
Three weather bureaux maintain this site, which together give 5-day forecasts for all US cities and several major cities

world wide. They also provide a
24-hour forecast for the USA and
Canada, the weather ahead, a beach
report, air quality, ski weather and
pollen count. However, there is a
disclaimer on the accuracy of all
information provided.
e-mail: feedback@raninorshine.com

Resort Cam

www.rsn.com/cams/copper/welcome.html
The web site reports current weather
and snow conditions with forecasts
on ski-related subjects for Copper
Mountain, Colorado, US.
e-mail: via online form

Times Union

www.timesunion.com/sports/ski/
Essentially weather information for ski
conditions in New York, Vermont and
Massachusetts with snowfall forecasts
and maps. It also has a ski resort chart
with web addresses and phone
numbers.
e-mail: via online form

TV Weather Dot Com

www.tvweather.com
On the home page is the current
weather information for the USA with
severe weather bulletins for all 50
States. The site also provides links to
weather-related companies, topics and
government weather offices. You can
add a favourite link if you think the
directory would benefit from more
information.
e-mail: info@tvweather.com

University of Illinois

www.atmos.uiuc.edu
The Department of Atmospheric
Science, University of Illinois, USA,
maintains this site. Apart from updated
weather reports for US cities, the site
explains their academic program and
research activities.
e-mail: via online form

US Government National Weather Service

tgsv5.nws.noaa.gov/
Weather news for the whole USA
from Uncle Sam himself, with storm
predictions, regional weather maps,
extended forecasts and marine weather.
There are links to other international
weather bureaux.
e-mail: via online form

World Climate

www.worldclimate.com
This Buttle and Tuttle web site does
not forecast weather. World Climate
contains over 85,000 records of world
climate data and historical weather
averages from a wide range of sources.
The home page gives detailed instructions
on how to search the site.
e-mail: via online form

WXUSA

www.wxusa.com/OR/Portland
This web site has weather reports for
major US cities. Reports include current
weather with hourly updates and a 4-day
forecast. It also issues avalanche and
hurricane warnings.
e-mail: via online form

World wide

CNN Weather

www.cnn.com/weather/index.html
CNN Weather web site has 4-day
forecasts for 8,000 cities world wide.
Designed for quick search, separate
search boxes are provided for US cities
and cities elsewhere. There are detailed
reports about weather related news,
weather maps, and storm centres.
e-mail: via online form

Intellicast

www.intellicast.com
Intellicast provide weather information
in a web site of 250,000 pages. By clicking
on weather reports, you get 4-day

forecasts for all US cities and other cities world wide, updated daily. There are links to other weather-related sites and centres.

e-mail: via online form

The Washington Post.com

www.washington.com/wp-srv/weather/
The web site is the weather bureau of the Washington Post, and information is updated daily. Select a region from the drop-down menu on the home page and you get the day's forecast and a 4-day outlook. You can also check sports, travel, health and local traffic information.

e-mail: via online form

The Weather Channel On The Web

www.weather.com
This excellent web site gives world weather reports in several formats, all well illustrated. The Weather Channel on the Web provides a round-the-clock television network devoted entirely to weather reports for all US cities and major cities world wide.

e-mail: via online form

Glossary

Acceptable Use Policy
The rules controlling the use of an
Access Provider, server or shared area.

access account
Your personal account with an **Internet
service provider**.

Access Provider
Any company that provides **Internet**
connections.

Acrobat
Computer program used to read **PDF files**.

active content
Any part of a program that enhances the
appearance and performance of a **web
page**.

ActiveMovie
A Microsoft **applet** for displaying video
from **MPEG, QuickTime** and **AVI** formats.

ActiveX
A program that is used to enhance the
appearance and performance of a **web
page**.

address book
A program used to keep details of
contacts, names, **e-mail addresses**
and so on.

ADSL
(Asymmetrical Digital Subscriber Line)
Digital technology for high speed data
transfer over telephone lines.

anonymous FTP server
Any **FTP** site which accepts a **log-in**
with a username of 'anonymous' and
a password which matches the **user's**
e-mail address.

anti-aliasing
A method of smoothing out the rough
edges of irregularly shaped images on
screen.

applet
A mini program which works together
with other programs.

application
Any computer program.

ARPAnet
The precursor to the **Internet**.

ASCII
**(American Standard Code for
Information Interchange)**
Computer coding system used to represent
letters and numbers on computers.

attachment
A **file** sent together with an **e-mail**
message.

auto-responder
A system that produces automatic
replies to **e-mail** messages.

avatar
A character you choose to represent you
in an **online virtual reality** environment.

AVI
A Microsoft format for audiovisual files.

backbone
A major **Internet** connection.

bandwidth
Gauge of the line available to transmit
data. The greater the bandwidth, the
more data can be sent at the same time.

banner ad
Small advertisements placed on **web
pages** with direct **links** to the advertiser's
own **web site**.

baud rate
Rate of change per second in the signal
used by a **modem** to transmit data.

BBS
Bulletin Board System.

Bigfoot
A search system used to locate **e-mail
addresses**.

binary file
A large unencoded **file attached** to a
newsgroup posting.

BinHex
A method of encoding **binary** data **files**
for transmission.

bookmark

A marked location within a **web page**, or the **Netscape Navigator** term for **user** designated **web addresses**.

boot up

To switch a computer on.

broadband

High speed **Internet** access.

browser or **web browser**

A program which allows you to search for and view **web pages** from the **Internet** on your computer. The most popular are **Netscape Navigator** and **Internet Explorer.**

cache

A temporary data store created by a computer program in order to speed up access to information.

capitals

To use capital letters when sending **online** messages, equivalent to SHOUTING.

CDF (**Channel Definition File**)

This holds the data for a **WWW** subscription **channel**.

CGI (**Common Gateway Interface**)

A programming system used on **web servers** to automate certain processes.

channel

A system for providing regularly updated data from a **web site** to a subscribing **browser**.

chat

Simultaneous **user** to **user** communication across the **Internet**, either with text or audio/video.

Chat room

A **web site** where members can communicate in real time.

click through

To click on a **banner ad** to visit the advertised **web site**.

client

Any program which accesses information across a **network**.

conferencing

Two or more computers connected to provide the sharing of information or resources.

cookie

A small data **file** stored on your computer by a **web server** in order to identify it.

crack

To circumvent a program's or a computer's security systems, or to fake a **user** ID.

crash

When a computer operating system or **program** ceases to function, or causes other programs to freak out.

cyberspace

The imaginary world created by the connection of computers, **modems** and telephones and the information they convey.

domain name

A unique name used to identify an organisation on the **Internet**.

download

To transfer a **file** from the **Internet** to your computer.

drill down

To go directly to the information you require, without going though intermediate pages of a **web site**.

dropout

Loss of signal on a data connection.

e-commerce

Commercial transactions carried out via the **Internet**.

e-mail

Electronic mail consisting of text, images and sound sent from one **user** directly to another via the **Internet**.

e-mail address
The unique address belonging to a **user**, used to direct **e-mail**.

emoticon
Icon used in text messages created with keyboard symbols to show an emotion when viewed from the side, for example: happiness :-) sadness :-(amazement :-o and so on.

encryption
The process of scrambling data in order to keep it confidential.

eye candy
Attractive graphic images used to enliven a **web page**.

e-zine
Online magazine.

FAQ (Frequently Asked Questions)
A list of commonly asked questions with answers.

Favourites
The way **Internet Explorer** notes your favourite **web sites**.

file
Any electronic document created by an **application** and stored on a computer.

firewall
A **network** security system for restricting internal and external access.

flame
To send abusive **e-mail** or **newsgroup** messages, often to a particular individual.

frag
To fragment or destroy, used in the world of **online** games.

freeware
Software available for free use.

FrontPage
Web authoring **software**.

FTP (File Transfer Protocol)
The normal method of **downloading files** or programs from a computer on the **Internet.**

GIF (Graphics Image Format)
A common format for graphic **files**.

GUI (Graphic User Interface)
The system of using **icons** to represent **applications** and **files** on a computer screen.

hacker
Someone who breaks into secure computer systems or programs.

hardware
The physical components making up a computer system, such as screen, processor, hard drive and so on.

history
A review of the past sequence of **web pages** visited by the **browser**.

home page
The main page of a **web site**, to which subsequent pages are **linked**.

host
A computer that offers information or services to network **users**.

HTML (HyperText Markup Language)
The computer programming language used to write **web pages**.

HTTP (HyperText Transport Protocol)
The system used to communicate on the **Internet**.

hyperlink
An area of a **web site** or portion of text which has been set up to take you directly to another **web page** when activated.

HyperText link
A text link from one **web page** to another, often shown underlined and in blue.

icon
A graphic device used to represent an **application** or **file** on a computer screen.

information superhighway
The media term for the **network** which provides access to the data and services on the **Internet**.

Internet
The sum of all the linked computers and the telephone **networks** which connect them around the world.

Internet Explorer
A popular web **browser**.

Internet Service Provider (ISP)
An ISP provides access to the **Internet**, using banks of computers connected by high speed data links to the **WWW**. Most **users** have an ISP account, which can be free or on subscription.

IP (Internet Protocol) address
A series of numbers allocated to each computer to identify it on the **Internet**.

IRC (Internet Relay Chat)
Simultaneous **user** to **user** communication across the **Internet**, either by text or audio/video.

ISDN (Integrated Subscriber Digital Network)
A standard for digital telephone communication.

Java
Programming language used to write programs to be used on all types of computer.

JPEG (Joint Photographic Experts Group)
A format for image **files**.

junk e-mail
Electronic junk mail.

Kbps
Kilobits per second, approximately one thousand bits per second.

LAN (Local Area Network)
An independent **network** of computers which in turn may be connected to the **Internet**.

link
A connection from one **web page** or **web site** to another.

log on/in
To connect to the **Internet**.

mail server
A **server** used to store and transmit **e-mail**.

MIDI (Musical Instrument Digital Interface)
Files containing music which can be played on a computer. Often used to play background music on **web sites**.

mirror site
A replica site set up at another location to permit easier access.

modem (MOdulator/DEModulator)
A device used to connect a computer to the telephone system in order to transmit and receive data.

metasearch engine
A **search engine** that uses other search engines in combination.

MP3
MPEG format for storing sound **files**.

MPEG/MPG
A format for audio visual **files**.

navigate
To find your way around a **web site**, or the whole **Internet**.

netiquette
How you should behave on the **Internet**.

Netscape Communicator
A popular program for sending and receiving **e-mail**.

Netscape Navigator
A popular **web browser**.

network
A system of computers connected to each other.

newbie
A new **Internet user**.

newsgroup
A system for posting messages for other **users** to read.

NNTP (Network News Transfer Protocol)
The standard used for **newsgroup** postings.

node
A specific point on a **network**.

offline
Not connected to the **Internet**.

offline browsing
Using your **browser** to view pages stored in the **cache** after disconnecting from the **Internet**.

online
Connected to the **Internet**.

online content provider
A company which provides information for **Internet users**.

Outlook Express
A popular program for sending and receiving **e-mail**.

patch
A temporary upgrade to a computer program.

parental control
Means of regulating the access to certain **web sites** from any **browser**.

PDF (Portable Document Format)
A format for **files** which can be read on many different computer systems.

plug-in
Small add-on program used to enhance the performance of another.

POP3 (Post Office Protocol)
A common format used by **e-mail servers**.

portal
A **web site** that acts as a **link** to other sites.

post
To put an electronic message on a **newsgroup** bulletin board.

PPP (Point to Point Protocol)
The system of allocating an address to your computer each time you **log on** to the **Internet**.

protocol
A recognised system used to permit communication of data between devices.

proxy server
A **server** used to store information before transmitting to the **user**.

QuickTime
A program used to play audiovisual **files**.

searchbot
A small search program which can be configured by the **user** to search for specific information.

search engine
A program used to search for information requested by a **user**.

server
A computer used to provide information or services to other connected computers.

shareware
Programs available for a small registration fee.

software
Any program or **file** stored on a computer.

spam
Junk **e-mail**. Beware.

surf
To use the **Internet**, going from **web site** to **web site**.

The Internet
The sum of all the computers and **servers** connected throughout the world.

thumbnail
A smaller version of an image **file**, usually linked to the full size image.

troll
Someone who thrives on causing controversy within a **newsgroup**.

upload
To transfer a **file** from your computer to the **Internet**.

URL (Uniform Resource Locator)
The address of a **web site**, usually prefixed by www.

user
Term for the person accessing information on the **Internet**.

UUencode
A method of encoding binary **files** for sending via **e-mail**.

V.90
Connection **protocol** used by many **modems**.

virtual reality
The imaginary world created using computer devices and **software** which mimics the real world.

virus
A mini program or string of code which attaches itself to your **software** with various results, usually bad.

WAP (Wireless Application Protocol)
Modified **web pages** for access by mobile telephones.

web address
The unique location identifying a particular **web site** or **web page**.

web authoring
Designing **web sites** and **web pages**.

webcam
A digital camera connected directly to the **Internet** and accessed via a **web site**.

web directory
Online database of **web sites** organised into categories.

web page
Single page of data published on the **World Wide Web**.

web site
A collection of electronic documents published on the **Internet**.

World Wide Web or WWW or the Web
The entire collection of electronic documents containing text, sound, graphics and video published on the **Internet**.

WYSIWYG
(What You See Is What You Get).
The way something appears on the screen is how it will appear if printed.

zip file
File compressed for transfer on the **Internet**.

Index

M

N

Notes

rainbowdirectories world wide travel

Thank you for purchasing this Internet directory. To help us produce the best directories for our readers, it would be very useful to know a little about you. We would therefore be very grateful if you complete the following information by ticking the appropriate boxes. To show our appreciation for your help, we will send you a free CD-ROM of this book, which includes hyperlinks to the Internet.

1. Your age: ☐ 16-25 ☐ 26-35 ☐ 36-45 ☐ 46-55 ☐ Over 55

2. Partner's age: ☐ 16-25 ☐ 26-35 ☐ 36-45 ☐ 46-55 ☐ Over 55

3. Marital Status: ☐ Single ☐ Married ☐ Single/Divorced
☐ Widowed ☐ Living with Partner

4. How many children live at home with you? ☐ under 1 ☐ 1-2 ☐ 3-5 ☐ 7-9

5. Please indicate their ages: ☐ 10-12 ☐ 13-15 ☐ 16-18

6. Do You:
☐ Own, or are you buying, a house, flat or maisonette?
☐ Rent a Private house, flat or maisonette?
☐ Rent a Council house, flat or maisonette?
☐ Live with parents/guardians?

7. When did you move to this address? Year _____ month _____

8. Occupation:

	You	Partner
Student	☐	☐
Housewife/husband	☐	☐
Manual/factory worker	☐	☐
Craftsman/tradesman	☐	☐
Office/clerical	☐	☐
Education/medical services	☐	☐
Shop worker	☐	☐
Middle management	☐	☐
Professional/senior management	☐	☐
Self-employed/business owner	☐	☐
Retired	☐	☐

Do you ever work from home? ☐

9. Which Computer Operating system do you use?
☐ Windows ☐ Macintosh ☐ Linux ☐ Other _____

10. What type of computer do you use?
☐ Desktop ☐ Laptop ☐ Palmtop ☐ Other _____

11. What do you use the Internet for? Please tick all that apply.
☐ Banking/Finance ☐ Job Seeking ☐ Travel ☐ Education
☐ Music ☐ Work ☐ Entertainment ☐ Online games
☐ E-mail ☐ Research ☐ Internet Chat ☐ Shopping
☐ Other _____

12. Please give your name and address.
Your free CD-ROM will be sent to this address.
1 ☐ Mr 2 ☐ Mrs 3 ☐ Miss 4 ☐ Ms 5 ☐ Other _____

Your surname: _____ Initials: _____

Address: _____

Town: _____ County _____

Postcode _____ Telephone No: _____

E-mail _____

If you have no objection, your details may be used by Dragon Publications Ltd. and other responsible organisations to contact you with information about themselves and offers, products or services that you may find interesting. Please tick this box if you would prefer not to share in this opportunity. ☐

➡ FOLD OVER   PLEASE ALLOW 32 DAYS FOR DELIVERY IN THE UNITED KINGDOM.

Dragon Publications Ltd.
PO Box 24076
LONDON
NW4 3ZR